FATHER GABRIEL OF ST. MARY MAGDALEN, O.C.D.

DIVINE INTIMACY

Volume I

First Sunday of Advent through
the Eighth Week of Ordinary Time

IGNATIUS PRESS   SAN FRANCISCO

This enlarged and revised edition was
previously published by Dimension Books, Inc.
Translated from the Sixteenth Italian Edition
Carmelite Monastery of Pittsford, N.Y.

With ecclesiastical approval
© Carmelite Monastery, Pittsford, N.Y. 14534
All rights reserved
Reprinted with permission of Dimension Books, 1987
ISBN 0-89870-142-2
Library of Congress catalogue number 86-83132
Printed in the United States of America

TABLE OF CONTENTS

ADVENT SEASON

FOREWORD

"Divine Intimacy" is a well known name throughout the world today, which would need no introduction now were it not for the revision of it that has been made in the light of Vatican II.

In actual fact, this present book is not new, and yet at the same time it is new.

Its author, Fr. Gabriel of St. Mary Magdalen, O.C.D. (1893-1953) was a teacher who excelled in the ways of God, joining an enviable experience with souls to a vast and profound knowledge of spiritual theology. He had had such a book under consideration for a long time, when, after weighing favorable and contrary opinions, he finally decided to sketch out a plan, convinced that through this projected work he would be able to reach a greater number of the faithful than through the treatise on ascetical-mystical theology upon which he had already been working for many years, which in its turn had been insistently asked for by many. What carried most weight for him was that it seemed, of the two, that *Divine Intimacy* would do more good by guiding innumerable souls to that loving colloquy with God, that dialogue in spirit and in truth, which, according to St. Teresa of Avila, "is the gate through which all good things enter;" it would be for the sanctification of the members of the Mystical Body of Christ, who are called to the spiritual banquet through prayer, in order to draw from it the theological charity which would radiate out from them to their brothers.

Once convinced of this, he sought to find time for the new enterprise in spite of every minute being consumed by the duties in which he was already engaged: teaching, editing the "Rivista di vita spirituale," collaborating professionally in various publications and dictionaries, preaching spiritual exercises and giving retreats, in addition to his priestly ministry. After he had studied the project and drawn up a carefully detailed plan, he sought the collaboration of the Carmel of S. Giuseppe in Rome which was especially dear to him. By the beginning of November, 1952 he was able to offer the public the first modest volume. Its simple, unpretentious appearance would scarcely lead one to imagine the burning outburst of grace that it would promote as one magnificent edition after another appeared, first in Italian, soon followed by versions in French, Spanish, German, English, Flemish, Polish,

Portuguese, Japanese and Croatian. The author himself, though endowed with a rich vein of natural and supernatural optimism, would never have dreamed of the extraordinary success that Divine Intimacy was destined to have.

Six modest volumes followed one another regularly despite the death of Fr. Gabriel, March 15, 1953. It seemed at first that this would put a stop to the work, but the valuable assistance he had sought from S. Giuseppe Carmel proved providential, and the work continued unabated. The numerous writings of Fr. Gabriel, preserved in the Teresian Carmel on the Via Ancillotto (now moved to Via della Nocetta) were an abundant source of material for planning the entire work, which was soon completed, following the author's guidelines and thought.

* * *

He had desired a gradual and meditative exposition of all the great truths of the spiritual life, one that would be grafted upon and incorporated into the liturgical year and its fundamental themes, so that the faithful might be united to the mystery of Christ and the Church. For this reason topics of spiritual theology were to be proposed and presented in the light of the various liturgical seasons, so that the truths which the liturgy set forth would stand out clearly through prayer. Fr. Gabriel had meditated long upon the "Mediator" of Pius XII, and was enthusiastic about it. For him the liturgy was not a collection of rubrics, but an encounter with God in the Church and with the Church, and he held that, as much as possible, personal prayer should be grafted onto the public prayer of the Mystical Body, by taking its tone and finding its starting point in the great stages of salvation history as presented by the liturgical year. The finished work corresponded to the ideal he had dreamed of, and many book-reviews, especially in German speaking countries, emphasized the liturgical value of Divine Intimacy, while, at the same time, pointed out that its liturgical spirit was directed toward promoting a personal contact with God. In its turn, the sure spiritual doctrine it contains inspires us to understand and live the treasures of the liturgy in a new manner.

With the flourishing of studies and fuller appreciation of liturgical life, all that Fr. Gabriel had planned could not but seem providential. Testimony to this, pouring in from all sides and from the most diverse parts of the world, bore witness to the author's wisdom, and manifested the deep gratitude of the many who considered themselves indebted to him for the richness of the spiritual teaching to be found in his work.

* * * *

Fr. Gabriel had been occupied for many years with theology, and during his last ten years, especially with spiritual theology.

For the most part he followed the teaching of St. Teresa of Jesus and St. John of the Cross, whose doctrine he made come alive through the clarity and directness of his explanations, which were made still more effective by his great experience in dealing with souls. For this reason, even when texts or expressions are not directly quoted, one soon discovers a constant echo of the words of these Doctors of Carmel, which had already long been the substance of his doctrine. This can be observed all through Divine Intimacy, where the teaching of St. Teresa and of St. John of the Cross, together with that of other masters of the Teresian Carmel, abounds, not only in numerous explicit citations from their writings, but also in the very flow of expression. This accounts for the effortless ease with which the liturgical text, enriched by facts of spiritual theology, is offered throughout the book, creating an harmonious and beneficial continuity between the liturgy and piety.

* * * *

This work has been revised and retouched many times, always keeping the spirit and way of thinking of the author in the forefront; he was ever a faithful son of the Church whom he loved with a true passion. For him "feeling with the Church" was the norm of life, and it is well known how and to what an extent he nurtured this "feeling" by an assiduous and careful reading of the documents which were promulgated by the hierarchy and especially by the Holy Father. How often, day after day, he could be seen in the choir in prayer, deep in meditation upon the great encyclicals or discourses of Pius XII! He would read carefully, then close the booklet and remain in peaceful, prolonged meditation. From the very outset, the pages of Divine Intimacy clearly bore the imprint of this pontifical teaching which he held to be a means of communion with the Church and an irreplaceable instrument of a sure theological updating.

For all these reasons we feel that this work, just as it is presented, in its spirit as well as in the changes required by the teaching of Vatican Council II and by the liturgical reform which followed it, can and must still be called the work of Fr. Gabriel of St. Mary Magdalen. The revision of the book fully corresponds with his spirit of fidelity to the Church, to which we have referred; it was a fidelity which made him at one and the same time a meditative reader and an outstanding executor of the pontifical documents. It will be easy for anyone who knew him to imagine the ready smile and the happy gleam in his eyes with which he would have welcomed having in his hand the statutes and decrees of Vatican II; how he would have meditated upon them, studied them, and made them a part of himself, zealously propounding their wealth to all the souls with whom he came in contact. He would have adhered with similar enthusiasm to the Church's directives for a deeper knowledge and assimilation of Sacred

Scripture as the basis of the spiritual formation of the faithful, and he would have wanted the meditations of Divine Intimacy to be inspired as much as possible by scriptural texts. All this is what this new edition has tried to do, in which the spirit, the thought, and the teaching of the author have been respected to the fullest degree. It is true that the work has been redrafted, but its prospectus and its general attitude remain unchanged, as also its themes and the explanatory thought of the individual meditations, although perhaps under different headings more in line with today's mentality.

It should also be noted that the new edition was made by the same faithful collaborators as before. The Discalced Carmelites of the Monastery of San Giuseppe, Rome, who had helped Fr. Gabriel in producing Divine Intimacy from the first pages of the modest little book that appeared toward the end of 1952, took upon themselves the burdensome task of revising, updating and drawing up the new text. This long and conscientious labor was performed in a spirit of utmost fidelity to him who they call "the Father," and who had transmitted to them the richness of his spirit along with his writings. Any one who knew Fr. Gabriel, or had the good fortune to be one of his disciples, or is acquainted with his teaching, can certify that the new pages, still in the freshness of the springtime of grace stirred up by Vatican II and by the renewed impulse given to a more vital return to Sacred Scripture and to liturgical reform, bear the mark and the unmistakable imprint of the great teacher. It is an achievement which redounds to the credit of Fr. Gabriel, and at the same time deserves the gratitude of all toward the hidden hardworking artisans who are responsible for the new edition, and have sought to disappear in order that he might speak.

Divine Intimacy has done an immense amount of good. It has spread quietly throughout the world, bringing everywhere in the name of the spirituality of the Teresian Carmel, a desire and renewed resolution for communion and dialogue with God, which is for the good of the entire Church. This new edition will undoubtedly continue in the same line. By inspiring the faithful to converse with God, it will make them more generous and more available in serving the Church and their brothers.

Fr. Valentino di S. Maria, O.C.D.
Rome, August 15, 1971

A WORD OF THANKSGIVING

As this new English edition of *Divine Intimacy* goes to press we feel it a duty to express our gratitude to the many friends thoughout the world who, by making known their interest in having a new edition, have played a real part in its publication.

We owe particular gratitude to Mr. J. Gregory Doyle who first suggested the project and who has assisted and encouraged us on every step of the way; to Gerard de Blasi whose invaluable cooperation with the translation from beginning to end has made our work much easier; in a special way to Fr. Gabriel Gates, O.C.D. who patiently reviewed the entire manuscript; and also to the ICS Publications in Washington, D.C. who gave permission to use excerpts from

The Collected Works of St. Teresa of Avila, Volumes I and II 1976, 1980

The Collected Works of St. John of the Cross, 1964 both translated by Kieran Kavanaugh, O.C.D. and Otilio Rodriguez, O.C.D.

The Story of a Soul, 1975, 1976

St. Therese of Lisieux: Her Last Conversations, 1977 both translated by John Clarke, O.C.D.

and last, but by no means least, a word of appreciation to Tom Coffey of Dimension Books, Inc. for his sustained help and guidance.

Monastery of Our Lady and St. Joseph of the
Discalced Carmelites in Pittsford, N.Y.
November 14, 1982

NOTICE

1. On the Sundays and Solemnities for which there is a triennial cycle of readings, three meditations are offered, respectively, for Year A, Year B, and Year C. In 1983 the meditations for Year C are used, and for the succeeding years according to the following table:

Year A	1984	1987	1990	1993	etc.
Year B	1985	1988	1991	1994	etc.
Year C	1986	1989	1992	1995	etc.

For Sundays and Feasts on which the first two readings or the Gospel are the same for the three years (e.g. Feast of the Holy Family, Palm Sunday, etc.) only one meditation is given.

2. During Lent and the weeks of Eastertime, the daily meditations are in harmony with the Liturgy; as also—although a little less strictly—during Advent and for the time between Ascension and Pentecost.

3. The colloquies—the prayers or elevations which follow each meditation—are almost exclusively taken from these sources: Holy Scripture, the Liturgy, the writings of the Saints or worthwhile spiritual writers. Although these texts are quoted with a certain freedom in order to make them more adapted to prayer, and not infrequently the explanatory form of the original has been changed into more direct colloquy, they have been kept as close as possible to the thought and letter of the author. When an accommodation has been necessary, it is indicated by the sign "cf."

PREFACE[1]

Mental prayer is indispensable to the spiritual life; normally it is, so to speak, its very breath. However, this spontaneity in prayer is usually realized only if the soul applies itself to meditation for some time by its own personal effort. In other words, one must learn how to pray. It is to teach souls this devout practice that various methods of meditation have arisen.

There are many methods, each with its own merit; among them is the Teresian method, so called because it is based on the teachings of St. Teresa of Jesus, the Foundress of the Discalced Carmelites and the great mistress of the spiritual life.[2]

The idea of mental prayer which St. Teresa has left us is well known today. In her *Life* she defines it as "an intimate sharing between friends, . . . taking time frequently to be alone with him who we know loves us" (Life 8).

In these words St. Teresa reveals the affective spirit of mental prayer which is its special characteristic. It is "a friendly sharing" and exchange of "mutual benevolence" between the soul and God, during which the soul "converses intimately with God"—intimacy, as we know, is the fruit of love—and the soul speaks with him whose love she knows. Each element of the definition contains the idea of love, but at the end the Saint mentions that the soul ought also to "know" and be conscious of God's love for her: this is the part which the intellect plays in prayer.

Therefore, according to St. Teresa, there is an exercise of both the intellect and the will in mental prayer: the intellect seeks to convince the soul that God loves her and wishes to be loved by

---

1This central portion of Father Gabriel's Preface to the first edition gives a clear idea of his thought and intentions.

2The proclamation of St. Teresa of Jesus as Doctor of the Church gives her teaching on prayer a universal value. Paul VI affirmed this in his discourse on the occasion of the conferral of the Doctorate, declaring that the Saint, now "adorned with the title of Doctor,(. . . has) a more authoritative mission to accomplish in the praying Church and in the world with her perennial and ever pertinent message: the message of prayer" (Osser. Rom. Sept. 28-29, 1970).

her; the will, responding to the divine invitation, loves. That is all. There could be no clearer concept of prayer.

But how translate it into practice? This is the task of the method.

* * * *

In order to understand the structure of the Teresian method clearly, we must keep in mind the definition of prayer given above; then we shall easily see that it is fully realized by such a method, that it truly means conversing lovingly with our Lord, once we understand that he loves us.

We cannot speak to God intimately unless we are in contact with him. For this reason, we make use of "preparation", which consists in placing ourselves more directly in the *presence of God*, turning to him by means of a good thought.

In order to convince ourselves that God loves us, we choose for the subject of meditation one of the truths of faith which can make his love evident: this is the purpose of the *reading* of an appropriate passage.

However, it does not suffice merely to read the matter, we must examine it thoroughly, and there is no better way of doing this than by reflecting upon it—by meditating.

All revealed truth can manifest God's love for me, but today I try to understand it by reflecting on the theme I have chosen in my reading. I make use of the good thoughts contained in the subject of the meditation to actually convince myself of his love, so that love for him will come spontaneously into my heart, and words perhaps, to my lips.

Thus my *colloquy* with God begins; I tell him in every way possible (using the words which come to me most spontaneously) that I love him, that I want to love him, that I want to advance in his holy love, and that I wish to prove my love for him by my actions, by doing his holy will.

And now we are at the center, *the heart of prayer*.

For many souls, nothing more is needed.

Some, however, prefer greater variety; therefore to facilitate the prolonging of our loving conversation with God, the three final steps of the method are offered. These, however, are *optional*.

Thanksgiving: After having told Our Lord again that we love him, we thank him for all the benefits we have received from him and show him we are grateful.

Offering: Aware of having received so many favors, we try to repay our debt as far as we can by making some good resolution. It is always useful to end our prayer in this way.

Petition: The consciousness of our weakness and frailty urges us to implore the help of God.

This is the whole Teresian method, divided into seven steps:

Two *introductory:* the preparation (presence of God) and reading.

Two *essential:* the meditation and the colloquy.

Three *optional,* to help in prolonging the colloquy: the thanksgiving, the offering, and the petition.

The meditations in this book are based on this method.

We begin with the *presence of God,* rather, with an appropriate thought which brings us into contact with God and orientates us toward him.

The *reading* provides the subject for the meditation. And as many spiritual persons apply themselves to meditation twice a day, each meditation offers two points.

The soul then begins to *reflect,* using freely the text already read.

In this way it will pass spontaneously to the *colloquy* which, according to the Teresian concept, is the "heart," the center of prayer.

That is why our meditations are directed toward helping souls especially on this point. To this end we have tried to give the colloquies a form that is sufficiently ample; nevertheless, they may be used freely as desired, each soul choosing whatever corresponds to the need of the moment. To make the colloquies more efficacious, we have selected suitable ardent expressions and thoughts taken by preference from the writings of the saints and other loving souls. Very often we have been obliged to make slight modifications in these texts, in order to adapt them to the intimate form of a colloquy. However we always indicate their source.

The colloquies consist of expressions of love, alternating with petitions, acts of thanksgiving, and transports of the soul toward God; these are made concrete in resolutions.

We hope that these meditations, written in this way, will help souls to apply themselves efficaciously to mental prayer according to the Teresian idea and method.

* * *

Teresian spirituality is the spirituality of divine intimacy, that is, it tries to nourish in souls the ideal of intimacy with God and it directs them toward this ideal, principally by means of mental prayer. Mental prayer should be attuned, therefore, to this great and lofty aspiration.

This is the "tone" we have tried to give our meditations, and the title, *Divine Intimacy,* indicates our intention to help souls as far as possible to attain this great end.

In addition, Teresian spirituality is also doctrinal. St. Teresa of Jesus, the great "mistress of the spiritual life," always desired—and endeavored to put her desire into practice—that the ascetical and mystical life of those who were dear to her be based on solid doctrine, for the Saint greatly loved theology. That is why we have desired to build these meditations upon a sound theological basis. We have attempted to arrange them in such a way that, in the course of one year, the most important problems of the spiritual life and all the supernatural realities met with in the interior life will have been reviewed.

May the Holy Spirit, the Spirit of love, who deigns to dwell in our souls in order to bring them gradually under his complete influence and direction, kindle in us, "with abundant effusion," that love of charity which will lead us to intimacy with God! May the Blessed Virgin Mary, Mother of fair love, whose soul, filled with grace, was ever moved by the Holy Spirit, obtain for us from this divine Spirit the favor of remaining docile to his invitations, so that we may realize, with the help of an assiduous, effective practice of mental prayer, the beautiful ideal of intimate union with God.

Fr. Gabriel of St. Mary Magdalen, O.C.D.
Rome, Feast of the Sacred Heart, 1952.

ADVENT SEASON

1 — FIRST SUNDAY OF ADVENT

YEAR A

"Come, let us walk in the light of the Lord" (Is 2:5)

The central theme of Advent is the coming of the Lord, considered under various aspects. First of all we see the expectation of the Old Testament, which is constantly directed toward the coming of the Messiah. The prophecies that the Liturgy presents to us during this season, all speak to us of his coming in such a way as to awaken in our hearts that deep desire and need of God which is so alive in the prophetic writings. At the same time they invite us to thank God for the great gift of salvation, which no longer appears on the horizon as a future event that is only promised and hoped for, but as one which has been a consoling reality ever since the incarnation of the Son of God and his birth in time. The Redeemer has come; in him the hopes of the Old Testament have been fulfilled and those of the New opened up. This then is the new expectation: the coming of the Savior must be actualized in the heart of each of us, for now all human history points toward the parousia, that is, to the return of Christ in glory at the end of time. It is in this context that we must listen to and meditate upon the readings of Advent.

Isaiah stresses the messianic era in which all peoples will converge on Jerusalem to adore the one God: "All nations shall stream toward it and say, 'Come, let us go up to the mountain of the Lord, to the house of the God of Jacob that he may teach us his ways'" (Is 2:3). Reunited in the one true faith, all men will become brothers and shall not "learn war anymore" (ib. 4). Jerusalem is the figure of the Church, constituted by God the "universal sacrament of salvation" (LG 48); she opens wide her arms to all men to lead them to Christ, so that by following his teachings they may live as brothers in harmony and peace. But how long a road still lies ahead of us before this can be fully realized! Every Christian should be a voice calling men with the ardor of Isaiah to the one faith and to brotherly love. The prophet concludes with a forceful invitation, "Come, let us walk in the light of the Lord" (2:5).

In the second reading, St. Paul tells us exactly what we must do to walk in that light: "cast off the works of darkness" (Rom 13:2), that is, sin in all its forms, and "put on the armor of light" (ibid) which means, clothe ourselves with virtue, especially with faith and love. This is all the more urgent "for salvation is nearer to us now" (ibid); in fact history is heading toward its last phase: the final coming of the Lord. The time that remains for reaching that goal must be expeditiously spent; the Lord who has already come in his earthly birth at Bethlehem, who is continuously present in the life of each and every man, and who is to come at the end of time, must be welcomed and followed and awaited in faith and hope, and in living and active charity. Jesus himself spoke of the attitude of vigilant expectancy which should characterize the entire life of the Christian: "Watch, you, therefore; for you do not know on what day your Lord is coming" (Mt 24:42). This indicates not only the parousia, but also that coming of the Lord which will take place for each of us at the end of our life, when we shall meet our Savior face to face, and which should be the most beautiful of days, the beginning of eternal life. "Therefore, you must be ready; for the Son of Man is coming at an hour you do not expect" (ib. 44).

We beg you, all-powerful God, to increase our strength of will for doing good that Christ may find us waiting for his coming and may call us to his side in the kingdom of heaven (Collect).

O Lord, may our Communion teach us to love heaven. May its promise and hope guide our way on earth. (After Communion).

Roman Missal

Our love for you, O Lord, rests upon the firm foundation of the love which is its reward. This love can no longer be doubted since it was shown so openly and with so many sufferings and trials, and with the shedding of your blood even to the point of death in order that we might have no doubt about it . . . Be pleased, Lord, to give us your love before you take us out of this life, for it will be a great thing at the hour of death, to see that we are going to be judged by you whom we have loved above all things. We shall be able to proceed securely with the judgment concerning our debts. It will not be like going to a foreign country but like going to our own, because it is the country of you whom we love so much and who loves us.

St. Teresa of Jesus, *Way* 40:7-8

YEAR B

O Lord, you are our father . . . Oh, that you would rend the heavens and come down! (Is 63:16-19)

Since the day of the first sin when God held out to Adam the promise of a redeemer, the hopes of mankind have been directed toward that longed-for salvation. The prophets were its untiring heralds. "You, Lord, are our Father, our Redeemer from of old is your name . . . You were angry and we sinned, in our sins we have been a long time . . . Yet, O Lord, you are our Father" (see Is 63:16; 64:5, 8). Man's deep sense of sin and of his powerlessness to raise himself up are mingled with his yearning for salvation and with his confidence in God, which is expressed in almost evangelical terms, "you are our Father." Isaiah seems to be trying, through his moving prayer, to hasten the coming of the Lord: "Oh, that you would rend the heavens and come down!" (64:1). We learn from history how this cry was heard and God's promise fulfilled: the heavens were really opened, and man received his Savior, the Lord Jesus. Yet Isaiah's prayer is still timely and the Liturgy cries out during Advent: "Oh, that you would rend the heavens and come down!" (64:1). The Son of God has already come historically; with his passion, death and resurrection he has already saved sinful mankind. Nevertheless, although this mystery is fulfilled in itself, it must be repeated for every man and continuously renewed in him until it brings him "into the fellowship of his Son, Jesus Christ, our Lord" (Cor 1:9). Until this fellowship is perfect, in fact, until we are completely possessed and transformed by grace, we are still waiting for our Savior. He comes continually through the Sacraments, in his word spoken by the Church, by interior inspirations and impulses. We must not cease welcoming him and desiring his coming in ways that are ever more intimate, profound and transforming. "The Spirit and the Bride (the Church) say: 'Come!' " and all the faithful repeat: "Come, Lord Jesus!" (Rev 22:17,20).

While St. Paul congratulates the Corinthians on the grace of God that they have received in Christ, because in him they have been enriched in everything and in him possess every gift, at the same time he summons them to prepare "for the revealing of our Lord" (1 Cor 1:4-7). The grateful remembrance of the birth of our Lord and of all the gifts we have received from him, and his glorious manifestation at the end of time are two pillars over which the arch of Advent extends. If this interval is really filled with vigilant expectancy, accompanied by good works, God himself, as the Apostle says, will make us who believe staunch to the end, "guiltless in the day of our Lord Jesus Christ" (ib. 8). To the fidelity of him who lives in expectation of his God, corresponds the fidelity of God who unfailingly keeps his promises.

Man's fidelity must be of the kind the Gospel proposes; a generous service in the fulfillment of duty without giving in to weariness or laziness. He must be like the diligent servant who does not go to sleep during his master's absence, but attends to the duties entrusted to him, so that when the master returns, "whether it be in the evening, or at midnight, or at the cock crow, or in the morning" (ib. 35) he will always be found at his post, intent on his work, not frightened like one who is caught in a fault, but happy to see him again. Since for the Christian God is not only master, but father, this meeting will be full of joy.

You, O Lord, are our Father, our Redeemer, from of old is your name. O Lord, why do you make us err from your ways and harden our heart, so that we fear you not? Return for the sake of your servants . . . O that you would rend the heavens and come down.

You meet him that joyfully works righteousness, those that remember you in your ways. Behold you were angry and we sinned . . . We have all become like one who is unclean, and all our righteous deeds are like polluted garments. We all fade like a leaf, and our iniquities, like the wind, take us away.

There is no one that calls upon your name, that bestirs himself to take hold of you; for you have hidden your face from us and have delivered us into the hand of our iniquities. Yet, O Lord, you are our Father; we are the clay, and you are our potter; we are all the work of your hand. Be not exceedingly angry, O Lord, and remember not our iniquity forever. Behold, consider we are all your people.

Isaiah 63:16-17; 64:1, 5-9

Show me, O Lord, your mercy and give me your salvation . . . O infinite Wisdom, come and lead me in the ways of heaven. O Splendor of the glory of the Father, come and enlighten me with the brightness of your virtue. O Sun of Justice, come and give light and the warmth of life to one who sits in the shadow of death. O King of Kings, come to rule me. O Teacher of the Nations, come teach me. O Savior of the world, come and bring me salvation.

Da Ponte, *Meditazioni* II, 15,2.

YEAR C

O Lord, confirm our hearts without blame, in holiness . . . at the coming of our Lord Jesus   *(1 Thes 3 :13)*

"Behold the days are coming—says the Lord—when I will fulfill the promise I made to the house of Israel . . . I will cause a righteous branch to spring forth for David" (Jer 33:14-15). Jeremiah announces God's intention of fulfilling the promise of the Savior who is to be born from the seed of David, here symbolized as a "righteous branch." He will reestablish "justice on earth," that is, he will save men from sin and lead them back to God.

The realization of the great event which was accomplished through the birth of the Savior by the Virgin Mary is one of the focal points of Advent. The Church is concerned that the people of God do not limit themselves to a superficial commemoration; instead she wants them to prepare themselves to relive in depth the

                                               Divine Intimacy

ineffable mystery of the Word of God made man "for our salvation" (Creed). And since salvation will be completed, or will have reached all mankind, only at the end of time, when "they will see the Son of Man coming ... with power and great glory" (Lk 21:27), the faithful are urged to live in a continual Advent. The remembrance of our Lord's birth must be lived "in the expectation of the blessed hope and coming of our Savior Jesus Christ" (RM). The Lord has come, is coming, and will come; we need to thank him, welcome him and wait for him. If the life of a Christian deviates from this orbit, it fails.

When the Church begins Advent by reading the Gospel that speaks of the end of the world and of the parousia of the Lord, her intention is not that of frightening her children, but of warning them that time is fleeting and earthly life is temporary; that the object of our hope and desire cannot be the earthly city, but the heavenly one. If the present world is convulsed by war, disorders, false philosophies and depraved customs, all this should be a warning that in rejecting God man perishes; by him alone can we be saved. Therefore, "look up, and raise your heads, because your redemption is drawing near" (Lk 21:28). The Church aims at awakening in our hearts the desire and need for salvation, and an ardent longing for the Savior. Instead of allowing ourselves to be overwhelmed and carried away by worldly pursuits, we need to dominate them and to live with the Lord's coming ever before our eyes. "Take heed to yourselves, lest your hearts be weighed down with dissipation and drunkenness and the cares of this life, and that day come upon you suddenly" (ib. 34). We need therefore to pray and "to watch at all times" (ib. 36) and make use of time to progress in love toward God and toward our neighbor. This is what St. Paul desires when he exhorts: Brothers, "may the Lord make you increase and abound in love to one another and to all men ... may he establish your hearts, unblamable in holiness ... at the coming of our Lord Jesus (1 Thes 3:12-13). The justice and holiness which the Lord came to bring upon earth must take root and grow in the heart of the Christian and from there spread over the world.

> "For you I wait all the day long, O Lord, Be mindful of your mercy, O Lord, and of your steadfast love for they have been from of old ... Good and upright is the Lord; therefore he instructs sinners in the way. He leads the humble in what is right, and teaches the humble his way. All the paths of the Lord are steadfast love and faithfulness for those who keep his covenant and his testimonies."
> Psalm 25:5-6, 8-10.

> Of what use is it to me, who am mindful of my sins, if you come, O Lord, and yet do not come into my soul and into my spirit; if you, O Christ, do not live in me, nor speak within me? It is to me that you must come, for me that your coming advent must become a reality.

*Your second coming, O Lord, will take place at the end of the world;
then we shall be able to say: For me the world has been crucified,
and I for the world.*

*Oh see to it, Lord, that the end of the world finds me ... oc-
cupied with heaven ... Then wisdom, virtue and justice, and the
redemption will all become truly present for me. O Christ, you indeed died but once for the sins of your people, but with the purpose
of ransoming them every day from their sins.*

cf. St. Ambrose, *Commento al Vangelo di S. Luca* (10:7-8)

2 — CALLED TO BE SAINTS

"Stir up your might, O Lord, and come to save us" (Ps 80:2)

1. With the fall of Adam, sin shattered the divine plan for
man's sanctification. Our first parents, created in the image and
likeness of God, in a state of grace and justice which made them
children of the Most High, fell into the depths of misery, dragging
all mankind with them. For centuries man groaned in his sin; it
dug an insurmountable abyss between humanity and God; man
lay in the depths of the abyss, powerless to raise himself up.

To do what man could not do, that is to destroy sin in him and
to restore himself to grace, God promised a Savior. This promise,
made and renewed down through the centuries, was not to be
restricted to the people of Israel; it involved all mankind. Isaiah
had already glimpsed it: "Many peoples shall come and say: Come,
and let us go up to the mountain of the Lord and to the house of
the God of Jacob, that he may teach us his ways" (Is 2:3). And
Jesus himself stated it clearly: "I tell you, many will come from
east and west and sit at table with Abraham, Isaac and Jacob in
the kingdom of heaven" (Mt 8:11).

The Lord Jesus came to save all peoples, to invite all to the
table of his Father in the heavenly kingdom, for God "desires all
men to be saved and to come to the knowledge of the truth" (1 Tim
2:4). In order that all may be saved, God has given us "his only
Son, that whoever believes in him should not perish, but have eternal life" (Jn 3:16); to such an extent has God loved the world.
Israel was the depositary of the divine promise and had the mission of transmitting it from generation to generation, but it was
not the only beneficiary. From the very beginning, in God's plan,
the promise was meant for the entire human family: no one was
left out. Jesus the Savior came for each of us, and to each he offers
the necessary means for salvation.

2. Writing to the Christians of Corinth, St. Paul addressed his
letter: to you who are "sanctified in Christ Jesus, called to be
saints together with all those who in every place call on the name
of our Lord Jesus Christ (1 Cor 1:2). All those who believe in

Christ, no matter to what nation they belong, are in fact "called to be saints," which in the words of the Apostle means above all to belong, to be consecrated to God through baptism, and then in the strength of this consecration, to become personally holy.

Holiness, like salvation, is offered to all men. "Be holy, for I am holy" (Lev 11:44), said God to the people of Israel; and Jesus specified: "You, therefore, must be perfect, as your heavenly Father is perfect" (Mt 5:48). Our Lord did not address these words to a select group, nor reserve them for his Apostles and close friends; he spoke them before the multitude that had followed him. He, the All-Holy One, came to sanctify all men and to offer each all the necessary means not only for salvation, but also for sanctification. "I came that they may have life, and have it abundantly" (Jn 10:10).

The Church never tires of repeating and of instilling into us this teaching of the Lord. "Let no one think that . . . (holiness) is the concern of only a few chosen men, while others can limit themselves to a lower level of virtue . . . Absolutely all . . . are included in this law, there are no exceptions" (Pius X1, AAS, 1923, p. 50). Vatican Council II reaffirmed in a particular way the universal calling to holiness: every one in the Church, whether "belonging to the hierarchy, or being cared for by it, is called to holiness . . . the Lord Jesus, the divine teacher and model of perfection, preached holiness of life to each and every one of his disciples, regardless of their situation; he himself stands as the author and finisher of this holiness of life" (LG 39:40). We cannot find the resources and energies for our sanctification within ourselves; God alone is holy and God alone can make us holy. God himself wants to be the sanctifier of his creatures, and in Jesus offers each of us the fullness of the means to holiness.

O my Lord, how obvious it is that you are almighty! There is no need to look for reasons for what you want. For, beyond all natural reason, you make things so possible that you manifest clearly there is no need for anything more than truly to love you and truly to leave all for you, so that you, my Lord, may make everything easy. It fits well here to say that you feign labor in your law. For I do not see, Lord, nor do I know how the road that leads to you is narrow. I see that it is a royal road, not a path; a road that is safer for anyone who indeed takes it. Very far off are the occasions of sin, those narrow mountain passes and the rocks that make one fall. What I would call a path, a wretched path and a narrow way, is the kind which has on one side, where a soul can fall, a valley far below, and on the other side a precipice: as soon as one becomes careless one is hurled down and broken to pieces.

He who really loves you, my Good, walks safely on a broad and royal road. He is far from the precipice. Hardly has he begun to stumble when you, Lord, give him your hand. One fall is not sufficient for a person to be lost, nor are many, if he loves you and not the things of the world. He journeys in the valley of humility. I cannot understand what it is that makes people afraid of setting out on the road to perfection. May the Lord, because of who he is, give us understanding of how wretched is the security that lies in such manifest dangers as following the crowd and how true security lies in striving to make progress on the road to God. Let them turn their eyes to him and not fear the setting of this Sun of Justice, nor, if we do not first abandon him, will he allow us to walk at night and go astray.

St. Teresa of Jesus, *Life* 35:13-14

3 — SANCTIFIED IN CHRIST JESUS

"Show us, O Lord, your steadfast love, and grant us your salvation"
(Ps 85:7)

1. "I give thanks to God always for you, because of the grace of God which was given you in Christ Jesus" (1 Cor 1:4), writes St. Paul to the Corinthians. It is only God's grace which justifies us and makes us holy: this grace comes to man through the infinite merits of our Lord Jesus, and is given freely to those who believe in him. "The followers of Christ," Vatican II teaches, "are called by God not according to their accomplishments, but according to his own purpose and grace. They are justified in the Lord Jesus ... truly become sons of God, and sharers in the divine nature. In this way they are really made holy. They must therefore hold on to, and complete in their lives this holiness which they have received" (LG 40).

Baptism has planted in us the seed of holiness; a most fruitful seed because it makes us participate in divine life, and therefore in God's holiness; a seed which is capable of producing the precious fruit of a holy life, and of eternal life when we second its development with good will. Every Christian has received this gift: we can each become a saint, and will become one, not in proportion to the works that we are able to accomplish, be they great or small, but in the measure in which, with the grace of God, we make the grace conferred by baptism bear fruit. Once baptized, we are saints by right; we must be so in fact also by leading a holy life, doing holy works worthy of a child of God who has been saved and redeemed by Christ, and worthy of a member of the Church which is the mystical body of Christ. God who has called us and sanctified us in his Son will give us all the necessary graces to bring to completion the work begun. "God is faithful," writes the Apostle, "by whom you were called into the fellowship of his Son, Jesus Christ our Lord" (1 Cor 1:9).

2. One day Jesus said to his disciples: "Blessed are the eyes which see what you see! For I tell you that many prophets and

kings desired to see what you see and did not see it, and to hear what you hear, and did not hear it" (Lk 10:23-24). During all the long centuries which preceded the birth of Christ, it had been the yearning of the people of Israel to see the Savior, to listen to his words of eternal life, and to be redeemed by him. All that had been the object of the burning desires of innumerable just men has become a reality for the new Israel, the Church of Christ, which for two thousand years has been living and growing through the sanctifying grace of her Lord. Now every Christian can enjoy its fullness; blessed are we if we know how to take advantage of it.

But for the grace of Christ to bear the fruit of holiness, it must possess and transform our entire being and activity, making us holy in every action: in our thoughts, desires, intentions and works, both in every detail and in the full totality of our life. As grace grows and matures in us who believe, it exercises a larger and deeper influence over us, and when its sanctifying influence effectively extends to all our activities, orientating us unfailingly toward the fulfillment of God's will and his glory, we shall indeed live in communion with Christ, intimately united to God, sharing in his life and holiness. This is the fullness of grace, the fullness of Christian life, authentic sanctity.

Holiness does not consist in the greatness of exterior works or in the richness of natural gifts, but in the full development of the grace and charity received in baptism, a development which is accomplished the more we open our hearts to the divine gift, and make ourselves fully available to God, ready and docile to his invitation and to his sanctifying action. So it is that a very humble Christian, who occupies only an unimportant place in the Church, possesses no outstanding human gifts, and has no great mission to accomplish, can reach a high level of holiness. In fact Jesus said he had come to save and sanctify in a special way these humble ones, these poor unknown ones, and he cried out; "I thank you, Father, Lord of heaven and earth, that you have hidden these things from the wise and understanding and revealed them to little ones" (Lk 10;21).

> *O eternal Father, for what reason did you hold man in such dignity? It was because of the priceless love with which you looked upon your creature in yourself and were enamored of him; for it was out of love that you created us and gave us being, so that we might enjoy your supreme and eternal goodness. Through our sin, we lost the dignity you had given us; through our rebellion we fell into conflict with your mercy, so that we became your enemies. Then, moved by the same fire of love which led you to create us, you desired to be reconciled with the human race which had fallen in that conflict, so that out of war great peace might come; you gave the Word, your Only-begotten Son, to be mediator between you and us. He was our justice, for he took upon himself the price of our injustice and obeyed your will in clothing himself with our human nature.*

O abyss of love! What heart can keep itself from breaking at the sight of the divine Majesty descending to the lowliness of our humanity? We are your image and you are ours, thanks to the union you have made with us, veiling your godhead in the miserable cloud and corruption of Adam. For what reason? Love! You, O God, became man, and man became God.

cf. St. Catherine of Siena, *Dialogue* 13 (pp. 36-37)

To you O Lord, I lift up my soul. O my God, in you I trust; let me not be put to shame. Let not my enemies exult over me. Let none that wait for you be put to shame; let them be ashamed who are wantonly treacherous. Make me know your ways, O Lord; teach me your paths. Lead me in your truth and teach me, for you are the God of my salvation.

Psalm 25, 1-5

4 — HOLINESS THROUGH CHARITY

O Lord, surely goodness and mercy shall follow me all the days of my life

(Ps 23 :6)

1. "The Lord God shall wipe away tears from every face" (Is 25:8), says Isaiah, referring to the work of salvation that God would one day carry out on behalf of his people. It is what was realized in the coming of Jesus: "Great crowds came to him, bringing with them the lame, the maimed, the blind, the dumb, and many others, and they put them at his feet and he healed them" (Mt 15:30). The work of Christ immediately showed itself as one of goodness and of infinite love for the relief of all human miseries. In such manner Jesus revealed to men God's intimate nature: love.

"God is love" (1 Jn 4:16), the apostle John would say later, drawing this assertion not from theoretical ideas, but from what he himself had seen with his eyes and touched with his hands of the Word of life, the Son of God (ib. 1): the sick cured, the dead restored to life, the oppressed and afflicted relieved, sinners absolved and brought back to spiritual life. Moreover John had listened to the Lord's discourses on the love of his heavenly Father, the love of which Jesus himself was the incarnation and by which he was led to give his life for the salvation of men. Under the inspiration of the Holy Spirit, the Apostle sums it up in a few simple words: "God is love."

The phrase though short has a most profound meaning. God is love; in other words, all that is in God, the whole being of God, is love: God is essentially love. Love, even human love, is a desire for what is good; it is the act by which the will is drawn toward the good. In God, infinite Being, love is an infinite will for the good and is directed toward infinite good which is God himself. In God,

Divine Intimacy

therefore, love is an infinite delight in his infinite goodness in which he finds his full happiness; and yet at the same time he does not shut up his love within himself, but pours it out, bringing innumerable creatures into existence in order to communicate to them his own goodness and happiness. He who is love creates men by an act of love, and by an act of love preserves them and leads them to their happiness by directing them toward himself, the highest good, and making them capable of loving him.

2. " 'God is love, and he who abides in love abides in God and God abides in him' (1 Jn 4:16). God has poured out his love in our hearts through the Holy Spirit who has been given us (cf. Rom 5:5); therefore the first and most necessary gift is charity, by which we love God above all things and our neighbor because of him" (LG 42).

The life of a Christian, like God's own life, must be essentially love: first of all, love for God, the infinite good, and then love for all men. This is possible for us because God has infused into our hearts a spark of his infinite love. Whoever cooperates with this divine love and lives in it "lives in God and God in him," precisely because he participates in the life of God which is love. But whoever opposes love with sin, extinguishes divine life within himself and falls headlong into death, for "he who does not love remains in death" (1 Jn 3:14). Charity and grace make up an inseparable unity; it is impossible to be "partakers of the divine nature" (2 Pet 1:4) if our hearts are closed to charity, because God is charity. On the other hand, the more we grow in love, the more we live in God, in intimate communion with him, to the point of no longer living for self but only for God (St. Thos 2-2, 16:6).

Since charity makes a soul a participant in the love that is God, it makes it like God, like his own Son, and unites it to himself; charity is therefore the greatest of the virtues, both in this life and in heaven. It will, in fact, endure for all eternity, and the eternal blessedness of each of the elect will depend on the intensity of each one's love.

Every Christian is holy, or rather participates in the holiness of God, in the measure in which he participates in his love. It follows that charity is truly "the first and most necessary gift" that God has given to man, and at the same time it is his first and greatest commandment: "You shall love the Lord your God with all your heart, and with all your soul, and with all your mind. This is the great and first commandment. And the second is like it: You shall love your neighbor as yourself" (Mt 22:37-39). Love is the essence of holiness, the dynamism of the Christian life and of the life of grace.

How easily we say: God is love! Indeed, the expression is brief: a simple sentence; but if you weigh it, how heavy it is! God is love . . . He who abides in love, abides in God and God in him. Make your abode in God and be yourself God's abode; abide in God and God will abide in you. God remains in you to hold you to himself; remain in God so as not to fall (1 Jn 9:1).

See Lord, how you excite me to love you. Would I be able to love you if you had not loved me first? Although I was once so indolent in loving you, do not let me be slow now in responding to your love. You were first in loving me . . . and not even after that am I ready to love you!

Although I was wicked you loved me and you destroyed my sinfulness; in spite of my sinfulness, you loved me, but you did not call me into the Church, because I continued in my sinful ways. You loved me when I was a sick person and came to visit me in order to cure me. Thus was your love for me made known, for you came into this world that I might have life through you (In 1 Jn 7:7).

I will not be alone in praising you, I will not be alone in loving you, I will not be alone in embracing you, for when I have embraced you there will still be room in your arms for others . . .

It would be shameful of me to want to bring you a jealous love . . . I will draw to your love my relations and all my household . . . in fact I shall draw as many as I can to you, through exhortations, prayers, discourses, arguments, all accompanied by gentleness and kindness. Yes, I shall lead them to love you, and to glorify you, and thus we shall all be united in glorifying you (In Ps 33,11,6-7).

St. Augustine

Love begets love. Even if we are at the very beginning and are very wretched, let us strive to keep this divine love always before our eyes and to waken ourselves to love. If at some time the Lord should favor us by impressing this love on our hearts, all will become easy for us, and we shall carry out our tasks quickly and without much effort. May His Majesty give us this love, on account of the love he bore us, and on account of his glorious Son, who demonstrated his love for us at so great a cost to himself.

St. Teresa, Life 22:14

5 — THE HOUSE ON THE ROCK

"Make me know your ways, O Lord; teach me your paths" (Ps 25:4)

1. The way which leads to holiness, and therefore to God, cannot be marked out except by God himself by his will. Jesus stated emphatically: "Not every one who says to me, 'Lord, Lord,' shall enter the kingdom of heaven, but he who does the will of my Father who is in heaven" (Mt 7:21). And in order to make it clear that those who are most closely united to him and most favored by him are precisely those who do God's will, he added: "Whoever

does the will of my Father in heaven is my brother, and sister, and mother" (ib. 12:50).

The saints found their inspiration in the school of Jesus. After St. Teresa of Jesus had experienced the most sublime mystical communications she did not hesitate to declare "the highest perfection consists not in interior favors or in great raptures or in visions or in the spirit of prophecy, but in the bringing of our wills so closely into conformity with the will of God that, as soon as we realize he wills anything, we desire it ourselves with all our might, and take the bitter with the sweet" (Fl 5:10). St. Therese of the Child Jesus echoes this: "Perfection consists in doing his will, in being what he wills us to be" (Autobiography).

True love of God consists in adhering perfectly to his holy will, not wanting to do or be anything in this life but what the Lord wishes, to the point that we become "a living will of God." When we view holiness in this light, it is possible for every soul of good will; indeed it is quite possible that one who leads a humble, hidden life may adhere to the divine will as well as, or perhaps even better than, a great saint to whom God has entrusted an important mission, and who has been enriched with special mystical graces. The more a soul does, and enjoys doing, the will of God, the more perfect and holy it is.

2. "Everyone who hears these words of mine and does them will be like a wise man who built his house upon the rock; and the rain fell and the floods came, and the winds blew and beat upon that house, but it did not fall, because it had been founded on the rock" (Mt 7:24-25). The will of God which is revealed in Sacred Scripture, especially in his commandments, is manifested in the concrete acts of Providence which supports and guides the entire life of man; it is the solid and secure rock upon which the edifice of Christian holiness must be built. Only upon such a foundation can it be built high without danger of falling under the fury of storms.

Whoever aspires to sanctity must always be on guard against the temptation of wanting to be a saint after his own fashion, according to his own views and plans and choices. That would be a contradiction, for only God, the one holy One, can make us holy, only he knows what is really profitable for our sanctification. The only path that infallibly leads to holiness is the one God has marked out. Therefore the first and indispensable condition for not working in vain is for the soul to abandon itself completely to the will of God, letting itself be led by him with entire docility.

St. John of the Cross teaches that in perfect union with God, and hence in the state of sanctity, "a man's will is so completely transformed into God's will that it excludes anything contrary to God's will, and in all and through all is motivated by the will of God" (Asc I 11:2). There is question here of a transformation through love through which a man does not want, seek, desire or do anything but the will of God, who is loved above all things, including self. Love in fact, leads to willing and not willing the same things, to an identity of affections, desires, ideals and actions.

And while the soul, with the help of grace, is endeavoring to adhere to the will of God in all things, this same will is sanctifying it and making it capable of an ever fuller adherence which will develop progressively into total conformity to the divine will. These are the souls who are pleasing to God, the just ones whom Isaiah prophesied would be the only ones worthy to enter the new Jerusalem: "Let the righteous nation which keeps faith enter in" (Is 26:2).

O my God, teach me not only what you want, but also what you are, because the more I know you the more I will love you, and loving you is my first duty, the thing you want most from me; it is also my greatest need... And together with your light give me the strength to follow it, my God; it is not enough to love you and to know your will, one must have the courage to serve you and to do what you want...

Cure me, Lord, I am blind and do not perceive your will; there are a thousand ways in which I do not know what you want from me; I do not see your beauty, and by not seeing you I do not love you enough... Enlighten my eyes, O God, cure my blindness, let me see your will and see your beauty... I am crippled too, O God; cure my weak feet! I have not the strength to come to you when you call me or to walk in your ways, no strength to put into practice what you show me: I drag my legs and hobble miserably when it comes to following you. O my God, cure me of this limp, make me run after you, following the scent of your perfume, instead of limping and dragging myself along in your footsteps...

Make me whole, give me the strength to carry my cross and follow you; the strength to do all you expect of me... O my God! And then, make me adore you with all the strength of my soul, and praise you from the bottom of my heart... Grant that I may be consumed and engulfed and lost in adoring you, my beloved Jesus! The light to see your will, the strength to carry it out, the love to lose myself in adoring you—these are the graces for you to pour out upon me... O my God, let me share abundantly in all three; you know how great is the need of this poor one who lies at your feet, so blind, so crippled, so cold.

C. de Foucauld, *Sulle feste dell'anno*, op. sp.

6 — LIVING IN GOD'S WILL

"Lead me in your truth, and teach me; for you are the God of my salvation."   *(Ps 25:5)*

1. "In that day the deaf shall hear ... the eyes of the blind shall see" (Is 29:18). The prophecy of Isaiah was fully verified in

the coming of Jesus, not only in the material sense, but in spiritual ways also: he prepared men's hearts to listen to the word of God and opened their eyes to recognize his ways and his will. The world always has need of this illumination. The sorrowful, trusting appeal of the two blind men of Jericho: "Have mercy on us, O Son of David" (Mt 9:27), is always timely, especially during Advent, which is a time of a renewed desire for salvation and sanctity. Besides it is always necessary for Jesus to come to free men from the "darkness and the shadow" that impede the recognition and full execution of the divine will.

The will of God is not manifested only through exact precepts; it is also written in the various circumstances of life which create for every man duties that he cannot escape. In the first place there are the duties of one's own state of life; they determine for each of us the manner of our daily conformity to the will of God. For the religious these are the duties prescribed by the Rule he has embraced and by the living voice of his superiors; for the priest, those which derive from his ministry in full union of mind and action with his bishop; for the laity, the obligations inherent in the family, in their various professions, and in the society in which they live. In addition there are duties connected with other situations which are ordered, or at least permitted, by God: health or sickness, wealth or poverty, aridity or spiritual comfort, failure or success, misfortunes or consolations. All is portioned out by the paternal hand of God who makes all things "work for good with those who love him" (Rom 8:28). It is according to all these circumstances that God presents to each of us our own particular duties of submission, patience, charity, and labor, and perhaps those of separation, sacrifice or generosity. If we follow the path of duty, we can be sure we are traveling in the way of God's will and are growing in his love.

"If love, as good seed, is to grow and bring forth fruit in the soul, each one of the faithful must willingly hear the word of God [even the silent word which is to be found in the circumstances of life], and with the help of his grace act to fulfill his will" (LG 42).

2. Holiness properly consists only in conformity to the divine will; it is expressed in continual and exact fulfillment of the duties of one's own state (Benedict XV. AAS 1920, p. 173). Yet holiness does not consist just in extraordinary undertakings; essentially it is to be found in the line of duty, and is therefore within the reach of every soul of good will. However it does require a generous and constant fulfillment of one's duty. Generous: that is, without negligence, anxious to please God in every act, ready to embrace with love each expression of his will. Constant: in all circumstances and situations, even in those that are less happy and pleasing, as also in dark moments of sadness, weariness and aridity, and all this, day after day. "What uncommon virtue is needed to accomplish ... with attention, piety and interior fervor of

spirit, the whole combination of common things which fill up our daily life" (Pius XI, Bertetto, vol. I, p. 759).

This exercise will be easier the more we learn to look at all the details of our life in the light of faith, getting used to recognizing in them signs of the will of God. As soon as one who really loves our Lord, notices that there is something God wants, he does it without hesitation, even if it costs him dearly. Certain delays and resistances stem not so much from unwillingness as from not understanding and recognizing the will of God. It is the spirit of faith that must illuminate us on this very important point.

"All of Christ's faithful, whatever be the conditions, duties and circumstances of their lives, will grow in holiness day by day through these very situations if they accept all of them with faith from the hand of their heavenly Father" (LG 41). Faith makes us go beyond the opaqueness of worldly affairs and see the hand of God who orders and guides everything for the sanctification of his elect. One never says no to God.

> *Now I freely give my will to you, O Lord, even though I do so at a time in which I am not free of self-interest. For I have felt and have had great experience of the gain that comes from freely abandoning my will to yours ... Your will, Lord, be done in me in every way and manner that you want. If you want it to be done with trials, strengthen me and let them come; if with persecutions, illnesses, dishonors, and a lack of life's necessities, here I am, my Father ...*
>
> *Oh what strength lies in this gift! It does nothing less, when accompanied by the necessary determination, than draw the Almighty so that he becomes one with our lowliness, transforms us into himself, and effects a union of the Creator with the creature ...*
>
> *And the more our deeds show that these are not merely polite words, all the more do you bring us to yourself and raise the soul from itself and all earthly things so as to make it capable of receiving great favors, for you never finish repaying this service in the present life. You esteem it so highly that we do not ourselves know how to ask for ourselves, and you never tire of giving. Not content with having made this soul one with yourself, you begin to find your delight in it, reveal your secrets, and rejoice that it knows what it has gained and something of what you will give it.*
>
> St. Teresa of Jesus *Way* 32:4, 10-12

> *O Lord, may your will be done in heaven and on earth, where we do not have pleasure unmixed with pain, nor roses without thorns, nor day not followed by night, nor spring not preceded by winter; on earth, O Lord, consolations are rare, and hardships innumerable. Nevertheless, O Lord, your will be done, not just in carrying out your commandments, your counsels and inspirations, which we must do, but also in the afflictions and sufferings which we must endure in order that your will may do with us, through us, and in us, all that is pleasing to you.*
>
> St. Francis de Sales, *Treatise on Love of God* IX, 1.

7 — MESSENGERS OF SALVATION

Praise the Lord, for he is gracious ... he gathers the outcasts, he heals the brokenhearted, and binds up their wounds   *(Ps 147, 1-3)*

1. "The Lord waits to be gracious to you; therefore he exalts himself to show mercy to you ... O people of Sion, ... you shall weep no more. He will surely be gracious to you at the sound of your cry; when he hears it, he will answer you" (Is 30:18-19). In words of tenderness, Isaiah describes God's untiring love for his people. But the full manifestation of this love is found in the person of the Messiah, who accomplishes and incarnates in the most sublime way all that the prophets have foretold. "Jesus went about all the cities and villages ... when he saw the crowds he had compassion for them: because they were harassed and helpless, like sheep without a shepherd" (Mt 9:35-36). Jesus is Emmanuel, God who has so loved men that he reaches out among them to bind up their wounds and heal their bruises (Is 30-26).

Jesus not only spends himself freely for all, but calls his friends to collaborate with him. Faced with the spectacle of the multitudes in need of guidance and help, "he said to his disciples: 'The harvest is plentiful, but the laborers are few. Pray therefore the Lord of the harvest to send out laborers into his harvest'" (Mt 9:37-38). "Pray!" this is the first collaboration asked of his followers: call upon the heavenly Father for enough workers to evangelize the whole world. There are even some to whom he entrusts a mission of perpetual prayer, for "no matter how urgent may be the needs of the active apostolate (these) will always have a distinguished part to play in the mystical Body of Christ ... by imparting a hidden apostolic fruitfulness" (PC 7). Others Jesus chooses to be workers and sends them to labor directly in the fields: then "he called to him his twelve disciples ... , he sent them out, charging them: 'Go ... preach ... saying, the kingdom of heaven is at hand'" (Mt 10:1,5-7).

All of us, whatever our walk of life, are called to collaborate in the work of salvation; "the Christian calling in fact is by its nature also a calling to the apostolate" (AA 2). Saved through Christ, we must in turn become in him and with him messengers and bearers of salvation.

2. When Jesus sent his disciples to preach the kingdom of heaven, he said: "You received without pay, give without pay" (Mt 10:8). The Master had called them to himself, had announced and brought salvation to them: the pardon of their sins and the free gift of his grace. Now it is their turn to do the same for their brothers: to preach the gospel, enlighten minds, and condition hearts for conversion. But not content with that, they must also, like Jesus, be concerned with men's material well-being: "Heal the sick, raise the dead, cleanse lepers, cast out demons" (ib.). The Son

of God who had willed to take human flesh knew only too well that we are not spirit alone, and he wants to save us in the fullness of our person. Just as we cannot cast aside our bodies, so we cannot effectively attain our spiritual good in isolation from the material part of our nature. When Jesus taught the multitudes and multiplied loaves of bread to feed them, forgave sins and healed their bodies, he was showing us that the work of salvation must embrace the whole man, and at the same time pointed out the easiest way to reach the human heart. The way that his infinite love took to reach us, is the way that we must follow in working for the salvation of our brothers.

Like Jesus, who in order to save mankind, became incarnate and adapted himself to all the concrete situations of men, apostles must know how to become one with their brothers in taking on their existential conditions. This is something to be expected not only of those who are apostles by profession—priests, religious, and all those consecrated to God—but of every faithful Christian. To do so it is not necessary to teach, but only to proclaim the Gospel, much more by life than by word, to bear witness to it with charity: with love, with a brotherly and generous service offered to whoever needs it. In this way we cooperate with the salvific will of God "showing every man through our earthly activities, the love with which God has loved the world" (LG 41).

> *Give ear, O Shepherd of Israel, you who lead (your people) like a flock! ... Stir up your might and come to save us! Restore us, O God; let your face shine that we may be saved! ... Turn again, O Lord of hosts! Look down from heaven and see; have regard for this vine, the stock which your right hand has planted ... Let your hand be upon the man of your right hand; the son of man whom you have made strong for yourself; give us life and we will call upon your name.*
>
> *Restore us, O Lord God of hosts! let your face shine that we may be saved.*
>
> *Psalm 80, 1-3, 14-19*

> *O God, you give me the strongest desire not to displease you in anything, however small, and the desire to avoid if possible every imperfection. For this reason alone, if for no other, I would like to flee people, and I greatly envy those who have lived in deserts. On the other hand, I would like to enter into the midst of the world to try to play a part in getting even one soul to praise you more ...*
>
> *Have pity on me, my God. Ordain that I may somehow fulfill my desires for your honor and glory. Do not be mindful of the little I deserve and of my lowly nature. You have the power, Lord, to make the great sea and the large river Jordan roll back and allow the children of Israel to pass ...*
>
> *Extend your powerful arm, Lord ... Let your grandeur appear in a creature so lowly, so that the world may know that this*

*grandeur is not hers at all and may praise you. This praise is what I
desire, and I would give a thousand lives—if I had that many—if one
soul were to praise you a little more.*

St. Teresa of Jesus, *The Interior Castle* VI 6:3-4

8 — SECOND SUNDAY OF ADVENT

YEAR A

O Lord, that I may bring forth fruit worthy of repentance. (Mt 3:8)

The figure of the Messiah becomes ever more clearly outlined
in prophecy. "There shall come forth a shoot from the stump of
Jesse, and a branch shall grow out of his root" (*Is* 11:1). Just when
the dynasty of David—the stock of Jesse—seems dead like a
dried-up tree trunk, the humble Virgin of Nazareth, who is espoused to Joseph of the family of David, gives birth to the Savior.
Isaiah presents him as full of the Holy Spirit, the peak of his gifts,
come to "judge the poor with justice" (ib. 4), and to raise up the
humble and oppressed who are to have a special place in his work
of salvation. Thus, under the allegory of a peaceful gathering of
animals who are enemies by instinct, the prophet speaks of the
peace that the Messiah will bring to the world, teaching men to
conquer the passions that make them act like wild beasts toward
one another, and instead, to love each other as brothers. Then "the
root of Jesse [Jesus the Savior] shall stand as an ensign to the people; him shall the nations seek" (ib. 10). It is the picture of universal salvation, which St. Paul takes up again in his letter to the
Romans, where he notes these last lines of Isaiah almost to the letter (*Rom* 15:12).

Christ, says the Apostle, came to save all men; he began his
mission first of all among the Jewish people, of whom "he became
a servant (ib. 8) in order to show God's faithfulness to the promises he had made to the Patriarchs; yet he did not reject the
pagans, but rather welcomed them so that his immense mercy
might be made manifest (ib. 9). He returns again to the theme of
reciprocal love: "Welcome one another, therefore, as Christ has
welcomed you, for the glory of God (ib. 7). The example of the Lord
who welcomes and saves all men is the basis for the good relations
they should have with one another. The love, harmony and peace
proclaimed by the prophets as prerogatives of the messianic era
are really the center of Christ's message; and yet after so many
centuries of Christianity, mankind is still rent by hatred and
discord and fratricidal strife. The world has not yet opened itself
up to the Gospel and been converted. The voice of the Baptist
which resounds throughout Advent is therefore more than ever
timely: Be converted, "for the kingdom of heaven is at hand" (Mt
3:2). All the prophets had preached conversion, but only the Bap-

tist was able to underline its urgency with the imminent approach of the kingdom of heaven through the presence of the Messiah in the world. To the people gathered to listen to him, St. John declares: "I baptize you with water ... but he who is coming after me, is mightier than I ... he will baptize you in the Holy Spirit and with fire" (ib. 11). Jesus has come, and has instituted baptism "with the Holy Spirit and with fire," the fruit of his passion-death-resurrection, but how many who have been baptized have been entirely converted to him, to his gospel, to his commandment of love? Advent again calls us all to a deeper conversion "for the kingdom of heaven is at hand!" It is closer today than ever before because Christ has been present and at work in the world now for centuries with his grace, with the Eucharist and with the sacraments; but we have not yet received him fully, we have not yet given him the whole of our hearts and lives.

Show us your power, O Lord, and help us with your great strength: let your love conquer the resistance of sin in us and hasten the moment of salvation.
Roman Missal, Collect of Thursday, 1st. week Advent

O Lord, if I loved you with all my strength, by virtue of this love I would love my neighbor as myself. Instead, I am so indifferent to his sufferings, while so touchy over the least of mine! I am reserved in showing him sympathy, slow in helping him, lukewarm in comforting him ... Where is the ardor or the tenderness of a St. Paul? To weep with those who weep, rejoice with the joyful, be weak with the weak; to suffer as if in a burning fire ourselves when some one is scandalized—where is all this?

O my God, if there is none of this in my heart, I have only to conclude that I do not love my neighbor as myself, and that I do not even love you with all my strength and all my heart ... O my God, make me understand the nature of my infirmity and how I need you in order to make use of my strength and energies so as to want what I really desire and to begin to want it.
J. B. Bossuet, Meditations on the Gospel, III, 48, v. 1, p. 225-226

YEAR B

"Show us your steadfast love, O Lord, and grant us your salvation"
(Ps 85:7)

A mighty cry rises from the Liturgy of Advent, summoning all men to prepare the way of the Lord who is to come. The prophet Isaiah had raised that cry in the old Testament: "A voice cries: in the wilderness prepare the way of the Lord, make straight in the desert a highway for our God! Every valley shall be lifted up and every mountain and hill made low" (Is 40:3-4). The immediate object of his prophecy was Israel's return from exile that was to be fulfilled under the guidance of God, foretold and awaited as savior of his people for whom the road through the desert was to be made ready. But as its final object the prophecy refers to the coming of the Messiah who is to free Israel and all mankind from the slavery of sin. He will be the shepherd who gathers the lambs in his arms and carries them in his bosom, who himself will gently lead those who are with young (ib. 11). It is the beautiful picture of Jesus, the good Shepherd, who will love his sheep so much that he will give his life for them.

In the Gospel of today the cry of Isaiah is repeated in exact words by John the Baptist: "the voice of one crying in the wilderness: Prepare the way of the Lord, make his paths straight" (Mk 1:3). The evangelist Mark thus introduces the forerunner who baptizes "in the wilderness, preaching the baptism of repentance for the forgiveness of sins" (ib. 4). The austere appearance of the Baptist reinforces his words; if he invites men to prepare the way of the Lord, he has prepared it first of all in his own person by withdrawing to the desert where he lives detached from all that is not God: he "was clothed with camel's hair . . . he ate locusts and wild honey" (ib. 6). Noisy revelling and softness of life do not make a favorable atmosphere either for proclaiming or answering the call to penance. The preacher must preach more by his life than by his words, and the listener must listen in a climate of silence and prayer and mortification. In a similar way we who believe must prepare ourselves to commemorate the coming of the Lord in the flesh, so that we may receive the blessings of Christmas with greater fullness.

By becoming holy in conduct and devotion (2 Pet 3:11-12) we also prepare ourselves for the coming of the Lord in glory. The expectation of the parousia made the early Christians impatient, while others, pointing out its delay, ridiculed it, and gave themselves up to a free and easy life. This is why St. Peter reminds us all that God does not measure time as men do; for him a thousand years is as a day (ib. 8). And if Christ's final coming is delayed it is not because God is unfaithful to his promises, but because he deals with us patiently . . . "not wishing that any should perish, but that all should reach repentance" (ib. 9). It is God's mercy that prolongs the time; each one of us ought to profit by it for his own conversion and to cooperate in that of others. Instead of becoming absorbed in worldly pursuits, we as believers ought to live with our hearts turned toward the "day of the Lord" that will surely come, but "like a thief" (ib. 10). We must behave so as to be "found without spot or blemish" (ib. 14) on that day, and, before that, on our own last day, when earthly life will yield to eternal life, the gift of Christ the Savior to those who believe in him.

All-powerful God, who command us to prepare the way for Christ the Lord, grant that in the extremity of our weakness we may not grow weary of waiting for the bright presence of the heavenly doctor. While we await the coming of your Son, give your people, O Lord, a spirit of great watchfulness, and following the teaching of our Savior, we shall go to meet him with our lamps lighted.

cf. Roman Missal, Collect, Wed. 2nd week Advent

O Lord, our early fathers in the faith waited for you as for the dawn. You will come at the end of time, when it pleases you, and when all will be in readiness for the last judgment. What have you still to give me, and what will be my eternal destiny? ...

You will give me pardon and also perseverance, that sublime gift which is hidden like a pearl beneath the bitterness of death and is the seal of liberation for your elect. I wait for it, I should prepare myself better for it and live in this blessed anticipation.

My God, on account of your definite coming, suppress in me the sin which hinders your work, destroy all that impedes it, triumph over every weakness; and come, at the hour you choose, like a long-desired master.

P. Charles, *La Priere de toutes les heures.*

YEAR C

"Prepare the way of the Lord; make straight his paths" (Lk 3:4)

"O Jerusalem, take off the garment of your sorrow and affliction, and put on forever the beauty of the glory from God ... Put on the robe of the righteousness from God ... For God will lead Israel with joy in the light of his glory, with the mercy and righteousness that comes from him." (Bar 5:1-2,9). In poetic language, Jerusalem, desolate and deserted through the exile of her children, is invited by the prophet Baruch to rejoice because the day of salvation is drawing near and her people will come back to her, led by God himself. Jerusalem is the figure of the Church. She, too, suffers on account of the estrangement and dispersal of so many of her children, and she, too, is incited in Advent to rekindle her hopes, confiding in the Savior, who mystically comes again each Christmas to lead her to salvation with all her people. Sin separates man from God and from the Church; the way back is prepared by God himself through the incarnation of his only Son. And in Advent the whole of the people of God goes forth to meet him.

The prophets spoke of a way in the desert that would make the return from exile easy. But when the Baptist takes up their teachings and appears on the banks of the Jordan like a "voice of one crying in the wilderness: Prepare the way of the Lord; make his path straight" (Lk 3:4), he no longer urges them to build roads, but instead, to prepare their hearts to receive the Messiah who has already come and is about to begin his work. It is for this that

John went about "preaching the baptism of repentance for the forgiveness of sins" (ib. 3). To be converted means to purify oneself from sin, straighten crookedness of heart and mind, shore up the sinking ground of inconstancy and caprice, knock down pretenses of pride, conquer the resistance of selfishness and destroy acrimony in our relations with our neighbor: it means, in short, to make our life a straight path which leads to God without crookedness or compromise. It is not a program to be exhausted in one Advent, but one which is to be carried out every Advent in a new and deeper way in order to make ourselves more ready for the coming of our Savior. Thus "all flesh, [that is every man] shall see the salvation of God" (ib. 6).

Personal conversion also includes the duty of working for the good of one's brothers and of the community; such is the conclusion we should draw from the second reading. St. Paul is rejoicing with the Philippians over their generous contribution toward the spread of the Gospel and prays that their charity may grow and become ever more splendid, so that they may be "pure and blameless for the day of Christ, filled with the fruit of repentance" (Phil 1:10-11). Eschatological expectation dominates this passage in harmony with the spirit of Advent, and there is a renewed call to hasten the conversion of self and of others which will only come to an end with "the day of Jesus Christ" (ib. 6). However we need to remember that our personal salvation and that of others is much more the work of God than of man. Man must collaborate diligently, but it is God who both begins the good work and carries it to completion (ib. 2:13). It is only with the help of grace that man can be rich "with the harvest of justice" on the final day, because justice, that is, holiness, is acquired only "in Christ Jesus" by opening oneself with humility and trust to his sanctifying action.

Stir up our hearts, O God: teach us to prepare the way for your only Son; and through the mystery of his coming, make us serve you with renewed spirit. (Coll. Thurs. II week Advent).

O Lord Jesus, in your first coming in the humble state of human nature, you fulfilled the ancient promise and opened the way to eternal salvation. Grant that when you come again in the splendor of your glory we may at last obtain, in the fullness of light, the promised salvation that now we only dare hope for in watchful expectation. (cf Preface of Advent I).

Roman Missal

O Lord, I do not boast of my works ... nor do I praise the works of my hands: I am afraid that when you examine them you may find more sin than merit. Only one thing do I ask, only one thing, I say, do I desire: that you scorn not the works of your hand.

Preserve in me your work, not mine; because by looking at mine you may condemn me; looking at yours, you will give me a crown. Since whatever is good in me all comes to me from you, it is therefore more yours than mine... Through your goodness I have been saved by means of faith, not through any merit of mine, but through your gift; not in virtue of my works lest I become proud. I am your creature, fashioned by your grace together with my good works.

St. Augustine, In Ps. 137,18.

9 — THE IMMACULATE CONCEPTION

December 8

Hail, full of grace; the Lord is with you. (Lk 1,28)

1. The feast of the Immaculate Conception is in perfect harmony with the spirit of Advent; it is only fitting that while the Church is preparing for the coming of the Redeemer we should think of her who had been conceived without sin because she was to be his mother.

The very promise of the Savior was joined to, or rather included in, the promise made to this "peerless Virgin." After cursing the serpent, God declared: "I will put enmity between you and the woman, and between your seed and her seed: he—(her offspring)—shall bruise your head" (Gen 3:15). The struggle between the offspring of the woman and that of the serpent began with Mary: war was declared from the first moment of her existence, for she was conceived without any stain of sin, and hence was in complete opposition to Satan. Hostility would continue to grow and would finally end in victory when Jesus appeared in the world and destroyed sin by his death. Mary's vocation is thus the first step in the history of salvation: she is mother of the Redeemer and at the same time the first of the redeemed, being preserved from the least shadow of guilt by virtue of the merits of Jesus.

The privilege of Mary Immaculate does not consist solely in the absence of original sin, but much more in being "full of grace." "The Mother of Jesus gave to the world that very life which renews all things . . . and was enriched by God with gifts befitting such a role . . . (She was) adorned from the first instant of her conception with the splendors of an entirely unique holiness" (LG 56). Gabriel's greeting, "Hail, full of grace, the Lord is with you!" is the strongest testimony of the Immaculate Conception of Mary, who would not be "full of grace" in the complete sense of the word if she had been stained by sin for a single moment.

Thus the Blessed Virgin began life with a richness of grace which far surpasses that which the greatest saints acquire at the end of their lives. When we also consider her absolute fidelity and her total availability to God, we can faintly imagine to what heights of love and communion with God she attained, far beyond "all other creatures in heaven and on earth" (LG 53).

2. In his letter to the Ephesians, St. Paul agrees with the Gospel in presenting Mary as "full of grace." "Blessed be God . . . " he says, "who has blessed us in Christ with every spiritual blessing in the heavenly places . . . (God) chose us in him before the foundation of the world that we should be holy and blameless before him . . . in love . . . to the praise of his glory" (Eph 1:3-6). The Blessed Virgin holds primacy of place in the blessing and choice of God; in the fullest and most absolute sense, she is the only holy and immaculate creature of God. In Mary the divine blessing has brought forth its most perfect and beautiful fruit. This was both because she had been blessed and chosen "in Christ" in anticipation of his merits, and because in the service of Christ, she was to be his mother.

Today the Church invites her children to praise God for the wonders accomplished in this humble virgin: "O sing to the Lord a new song, for he has done marvelous things (Ps 98:1)—that prodigious "thing" of breaking the chain of original sin that binds all other children of Adam, for to Mary was applied, in anticipation, the work of salvation that would be accomplished by Jesus who was to be born of her.

The Virgin of Nazareth is thus the first of all the host of the redeemed: with her begins the history of salvation in which she herself collaborated by giving to the world him by whom all men will be saved. Those who believe in the Savior have only to follow her; after Mary, and through her mediation, they have been blessed and chosen "in Christ" by God to be holy and immaculate . . . in charity. If this divine plan was fulfilled in Mary with a singular and privileged fullness, it must also be accomplished in every one of us according to the measure set by God. For that to come about, we have only to model our lives on that of the Immaculate Virgin: to imitate her in fidelity to grace, and in unceasing opening and consecration to God. Just as in Mary the fullness of grace blossomed into fullness of love for God and man, so in every one of us grace should ripen into charity toward God and our fellow-man to the glory of God and the advancement of the Church.

It is right and just, O Almighty God, that we give you thanks, and with the help of your power, celebrate the feast of the Blessed Virgin Mary. Indeed from her sacrifice blossomed the stalk which was to nourish us with the Bread of the angels. Eve ate of the fruit of sin, but Mary gave us instead the sweet fruit of the Savior. How different the deeds of the serpent from those of the Virgin! From the former the poison poured out that separated us from God, in Mary the mystery of our redemption had its beginning. Through Eve the wickedness of the tempter prevailed; in the grace of Mary the Savior's majesty found cooperation. By her sin Eve killed her own offspring, which rose again in Mary in the grace of the Creator who freed our human nature from slavery and restored it to its former liberty. Whatever we lost in our common father Adam, we have recovered in Christ.

Ambrosian Preface from *Maria Regina della Chiesa.*

Through you, O Mary, blessed finder of grace, may we have access to your Son, that through you we may be received by him who through you was given to us.

May your integrity and purity excuse before him the stain of our corruption; may our humility, so pleasing to God, obtain from him the pardon of our vanity.

May your abundant charity cover the multitude of our iniquities, and your glorious fruitfulness supply our indigence of merits.

Our Lady, our Mediatrix, our Advocate, reconcile us to your Son, commend us to your Son, present us to your Son.

By the grace you have found, by the prerogative you have merited, by the Mercy you have brought forth, obtain, O blessed one, that he who vouchsafed to become partaker of our infirmity and misery, may through your intercession, make us partakers of his blessedness and glory.

St. Bernard, *In Advent* II:7.

10 — THIS IS THE WAY

"Come, let us go up to the mountain of the Lord, ... that he may teach us his ways"   *(Is 2:3)*

1. The words of Isaiah still echo through our Advent weeks: "Say to those who are of fearful heart: Be strong, fear not! ... a highway shall be there, and it shall be called the holy way ... The redeemed shall walk there ... and come to Sion with singing" (35:4, 8-10). Just as the people of Israel were urged not to lose faith because of the defeats and the exile they endured, but to trust that God would save them and lead them back to Jerusalem when it was at last saved and reestablished in peace, so now we are urged to prepare ourselves with trusting hearts for the new coming of Jesus, our Savior. For us too, there stretches out "a way ... the holy way" which, under the guidance and in the footsteps of Christ, will lead us, not indeed to the earthly Jerusalem, but to the more sublime goal of holiness.

St. John of the Cross has synthesized the whole way which leads to holiness in a very expressive drawing. At the top is a circle, the symbol of a mountain whose summit represents Christian perfection; from the base three paths lead toward the top, but only one, the narrowest, reaches it: the saint called it "the way of nothing," and it is the only one which leads directly to where is written: "only the honor and glory of God abide here." It is the way of nothing, because to follow it one must abandon all that stands in the way of seeking and loving God above all things, all that engages the heart in the desires and goods of the world, or delays it in a selfish search for spiritual satisfaction. In the language of Isaiah, this path would be called a "straight way," a "holy way." Cleansed of every trace of sin, of all disordered seeking of creatures or of one's self, the soul is wholly directed toward seeking God, his honor and his glory.

This is the road that Jesus our Savior opened to every man, first traveling it himself, who "though he was in the form of God, did not count equality with God a thing to be grasped, but emptied himself, taking the form of a servant, being born in the likeness of men" (Phil 2:6-7); again he said: "If any man would come after me, let him deny himself" (Mt 16:24).

2. At either side of the "way of nothing," there are two other easier, more comfortable roads which St. John of the Cross calls the ways "of the imperfect spirit"; these come to an end half way up the mountain, making it impossible to reach the top. The imperfect spirit is one that is "attached" to the goods of earth or even to spiritual goods used with a view to personal satisfaction.

To get out of "the path of the imperfect soul" it is necessary not to love or want anything that is not in full conformity with the will of God. Every object loved for itself, and not according to the divine will, becomes a source of desires and preoccupations; it moves the heart of man and impels him to act only for his own satisfaction. In one who is still attached to earthly things or to himself, there are so many principles of action very unlike the will of God. Such a soul is traveling along on just these "paths of the imperfect," which will never lead it to holiness. For that reason, the mystical Doctor wrote next to these paths, in his drawing: "neither the goods of earth, nor of heaven"; therefore, *nothing*.

We are not speaking of a nothing that leads to emptiness and to death, but rather to everything, to fullness, to life: to life renewed in Christ, refinding in him with a pure heart all the goods of earth and of heaven. It is like a rebirth from which a man comes out a new creature, re-clothed in Christ, through the merits of him who being God willed to live among men, a man like themselves. Every Christmas, the commemoration of the birth of Jesus should mark a genuine spiritual rebirth for us. On this road, the way of the nothing, the straight and holy way which leads to holiness, we shall encounter struggle and rejection, but we must not yield to discouragement for we are not alone. "Though the Lord give you the bread of adversity and the water of affliction yet your teacher will not hide himself any more: but your eyes shall see your teacher. And your ears shall hear a voice behind you, saying 'This is the way; walk in it!' " (Is 30:20-21). Jesus, the teacher is with his disciple: the disciple has no reason to fear.

Now I love you alone: You alone do I follow: You alone do I seek:

You alone am I ready to serve, for You alone have just dominion; under your sway do I long to be. Order, I beg you, and command what you will; but heal and open my ears, so that with them I may hear your words. Heal and open my eyes so that with them I may perceive your wishes. Banish from me my senselessness, so that I may know you. Tell me where I should turn that I may behold you: and I hope I shall do all you have commanded me.

Look, I beseech you, upon your prodigal, O Lord, kindest Father; already have I been punished enough: long enough have I served your enemies whom you have beneath your feet; long enough have I been the plaything of deceits ... I realize I must return to you. Let your door be open to my knocking. Teach me how to come to you. I have nothing else but willingness. Naught else do I know save that fleeting and perishable things are to be spurned, certain and eternal things to be sought after. This I do, O Father, because this is all I know, but how I am to reach you I know not. Do you inspire me, show me, give me what I need for my journey. If it is by faith that they find you who have recourse to you, give me faith; if it is through virtue, give me virtue: if it is by knowledge, give me knowledge. Grant me increase of faith, of hope and of charity.

St. Augustine, *Soliloquy* I:5

O Lord, how gentle are your ways! But who will walk them without fear? I fear to live without serving you; and when I set out to serve you, I find nothing that proves a satisfactory payment for anything of what I owe. It seems I want to be completely occupied in your service, and when I consider well my own misery I see I can do nothing good, unless you give me this good. O my God and my Mercy! What shall I do so as not to undo the great things you have done for me?

Do not abandon me, Lord, because I hope that in you my hope will not be confounded; may I always serve you; and do with me whatever you will.

St. Teresa of Jesus *Soliloquies* I:1-2; XXVII:6.

11 — THE GIFT OF GOD

Sing to the Lord, bless his name; tell of his salvation from day to day
(Ps 96,2)

1. "Behold the Lord God comes with might, and his arm rules for him . . . He will feed his flock like a shepherd: he will gather the lambs in his arms, he will carry them in his bosom, and gently lead those that are with young" (Is 40:10-11). The majestic figure of God coming in power to deliver Israel is followed by that of the meek and gentle Lord who guides his people with the affectionate concern of a shepherd for his flock. This latter image was so dear to the prophets of old that they used it to express God's love for

Israel. Jesus took it up and applied it to himself, the good shepherd who leaves the ninety-nine sheep in the mountains and goes in search of the one who is lost, because he does not want a single "one of these little ones to perish" (Mt 18:12,14). Jesus the good Shepherd who will give his life for his sheep, loves and knows each one individually and wants to establish with each a relationship of affectionate intimacy like that which exists between his Father and himself (Jn 10:14-15). Not even the least is forgotten: the Lord wants to gather all men around him, not only to save them, but also to offer them his friendship in order to admit them into intimate communion with himself. He promises all: "If a man loves me . . . my Father will love him and we will come to him and make our home with him" (Jn 14:23).

Israel had enjoyed the great privilege of God's presence among his people: God had accompanied them across the desert, protected them in battle, and guided them in their return from the Babylonian exile; he had taken up his abode in the holy ark, and later in the temple at Jerusalem. Jesus openly reveals to the new Israel an immensely greater privilege: the indwelling of the Trinity in each of those who love him. God is not only the shepherd, the defender who guides, comforts, protects and saves his people, he is the friend, the host who wants to make his dwelling in their hearts and to live with them in sweet intimacy.

2. God is necessarily present in all his creatures. Indeed, in order to exist, they need not only his creative act, but also his providence to keep them in existence; in fact, he sustains them by acting within them, that is, by continually communicating existence to them. Since he acts by his substance, he is present wherever he acts, and is therefore in all his creatures. Thus God is everywhere, even in the souls of unbelievers and sinners.

But in the soul living in grace and charity, God makes himself present in a special way, in the way precisely promised by Jesus: that presence which is called *indwelling*. "The divine Persons are said to be *indwelling* in as much as they are present to intelligent creatures in a way that lies beyond human comprehension, and are known and loved by these in a purely supernatural manner alone that transcends all created nature" (Pius XII *Mystici Corporis*). The three divine Persons are present in the soul that is in the state of grace so that it may know them by faith and love them by charity; they invite it to live in communion with them, that is, in intimate friendship with the Father, the Son and the Holy Spirit. Jesus repeats: "Abide in me and I in you" (Jn 15:4). "As you, Father, are in me, and I in you; that they also may be (one) in us" (ib. 17:21); where the Father and Son are, there is the Holy Spirit: "the Spirit of truth . . . dwells with you and will be in you" (ib. 14:17).

"The dignity of man"—according to Vatican II—"consists above all in this call to communion with God" (GS 19), a commu-

nion which is attained precisely through the mystery of the indwelling of the Trinity in those who love God. In regard to each of
these souls we can repeat with full truth the words which made
such an impression on Sister Elizabeth of the Trinity: "The Father
is in you, the Son is in you, the Holy Spirit is in you." What a
tremendous gift! "If you knew the gift of God" (Jn 4:10).

*O my Lord and my God! I cannot say this without tears and
great joy of soul. How you desire, Lord, thus to be with us and to be
present in the Sacrament (for in all truth this can be believed since it
is so, and in the fullness of truth we can make this comparison); and
if it were not for our fault, we could rejoice in being with you, and
you would be glad to be with us since you say that your delight is to
be with the children of men. O my Lord, what is this? As often as I
hear these words, they bring me great consolation; they did so even
when I was very far gone. Is it possible, Lord that there be a soul
that reaches the point where you bestow similar favors and gifts,
and understands that you are to be with it, that goes back to offending you after so many favors and after such striking demonstrations
of the love you have for it which cannot be doubted since the effects
of it are obvious? Yes, there certainly is one, and not one who has
done this once, but done it many times—for it is I. And may it please
your goodness, Lord, that I might be the only ungrateful one and the
only one who has done such terrible evil and shown such excessive
ingratitude. But even from this evil, your infinite goodness has
drawn out something worthwhile; and the greater the evil, the more
resplendent the wonder of your mercies. And how many are the
reasons I can sing your mercies forever!*

St. Teresa, *Life* 14:10.

*My God, I am dismayed and want to say: "Depart from me, O
Lord, for I am a sinner," but I do not say it; oh! no, quite the contrary: "Stay with us, Lord, for night is coming." I am in the night of
sin, and the light of salvation can come only from you; stay, O Lord,
because I am a sinner, but I am discouraged at seeing all the imperfections I am committing in your sight every hour, at every moment, continually ... You are within me; and before you and in you,
at every moment from morning until night, I am committing faults
and omissions without number, in thought, word, and deed ...
This is part of what has held me back for a long time from looking for you within myself so that I could adore you and kneel at your
feet. I was dismayed, too, at feeling you thus within me, so close to
my misery and to my innumerable imperfections.*

C. de Foucauld, *Sulle feste dell'anno,* Op. Sp.

12 — COME TO ME

As a father pities his children, so the Lord pities those who fear him.
(Ps 103:13)

1. "Come to me all who labor and are heavy laden and I will give you rest ... and you will find rest for your souls" (Mt 11:28-29). Jesus, who came "to preach good news to the poor ... and to proclaim release to the captives ... and to set at liberty those who are oppressed" (Lk 4:18) calls all to him, especially those who are suffering in body and in soul, those who are worn out with the troubles of life: he will console them, give them strength, grant them comfort and rest.

People today, driven by unbridled activity, seem almost incapable of pausing, yet their souls have an immense need of a refreshing respite. There is no question here of the kind of rest that makes one lazy, but of that which is born of solitude, silence and prayer, the indispensable conditions required for entering into oneself and meeting with God. Jesus invites and calls us to repose, to a face to face intimacy with him: "Come away by yourselves to a lonely place, and rest a while" (Mk 6:31). Without such pauses for recollection, it is an illusion to aspire to living the most elementary interior life. Every activity, however important and urgent, must be contained within certain limits in order to leave enough room for the supreme activity of prayer. These periods of rest are sacred and cannot be sacrificed without running the risk of harming true spiritual life. The word of Jesus applies here: "Seek first the kingdom of God" (Lk 12:31, Douai). In a certain sense the kingdom of God is already in the heart of the Christian where the most Holy Trinity dwells; but this kingdom cannot be discovered without moments of escape from everything and everyone, in order to concentrate in silence and solitude on prayer, the intimate and personal dialogue with God.

2. "When you pray, go into your room, and shut the door and pray to your Father who is in secret," says St. Matthew (6:6). Vatican Council II reiterates these words and affirms: "The Christian is assuredly called to prayer with his brethren, but he must also enter into his chamber to pray to his Father in secret" (SC 12). Some definite form of solitude, of effective withdrawal from the noise and preoccupations of life is indispensable for prayer, in which one has ears only to listen to God and voice only to speak to him. But solitude and material retirement will not suffice if they are not accompanied by interior recollection. John of the Cross comments on the Lord's words: "Closing the door behind you (your will to all things), you should pray to your Father in secret" (Sp. Cant. 1:9). It is not enough to shut only the material door of our room, we must close our will to everything: business, worries,

thoughts, desires, affections; we must make room to pay attention only to God; all our powers must be free to concentrate on him.

St. Teresa of Jesus writes: "This little bit of time that we resolve to give him, which we spend on ourselves ... let us give it to him since we desire to do so, with our thoughts free of other things, and unoccupied by them. And let us be determined never to take it back from him, neither because of trials on this account, nor because of contradictions, nor because of dryness" (*Way* 23:2). Only then can the soul meet God effectively and find refreshment in him for its tired spirit, so often embittered by the anxieties of life; every day, in intimate contact with God, it can draw light and strength to continue on its way in full harmony with the gospel. God "gives power to the faint, and to him who has no might he increases strength. Even youths shall faint and be weary, and young men shall fall exhausted: but they who wait for the Lord shall renew their strength ... They will run and not be weary, they shall walk and not faint" (Is 40:29-31).

O my God, Trinity whom I adore! Help me to become utterly forgetful of self, that I may bury myself in you, as changeless and as calm as though my soul were already in eternity. May nothing disturb my peace or draw me out of you, O my immutable Lord! but may I at every moment penetrate more deeply into the depths of your mystery!

Give peace to my soul; make it your heaven, your cherished dwelling place, your home of rest. Let me never leave you there alone, but keep me there, all absorbed in you, in living faith, adoring you and wholly yielded up to your creative action!

Elizabeth of the Trinity, *Spiritual Doctrine,* Philipon p. 53-54.

I consider it impossible for us to pay so much attention to worldly things if we take the care to remember we have a Guest like you within us, for we then see how lowly these things are next to what we possess within ourselves ...

Though it was obscure for some time, I understood well that I had a soul. But what this soul deserved and who dwelt within it I did not understand because I had covered my eyes with the vanities of the world. For, in my opinion, if I had understood as I do now that in this little palace of my soul so great a King as you, my Lord, made his dwelling, I would not have left you alone so often. I would have remained with you at times and striven more so as not to be so unclean. But what a marvelous thing, that you who would fill a thousand worlds and many more with your grandeur would enclose yourself in something so small! ... Since you are Lord you are free to do what you want, and since you love us you adapt yourself to our size ... You are free to do what you want since you have the power to make this palace a large one. The whole point is that we should give ourselves to you with complete determination, and we should

empty the soul in such a way that you can store things there or take
them away as though it were your own property.

St. Teresa of Jesus, *Way* 28:10-12

13 — IN SEARCH OF GOD

Lord, "may all who seek you rejoice and be glad in you" (Ps 70:4)

1. "For I, the Lord your God hold your right hand: it is I who say to you, 'Fear not, I will help you!' " (Is 41:13). So did God assure Israel of his continual presence and protection.

If the ancient people of God had every reason to trust in the Lord and to feel that he was always near at hand, how much stronger are the grounds his new people, the Christian people, have for this. Not only is God close to every believer, guiding him with fatherly providence; he has made his temple within him: "Do you not know that you are God's temple, and that God's Spirit dwells in you?" (1 Cor 3:16). The infallible word of Jesus resounds continually in the heart of every Christian: "If a man loves me . . . we will come to him and make our home with him" (Jn 14:23).

Just the same there still remains a great question: if God abides in every person who lives in the state of grace, why does such a person have such difficulty in finding him and in recognizing his presence? John of the Cross answers: "It should be known that the Word, the Son of God, together with the Father and the Holy Spirit is hidden by his essence and his presence in the innermost being of the soul. A person who wants to find him must leave all things through affection and will, enter into himself in deepest recollection and regard things as though they were nonexistent" (Sp C 1:6). The answer is clear: God is within us, but he is *hidden.* In order to find him we must go forth from everything as regards *affection and will.* That means to detach ourselves, to renounce ourselves, annihilate ourselves, to die spiritually to ourselves and to all things, not so much, or only, by a physical withdrawal, but especially by detachment of the affections and the will. It is the path of the "nothing," or complete detachment; it is the death of the old man, the indispensable condition for putting on Christ, for life in God. St. Paul, too, has said: "You have died, and your life is hid with Christ in God" (Col. 3:3).

The loving search for God present in our heart goes hand in hand with this dying to the world and to ourselves. In this sense, the more we die to ourselves, the more we find God.

2. The soul . . . "in order to speak to its eternal Father and to find its delight in him has no need to go to heaven . . . neither is there any need for wings to go to find him. All one need do is to go into solitude and look at him within us" (St. Teresa, *Way* 28:2).

But in actual fact, Christians, even those consecrated to God, are very often satisfied with a superficial life, pretty much an exterior one, which makes them incapable of recollecting themselves interiorly in order to come into contact with God. We have in us a host of inclinations, ideas, and strong passions which make us turn toward creatures and induce us to give them our heart, to build our hopes on them and find consolation in their presence and remembrance. All this can make us go so far as to forget, or at least neglect the great treasure that we carry within us: God, living and present, who urges us on to a life that is deeper and truer, a life of intimate communion with him. The Lord awaits us there, in the depths of our soul, where he has set up his abode; but we find it very difficult to recollect ourselves at such a depth, and continue to let ourselves be taken up with a thousand external matters to which we give all our interest.

"Anyone who is to find a hidden treasure," warns St. John of the Cross, "must enter the hiding place secretly, and once he has discovered it, he will also be hidden just as the treasure is hidden. Since, then, your beloved Bridegroom is the treasure hidden in a field, for which the wise merchant sold all his possessions (Mt 13:44) ... in order to find him you should forget all your possessions and all creatures and hide in the interior, secret chamber of your spirit" (Sp C 1:9). Without a certain avoidance of the outer world, of the superficial life, it is impossible to reach God who is present, but hidden, in us; it is impossible to live in communion with him who never abandons us unless we first abandon him.

> *O then, soul, most beautiful among all the creatures, so anxious to know the dwelling place of your Beloved that you may go in quest of him and be united with him, now we are telling you that you yourself are his dwelling and his secret chamber and hiding place. Rejoice, and see that all your good and hope is so close to you as to be within you, or better, that you cannot be without him ...*
>
> *What more do you want, O soul! What else do you search for outside, when within yourself you possess your riches, delights, satisfactions and kingdom—the Beloved whom you desire and seek. Be joyful in your interior recollection with him ...! Desire him there, adore him there. Do not go in pursuit of him outside of yourself. You will only become distracted and wearied, and you shall not find him nor enjoy him more securely, nor sooner, nor more intimately than by seeking him within you.*
>
> St. John of the Cross, *Spiritual Canticle*, 1:7-8.

> *A soul which listens to self, which is preoccupied with its feelings, which indulges in useless thoughts or desires, scatters its forces. It is not completely under God's sway. Its lyre is not in tune, so that when the Master strikes it, he cannot draw forth divine harmonies; it is too human and discordant.*

Divine Intimacy

The soul which reserves anything for self in its interior kingdom, whose powers are not all "enclosed" in God, cannot be a perfect "Praise of Glory,"... because it is not in unity. So that, instead of persevering in praise, in simplicity, whatever may happen, it must be continually tuning the strings of its instrument, which are all a little off key. How necessary is this blessed unity for the soul that desires to live here below the life of the blessed—that is, of simple beings, of spirits.

Elizabeth of the Trinity, *2 Retreat* 2.

14 — LIFE WITH GOD

"He who follows me, will not walk in darkness"   *(Jn 8:12)*

1. Jesus compares men to capricious children, whom nothing pleases or satisfies. "John came neither eating or drinking, and they say: 'He has a devil.' The Son of Man came eating and drinking, and they say: 'Behold a glutton and a drunkard, a friend of tax collectors and sinners' " (Mt 11:18-19). History repeats itself; today also, men find it easier to criticize the gospel and the Church than to follow Christ the savior, who is light and infinite truth.

Those who consider themselves believers do not always give evidence of complete adherence to Christ; often their way of life fluctuates between the caprices of wanting and not wanting, in inconsistency between faith and works. Only a full participation which embraces and engages our entire life will permit us to achieve a living contact with God. "If a man loves me he will keep my word ... we will come to him and make our home with him" (Jn 14:23).

We cannot always keep ourselves in solitude and in prayer in order to live with God present in our heart. There are occupations and contacts with others which are connected with the duties of our state of life and are therefore expressly willed by God; if these activities are attended to in the measure required by the divine will, they cannot of themselves be obstacles to our union with God. However we must always keep within the limits of God's will and so be guided by a single purpose: to do our duty in order to give pleasure to God. When, on the other hand, although doing our duty, we look for a little personal satisfaction as well—such as gratifying curiosity or our natural desire for affection, trying to gain some selfish advantage or to win the esteem of others—at that point we stray from the path of God's will, our heart becomes attached to this and that, we waste our energies in useless chatter and empty desires, and make ourselves incapable of living in communion with God. A constant and generous effort is necessary if we are to free ourselves of these weaknesses; above all we need that great uprightness of intention through which a Christian soul seeks God and is united to him in no matter what occupation.

"Whatever you do, in word or deed," urges St. Paul, "do everything in the name of the Lord Jesus" (Col 3:17).

2. "I am the Lord your God, who teaches you profitable things and guide you on the way you walk. Oh, that you would hearken to my commandments . . . " (Is 48:17-18). All our troubles and all our errors come from not following fully God's teachings, his guidance, his commandments. And conversely, all our good follows from perfect compliance with every least sign of God's will. "You are my friends if you do what I command you" (Jn 15:14). The greatest good that comes from friendship with God and from communion with him, is precisely the fruit of generous availability to the divine wishes; an availability which should not be limited to the moments of intimacy in prayer, but should extend to every area of life.

Union with God in this world is achieved much more by means of the will than by the intellect. Even when our duty—study, work, teaching, the apostolate—requires intense application of the mind, and dedication to the work at hand, we can still remain oriented to God by the affection of the heart, that is, "with the desire of charity" that unceasingly urges us to seek God, and his will and glory. If the charity of Christ is urging us, nothing will be able to separate us from him. In that case, all our actions, affairs and works, instead of distracting us from God, will become means of uniting us to him. Vatican Council II affirms: "Everything . . . works, prayers, and apostolic endeavors, ordinary married and family life, daily labor, mental and physical relaxation, if carried out in the Spirit, even the hardships of life when patiently borne—all these become spiritual sacrifices acceptable to God through Christ Jesus" (LG 34). "Spiritual sacrifices pleasing to God" fortify our friendship with God more and more. But in order to do this, they must be "carried out in the Spirit," that is, in conformity with the Holy Spirit who guides us in a single direction: perfect compliance with the will of God. For this to be reality and not utopia, we must go beyond practicing detachment to cultivating interior recollection. Then even in the midst of a busy life, we shall be able to catch the voice of the Spirit—his inspirations and invitations—and then follow them with an open heart.

O Jesus, to do your Father's will, to do everything in his sight was what you lived for . . . May this also be our food and our life: to act incessantly in your sight, to live on this, to live on the thought of your will, on the thought of your glory, of this search and this realization . . . To have your will and your glory unceasingly before our eyes. This is our life, our daily bread, our nourishment at every moment, following your example, O my Lord and my God.
C. de Foucauld, *Meditazioni sul Vangelo*, Op. Sp.

Blessed are those whose way is blameless, who walk in the law of the Lord. Blessed are those who keep his testimonies, who seek him with their whole heart, who also do no wrong, but walk in his ways.

You have commanded your precepts to be kept diligently. Oh! that my ways may be steadfast in keeping your statutes . . .

I will meditate on your precepts, and fix my eyes on your ways. I will delight in your statutes; I will not forget your word.

Give me understanding that I may keep your law; and observe it with my whole heart. Lead me in the path of your commandments; for I delight in it. Incline my heart to your testimonies, and not to gain. Turn my eyes from looking at vanities, and give me life in your ways.

Psalm 119:1-5, 15-16, 34-37.

15—THIRD SUNDAY OF ADVENT

YEAR A

Come, O Lord, and save us   (Is 35:4)

By the Third Sunday of Advent the Liturgy is dominated by the thought of the near approach of Christmas, which gives it a festive tone. In fact Christmas, the commemoration of the incarnation of the Son of God, marks the beginning of salvation: mankind sees the ancient promise fulfilled and has its Savior. Today's readings are a message of consolation and comfort: "Say to those who are of a fearful heart, 'Be strong, fear not. Behold your God . . . will come and save you.' Then the eyes of the blind shall be opened, and the ears of the deaf unstopped. Then shall the lame man leap like a hart, and the tongue of the dumb sing for joy" (Is 35:4-6). The words of Isaiah were directed toward comforting the exiled people of Israel, but can equally be applied to all who want to be more deeply converted to God, yet feel incapable of breaking the bonds of sin and mediocrity and worldly vanity; all are encouraged to have confidence in the Savior. He will come to give strength and to sustain the weak, healing the wounds of sin and bringing salvation to all.

With the coming of Jesus, prophecy was literally fulfilled, and he himself made use of it to prove his Messiahship. The Baptist has been following Jesus' movements from the prison where Herod imprisoned him; he knows Jesus is the Messiah, yet his behavior, so different from what had been foretold had perhaps confused him; besides, John's disciples need enlightenment; so he sends them to ask the Lord: "Are you he who is to come,or shall we look for another?" (Mt 11:3). In answer Jesus points to the miracles he has worked: "Go and tell John what you hear and see: the blind receive their sight, and the lame walk, lepers are cleansed and the deaf hear, and the dead are raised up, the poor have good news preached to them" (ib. 4-5). The fulfillment of Isaiah's prophecy is evident. But Jesus continues: "Blessed is he who takes no offense at me" (ib. 6). Jesus accomplishes his work as Savior without any ostentation, simply and humbly; he does not present himself as a conqueror, but rather as one who is meek; as a poor man who has come to preach the gospel to the poor, to heal the sick, and to save sinners. His manner might scandalize those who were looking for a powerful and glorious Messiah, but it brought great encouragement to those who felt themselves poor, little and sick, in need of salvation. Hearts swelled with hope before the Savior's kindness and meekness.

All this is reinforced in the second reading: "Establish your hearts, for the coming of the Lord is at hand" (Jas 5:8). The sentiments of faith with which we prepare for Christmas are identical with those which should dispose us for the glorious return of the Lord when he will come not only as Savior, but also as Judge. While waiting we need to practice his commandment of love which will make us well-disposed and merciful toward all; we should "take the prophets who spoke in the name of the Lord . . . as an example of suffering and patience" (ib. 10). Just as the prophets kept their eyes constantly turned toward the promised Redeemer, so ought we live with hearts turned toward the coming of Jesus, renewing this disposition every day through grace and the Eucharist, and deepening it into greater intimacy through the devout celebration of Christmas, until it becomes final and beatifying on the last day.

O Lord, you are gracious and merciful, slow to anger and abounding in steadfast love. The Lord is good to all and his compassion is over all that he has made . . . The Lord is faithful in all his words and gracious in all his deeds. He upholds all who are falling, and raises up all who are bowed down. The eyes of all look to you . . . The Lord is near to all who call upon him, to all who call upon him in truth. He fulfills the desire of all who fear him, he also hears their cry, and saves them . . . My mouth will speak the praise of the Lord—let all flesh bless his holy name forever and ever.
Psalm 145, 8-9, 13-15, 18-19, 21

O Jesus, you are he who was to come! O my Jesus, you have come! O Jesus, you have still to come on that last day to gather your chosen ones into your eternal rest. O Jesus, you are coming and going continually! You come int our hearts and make your presence felt there as something so sweet and gentle and yet so powerful! "Both the Spirit and the Bride say: 'Come' . . . and he that thirsts, let him come." Because O Jesus, you come to us just as we come to you. "Yes," you say, "I come quickly." "Come, Lord Jesus!" Come, you who are the desired of the nations, our love and our hope, our strength and our refuge, our consolation during our journey, and our eternal repose in our fatherland.
J.B. Bossuet, Elevazioni a Dio sui misteri 10,6

YEAR B

"I will greatly rejoice in the Lord, my soul shall exult in my God, for he has clothed me with the garments of salvation, he has covered me with the robe of righteousness" (Is 61:10). The joyful song of Jerusalem after she has been freed and rebuilt after the exile is applied to the Church which rejoices and gives thanks for the salvation brought to her by Christ her Redeemer. His mission is traced out in Isaiah's prophecy: "The spirit of the Lord is upon me because the Lord . . . has sent me to preach to the lowly and to heal the contrite of heart, to proclaim liberty to the captives and deliverance to the prisoners" (ib. 1). When Jesus reads this passage in the synagogue of Nazareth, he will apply it to himself (Lk 4:17-21), for indeed this prophecy was completely fulfilled only in himself. Only Christ has a power of universal salvation which power is not limited to healing the misery of one small nation, but reaches out to cure that of all mankind, most of all to freeing men from that most fearful wretchedness, sin, thereby teaching them how to transform suffering into eternal beatitude. Blessed are the poor, the afflicted, the hungry, those who are persecuted, for "theirs is the kingdom of heaven" (Mt 5:10). This is the inner meaning of his redemptive work. We must become its messengers and make it understandable to our brothers by helping to relieve their sufferings through active generosity. Then the birth of the Savior will take on meaning for those who are far away and will bring joy to the world.

It is just this mission of goodness and happiness entrusted to us that St. Paul mentions in today's reading: "Rejoice always . . . test everything; hold fast what is good. Abstain from every form of evil" (1 Thes 5:16-22). Not only specifically bad actions are evil; the omission of good ones is also evil when the omission is due to selfishness, coldness or indifference toward our needy neighbor. But to be always ready to do good to all requires living in communion with Jesus, and trying to penetrate his sentiments of kindness, love and mercy. Prayer is the climax of this communion, and so the Apostle says "Pray constantly" (ib. 17).

Our own living faith and active kindness toward our brothers are powerful means of bearing witness to Christ and of making him known to the world . . . Again, in words that are still all too sadly true today, we hear the voice of the Baptist declaring: "Among you stands one whom you do not know" (Jn 1:26). Jesus is in our midst: in his Church, in the Eucharist, in the grace that makes him present and active in the baptized; but the world does not know him—not only because it closes its eyes, but also because there are too few who give witness to the living gospel, to the goodness which reveals the Savior's goodness. And his own faithful know him too little because their communion with him is superficial, too little nourished by prayer, without intimacy: they know him too little because they do not recognize him where he is hidden: among the poor, the afflicted, those suffering in body and soul. The Baptist appears during Advent as the model witness to Christ; with his strong faith, his austere life, his indifference to self, his humility and charity he came "to bear witness to the light, that all might believe through him" (ib. 7).

O God, may we, your people, who look forward to the birthday of Christ: experience the joy of salvation and celebrate that feast with love and thanksgiving.

Roman Missal, Collect

How priceless is the love of this Master! When he saw that the water of the prophets was not living enough to give us life, he drew from himself and offered to us is only Son, the Word made flesh: he gave him power and strength, and made him the corner-stone of our house: without him we cannot live. He is so sweet that everything bitter becomes sweet to us through his sweetness.

St. Catherine, *Epistolario* 181, v.3

Your coming is truly necessary for us, O God, our Savior; O Christ, we need your presence. In your immense kindness come to us! Abide in us through faith and enlighten our blindness: stay with us and help our weakness; take our side and protect and defend our frailty. If you are in us, who will be able to deceive us? If you are in us, what can we not do in you who strengthen us? If you are for us, who can be against us? For this you come into the world: dwelling in us men, with us and for us, taking our part, you desire to light up our darkness, to relieve our weariness, to keep all danger far from us.

cf. St. Bernard, *De Adventu* 7:2

YEAR C

"Behold, God is my salvation; I will trust and will not be afraid"
(Is 12:2)

With Christmas drawing near, the Liturgy invites us to be joyful because of the great salvific event we are soon to celebrate, and simultaneously exhorts us to conversion. The first two readings both speak of joy. "Sing aloud, O daughter of Zion! Shout, O Israel! Rejoice and exult with all your heart, O daughter of Jerusalem!" (Soph 3:14). The motive for such happiness is not only the restoration of Jerusalem, but the promise of a Messiah, which gives the prophet a foretaste of the presence of God among his people: "On that day it shall be said . . . the Lord your God is in your midst," a mighty Savior (ib. 16-17). "That day" will be the day that Jesus is born at Bethlehem; then the Lord will be present in the world in the most concrete way, become man among men in order to be the powerful Savior of all. If Jerusalem rejoiced in awaiting "that day," the Church now commemorates it every year with an immensely greater joy. Then it was promise and hope; now it is reality, an accomplished fact. Still, this does not exclude hope, for man is always on the way toward God who, although already come in the flesh, will come again in glory at the end of time. The pathway of the Church stretches between these two events; just as she rejoices in the former, so she also rejoices in the latter and urges her children to be happy with her: "Rejoice in the Lord always! Again I will say, rejoice! . . . The Lord is at hand" (Phil 4:4-5). He is near because he has already come, he is near because he will come again; he is near, because for any one who seeks him in love each Christmas brings a new grace for discovering him and being united with him in a new and deeper way.

As preparation for the Lord's coming St. Paul recommends goodness as well as rejoicing. Let all men know your forbearance (ib. 5). The Gospel insists on this theme through the preaching of the Baptist, which is aimed at preparing for the coming of the Messiah. "What then shall we do?" (Lk 3:10), asked the crowds who gathered to hear him. He answered: "He who has two coats, let him share with him who has none; and he who has food, let him do likewise (ib. 11). The main point of conversion is charity towards our neighbor united with the love of God; the selfish person who is concerned only with his own affairs must alter his course and apply himself to the needs and welfare of his brothers. To the soldiers and publicans who questioned him, John also proposed a program of justice and charity: do not exact more than is owed, do not bully or exploit your neighbor, be content with your pay. The Baptist did not ask for great deeds, but for love of neighbor, expressed in concrete ways, for generosity toward the needy and for the honest practice of one's own profession. It was the prelude to the commandment of love upon which Jesus was to insist so much. To set oneself solidly in this direction would be enough for a worthy preparation for Christmas. Jesus wants to be welcomed on his birthday not only in his own person, but in every man, especially in the poor and the oppressed with whom he loves to identify himself. "I was hungry and you gave me food . . . naked and you clothed me" (Mt 25:35-36).

> We await the day of your birth, O Jesus, and according to your promise, we shall see it soon . . . Make our souls rise above self, and rush, foolish with joy, to meet you, straining forward with impatient ardor in the desire to behold the future . . .
>
> O Lord, come to us even before your advent; before you appear to the whole world, come visit us in intimacy . . . Come visit us now in the time between your first and last coming, so that the first one may not be in vain for us, and the last not bring upon us a sentence

of condemnation. By your present coming, you seek to correct our pride by making us conformable to your humility, such as you revealed it at your first coming; then you will be able to transform our humble bodies, making them like your glorious one as it will appear at the moment of your final return. Therefore we beg you with fervent prayer and zeal: prepare us to receive this personal visit which gives us the grace of the first advent and promises us the glory of your last coming. For you, O God, love mercy and truth, and will give us grace and glory: in your mercy grant us grace, and then in your truth you will give us glory.

cf. Guerrico d'Igny, *De Adventu Domini* 2:3

16 — THE DESERT

"Lead me in your truth and teach me, for you are the God of my Salvation"　　　　　　　　　　　　　　　　　　　　　　*(Ps 25:5)*

"What did you go out into the wilderness to see? A reed shaken with the wind? . . . a man clothed in soft raiment?" (Mt 11:7-8); Jesus is praising his precursor. He is not a weakling swaying in the wind like a reed, nor a man in comfortable circumstances who takes pleasure in the conveniences of life; he is a strong man, sturdy in faith, austere of habit, wholly given to God. He is a prophet "and more than a prophet' (ib. 9); he has chosen to live in the desert where, removed from the attractions of this world and given to prayer and penance, he has been preparing to fulfill his mission, which is to announce the coming of the Savior and to prepare his way.

Every form of Christian life requires the desert, at least to some extent: the desert of mortification, penance, giving up of conveniences. Advent, the time in which the Baptist holds a pre-eminence of place, is an urgent summons to this duty, which is presented to us as the indispensable means for getting ready for the Lord's coming.

Without doubt, the most important penance is interior: the conversion of the heart; but the sincerity of this conversion must also be manifested in exterior penance. "The pre-eminently interior and religious character of penance . . . neither excludes nor weakens in any way the external practice of that virtue: in fact it recalls, with special urgency, its necessity, and impels the Church . . . to seek, besides abstinence and fasting, new expressions more suited to bring about . . . the very purpose of penance . . . The need for mortification of the body is clear if we consider the frailty of our nature, in which since Adam's sin the flesh and the spirit have desires which oppose each other" (Paul VI, Paen 8). Modern civilization offers many comforts and sensible pleasures which can be had easily; when we indulge in these without setting any limits, we run the risk of weakening our will and of making our way of life commonplace. It is necessary to impose some discipline on ourselves to be able to renounce such unnecessary pleasures; we have to resist our tendency to want to see, enjoy and try everything. When we do this "the human spirit grows increasingly free of its bondage to creatures and can be more easily drawn to the worship and contemplation of the Creator" (GS 57).

2. The spirituality of the desert does not consist only in self-denial and renunciation, but also in recollection and silence, which make us open to God, ready to listen to his word and to contemplate his mysteries. A prophet is one who hears the word of God (Num 24:4), and having heard it, proclaims it. Such were the ancient prophets, such was the Baptist, who was sent to announce the Messiah. Every Christian has a prophetic vocation in that he is called to listen to the word of God within him, then to embody it in his own life, and finally to communicate it to his brothers. This presupposes silence and recollection: silence in regard to creatures in order to listen to God and fathom his word. If we are always chattering ourselves, we cannot hear what others are saying nor, much less, the voice of God, which itself is noiseless and lets itself be heard only in silence.

Although relations between men require dialogue and speech, talking must not go so far as to make us incapable of keeping quiet and listening. Moreover, the silence which leads to interior reflection, makes us more able to listen to and understand others, and to know how to say the right enlightening word at the right time. Foolish conversations and unbridled talkativeness do not open the way to the intelligent, persuasive dialogue which is suited to bringing the word of the Lord to our brothers.

For a special relationship—intimacy—with God, there is a special need of silence, not only exterior, but interior as well. Commenting on the spiritual meaning of the verse of the psalm: "Hear, O daughter, consider, and incline your ear. Forget your people and your father's house" (Ps 45:10), Sister Elizabeth of the Trinity writes: "in order to listen we must forget our 'father's house,' that is, whatever pertains to the natural life . . . To forget our people is more difficult because these 'people' are that world which is, as it were, a part of ourselves. It involves our feelings, memories, impressions and so on. In a word it is *self*. We must forget it, give it up" (2 Retreat, 10). Then the soul enters into interior silence, and in that silence God communicates himself to it and makes himself known.

Lord, where do you live? My child, I do not live far from you, I am infinitely nearer to you than you think: I am called the unknown Guest, I live within you; seek me in purity of soul, and you will find me.

Lord, how can I enter into myself in purity, since I am wide open to my senses and all turned to the exterior?

Follow behind me in my footsteps ... to sleepless prayer, to the desert where there is neither animal's lair nor nest of bird, to the baptism of the cross; and you will find the inner dwelling where I live hidden within you: because only by following me can you enter within yourself.

G. Canovai, *Suscipe Domine*

I am sure, my God that the time will come, when I shall have exhausted all the enjoyment the world can give. Only you, my Lord, are the food for eternity, and you alone ... In your presence are torrents of delight, which whoso tastes will never let go. This is my true portion, O Lord, here and hereafter!

My God, how far am I from acting according to what I know so well! I confess it, my heart goes after shadows. I love anything better than communion with you. I am ever eager to get away from you. Often I find it difficult even to say my prayers. There is hardly any amusement I would not rather take up than set myself to think of you. Give me grace, O my Father, to be utterly ashamed of my own reluctance! Rouse me from sloth and coldness and make me desire you with my whole heart. Teach me to love meditation, sacred reading and prayer. Teach me to love that which must engage my mind for all eternity.

J. H. Newman, *Meditations on Christian Doctrine* III, 1, p. 328

17 — SALVATION PROMISED TO THE POOR

This poor man cried and the Lord heard him, and saved him out of all his troubles. (Ps 3 4:6)

One day Jesus reprimanded the Pharisees and the leaders of the people severely: "John came to you in the way of righteousness, and you did not believe him: but the publicans and harlots believed him" (Mt 21:32). The publicans had indeed submitted to the Baptist's preaching, they had confessed their sins and begged for the baptism of penance, asking: "What shall we do?" (Lk 3:12). But not the Pharisees; they "did not believe him" (Mt 21:32). Pride blinded them, and just as it had prevented them from believing in the Precursor, it closed their minds and made them hostile to Christ. Therefore Jesus would say: "The tax collectors and harlots (shall) go into the kingdom of God before you" (ib. 21:31). Certainly it is not a person's sins as such that give the right to enter the kingdom; it is rather humble repentance for sin, the humble consciousness and confession of our own moral misery and need to be saved. It was humility that opened the hearts of the tax collectors and sinners to accept salvation, and that gave them precedence in the kingdom of God. The position of the

Pharisees was diametrically opposite: not only did they not recognize and confess their sin of pride, but they considered themselves just and not in the least need of forgiveness; salvation was offered to them and they rejected it: "the Pharisees and the lawyers rejected the purpose of God for themselves" (Lk 7:30). The one same salvation is offered to everyone, but only the humble, the poor, and the little ones are prepared to embrace it.

The prophecy of Isaiah that Jesus read and applied to himself in the synagogue at Nazareth continues to be fulfilled: "The spirit of the Lord . . . has anointed me to preach the gospel to the poor" (Lk 4:18). He is referring not only to the disinherited and the hungry, but above all to those who realize their own moral insufficiency, to those who recognize their own spiritual poverty, to those who feel a deep need of being saved, redeemed and purified, and who therefore call upon and await the Savior with all their hearts. "The Lord is near to the broken-hearted, and saves the crushed in spirit" (Ps 34:18).

2. In order to find God we must go to him poor in spirit. God offers us salvation, calls us to holiness, to communion with himself; but we must accept all these immense gifts of God with a humble heart, convinced that we can do nothing without divine help, since from God alone come the power and the will. St. Therese of the Child Jesus used to say: "Holiness does not consist in this or that practice; instead, it consists in the inclination of the heart which makes us humble and little in God's arms, aware of our own weakness, and trusting, in a way bordering on boldness, in his goodness as our Father" (NV 3-VIII, Aug. 3, 1927 French ed.). The saint drew light and encouragement for her "little way" of evangelical simplicity from the words of Holy Scripture: "you shall be carried like little children and caressed on the lap; as a child whom the mother comforts, so will I comfort you" (Is 66:12-13). God is ready to do everything for a soul who seeks him without pretense in true poverty of spirit, for one who is convinced that even to seek and desire him is a gift, and that its own powers are absolutely inadequate for salvation and sanctification, and for bringing it to intimacy with God. The more we realize our own powerlessness, the more God draws us to himself.

When the Son of Man came into the world he wanted to be surrounded by the poor and the humble. Although Mary and Joseph were descended from the house of David, they were so unknown and poor that there was no room for them in the inn; the shepherds were despised as people of no account and were often shunned, mistrusted and repulsed. Throughout his ministry Jesus sought out the poor, the oppressed, sinners, the little ones, and he tells us: "I am not come to call the righteous, but sinners" (Mt 9:13). Whoever thinks himself righteous, feels satisfied with his own virtue and perhaps scorns others, judging them to be inferior to himself—such a one will derive no benefit from Christmas. Jesus the Savior comes for all, but in a heart which is full of self there is no room to welcome him, or at least too meager a space. Only those who go to Christ poor in spirit offer him room enough to pour out his grace and love, and are fit to receive redemption, "the consolation of Israel" (Lk 2:25) for themselves and for the whole Church.

My soul makes its boast in the Lord; let the afflicted hear and be glad ... I sought the Lord, and he answered me ... This poor man cried and the Lord heard him, and saved him out of all his troubles ... Taste and see that the Lord is good! Happy is the man who takes refuge in him ... The rich suffer want and hunger; but those who seek the Lord shall lack no good thing ...

The Lord is near to the broken-hearted, and saves the crushed in spirit. Many are the afflictions of the righteous, but the Lord will deliver him out of them all ... The Lord redeems the life of his servants, none of those who take refuge in him will be condemned!

Psalm 34:2-10, 18-19, 22

Though our iniquities testify against us, act, O Lord, for your name's sake, for our backslidings are many: we have sinned against you ... You are in the midst of us, O Lord, and we are called by your name: leave us not!

We acknowledge our wickedness, O Lord, and the iniquity of our fathers, for we have sinned against you. Do not spurn us, for your name's sake; do not dishonor your glorious throne. Remember and do not break your covenant with us ... Are you not he, O Lord our God, on whom we set our hope?

Jeremiah 14:7, 9, 20-22

O Lord Jesus Christ, who came into this world to seek and save that which was lost, if I, man, had not been lost, you, Son of man, would not have come; but since I, man, was lost, you who are God and man came, and I was found again. I, man, had lost my way through my free will; you, God and man, came with saving grace. Pride caused the downfall of the first man ... where would I be, O second Man, if you had not come?

St. Augustine, *Sermon* 174,2

18 — SEEKING GOD IN FAITH

Lord, increase our faith (Lk 17:5)

1. "Blessed is he who takes no offense at me" (Lk 7:23). These words of Our Lord contain a great lesson for us. When he showed himself to the world it was not as a powerful, glorious savior, but as one who was humble, poor, and meek. His appearing in so

modest a manner, simply a man like every other man, has been a stumbling block for any who, not knowing how to go beyond the human aspect, have failed to recognize in Christ the promised Messiah. Rather than believe in the word of God as revealed through the prophets or in the miracles performed by Jesus, they have preferred to trust in their own limited understanding, judging it absurd that the Savior of the world should identify himself with man and be like a man in everything.

To accept Christ and to believe in him, to seek and to find God, we need faith. Faith is "the assurance of things hoped for (Heb 11:1). It is based, not upon data furnished by the senses that can be tested by man, but upon the word of God, upon what he in his love has revealed of himself and his mysteries. "The obedience of faith must be given to God who reveals, an obedience by which man entrusts his whole self freely to God, offering the full submission of intellect and will to God who reveals, and freely assenting to the truth revealed by him" (DV 5). Faith does not supply the evidence of divine reality, but it gives us certainty, grounded on the word of God-Love.

Faith tells us that Jesus of Nazareth, who was thought by his contemporaries to be "Joseph's son" (Lk 4:22), is the Son of God, the promised Savior. The more living our faith, the more lovingly we shall welcome Jesus and the more truly accept him as God-Man; and, accepting his message, we shall base our life upon it.

Jesus said: If anyone loves me, "my Father will love him; and we will come to him and make our home with him" (Jn 14:23); it is faith that gives us the certainty of this sublime truth, which nevertheless escapes the control of our senses and of our human understanding. Faith tells that the mystery of the indwelling of the Trinity in the baptized is a reality infinitely more real than those many transitory truths which can be verified by human science; when a soul is fully convinced of this, it becomes capable of setting this divine truth above all earthly reality.

2. John of the Cross says to every one who longs for God: "listen to a word abounding in substance and in inaccessible truth: seek him in faith and love, without desire for satisfaction in any other thing" (Sp C 1:11). A life of union with God cannot be based on feeling; it must be based on the theological virtues alone. Therefore we need to begin our search for God by putting aside every pleasure and consolation, even when spiritual, in order to walk in the way of "pure faith." Much more than any experience of the senses, or any knowledge or reasoning, faith puts us into direct contact with God. Faith "is the only proximate and proportionate means to union with God. For the likeness between faith and God is so close that no other difference exists than that between believing in God and seeing him" (Asc II, 9:1). Faith proposes God to us as he is, not by making us see him, but by making us believe in his essential reality; thus it puts our human intellect

into contact with God. "Only by means of faith, in divine light exceeding all understanding, does God manifest himself to the soul. The more intense a man's faith, the closer is his union with God" (ib.). Faith unites us to God, even when we do not enjoy any consoling experience; in fact God often deprives those who seek him of any spiritual consolation so that their relations with him may not depend on feeling, but on faith, and that they may grow in faith.

"Whoever would draw near to God must believe that he exists" (Heb 11:6). In the measure that we live by faith, we draw near to God, are united to him, and believe in his love. "This is our great act of faith," says Sister Elizabeth of the Trinity: to believe in God's love and to believe it firmly even in the midst of trials and darkness. Then the soul "no longer stops at tastes and feelings. Henceforth it cares little whether it feels God or not, whetherhe sends it joy or suffering; it believes in his love" (2 Retreat 8:20). But to reach this "firm faith" we need to practice it; we must pray: Lord "increase our faith!" (Lk 17:5).

O Lord Jesus Christ, I believe in you, but make me believe in such a way that I may love you. To believe in you truly is to love you: not as the demons believed, for they did not love, and therefore, although they believed, they said: "What have we to do with you, Jesus, Son of God?"

Oh! that I may believe, and believe in such a way that my belief leads to loving you, not to saying: "What have I to do with you?" but rather; "You have redeemed me, and I want to be yours" (In Ps 130,1).

I want to call out to you, but help me not to do it only in the sound of my voice while remaining silent in my manner of living. I want to call out to you through despising the world; I want to call out to you by trampling on the pleasures of the world. I want to call out to you, not with my tongue, but by my life, that the world is crucified to me, and I to the world. I want to call out to you by giving freely to the poor. (Sir 88:12).

To right belief I will join right living, so that I may give you glory in words by speaking the truth, and in deeds by living as I should. (Sir 183:13).

St. Augustine

When a soul really believes in this exceeding love overshadowing it, we may say of it what was said of Moses, that he "endured as seeing Him that is invisible."

Oh Lord, may I no longer stop at tastes and feelings. I care little whether I feel you or not, whether you send me joy or suffering; I believe in your love.

The more we are tried, the stronger is our faith, for it overleaps, as it were, all obstacles and finds its rest in the bosom of infinite love, which can do naught but works of love. Then to this soul, vivified by faith, you can whisper in secret, O my Master, the words you once spoke to Mary Magdalen: Go in peace, your faith has made you safe."

Sr. Elizabeth of the Trinity, *Spiritual Doctrine,* (Philipon) 2 Retreat
8:2

19 — SEEKING GOD IN LOVE

Lord with great compassion you have taken me back;with everlasting love you have had pity on me.   (Is 54:7-8)

1. "For the mountains may depart, and the hills be removed, but my steadfast love shall not depart from you, and my covenant of peace shall not be removed, says the Lord who has compassion on you" (Is 54:10). Thus did the Lord reveal to Israel the eternal faithfulness of his love. His love prevails over his omnipotence, his greatness and his infinite justice; or rather, in God all is love. "God is love" (1 Jn. 4:16), and he wants us to return his love. If the highest act of faith is to believe in God's love, then the highest act of love is to dedicate our life to returning his love.

Faith and love, says John of the Cross "will lead you along a path unknown to you, to the place where God is hidden. Faith . . . is comparable to the feet by which one journeys to God, and love is like one's guide" (Sp C 1:11). In this life faith and charity go in step with each other; one depends on the other, and makes progress as the other makes progress: we cannot love God if we do not believe in him, and we cannot believe in God efficaciously, unless our faith blossoms from love and in love. Faith and love permit us to find God and to establish a relationship of intimate friendship with him.

One who believes with all his strength that God is God, the supreme Lord upon whom everything depends, and to whom we owe all our love, "will merit through love the discovery of the content of faith" (ib.). Jesus himself said: If anyone "loves me . . . I will love him and manifest myself to him" (Jn 14:21). The theological virtue of charity becomes the vehicle for our knowing God and his mysteries in a much deeper way than through study. This is what happens in contemplative prayer where God draws the soul to himself and gives it the feeling and, as it were, the experience of his goodness and infinite greatness. But man could not have the capacity for loving God if God himself had not infused this power in him; "he sent the Holy Spirit upon all men that he might inspire them from within, to love" (LG 40). The gift of love is bestowed on every Christian at his baptism; now it is for him to open wide his heart and his life to this divine gift, so that it may grow and mature into a deep friendship with God.

2. The Lord your God is the only Lord. Therefore "you shall love the Lord your God with all your heart, and with all your soul,

and with all your mind and with all your strength" (Mk 12:29-30). This is the great commandment of the Lord that St. Paul stresses: "walk in love" (Eph 5:2). Theological love, a divine gift which enables man to love God, is pure benevolence: its purity is the condition of its intensity: in fact this love must consist in a single-minded desire to please God and to do his will without any seeking of personal satisfaction.

The love with which we must go to God does not consist in feeling; it is an act of the will. To love God is "to wish well to God," and the good that man is able to wish for God is the one that Jesus himself taught us to ask: "hallowed be thy name: thy will be done." Since he is God, the infinite Good on whom everything depends, the good that he desires is none other than his own glory and the fulfillment of his will.

In practice, we love God to the extent that we apply ourselves to fulfilling the divine will, without any personal preoccupation or self-seeking. Whoever seeks his pleasure and consolation in God "would no longer love God purely, above all things," declares John of the Cross, but loves his own comforts together with God; therefore his heart is divided between love for God and love for self, and he is incapable of "surrendering his whole will to God." (Let 12). On the other hand, he who seeks only the will of God in all things, truly seeks God with love, is united with him and lives in communion with him, even though he may enjoy no sweetness. Since it is always true that "if a person is seeking God, his Beloved is seeking him much more" (L Fl 3:28), he may sometimes draw us to him by making us taste the sweetness of his love; we should use this only to give ourselves to God with even greater resolution and generosity.

O supreme and eternal Good, who has moved you, infinite God, to illuminate me, your finite creature, with the light of your truth? You, O Fire of love, are the cause, because it is always love that constrained and constrains you to create us in your image and likeness, to be merciful to us by giving infinite and immeasurable graces to your rational creatures. O Goodness above all goodness! You alone are supremely good; and nevertheless you sent the Word, your only-begotten Son, to converse with us ... What was the reason? Love, for you loved us before we were. O good and eternal Greatness, you made yourself lowly and small to make men great. Wherever I turn, I find nothing but the abyss and fire of your love.
St. Catherine of Siena, Dialogue 134 (p. 296)

Love alone is what gives value to all things: and a kind of love so great that nothing hinders it is the one thing necessary. But how can we possess, my God, a love in conformity with what the Beloved deserves, if your love does not join love with itself? Shall I complain? ... I have no reason at all, for I have always seen in my God much greater and more extraordinary signs of love than I have

known how to ask for or desire! If I don't complain about the many
things your kindness has suffered for me, I have nothing to com-
plain about. What, then, can so miserable a thing as I ask for? That
you, my God, give to me what I might give to you, as St. Augustine
says, so that I may repay you something of the great debt I owe you:
that you remember that I am the work of your hands; and that I
may know who my Creator is in order to love him . . .

I have only words, because I am not good for anything else!
May my desires be worthwhile, my God, before your divine
presence, and do not look at my lack of merit. May we all merit to
love you, Lord. Now that we must live, may we live for you, may our
desires and self-interests come to an end.

St. Teresa of Jesus, Soliloquies, 5:2; 15:3

20 — A BURNING AND SHINING LIGHT

That we may know your way upon earth . . . Let the peoples praise
you, O God: let all the peoples praise you.   (Ps 67:3-4)

1. "He was a burning and a shining light," said Jesus speaking of the Baptist; "he has born witness to the truth" (Jn 5:35, 33).
One should be able to say of every Christian that each of us is "a
bright and shining light" capable of enlightening others through
our living faith, and able to warm cold and indifferent hearts by
our burning love. Our faith and love should give witness to God's
truth and love, not just when we are engaged in prayer and purely
religious acts, but in every aspect of our lives. This is only possible
when we ceaselessly tend toward God and seek him in all our actions and in every activity.

Vatican Council II recommends to the laity that "while properly fulfilling their secular duties in the ordinary conditions of
life, they do not disassociate union with Christ from that life.
Rather, by performing their work according to God's will they can
grow in that union" (AA 4). Every Christian has the duty to bring
Christ to the world, and we do so in the measure in which we keep
close to him, not only in times of prayer, but also in our daily work,
no matter what duty may be involved. This union with Christ in
our daily activities demands interior recollection and self-control
so that our hearts may remain oriented toward God, always
desirous of pleasing him and of acting in accordance with his will.

But when we rush precipitously into action in such a way that
we are carried along by it, we make ourselves incapable of ruling
and ordering our actions according to God. Then there can be real
distortion: after declaring to God in prayer that we want to love
him above all things and to do his will alone, we forget all about
this when we come to action, and we, Christians, may go so far as
to act like pagans, guided in our decisions by the spirit of the

world instead of by the gospel. When this happens we are no longer "burning and shining" lights, and our lives do "not give testimony to the truth."

2. St. John of the Cross wrote to a religious: "whether you eat or drink, or speak, or converse with lay people, or do anything else, you should always do so with the desire for God and with your heart fixed on him" (Counsels 9). This is precious advice for every one who wants to live in union with God and bring God to his brothers. It requires that even when engaged in active works, we must know how to recollect ourselves from time to time in order to reawaken the thought of God, and even more the desire for God; to become conscious of the divine presence, and put ourselves into contact with God dwelling in our heart. St. Tersa of Jesus says that "we must need be careful in doing good works, even those of obedience and charity, not to fail to have frequent interior recourse to our God, but to withdraw within ourselves with our God, often" (F 5:17).

When our exterior activity is regulated by duty or obedience, or when some work is undertaken through the motive of charity, we already have the security of being united with God, because we are operating within the ambit of his will; all the same, we must always pay attention to making this union as actual and conscious as possible, profiting by little ingenuities to make it grow. This is the way to make use of those moments, fleeting yet frequent enough, when we can retreat within ourselves to meet God. They are, as it were, the bulwark of the interior life, and in reality defend it against the danger of our exhausting and dissipating it in external activity. Those who plunge into the active life without caution will soon lose sight of God and God's purpose, and will end up by behaving in purely human fashion: often they will lose tranquility, and become upset and incapable of recollection.

Jesus chided Martha, not because she was busy, but because she fretted: "Martha, Martha, you are anxious and troubled about many things" (Lk 10:41). God wants us to be active, wants us to serve our brothers with generosity, but he does not want anxiety, because in all this only one thing counts: union with God. The more we can achieve a life of close union with God, the more our conduct gives witness to God, embodies the spirit of the gospel and becomes for our brothers a "burning and shining light" to lead them to God.

O Lord, I am not a light for myself; I can be an eye, but not light. Of what use are good healthy eyes when there is no light? I cry out to you, O Lord, give light to my lamp; with your light, O Lord, you will light up my darkness. Of myself I have but darkness, but you are light that scatters the darkness and enlightens me. No light comes to me from myself, my only light is in you . . .

The wise and the learned think they are light, but they are darkness; and since they are darkness and think they are light, they cannot be enlightened. But those who are darkness and admit it, who stay little with no inclination for putting on airs, they are humble, not proud . . . They know themselves and give praise to you, O Lord, and so they do not stray from the road that leads to salvation. They praise you and call upon you and are safe from their enemies.

Turning to you, O Lord God, almighty Father, with all the sincerity of heart that my meanness permits, I give you most ardent and abundant thanks, and with all my heart beg you in your great goodness to look kindly on my petitions: by your power drive the enemy from my actions and intentions, increase my faith, govern my mind, grant me holy thoughts and lead me to the possession of your beatitude.

St. Augustine, *Sermon* 67:8-10

My God, it seems nothing can distract me from you when I act only for you, always in your sight and under your divine gaze which penetrates to the depths of my soul. Even in the midst of the world you can be heard in the silence of the heart of one who wants only to be yours.

It all depends on our intention, by which we can sanctify the least little thing! It can transform the most ordinary acts of life into divine acts! A soul that lives united to you, my God, performs nothing but supernatural acts; and the most commonplace actions, instead of separating it from you, bring it all the closer to you.

Elizabeth of the Trinity, *Lettres* 38;261

21 — SEEKING GOD IN CREATURES

O Wisdom of the Most High, mightily and sweetly disposing all things, come and teach us the way of prudence.   (Lectionary)

1. Today's Liturgy resounds with the first of the great Advent antiphons which are drawn from the books of wisdom. "I came forth from the mouth of the Most High" (Sir 24:3), says Wisdom of herself, presenting herself as a person, and the holy writer adds in praise: "She reaches mightily from one end of the earth to the other and orders all things well" (Wis 8:1). In Wisdom, proceeding "from the mouth of the Most High" and appointed to direct all created things, Catholic tradition has seen prefigured the Word, the substantial Word of God, the Second Person of the Blessed Trinity, eternal and uncreated Wisdom through whom all things were made, and who one day became incarnate for the salvation of mankind. Therefore the Church calls out during Advent: "O Wisdom of the Most High . . . come, teach us the way of prudence."

Man has an immense need to understand that all things—all creatures—come from God and are guided by his infinite Wisdom.

Every created thing bears the imprint of uncreated Wisdom, every being reveals some aspect of it, and no creature or happening escapes its control. To recognize the imprint of God in every creature, to acknowledge Wisdom's plan in human events is highest wisdom and greatest prudence.

Man especially, who is created in God's image, is to be regarded and treated as the masterpiece of eternal Wisdom. The divine image can be disfigured in him by sin, the plan of infinite Wisdom can be altered and upset by a multitude of moral miseries; but both the image and the plan still continue to exist, and whoever discovers them has the joy of finding God in every one of his brothers. Then, relations with our neighbor will not distract us from God, but will become so many occasions for seeking and finding God, and for loving and serving him in his creatures. However this is not possible unless we have first filled our hearts with God, fixed our interior gaze upon him for a long time, and learned to know him in the intimacy of prayer.

2. When the eternal Wisdom of God took flesh and appeared in the world in human form with the name of Jesus, the Savior, foretold for centuries, most men did not recognize him. "The darkness did not comprehend . . . He came to his own home, and his own people received him not" (Jn 1:5,11). An eye clouded by sin is not capable of perceiving in Christ the Son of God made man to save "his people from their sins" (Mt 1:21); a mind blinded by passion is not capable of understanding the word of him who is the Word of the Father.

By analogy, a man without a pure heart or clear sight is not capable of recognizing God nor of recognizing Christ in his brothers. "Blessed are the pure of heart, for they shall see God" (Mt 5:8); these will see hm openly in eternity, but through faith they begin to see him even in this life, not only in himself and his mysteries, but also in his works and in his creatures. "Only by the light of faith"—teaches the Council—"and by meditation on the word of God can one, always and everywhere, recognize God in whom 'we live and move and have our being' (Acts 17:28), seek his will in every event, see Christ in all men, whether they be close to us or strangers" (AA 4). This light of wisdom which enables us to discover God in every event of our lives and in every creature, which makes us see Christ in every brother, profoundly transforms our relationships with our neighbor. Instead of stopping on their purely human level with the inevitable shortcomings and defects which are more or less irritating, our gaze is fixed on what in them reveals God. In that way we go beyond all diversity of race or nationality, of political party or social class, all distinction between what is pleasant or unpleasant, friend or not, believer or unbeliever—all this is overcome, and in every person we see, respect and love the image of God, and we seek and recognize the face of Christ. Even those who live far from God and are perhaps in rebellion against him are still his creatures and his children, if not through grace, then at least through their calling to grace; they are always brothers of Christ, by right if not in fact, because for them too did Christ become man, die, and rise again. Thus our relations with others become relations with God; to deal with them is to deal with Christ, to serve our brothers is to serve Christ.

O Lord, our Lord, how majestic is your name in all the earth!... What is man that you are mindful of him? And the son of man that you care for him? Yet you have made him little less than God, and crowned him with glory and honor. You have given him dominion over the works of your hands. You have put all things under his feet... O Lord, our Lord, how majestic is your name in all the earth!

Psalm 8:1,4-9

My God, grant me the grace of seeing only you in creatures and of never being stopped by them; of considering their physical or spiritual beauty, not as something belonging to themselves, but only as a reflection of you. Grant that I may go beyond the obscurity... and see you beneath all appearances, you who are essential Being, who possess the fullness of being and have transfused a tiny particle of it into the creature that attracts me.

To stop at creatures would be improper and ungrateful, an abuse of your trust, because you do not give them beauty nor allow me to feel its fascination except to let me catch a glimpse of you and be attracted to you; to arouse my gratitude for your goodness, and my love for your beauty. Thus you invite me to ascend even to your throne and to establish my soul there in adoration, in ecstatic contemplation and gratitude... May my conversation be only in heaven, because what I see on earth only lets me guess at your beauty and tenderness.

Created beings in whom I admire some reflection of your perfection, upon whom falls a faint ray of your light, O infinite Sun—these are outside me, distant and separate from me; but you, my God, O perfection, goodness, truth, infinite and essential love, you are within me, you envelop me, you fill me fully.

C. de Foucauld,
Retreat at Nazareth (Meditations of a Hermit, p. 40)

22 — FOURTH SUNDAY OF ADVENT

YEAR A

"Let the earth open that salvation may sprout forth." (Is 45:8)

Today's Liturgy is entirely directed toward the birth of our Savior. First of all there is the famous prophecy about Emmanuel, which had been proclaimed at a time that was particularly difficult for the kingdom of Judah. When the wicked king Achaz refused to believe that God could remedy the situation, Isaiah answered with a strong reprimand and, as if to prove that God could do still greater things, added: "Therefore the Lord himself will give you a sign: . . . a virgin shall conceive and bear a son, and shall call his name Emmanuel" (Is 7:14). Although his prophecy referred immediately to the birth of the heir to the throne, its complete fulfillment would come only seven centuries later in the miraculous birth of Jesus, who alone would satisfy its full meaning. The Gospel of St. Matthew confirms this interpretation; in fact he concludes his account of the virgin conception of Jesus by saying: "All this took place to fulfill what the Lord had spoken by the prophet: a virgin shall conceive and bear a son, and his name shall be called Emmanuel" (Mt 1:22-23).

When he traces Jesus' ancestry, Matthew is showing that he is true man; when he speaks of his birth by the Virgin Mary, who had become a mother through the power of the Holy Spirit (ib. 18), he is attesting that he is true God; and finally by relating Isaiah's prophecy, he is declaring that he is the Savior promised by the prophets, Emmanuel, God-with-us. In the context of this essential background, Matthew lifts the veil on one of the most human and delicate circumstances of the birth of Jesus: the agonizing doubt of Joseph and his behavior in accepting the mission entrusted to him by God. Faced with the mysterious motherhood of Mary, he was greatly troubled and was minded to put her away privately. But when the angel of the Lord reassured him and commanded him to take her with him because "that which was conceived in her was of the Holy Spirit (ib. 20), Joseph, a just man who lived by faith, obeyed by taking upon himself with humble simplicity the extraordinary responsibility of being husband to the Virgin Mother and chaste father to the Son of God. Thus the life of the Savior blossomed, protected by the faith, obedience, humility and self-denial of the carpenter of Nazareth. They are the same virtues with which we should welcome the Lord who is about to come.

In the second reading St. Paul joins the prophets in proclaiming Jesus to be "descended from David according to the flesh" (Rom 1:3), and follows Matthew in declaring him to be "Son of God" (ib.). The Apostle, who called himself "a servant of Jesus Christ" (ib. 1) and was chosen to preach his gospel, succinctly summarizes the entire life and work of the Savior in two phases: his life from his birth in the flesh up to his glorious resurrection and his power to sanctify men. In fact, the incarnation, passion, death and resurrection are one single mystery which has its beginning in Bethlehem and its climax at Easter. Yet Christmas sheds light on Easter in making known the origin and nature of him who will die on the cross for the salvation of the world: he is the Son of God, the Word made flesh.

Father, all powerful and ever-living God, we do well always and everywhere to give you thanks, through Jesus Christ our Lord.

His future coming was proclaimed by all the prophets. The virgin Mother bore him in the womb with love beyond all telling. John the Baptist was his herald and made him known when at last he came. In his love he has filled us with joy as we prepare to celebrate his birth, so that he may find us watching in prayer, our hearts filled with wonder and praise.

Roman Missal, Preface of Advent II

You were a good and faithful servant, Joseph, to whom Mary, the Mother of the Savior was espoused; a faithful and prudent servant whom our Lord chose for the comfort of his Mother and the nurse of his childhood, as well as the only and most trustworthy cooperator in his great plan of salvation.

You were of the house of David and truly the son of David... Like another David, you were a man according to God's own heart, to whom he entrusted his most precious secret; to whom, as to David, he made manifest the uncertain and hidden things of his wisdom, and to whom he revealed a mystery hidden from the great ones of the world. To you it was given to behold him whom many kings and prophets had desired to see and had not seen, to hear and had not heard. And not only were you allowed to behold him and listen to his words, but you were able to bear him in your arms, guide his steps, embrace and caress him, feed and protect him.

St. Bernard, On the "Missus Est" 2:13-14

YEAR B

O Lord and guide of the house of Israel ... save us with the might of your arm. (Lectionary)

Today the Liturgy of the Word offers us one of the most important messianic prophecies and its fulfillment. King David wanted to build "a house," a temple, to the Lord; but the Lord has Nathan tell him that his will is otherwise; instead it will be God himself who will concern himself with the "house" of David by prolonging the line of descendants, because from it the Savior is to be born. "Your house ... and your throne shall be established forever" (2 Sam 7:6). Many times in the course of history it seemed that the family of David was about to die out, but God always saved it since from it was to come "Joseph, the husband of Mary, of whom Jesus was born who is called Christ" (Mt 1:16); "the Lord God will give to him the throne of his father David, and he will reign ... forever; and of his kingdom there will be no end" (Lk 1:32-33). All that God had promised has been accomplished, in spite of the vicissitudes of history, the sins of men, the offenses and wickedness of David's successors themselves. God is always faithful: "I have made a covenant with my chosen one: I have sworn to David my servant I will keep my steadfast love for him forever; and my covenant will stand firm for him" (Ps 89:3,28).

The liturgy today presents the faithfulness of Mary, in whom the Scriptures were fulfilled, on a parallel with the faithfulness of God. In God's eternal plan all had been foreseen, and everything as already prepared for the incarnation of the Word in the womb of a virgin descended from the house of David, but when the moment came for this plan to be accomplished "the Father of mercies willed that the consent of the predestined mother should precede the incarnation" (LG 56). St. Luke records the sublime conversation between the Angel and Mary, which ends with her humble and unconditional acceptance: "Behold the handmaid of the Lord, be it done to me according to your word." God's "fiat" created all things out of nothing: Mary's "fiat" set in motion the redemption of all creatures. Mary is the temple of the New Alliance, immensely more precious than the one David had wished to build for his Lord, a living temple that contains within it, not the holy ark, but the Son of God. Mary is the most faithful one, completely open and available to the will of the Almighty; and it is precisely through her faithful concurrence that the mystery of universal salvation in Christ Jesus is carried out.

St. Paul exults in this great mystery, kept secret from eternity, but now made known and announced to all the nations through the prophetical writings in accordance with the ordinance of the eternal God, (Rom 16:25-26) no longer reserved exclusively for the salvation of Israel, but directed to the salvation of all peoples: he makes it clear that the purpose of this revelation is that all men may have the "obedience of faith" (ib.). Faith alone makes a man capable of welcoming and adoring the mystery of God made man, and his faith must be modeled on that of Mary who accepted the unbelievable: becoming a mother while remaining a virgin, made mother of the Son of God although a creature—all with absolute trust" (LG 63).

"To the only wise God" (Rom 16:27) belongs the glory for the great mystery of salvation, the glory offered him "through Jesus Christ" (ib.) while to the humble Virgin of Nazareth, the obedient and docile instrument in the accomplishment of the divine plan, belongs the gratitude of every soul saved in Jesus Christ.

At the message of an angel, O God most high, the pure Virgin welcomed your eternal Son; and filled with the light of your Spirit, she became the temple of your Word; help us to adhere to your will in all humility, just as the Virgin entrusted herself to your word.
cf. *Roman Missal, Collect,* Dec. 20

O Virgin, you will indeed give birth to a little One, you will nourish a little One; but while you look upon him as little, think upon him as great. He will be great, because God will magnify him

Divine Intimacy

*in the sight of kings; wherefore let all kinds adore him and all na-
tions serve him. Let your soul magnify the Lord, for "he shall be
great and shall be called the Son of the most High." He shall be
great; and "he that is mighty shall do great things for you, and holy
is his name."*

*What name is holier than "Son of the most High?" This great
Lord will be magnified also by us little ones, for he became a little
One that he might make us great. "A child is born to us, a Son is
given to us."*

*Born "to us" not to himself; for he who before all ages was much
more nobly born of his Father needed not in time to be born of a
mother. Nor was he born and given to the angels. They who possessed him in his greatness did not require him in his lowliness. To
us, then, is he born, because only by us is he so greatly needed.*

St. Bernard, *On the "Missus est"* 3:13

YEAR C

I have come to do your will, O God   (Heb 10:7)

The Liturgy now takes on the tone of a birthday eve. The prophecies concerning the Messiah become more precise in Micah,
who names as his birthplace a small village in the country of
David, from whose family line the Savior was expected. "But you,
O Bethlehem-Ephrathah, who are little to be among the clans of
Judah; from you shall come forth for me one who is to be ruler in
Israel" (Mic 5,2). And in the words that follow: his "origin is from
of old, from ancient days" (ib. 2-3), we find an illusion to his eternal
origin and therefore of the Messiah's divinity. This is St. Matthew's interpretation, who gives this prophecy as the answer of
the high priests regarding the birthplace of Jesus (Mt 2:4-6). Like
Isaiah (7:4), Micah also speaks of the mother of the Messiah:
"when she who is in travail has brought forth" (Mic 5:3) with no
mention of his father, thus allowing his extraordinary birth to be,
at least indirectly, foreseen. Finally he indicates what his work
will be: he will save and reunite "the remnant" of Israel, and guide
it as a shepherd with "the strength of the Lord"; he will extend his
domain "to the ends of the earth" and bring peace (ib. 2:4). The image of Jesus, born humble and unknown in Bethlehem, yet nevertheless Son of God who has come to redeem the "remnant of
Israel" and to bring salvation and peace to all men, stands out
sharply in Micah's prophecy.

St. Paul gives us a more interior picture, which emphasizes
the intentions of the Son of God from the moment of his incarnation: "I have come to do your will, O God (Heb 10:7). The ancient
sacrifices were not capable of expiating the sins of men nor of
rendering to God worship that was worthy of him. Then the Son
offers himself: he takes to himself the body which the Father has

made ready for him and in that body he is born and lives in time as a victim who is offered in an uninterrupted sacrifice, which is to be consummated on the cross. It is the only sacrifice which is able to satisfy God, which is capable of redeeming men, and which does away with all other sacrifices. "Behold, I come": obedience to the will of the Father is the underlying motive of the whole life of Christ, from Bethlehem to Golgotha to the Resurrection. Christmas is already linked with Easter: the one and the other are but two moments of a unique holocaust directed toward the glory of God and the salvation of mankind.

The "behold I come" of the Son is perfectly echoed in the Mother's "behold the handmaid of the Lord." Mary's very life is a continual offering to the will of the Father, carried out in an obedience guided by faith andinspired by love. "Through her faith and obedience she begets on earth the very Son of the Father" (LG 63); because of her faith and obedience, she hurriedly leaves, immediately after the angel's annunciation, to visit her cousin Elizabeth and offer her help as "handmaid" of men as well as of God. The great service of Mary to mankind is therefore to bring Christ to man just as she brought him to Elizabeth. Through the Virgin-Mother, the Savior visits the house of Zachary in very fact, and fills it with the Holy Spirit, so that Elizabeth discovers the mystery being accomplished in Mary, and John rejoices in his mother's womb. All this takes place because the Blessed Mother believed God's word, and, believing, offered herself to the divine will: "Blessed is she who has believed" (Lk 1:45). The example of Mary teaches us how a simple creature can join in the mystery of Christ and bring Christ into the world through her "yes"—a "yes" which is continually repeated in faith and lived in loving obedience to God's will.

O God, Creator and Redeemer of mankind, you decreed and your Word became man, born of the Virgin Mary. May we come to share the divinity of Christ, who humbled himself to share our human nature.

Roman Missal, Dec. 17

O Mary, you did not doubt, you believed and received the just reward of your faith. "Blessed are you that have believed." But we too are blessed because we have heard and have believed: every soul that believes, conceives and begets the word of God, and recognizes his works.

O Mary, obtain for each of us your spirit of glorifying the Lord; that each of us may have your spirit of rejoicing in God. Though you alone are mother of Christ physically, yet through faith Christ is begotten by all; help me, O Mary, to receive within me the Word of God.

cf. St. Ambrose, *Commento al Vangelo di S. Luca* II, 26

23 — O ROOT OF JESSE

"O root of Jesse, exalted as a sign to all peoples, come deliver us, and tarry now no more."   (Lectionary)

1. The great antiphons which follow each other on the last ferias of Advent, all implore in different ways the coming of the Savior, applying to him the most significant titles, drawn from the Messianic prophecies, and throwing light on the various prerogatives of his salvific work. Two of these antiphons,—O Root of Jesse, and O Key of David—reaffirm in a special way Christ's descent from David's line, and welcome in him the fulfillment of the promises made to the king of Israel. Isaiah had said: "There shall come forth a shoot from the stump of Jesse, and a branch shall grow out of his root . . . the root of Jesse shall stand as an ensign to the peoples; him shall the nation seek" (Is 11:1,10). Jeremiah also said: "Behold, the days are coming when I will raise up for David a righteous branch. He shall reign as king, and deal wisely and shall execute justice and righteousness in the land" (Jer 23:5). All this will become fact when, from the root of Jesse, David's father, Jesus the Savior is born: he is set before all the peoples as the sign, the banner of salvation. Every nation looks longingly to him, seeks him, waits for him, calls upon him: "Come and free us, do not delay!"

The world waited for him for thousand of years, yet now that he has been with us for other thousands, it hardly recognizes him or accepts him as Savior, as the Son of God, true God and true man. Yet the world has sore need of him; today as yesterday, and tomorrow as today, Christ is, and will always be, the only sign of salvation through which we will be saved. The great antiphons, like the prophecies, point out his descent from a human family line in order to stress that if he is "Wisdom coming forth from the mouth of the Most High," if he is the Word, the Son of God, he is also Son of man. Christ belongs to the race of man and at the same time is at its summit; he is "the key, the focal point and the goal of all human history" (GS 10). He became man in order that man might find God again in him.

2. "O Key of David . . . " Keys indicate power, and therefore the kingdom, in this case the kingdom of David conferred on Christ. In the Apocalypse also, Christ is presented as "the holy one . . . who has the key of David, who opens and no one shall shut, who shuts and no one opens" (Rev 3:7). It is evident that his power is not exercised only over the kingdom of David by reason of his descent, but that, over and beyond every earthly kingdom, it extends to the kingdom of heaven of which he is the eternal Lord, and to which he wants to lead us all. Christ is the supreme King with power to open his Father's kingdom to men; he does this not by an act of authority, but through an act of merciful love which makes him a man among men, and impels him to give his

life to obtain anew for them the right of entry into his Father's house. By the abasement of the Incarnation, by the sufferings of his Passion, by his Death and Resurrection, Christ became "the key" to the kingdom of heaven.

When, at the birth of his son, Zachary regains the power of speech which he had lost by his incredulity, he immediately bursts into a song in which he praises the Messiah of whom John will be the forerunner. "Filled with the Holy Spirit" delineates the Messiah's mission: he will visit us with light from on high "to give light to those who sit in darkness and in the shadow of death" (Lk 1:78-79). The Liturgy takes up these words and uses them in the fourth great Advent antiphon: "O Key of David . . . come and lead the captive from prison where he sits in darkness." In order to lead men into his Father's kingdom, Christ must first tear them away from the prison of sin, from the shadows of death. He, eternal light, splendor of the Father, desires to light up their minds and their hearts by removing them from the shadows of evil and freeing them from the slavery of Satan. To prepare for Christmas means to open ourselves to the light of Christ, to let ourselves be enlightened by his words and by his gospel, by rejecting the darkness and following him who is the Light that comes from above to visit us.

> There shall come forth a shoot from the stump of Jesse, and a branch shall grow out of his roots and the Spirit of the Lord shall rest upon him, the spirit of wisdom and understanding, the spirit of counsel and fortitude, the spirit of knowledge and the fear of the Lord . . .
>
> You will say on that day: "I will give thanks to you, O Lord, for though you were angry with me, your anger turned away, and you have comforted me. Behold, God is my Savior; I will deal confidently and will not be afraid, for the Lord God is my strength and my song, and he has become my salvation. With joy you will draw waters from the wells of the Savior."
>
> Isaiah 11:1-2; 12:1-3

> O let the Truth, the Light of my heart, not mine own darkness, speak unto me. I fell off into that and became darkened; but even thence, even thence I loved you. I went astray, and remembered you. I heard your voice behind me, calling to me to return, and scarcely heard it, through the tumultuousness of the enemies of peace. And now, behold, I return in distress and panting after your fountain. Let no man forbid me! Of this will I drink, and so live. Let me not be my own life; from myself I lived ill, death was I to myself; and I revive in you (Confess XII 10,10).
>
> Lord, I thirst! Fount of life, satisfy me fully! . . . Come, O Lord, and do not delay. Come, Lord Jesus, come visit us in peace. Come and free this prisoner from his prison, so that we may rejoice before you with full hearts. Come, our Savior; come, the Desired of all the nations . . . Show us your face, and we shall be saved. (Ps Sol 35).
>
> St. Augustine

24 — THE VIRGIN OF THE INCARNATION

"O Key of David, who opens the gates of the eternal kingdom, come and wrest from prison the captive lying in darkness."   *(Lectionary)*

1. If Mary's whole life was one of recollection and concentration on God, it must have been especially such at the time when, by the power of the Holy Spirit, the Word became incarnate within her. The angel Gabriel found her in solitude and recollection, and in that atmosphere he revealed God's plan to her: "The Holy Spirit will come upon you and the power of the Most High will overshadow you; therefore the child to be born will be called holy, the Son of God" (Lk 1:35).

Long meditation had prepared the Virgin to be receptive to hearing the divine message and assenting to it, and to be quick to offer herself unconditionally. At the moment she "welcomed into her heart and into her body "the Word of God" (LG 53), God made himself present in Mary in a very special way which far surpassed his presence in any other creature. Thus does the humble Virgin become the tabernacle of the eternal Word; she is fully conscious of it and proclaims it in her sublime canticle: "My soul magnifies the Lord ... he who is mighty has done great things for me" (Lk 1:46-49). Still, she keeps the divine mystery hidden in silence, and lives with it, recollected and adoring in the intimacy of her heart. The day will come when Joseph will realize her condition and not know how to behave in the situation, but Mary does not think it proper to break her silence, neither to justify herself nor to give any explanation. God who has spoken to her and is working within her, will know how to protect his mystery, and when to intervene. Mary is sure of that; she rests her case with him, and though suffering, she continues to be silent, a faithful depositary of God's secret. How that silence must have touched the heart of the Most High; for behold, an angel of the Lord appears to Joseph in a dream and says to him: "Joseph, son of David, do not fear to take Mary your wife, for that which is conceived in her is of the Holy Spirit" (Mt 1:20). God cannot hold out against a silence that is all faithfulness, unconditional trust, and total commitment of a soul into his hands.

2. To no creature did God "give" himself more fully than to Mary; but no creature ever understood better than she the grandeur of the divine gift, nor has there ever been a more loving and faithful guardian of it. Sister Elizabeth of the Trinity says, "If you but knew the gift of God! ... There is one created being who knew this gift of God, one who never lost a particle of it ... the faithful Virgin, who kept all things in her heart ... The Father, inclining toward this creature so beauteous, so unaware of her beauty, decreed that she should be the Mother in time of Him who is his Son in eternity. Then the Spirit of Love, who presides at all the

workings of God, came upon this Virgin and she uttered her 'Fiat!' 'Behold the handmaid of the Lord: be it done unto me according to your word.' The greatest of mysteries was accomplished, and through the descent of the Word into her, Mary was forever seized upon and held by God." (1 Retreat 10:1).

And while Mary adores in silence the mystery that is being accomplished within her, she does not neglect the humble duties of life; her life with God living within her does not draw her away from the concrete facts of daily existence. But her manner is always that of an adorer of the Most High. "In what peace, what recollection Mary went to and lent herself to everything! How the most commonplace things were divinized by her—for she remained ever in adoration of the Gift of God. Yet that did not hinder her from spending herself externally when there was question of practicing charity . . . To me"—concludes Elizabeth of the Trinity—"Our Lady's attitude during the months intervening between the Annunciation and the Nativity is the model for interior souls, those beings chosen by God to live in the depths within themselves."

Mary teaches us the secret of the interior life, concentrated on God present in our hearts. It is recollection, which is accomplished by avoiding curiosity, idle words, and useless occupations, and is nourished by silence, by a sense of the divine Presence, by adoration. This silence is not poverty, but fullness of life, it is intensity of desire, it is a loud cry which calls out to God, and appeals to the Savior not for ourselves alone, but for all. O Key of David, who opens the gates of the eternal kingdom, come and deliver us from the prison of sin. (Lectionary).

O Mary, Mary, temple of the Trinity. O Mary, bearer of the fire within, Mary, who offer us mercy . . . Mary who buy back the human race because you bear within you the Word who paid the price of the world! Christ bought it back by his passion; and you with your sorrows of body and soul. O Mary, peaceful sea, giver of peace, fruitful earth! You, O Mary, are that new plant which gives us the perfumed flower, the Word, the Only-Begotten Son of God, who was planted in you, O fruitful earth! You are the soil and you are the plant. O Mary, bearer of the inner fire, you carried this fire hidden and veiled under the ashes of your humility.

St. Catherine of Siena, *Preghiere ed Elevazioni*

O Mary, after Jesus Christ, of course in the measure in which the finite is distant from the infinite, you are also the great praise of glory of the Blessed Trinity . . . You were always holy and spotless and irreproachable in the sight of the thrice holy God. Your soul is so simple, its movements are so profound that one cannot comprehend them. Your whole life can be summed up in these few words: "Mary kept all these words, pondering them in her heart." You dwelt within your heart, so deep as to be lost to our gaze. When

Divine Intimacy

I read in the Gospel that you went with all haste into the hill country of Juda to fulfill your duty of charity to your cousin Elizabeth, I see you pass on your way, so beautiful, so calm and majestic, so recollected in the presence of the Word of God within you! Your prayer like his was always 'Behold, here I am!' Who? 'The handmaid of the Lord,' the least of his creatures, his Mother!

You were truly humble because you were always oblivious of self, unconscious of self, freed from self! Therefore you could sing: "He who is mighty has done great things for me; henceforth all generations shall call me blessed."

Elizabeth of the Trinity, 2 *Retreat* 15

25 — O RADIANT DAWN . . .

"O radiant Dawn, splendor of eternal light and sun of justice, come and enlighten those who sit in darkness and in the shadow of death." (Lectionary)

1. "The voice of my Beloved! Behold he comes, leaping upon the mountains, bounding over the hills . . . My beloved speaks . . . to me, 'Arise, my love, my fair one, and come! ' " (Cant 2:8,10). Under the metaphor of marriage, Holy Scripture shows us God as a bridegroom who takes the initiative in drawing near to his loved one, to Israel, the people he chose and sought after as his bride. We can regard this as a figure of what took place when the eternal Word, the Son of God, espoused human nature by joining himself to it in the virginal womb of Mary.

Although through this sublime union Christ became the mystical bridegroom of the Church, and through it, of every soul whom he redeemed, the Virgin of Nazareth is beyond all others the Beloved whom the Son of God calls and chooses as his own. "Arise my love . . . and come" (ib. 13). Mary answers the invitation and the Word gives himself to her as a mystical bridegroom and at the same time as a real son. But while the Virgin is absorbed in adoration of so sublime a mystery, she senses that this ineffable gift is not for her alone; she is conscious of being its depositary in order to share it with all mankind. Attentive and submissive to her interior summons, she arises and goes into the hill country in haste (Lk 1:39), to the home of her cousin Elizabeth, whose coming motherhood had been revealed to Mary by the angel. She is not alone: the Word made flesh is with her, and with her literally crosses the mountains and hills to meet his creatures whom he has come to save. So Mary begins her mission of bringing Christ to the world. She carries him in silence, but God living in her reveals himself. "When Elizabeth heard the greeting of Mary, the babe leaped in her womb, and Elizabeth was filled with the Holy Spirit" (ib. 41).

Mary teaches all who believe, nad especially apostles, that we bring Christ to our brothers not so much by word, as by a life of union with him, making room for him and letting him grow in our own hearts.

2. Mary bears Christ, who is about to rise upon the world as the "brightness of eternal light and the sun of Justice." His splendor is so great that it cannot stay hidden, but acts through his mother, for as soon as "the voice of your greeting came to my ears"—says Elizabeth—"the babe in my womb leapt for joy" (Lk 1:44). What the angel had predicted to Zachary comes true: "Your wife Elizabeth will bear you a son . . . he will be filled with the Holy Spirit even from his mother's womb." The Precursor is sanctified before his birth through the mediation of Mary, who, by being Mother of the Son of God, is also mediatrix of grace and holiness, not just for John the Baptist, the greatest among those born of woman (Lk 7:28), but for all men of all times and all peoples.

The Virgin Mary is so pure, so transparent, that her very presence reveals the splendor and the light of Christ. Men "who sit in darkness and in the shadow of death," deprived of light and incapable of welcoming it, have such need of recourse to her motherly intercession. Mary is the way that leads to Christ, she is the mother who dispels darkness, who prepares hearts to receive the Redeemer. At the same time she is a model for every Christian, who, once he has received Christ, must give him to his brothers. Likewise the life of a Christian ought to be so pure, so bright, and genuine that it reveals the Lord in every action. Christ, "splendor of eternal light and sun of justice" should shine out in our conduct as Christians, and by this dispel the darkness, doubts, errors, prejudices and uncertainties on the part of so many who perhaps do not believe because they have not met any one who knew how to give an effective witness to the gospel. The Christian prays for himself and for all his brothers by trusting all to Mary's powerful intercession: "O radiant Dawn, splendor of eternal light, sun of justice, come and enlighten those who sit in darkness and in the shadow of death" (Lectionary).

O beloved Mother, you who carried Jesus, teach us to carry him within us . . . when we receive him in Communion he is within us in his body, just as he was within you; he is always within us in his divine essence as he was within you.

Teach us to carry him with the same love as you did, with your recollection, your contemplation and your continual adoration . . .

Teach us, O Mother, to carry him as you did, completely oblivious of material things, with the eyes of your soul fixed unceasingly on Jesus within you, contemplating and adoring him in continual wonder. You passed in the midst of created things as in a dream, seeing everything that was not Jesus as though through

*mist, while he shone and scintillated in your soul as resplendent as
the sun, and encompassed your heart and enlightened your mind.
Teach us how to act on our little excursions in this world and indeed
on our whole journey through life so that we may walk as you did, on
your travels and every day, seeing external things as though they
were plunged in deep darkness, with our eyes fixed only on your
Jesus who illuminates our souls like a flash of fire. "For darkness is
as light with you" (Ps 139:12). Ah yes, my God, let all that is not you
be like darkness; light up the depths of our souls with the
delight of your glory.*

C. de Foucauld, *Sulle feste dell'anno*, Op. sp.

*O Lord, I do not ask you to repeat your birth as man which has
already taken place, but I beg you to let me be born into your divinity. Grant that what your grace alone accomplished corporally in
Mary, may be brought about now in the Spirit and in your Church.
May the unshakeable faith of your Church conceive you, her
spotless understanding give you birth, her spirit, protected by the
strength of the Almighty, preserve you forever!*

Mozarabic Missal PL 85, 187.

26 — THE GREAT MYSTERY

*"O King of nations and cornerstone of the Church, come and save
man whom you formed out of dust."*   (Lectionary)

1. The Liturgy is filled with ever growing expectation of the
Savior and stresses the longing desire of all the men who have
waited for him through the ages: "O King of nations . . . come!"
This yearning, always present in everyone who is aware of his
need for salvation, impels him to probe ever deeper into the
mystery of the Savior. And this means penetrating the mystery of
the infinite love which alone can explain it.
    God is love; everything he does, both in himself and outside of
himself, is a work of love. Being the infinite good, he cannot love
anything outside of himself from the desire of increasing his happiness; in himself he possesses all. Therefore, in God, to love, and
hence to will creatures, is simply to extend, outside of himself, his
infinite goodness, his perfections, and to communicate to others
his own being and happiness. Thus God loved man with an eternal
love and, loving him, called him into existence, giving him both
natural and supernatural life. Through love, God not only brought
man out of nothing, but chose him and elevated him to the state of
divine sonship, destining him to participate in his own divine life,
in his eternal beatitude. This was the first plan of the immense
charity of God with regard to man. But when man fell into sin,
God, who had created him by an act of love, willed to redeem him
by·an even greater act of love.

See then, how the mystery of the Incarnation presents itself to us as the supreme manifestation of God's exceeding charity toward man (Eph 2:4). "In this the love of God was made manifest among us, that God sent his only Son into the world, so that we might live through him. In this is love, not that we loved God but that he loved us and sent his Son to be the expiation for our sins" (1 Jn 4:9-10). After giving us natural life, and destining us for supernatural life, what more could God give us than to give himself, his Word made flesh for our salvation?

2. God is love. It is not surprising, therefore, that the story of his benevolent action on behalf of man is all a poem of love, of merciful love. The plan of creation and redemption "flows from 'that fountain of love' or charity within God the Father, who . . . freely creates us out of his surpassing and merciful kindness, and graciously calls us moreover to communicate in life and glory with himself" (AG 2). The first stanza of this poem was our eternal predestination to the vision and to the fruition of the intimate life of God. The second stanza relates, in an even more touching way, the sublimity of mercy: the mystery of the Incarnation.

The sin of our first parents had destroyed God's original plan for our elevation to a supernatural state; we had forfeited our claim, and we could never atone for the sin: "since all have sinned and fall short of the glory of God," says St. Paul (Rom 3:23). God could have pardoned all, but it was becoming to his holiness and infinite justice to exact an adequate satisfaction: man was absolutely incapable of providing this. Then the most sublime work of God's mercy was accomplished: one Person of the Blessed Trinity, the second, came to do for us what we could not do for ourselves. Behold the Word, God's only-begotten Son; "for us men and for our salvation he came down from heaven: by the power of the Holy Spirit he was born of the Virgin Mary, and became man" (Creed). The merciful love of God thus attains its highest manifestation. If there is no ingratitude and misery greater than sin, there can be no love greater than that of him who inclines over so much ingratitude and abjection to restore it to its primal splendor. God did this, not by the intervention of a prophet or the highest of the angels; he did it personally: all three Persons of the Blessed Trinity acted in the Incarnation, the end of which was to unite a human nature with the Person of the Word. The Son of God comes to save man whom he himself has made from dust. It is the Creator, the King of all peoples, who personally restores the work of his hands and lays the foundation of the Church in which he desires to reunite all his scattered children.

O my God! make me worthy to understand something of the mystery of the burning charity which is in you, which impelled you to effect the Incarnation, which is the root and source of our salvation and brings us this outpouring of love and the assurance of

Divine Intimacy

salvation. How ineffable is this charity! Truly, there is no greater than this, that the Word was made flesh in order to make me like unto God! O devoted love! To renew me you made yourself nothing, but though you took the form of a slave, you did not lessen your substance, nor injure your divinity; but the depths of your humility pierce my heart and make me cry out: 'O incomprehensible One, made comprehensible because of me! O uncreated One, now created! O inconceivable One, made conceivable! O inaccessible One, become palpable to touch! O Lord, make me worthy to understand your ineffable charity which was transmitted to us in the Incarnation.

Bl. Angela of Foligno, *Il libro della B. Angela* III

With what words shall we praise the love of God? What thanks shall we give? He so loved us that for our sakes he, through whom time was made, was made in time; and he, older by eternity than the world itself, was younger in age than many of his servants in the world; he who made man, was made man; he was given existence by a mother whom he had brought into existence; he was carried in hands which he had formed; he nursed at breasts which he had filled; he cried like a babe in the manger in speechless infancy—this Word without which human eloquence is vain!

St. Augustine, *Sermon* 188,2

27 — THE WORD WAS MADE FLESH

"O Emmanuel, our King and Lawgiver, come to save us, O Lord our God!" (Lectionary)

1. The Word is the second Person of the Blessed Trinity. In the bosom of the one divine nature, there are three Persons, three subsistent relations. We too are "subsistent": "subsistence" is that which permits me to say "I," and to attribute to the "I" the various acts that I perform as a person. In God, in the divine nature, there are three relations who can say "I" in regard to the external divine operations, operations which are common to all three, because they proceed from the one single nature possessed by all and by each of the three divine Persons. The Word possesses the same divine nature as the Father and the Holy Spirit; he possesses the same divine attributes, such as infinity, eternity, omnipotence, omniscience—all the divine grandeur and perfections belong to the Word as well as to the other two Persons. The word, the only-begotten Son, is distinguished from the Father only because he is generated by him, and from the Holy Spirit in that he, the Spirit, is the "spiration" of the Father and the Son. But in all other aspects the Word is absolutely identical with the Father and the Holy Spirit and performs the same divine actions: he knows and loves in an infinite manner, he creates and preserves the universe.

The Word is God! St. John the Evangelist, in the beginning of his Gospel, before speaking of the temporal birth of Jesus, presents to us the eternal generation of the Word, existing from all eternity in the bosom of the Father, equal to the Father in all things, but distinct from him. "In the beginning was the Word, and the Word was with God, and the Word was God" (Jn 1:1). The word is the one utterance of the Father—he expresses the Father *completely.* The Father, in giving the Word his whole essence and divine nature, also communicates to him all the divine activity. Thus the Word is the efficient *cause,* the first principle of all natural and supernatural life: "All things were made through him, and without him was not anything made that was made" (ib. 1:3). But the Word, the splendor of the Father, is not only life; he is also light, the light which reveals the greatness and the mystery of God to men: "In him was life, and the life was the light of men" (ib. 1:4). Natural life and the life of grace, light and knowledge of God—all come from the Word, who is God, together with the Father and the Holy Spirit.

2. "The Word was made flesh" (Jn 1:14). As God, the Word is eternal and immutable: therefore, of necessity, he always remains what he was: *manet quod erat*! But nothing prevented him, together with the Father and the Holy Spirit, from creating in time a human nature, which, instead of having a weak, limited ego like ours, was completely governed by its divine Person. And so it was done: the human nature assumed by him is the same as ours, but instead of belonging to a human person, it belongs to a divine Person, to the subsistent Person of the Word; therefore, even the operations and passions of this human nature belong to the Word. Since the Incarnation, the Word has a two-fold nature: the unique divine nature, which he possesses in common with the Father and the Holy Spirit, and the human nature, which is of the same quality and has the same properties as ours.

The Word remains what he was—perfect God. Nevertheless, he does not disdain to assume our poor human nature, fallen through sin, "but emptied himself, taking the form of a servant, being born in the likeness of man. And being found in human form he humbled himself" (Phil 2:7-8). Thus the eternal Word truly became Emmanuel, "God with us," came to dwell in the midst of men, made like to them in all things in order to free them from the slavery of sin, from the yoke of Satan.

All this was wrought by the immense charity of God. Full of mercy for his creature so sunk in the abyss of sin, he did not hesitate to decree the redemptive incarnation of his only-begotten Son. "For Jesus Christ was sent into the world as a real mediator between God and men . . . Therefore the Son of God walked the ways of a true incarnation that he might make men sharers in the divine nature" (AG 3). This is the fruit of the exceeding charity with which God has loved us (Eph 2:4).

O great and eternal Trinity . . . we are trees of death, you are the tree of life. O eternal Deity, highest purity, what a wondrous thing to look in your light at the tree of your creature, such as it came from you in unadulterated innocence, which you united to the human nature you had formed from the slime of the earth! But this tree of life, born in innocence, fell through disobedience and from being a tree of life became a tree of death—wherefore it could bring forth only fruits of death. Then O great and eternal Trinity, as if intoxicated with love and gone mad over your creature, seeing that since it was separated from you who are life, it could produce only the fruit of death, you provided a remedy for it with the same love with which you had created it, and grafted your divinity on to the dead tree of our humanity. O sweet and gentle grafting! You who are greatest sweetness deigned to unite yourself to our bitterness; you, who are brightness, with darkness; you, wisdom, with foolishness; you, life, with death; you, who are infinite, with us who are finite. What constrained you to this in order to restore us to life, after your creature had so injured you? Only love—for through this grafting, death is vanquished.

St. Catherine of Siena, *Preghiere ed Elevazioni*

O divine Word . . . whom I love. Coming into this land of exile, you willed to suffer and to die in order to draw souls to the bosom of the eternal fire of the most holy Trinity; ascending once again to the inaccessible light, henceforth your abode, you remain still in the "valley of tears," hidden beneath the appearances of a white host. You desire to nourish me with your divine substance, and yet I am but a poor little thing, who would return to nothingness if your divine glance did not give me life from one moment to the next.

O Jesus, allow me in my boundless gratitude to say to you that your love reaches unto folly. In the presence of this folly, how can you not desire that my heart leap toward you? How can my confidence, then, have any limits?

St. Therese of the Child Jesus, *Autobiography*, p. 199-200

28 — GOD WITH US

"Tomorrow the iniquity of the world shall be blotted out; the Savior of the world shall rule over us."   *(Lectionary)*

1. Of all the works accomplished by God in time and outside himself, the redemptive Incarnation of the Word is the greatest. It is the greatest because it has as its end not a mere creature, however sublime, but God himself, the eternal Word who, in time, assumed human nature. It is the greatest because it is the supreme manifestation of the merciful love of God, and the work which above all others glorifies him: and it glorifies him precisely in reference to charity which is his very essence. It is also the

greatest of his works because of the immense good it brings to mankind. The remission of sins, salvation, and the eternal happiness of the whole human race depend wholly on the Incarnation of the Word, upon Jesus the incarnate Word.

God the Father "chose us in him before the foundation of the world, that we should be holy and blameless before him. He destined us in love to be his sons through Jesus Christ . . . In him we have redemption according to the riches of his grace . . . But God who is rich in mercy, out of the great love with which he loved us, even when we were dead through our trespasses, made us alive together with Christ . . . and raised us up with him and made us sit with him in the heavenly places" (Eph 1:4-7; 2:4-6).

Jesus, the incarnate Word, is the one source of our salvation and our sanctification. "He who is 'the image of the invisible God' (Col 1:15), is himself the perfect man. To the sons of Adam he restores the divine likeness which had been disfigured from the first sin onward" (GS 22). Without Christ man would not be able to call God by the name of Father; he could not love him as a son loves his father, nor could he hope to be admitted to his intimacy; there would be no grace, no beatific vision. Without Jesus man would be imprisoned within the limits of a purely human life, deprived of every supernatural horizon, in time and in eternity.

2. God's greatest work, the Incarnation of the Word, destined to enlighten and save the whole world, takes place in obscurity and in silence, under the most humble and most human conditions. Caesar's edict obliges Mary and Joseph to leave their little home in Nazareth. They travel on foot like the very poorest in spite of the discomfort of Mary's condition. They do not think of objecting to the trip; they make no complaint, but obey with promptness and simplicity. He who commands is a man, but their profound spirit of faith discovers God's will in the command of the pagan emperor. So they go, trusting in God's providence. God knows and God will provide: for "in everything God works for good with those who love him" (Rom 8:28).

Nothing happens by chance: even the place of the Savior's birth had already been indicated by the prophet: "And you, O Bethlehem Ephrata, who are little . . . from you shall come forth for me one who is to be ruler in Israel" (Mic 5:2). The prophecy is fulfilled through the obedience of the humble pair. When they arrive in the little town, they look for lodging, but "there was no place for them in the inn" (Lk 2:7), and all they can do is seek shelter in a cave of the countryside. The squalor of this refuge for animals does not dismay or scandalize them: They know indeed that the child who is about to be born is the Son of God, but they know also that the ways of God are very different from those of men. And if God wills that this greatest work be accomplished there in that wretched cave in the extreme of poverty, Mary and Joseph have no objection to offer. It would have taken only a little human reasoning to make them feel disconcerted and dismayed, to make them question . . . Mary and Joseph are profoundly humble, and because of that, obedient and full of faith in God. And God, following his wonted way, makes use of what is humble and contemptible in the world's eyes to accomplish the greatest of his works.

In silence and darkness of night, Mary will give birth to a son: "the Son of the Most High" (Lk 1:32). And so will finally come to pass what had been foretold: "Behold a virgin shall conceive and bear a son, and his name shall be called Emmanuel, which means, God with us" (Mt 1:23).

O highest, transformed Love! O divine Vision! O ineffable One! O Jesus Christ, when you make me realize that you were born for my sake, how wonderful it is to understand it! Indeed, to comprehend that you were born for me fills me with every delight. The certitude that comes to us from the Incarnation is the same as that which flows from your birth, for the reason you became incarnate is also the reason for your birth. O admirable One, how wonderful are the works you have worked for us!
B. Angela of Foligno, *Il Libro della B. Angela III*

Make haste, O Jesus, I offer you my heart; my soul is poor and bare of virtues, the straws of so many imperfections will prick you and make you weep—but, O my Lord, what can you expect? This little is all I have. I am touched by your poverty, I am moved to tears . . . Jesus, honor my soul with your presence, adorn it with your graces. Burn this straw and change it into a soft couch for your most holy body.

Jesus, I am here waiting for your coming. Wicked men have driven you out and the wind is like ice. Come into my heart. I am a poor man but I will warm you as well as I can. At least be pleased that I wish to welcome you warmly, to love you dearly and sacrifice myself for you. But in your own way you are rich and you see my needs. You are a flame of charity and you will purge my heart of all that is not your own most holy Heart. You are uncreated holiness and you will fill me with those graces which give new life to my soul. O Jesus, come, I have so much to tell you, so many sorrows to confide, so many desires, so many promises, so many hopes. I want to adore you, to kiss you on the brow, O tiny Jesus, to give myself to you once more, for ever. Come my Jesus, delay no longer, come, be my guest.
John XXIII, *Journal of a Soul* 1902, p. 99

CHRISTMAS SEASON

29 — THE NATIVITY OF OUR LORD

December 25

"A holy day dawns upon us! Come, let us adore the Lord!"
(Lectionary)

1. "Today is born to you a Savior who is Christ the Lord" (Lect). The prophets beheld this "today" from the distance of many centuries and described it with a profusion of imagery: "The people who walked in darkness have seen a great light ... " (Is 9:2). The light that shatters the darkness of sin, and of slavery and oppression, is the prelude to the coming of the Messiah, who brings freedom, joy and peace: "A child is born to us, a son is given to us" (ib. 6). The prophecy goes far beyond simply anticipating a new David to be sent by God to free his people, and is focused on Bethlehem, lighting up the birth, not of a powerful king, but of the "mighty God" made man; he the "child" who is born for us, the "Son" who is given to us. He alone can be called "Wonderful Counsellor, Mighty God, Everlasting Father, Prince of peace" (ib.). When the prophecy came to pass in the brilliance of an infinitely greater light the announcement was no longer made by an earthly messenger, but by one from heaven. While shepherds were tending their flocks by night, "an angel of the Lord appeared to them and the glory of the Lord shone around them ... I bring you good news of a great joy which will come to all the people: for to you is born this day ... a Savior, who is Christ the Lord" (Lk 2:9-11). The Savior who had been promised and awaited during long ages, is now living and breathing among men: "you will find a babe wrapped in swaddling clothes, and lying in a manger" (ib. 12). In that baby the new people of God possess the Messiah, so longed for from of old: immeasurable hope has become immeasurable reality.

Contemplating this, St. Paul is moved to cry out: "The grace of God has appeared for the salvation of all men ... When the goodness and loving kindness of God our Savior appeared ... he saved us" (Tit 2:11; 3:5). That goodness and kindness appear in the sweet Child resting on the lap of his Virgin Mother: he is our God, God with us, made one with us, "training us to renounce irreligion and worldly passions, and to live soberly ... awaiting our blessed hope, the appearing of the glory of our great God and Savior Jesus Christ" (ib. 2:12-13). See here the arch of Christian hope extending between two poles: the Nativity of Jesus, which is the beginning of all salvation, and his return at the end of time, the goal toward which all Christian life is directed. When we contemplate and adore the birth of Jesus, we are not closing our lives off from reality and hope, but opening them to eternal hope in the expectation of one day meeting our Lord and Savior.

2. The Liturgy of the first two Christmas Masses especially celebrates the birth of the Son of God in time; while that of the third Mass ascends to his eternal generation in the bosom of the Father. "In the beginning was the Word, and the Word was with God, and the Word was God" (Jn 1:1)—God as Father, the Word who always was, and who from the beginning of time presided over the work of creation, in the fullness of time "became flesh, and dwelt among us" (ib. 14). An unheard-of, inexpressible mystery; yet it is not myth nor figure, but documented historical reality: "we beheld his glory, the glory as of the only begotten Son from the Father . . . full of grace and truth" (ib.). The evangelist knew Jesus, lived with him, listened to his words, touched him, and recognized in him the eternal Word who took flesh in our humanity.
John lifts a little of the veil of mystery: the Son of God, in becoming man, put himself on man's level in order to raise man to his dignity: "as many as received him, he gave them power to be made sons of God" (ib. 12). Not only that; he became man to make God accessible to man, to make man acquainted with God: "No one has ever seen God at any time; the only Son, who is in the bosom of the Father, he has made him known" (ib. 18). St. Paul repeats and develops the thought: "God . . . spoke of old by the prophets; but in these last days he has spoken to us by his Son" (Heb 1:1-2). The prophets transmitted the word of God, but Jesus is the Word itself, the Word of God: the incarnate Word who translates God into human language, especially by revealing his infinite love for men. The prophets had said wonderful things about God's love, but the Son of God incarnates this love and shows himself, living and able to be touched by human hands. The child "wrapped in swaddling clothes and lying in a manger" (Lk 2:12), is telling men that God loves them so much that he gives his only-begotten Son for their salvation. This message, once announced to the shepherds by angels, is proclaimed today to all—especially to the poor, the humble, the despised and the afflicted—no longer by angels, but by believing men. What good would it do to celebrate the birth of Jesus, if we Christians did not know how to announce it to our brothers by the example of our own lives? We really celebrate Christmas when we welcome the Lord into ourselves in ever deeper faith and love, and when we let him be born and live in our hearts so that he can show himself to

the world through the goodness, kindliness and self-surrender of those who believe in him.

The people who walked in darkness have seen a great light; to them who dwelt in the region of the shadow of death a light has risen... For a child is born to us, and a son is given to us; the government is upon his shoulder and his name shall be called Wonderful, Counselor, God the mighty, the Father of the world to come, the Prince of peace.

Isaiah 9:2,6

O how blessed that birth, when the Virgin Mary, made fruitful by the Holy Spirit, gave birth to our salvation, and the Child, the Redeemer of the world, showed his divine face. May all the heavenly host sing: oh sing, all you angels! May every power in the universe sing praise to God; let no tongue remain silent, let every voice be joined in harmony. Behold he appears, of whom the prophets sang centuries ago, he whom their truthful message announced, the promised one of all the ages; may all things together sing his praise!

Aurelio Prudenzio, *Inni della giornata*

O God, who in marvelous fashion created human nature, and have still more marvelously renewed it with the coming of your Son, grant that we may be made partakers of his divinity who vouchsafed to become partaker of our humanity.

Prayer (Roman Missal)

Today in him Christ the Lord, a new light has dawned upon the world: God has become one with man and man has become one again with God. Your eternal Word has taken upon himself our human weakness, giving our mortal nature immortal value. United to you, O holy Father, in a wonderful communion, man shares your everlasting life.

Preface III Roman Missal

O sweet Child of Bethlehem, grant that we may share with all our hearts in this profound mystery of Christmas. Put into the hearts of men this peace for which they sometimes seek so desperately, and which you alone can give them. Help us to know one another better and to live as brothers, children of the same Father. Reveal to us also your beauty, holiness and purity. Awaken in our hearts love and gratitude for your infinite goodness. Unite us all in charity. And grant us your heavenly peace. Amen.

John XXIII, *Prayers and Devotions*, p. 318

30 — FEAST OF THE HOLY FAMILY

Sunday within the octave of Christmas

Blessed is every one who fears the Lord, who walks in his ways.
(Ps 128:1)

1. The feast of the Holy Family, fixed by the Liturgy in the midst of the Christmas season, makes it clear that when the Son of God came into the world, he wanted to be part of a family group like every other man, even though his family was an entirely exceptional one due to the unusual situation of Mary and Joseph in relation to him. When he became man, he wanted to be like all other men: to have a country and an earthly family: a family so simple and humble as not to be distinguishable exteriorly in any way from other Jewish families. All the same, the gospel recounts some episodes which show it had a spiritual character that made it unlike any other family.

Forty days after the birth of Jesus, Mary and Joseph went to the temple in Jerusalem "to present him to the Lord, according to the law of Moses" (Lk 2:22-23). Enlightened by the Holy Spirit, Simeon recognized in the baby "the Christ of the Lord . . . He took him up in his arms and blessed God" then, turning to his mother, he spoke to her of her Son's mission and added: "A sword will pierce through your own soul also" (ib. 26,28,35). Besides fulfilling a formal prescription of the law by presenting Jesus in the temple, Mary and Joseph were renewing the gift of their absolute surrender to God, and, in the very words of Simeon, receive the assurance that God has accepted their act. The sign of this will be the "sword," or rather, the suffering that will accompany their steps and by means of which they will participate in the Son's mission. In this spirit the holy pair will embrace all the tribulations of their never easy life: the discomforts of the sudden flight to Egypt, the uncertainty attendant on settling in a strange country, the fatigues of hard work, the privations of a life of poverty, and later the anguish of losing their Son on a pilgrimage to Jerusalem. Jesus himself will explain to them then the deep reason of their suffering when he says: "Did you not know I must be in my Father's house?" (ib. 49). He belongs to his heavenly Father before he belongs to them; Mary and Joseph have the duty of preparing him for the mission the Father has entrusted to him. Such a situation demands the greatest unselfishness from them and gives their life a direction of total service to God in intimate collaboration with the salvific mission of the Son.

Meanwhile, the Gospel points out that after returning to Nazareth, Jesus "was obedient to them . . . and increased in wisdom and age and in favor with God . . . " (ib. 51-52). This is a precious remark indicating how children should grow up under the eyes of Christian parents.

2. The Church holds up the Holy Family as the model for every Christian family. First of all because the supremacy of God is strongly acknowledged: in the house of Nazareth God is always first, everything is subordinated to him: nothing outside his will is ever desired or done. Suffering is embraced in a deep spirit of faith because in every event they see the fulfillment of a divine plan even though often surrounded by mystery. The harshest and most painful vicissitudes do not trouble their peace, prcisely because everything is looked at in God's light, because Jesus is the center of their affections, and because Mary and Joseph gravitate around him, forgetful of themselves and wholly involved in his mission.

When the life of a family is inspired by such principles, its whole life-style is well ordered: obedience to God and his laws leads children to honor their parents, and causes the latter to love each other, and consequently to understand each other, and to love and bring up their children with respect for God's claims upon them. The Scripture readings of the feast stress two very important points; the first is the respect of children for their parents: "The Lord honored the father above the children . . . whoever honors his father atones for sins; whoever glorifies his mother is like one who lays up a treasure . . . My son, help your father in his old age and do not grieve him as long as he lives" (Sir 3:3-5,12). The ancient maxims of Sirach are an effective amplification of the fourth commandment; after so many centuries, they still possess an indisputable timeliness today—well worth meditating upon in prayer.

The second point is underlined by St. Paul in writing to the Colossians when he treats of the mutual love which should make the Christian family an ideal community: "Brothers . . . put on, then, compassion, kindness, lowliness, meekness, and patience, forbearing one another . . . and forgiving one another (Col 3:12-13). If the family is not founded on Christian love, it is very difficult for it to persevere in harmony and unity of heart. Every difficulty can be overcome and accepted when we love each other, but everything becomes an enormous burden when mutual love cools. And the only love which lasts, in spite of all the differences that are possible even in a family, is the love founded on the love of God.

Thus built on the gospel, the Christian family is truly the primary nucleus of the Church: in the Church and with the Church it collaborates in the work of salvation.

O God, Father of us all, you have given us a model of life in the Holy Family of Nazareth; grant that in our own families we may imitate their virtues and their love, until gathered together in your house, we may enjoy happiness without end.

Roman Missal, Collect

O Jesus, you return to Nazareth; there you spend your childhood and young manhood until your thirtieth year. You remain there to live for us, for our love ... You live there to teach us; during those thirty years you never tire of instructing us, not yet by word, but by your silence and your example ... You especially teach us that one can do good to others, much good, unending divine good, without any words or discourses, without noise, in silence, by giving good example ... the example of piety, of obligations to God lovingly fulfilled, of goodness toward others, of affection toward those near us, of family duties carried out in a holy manner; by the example of poverty, work, humiliations, recollection, retirement, of a life hidden in God, a life of prayer, of penance, a life of retreat, abandoned to God and engulfed in him. You teach us to live by the work of our own hands, so as not to be a burden on anyone and to be able to give something to the poor; you confer an incomparable beauty to this manner of life ... that of imitating you.

C. de Foucauld, *Eight Days at Ephrem,*
(Meditations of a Hermit, p. 103)

Truly, my Savior, you are a hidden God. Doubtless, O Jesus, you grow "in wisdom, age and grace with God and men;" your soul possesses the fullness of grace from the first moment of your entrance into this world, and all the treasures of knowledge and wisdom and this grace are only manifested little by little; you remain a hidden God in the eyes of men; your divinity is veiled beneath the outward appearance of a workman. O Eternal Wisdom, who to draw us out of the abyss into which Adam's proud disobedience had plunged us, chose to live in a humble workshop and therein to obey creatures, I adore and bless you!

C. Marmion, *Christ in his Mysteries,* 9, p. 168

31 — BELIEVING IN LOVE

December 26

I will sing of your steadfast love, O Lord for ever.   (Ps 89:1)

1. When creating us, God loved us so much that he made us to his own image and likeness; when redeeming us, he loved us so much that he made himself to our image. The Son of God, "born of the Virgin Mary ... has truly been made one of us, like us in all things except sin" (GS 22).

Christmas is preeminently the feast of love—the love that is revealed, not in the sufferings of the cross, but in the lovableness of a little child, our God, stretching out his arms to make us understand that he loves us. If the consideration of infinite justice can rouse us to greater fidelity in his service, how much more does the consideration of his love incite us! To run in the path of God's commandments we must be thoroughly convinced of God's infinite love for us; and precisely in order to reach this conviction we immerse ourselves in contemplation of the mystery of the Nativity. "The Word was made flesh, and dwelt among us, and we saw his glory, the glory as it were of the only begotten of the Father, full of grace and truth" (Jn 1:14). But in Bethlehem the glory of the eternal Word, consubstantial with the Father, and like him eternal, omnipotent, omniscient, and creator of the universe, is found hidden in a child, who from the very first moment of his earthly existence not only gladly takes on all our human miseries, but experiences them in the most wretched and abject conditions. "Remember, O Creator of all things"—sings the Liturgy of the Nativity—"that being born in time of the most pure Virgin, you took a body like our own . . . You came from the bosom of the Father to save the world" (RB). This touching prayer speaks to the heart of God and to the heart of the faithful soul; it reminds God of the wonders he accomplished for the salvation of mankind through his love, it repeats to us the wonderful truth: "God is love." Before the manger of Bethlehem let us repeat again and again: "We know and believe the love God has for us" (1 Jn 4:16).

2. "God is love!" (1 Jn 4:16). An immense treasure is contained in these words of Holy Scripture; it is the treasure which God discloses to souls who know how to concentrate on contemplating the incarnate Word. Until we comprehend that God is infinite love and infinite benevolence, who gives himself and extends himself to all men in order to communicate to them his goodness and his happiness, our spiritual life has still just begun; it has not yet developed or deepened. Only when the soul, enlightened by the Holy Spirit, has penetrated the mystery of divine love, only then does its spiritual life attain to full maturity.

There is no better way of understanding God's infinite love than by drawing near to the humble manger where he lies, made flesh for us. Jesus, The Word, the spoken Word of the Father, tells each and every one of us this great fact: God loves you!

The virtues and divine attributes are to be discovered in God through the sublime mysteries of God made man; so teaches St. John of the Cross (Sp C 37:2); among these attributes the first is charity, which constitutes the very essence of God. From the silent loving contemplation of the Infant Jesus there is easily aroused in us a more profound and penetrating sense of his infinite love; we no longer merely believe, but, in a certain way, we know by experience God's love for us. Then our will fully accepts what faith teaches; it accepts it with love, and with all its strength, and our soul believes unreservedly in God's infinite love. God is love, this truth, fundamental for all Christian life, has penetrated to the depths of the soul; it feels it and lives it, because it has, so to say, almost touched its incarnate God. One who so believes in infinite love, will know how to give itself to him without measure—to give itself totally.

It was in this way that the proto-martyr, St. Stephen, believed and offered himself. The Church presents him to us today to show us a most authentic response to God's love: martyrdom embraced in order to keep faith with him who had come to save him.

You, O eternal God . . . have come down from the great height of your divinity to the mire of our humanity, because the lowness of my intellect could neither understand nor behold such height. In order that my littleness might see your greatness, you became a little child, concealing the greatness of your deity in the littleness of our humanity. And so you manifest yourself to us in the Word, your only-begotten Son; thus have I known you, O abyss of charity! Oh blush with shame, blind creature, so exalted and honored by your God, not to know that God, in his inestimable charity, came down from the height of his infinite deity to the lowliness of your humanity! O inestimable love! What do you say, O my soul? I say to you, eternal Father, I beseech you, most benign God, that you give us and all your servants a share in the fire of your charity.
St. Catherine of Siena, *Preghiere ed Elevazioni*

O my Lord, how ill we profit from all the blessings which you have granted us! You seek methods and ways and inventions by which to show us what love you have for us; yet we, inexperienced in loving you, set so little store by them that, unpractised as we are, our thoughts pursue their habitual path and cease pondering on the great mysteries hidden in this language used by the Holy Spirit. What amazes and bewilders me more, considering what we are, is the love which he had for us and still has. Yet such love he has, and there can surely be no words with which he can express it as clearly as he has already expressed it by his actions.
cf. St. Teresa of Jesus, *Meditations on the Song of Songs* I:4,7

32 — RETURNING LOVE FOR LOVE

December 27

At your birth, O Lord we sing you hymns of love and praise. (Brev)

1. "Though he was in the form of God . . . he emptied himself, taking the form of a servant, being born in the likeness of men" (Phil 2:6-7). To assume human nature, the eternal Word concealed his divinity, majesty, power, and infinite wisdom: behold the divine Infant who can neither speak nor move by himself, who in all things depends on his mother, his creature, and to whom he looks for everything.

True love overcomes every obstacle, accepts every situation, makes any sacrifice to unite itself with him whom it loves. If we wish to be united to God, we must do exactly what the Word did to become united to human nature: he followed a path of prodigious self-abasement, of infinite humanity. Here these open before us the path of total abnegation, "the way of the nothing." "All, nothing, all, nothing!" is the lullaby that St. John of the Cross sings to his God made man. "To come to possess all, desire the possession of nothing ... Because if you desire to have something ... your treasure in God is not purely your all" (Asc I, 13:11-12). God will be our everything, the soul's only treasure, when the soul, in order to possess him, is able to renounce every earthly good, even itself, in a perfect spirit of poverty and humility. Compared to the annihilation of the eternal Word, this program should not appear to us too austere and exacting. For anyone who loves Jesus, there can be nothing more spontaneous and desirable than to follow him and adapt oneself to him. To repay his infinite love, to prove our love for him, let us resolve to strip ourselves above all of selfishness, pride, vanity, all our righteous pretensions. What a striking contrast between these vain pretensions of self and the touching humility of the incarnate Word! St. Paul repeats: "Have this mind among yourselves, which was in Christ Jesus, who though he was in the form of God ... emptied himself, taking the form of a servant" (Phil 2:5-7). Who would not love him who loves us so much?

2. "You know the grace of our Lord Jesus Christ: that though he was rich, yet for your sake he became poor, so that by his poverty you might become rich" (2 Cor 8:9). Out of love for us, to enrich us with his own divine gifts, Jesus chose the utmost poverty for himself: Mary "wrapped him up in swaddling clothes and laid him in a manger, because there was no room for them in the inn" (Lk 2:7). "He let himself be laid on hay, he did not abhore the manger," we sing in the Christmas liturgy. If we wish to follow Jesus more closely, we must voluntarily, for love of him strip ourselves of our love of riches, of our attachment to material well-being; we must willingly renounce our comforts and everything that is superfluous. The vow of poverty obliges this detachment in a special way, but even without this obligation, how can we calmly live a life of ease, when the Son of God has voluntarily embraced so much poverty and hardship? Looking at the manger, one feels that the way of nothing does not ask too much. "Endeavor to be inclined always: not to look for the best of temporal things, but for the worst and to desire to enter into complete nudity, emptiness and poverty in everything in the world" (Asc I, 13:6). By this path we arrive quickly at Bethlehem, where the Son of God has united himself to our humanity in the most intimate personal way, there where he awaits us to unite our souls to himself.

Just as humility and poverty dispose the heart for a more perfect love of God and a more intimate communion with him, so do they also dispose us to a more perfect love of neighbor, to a more cordial brotherly communion. St. Paul suggests that the faithful imitate Jesus' sentiments of humility, so that by rejecting self-love they may come to be "of the same mind, having the same love" (Phil 2:2). He proposes the example of the Lord's poverty, so that they may learn to become poor like him for the benefit of the more needy. Love for God is perfect only when love for our brothers is also perfect. The apostle John whom the Church honors today is the herald of the great truth: "He who loves God, should love his brother also" (1 Jn 4:21).

O uncreated God, make me worthy to understand your deep love and ardent charity and give me the grace to understand that ineffable love which you communicated to us when you showed your Son in his Incarnation, and when your Son revealed himself to us. O admirable and joyous love, truly in you is every savor, every sweetness and joy! This is the contemplation that raises the soul from the world, and supports it above itself in a state of peace and tranquillity.
B. Angela of Foligno, *Il libro della B. Angela* III

O Lord, the will is inclined to love after seeing such countless signs of love; it would want to repay something; it especially keeps in mind how you, its true Lover, never leave it, accompanying it and giving it life and being. Then the intellect helps it realize that it could not find a better friend, even were it to live for many years, that the whole world is filled with falsehood, and that so too these joys the devil gives it are filled with trials, cares, and contradictions . . .

But oh, my Lord and my God, how the whole world's habit of getting involved in vanities vitiates everything! Our faith is so dead that we desire what we see more than what faith tells us. And, indeed, we see only a lot of misfortune in those who go after these visible vanities . . . Ah, my Lord! Your help is necessary here; without it one can do nothing. In your mercy do not consent to allow this soul to suffer deception and give up what was begun. Enlighten it that it may see how all its good is within this castle.
St. Teresa of Jesus, *Interior Castle* II 4-6

33 — GLORY TO GOD

December 28

"Glory to God in the highest! Glory to you, O Jesus, born of the Virgin"   *(Lk 2:14; RB)*

1. "Suddenly there was with the angel a multitude of the heavenly host, praising God and saying: 'Glory to God in the highest' " (Lk 2:13-14). The Son of God became man for our salvation and happiness; he came to save that which was lost. However the primary end of the Incarnation is God's glory, which is the end of all his works. He, the one absolute good, cannot will anything apart from his glory. By sending his only Son to save man, he

wished to glorify his infinite goodness, to glorify himself in our salvation, accomplished by means of this supreme act of his infinitely merciful love. The work of creation glorifies God in his wisdom and omnipotence; the work of the Incarnation glorifies him in his charity. And God could not manifest greater mercy and charity than by giving his Son for our salvation, so none of his works can give him greater glory than the Incarnation of the Word. Hence, the angels sang at the birth of the Redeemer, "Glory to God in the highest!" The church takes up this hymn and amplifies it in the Gloria which is sung in every feast-day Mass: "Lord God, heavenly King . . . we worship you, we give you thanks, we praise you for your glory." At no time more than at Christmas do we feel the need of repeating this song, more with our heart than with our lips. The soul feels more than ever incited to praise its God, so immense, so great, so beautiful, but also so good, so merciful, so full of charity. "Father, we acknowledge your greatness: all your actions show your wisdom and love . . . you so loved the world that in the fullness of time you sent your only Son to be our Savior" (IV Euch. Prayer). Song does not suffice: the soul would wish to be transformed into an incessant "praise of his glory."

2. We have been destined in Christ "to live for the praise of his glory" (Eph 1:12). As Christians, we are, of ourselves, proofs of Christ's glory; our elevation to a supernatural state, our sanctification, and our eternal happiness have for their supreme end the glory of him who has redeemed us. Christians, and with even greater reason, consecrated souls, must act in such a way that all their works and their whole lives may be a praise of glory to the Trinity and to Christ our Lord.

Today the Church presents to us the "first fruits" of these "true Christians," those who by their works, and even by their death, have sung the glory of the Redeemer. We see them in the retinue of the divine Child, like angels on earth, who unite their hymn to that of the angels in heaven. St. Stephen, the protomartyr, teaches us that a faithful, loving soul must be ready to give up everything, itself, and even its life, for the glory of its God. St. John the Evangelist, "the blessed Apostle to whom heavenly secrets were revealed," and who penetrated so deeply into the mystery of God as infinite charity, shows us that love for our neighbor "is the precept of the Lord; if this only be done, it is enough" (RB) to give glory to him who is infinite Love.

The Holy Innocents, "the flowers of the martyrs, the first tender buds of the Church," demonstrate that the voice of innocence is a hymn of glory to God, resembling that of the angels: Out of the mouths of babes and infants you have perfected praise to the confusion of your enemies (cf Ps 8:3). But this hymn becomes much more powerful and eloquent when it is united to the sacrifice of their blood: the Holy Innocents celebrated the glory of

God "not by words, but by their death." May the life of every Christian be a hymn of praise to God, not by word, but by deed, so that we may bear witness by our lives to the faith we profess with our lips (MR).

O eternal and infinite Good, O extravagance of love! you need your creature? Yes, it seems to me; because you behave as if you could not live without it, although you are life and all things receive life from you, and without you nothing lives . . . You fell in love with your own workmanship and delighted in it as if enraptured with its well-being; it flees from you and you go searching for it; it goes away from you and you draw near; you could not have come any nearer than in assuming its very humanity.
St. Catherine of Siena, *Dialogue* 153

You, who were great and rich, made yourself little and poor for our sake, you chose to be born outside a house in a stable, to be swaddled in rags, to suck virgin milk, to be placed in a manger between an ox and a donkey. "Then there dawned for us the day of the new redemption, the day of eternal happiness; then for the entire world the skies distilled honey!" My soul, embrace that divine manger, press your lips to the Babe's small feet and kiss them both. Besides that, meditate on the shepherds' watch, look at the onrushing army of angels, join them in your part of the heavenly melody, singing with your voice and your heart: Glory to God in the highest, and peace on earth to men of good will.
St. Bonaventure, *The Tree of Life 4*

O God, in order to be a praise of glory, I must love you with a pure, disinterested love, without seeking myself in the sweetness of your love; I must love you above all your gifts. Now, how shall I desire and effectively will good to you, except by fulfilling your will, since this will orders all things for your greater glory? I ought, therefore, to surrender myself completely, blindly, to that will, so that I cannot possibly will anything but what you will."
Elizabeth of the Trinity, *I Retreat* 13:3

34 — PEACE TO MEN

December 29

O Jesus, Prince of peace, give me your peace! (cf Is 9:6)

1. At Bethlehem the angels announced two things: glory to God and peace to men. No one glorifies God as much as that little Babe lying on the straw; he alone, being the eternal Word, can give God perfect, infinite love that is worthy of him. And no one brings peace to men more than Jesus, our Savior; by making

reparation for sin, he reconciles man with his Creator and establishes a new covenant between them: the Creator becomes Father, and man, his son.

"In order to establish peace or communion between sinful human beings and himself, as well as to fashion them into a fraternal community, God determined to intervene in human history in a way both new and definitive. For he sent his Son, clothed in our flesh, in order that through this Son he might snatch men from the power of darkness and of Satan and that in this Son he might reconcile the world to himself" (AG 3). The primary and special peace that man needs is precisely good relations with God, filial relations of love and friendship. When the angels sing: "peace on earth to men of good will," they are announcing that the heavenly Father not only forgives sin, but welcomes men as his children, and readmits them to communion with himself. It is the "good will," or rather, the infinite benevolence of God which stoops down to men offering them his peace, a peace in which is contained every good and all salvation. This peace is offered to men through Christ the Savior, announced long before as the "Prince of peace" (Is 9:6). From peace with God and from the fact of feeling that we are all his children and the object of his love, comes peace among men. This peace is also the fruit of Christ's mediation: "he is our peace" . . . says St. Paul, "he came and preached peace to you who were far off and to you who were near. For through him we both have access in one Spirit to the Father" (Eph 2:14, 17-18).

2. "Peace to men of good will." If "good will" means above all the benevolence of God toward men, it also means the benevolence of men, that is, the good will with which they must receive the peace brought to earth by the Messiah.

The angels promised peace "to men of good will." Our will is "good" when it is upright, docile, and resolute. It is *upright* when it is sincerely and entirely oriented toward good; *docile,* when it is always ready to follow every indication of God's will; *resolute,* when it is prompt to adhere to the will of God, even though difficulties and obstacles arise, and sacrifices are required. The Lord is continually urging us to generosity and abnegation in all the circumstances of life, even the smallest ones. We must give ourselves to God without hesitation, certain that if God asks anything of us he will also give us the strength to carry out his wishes. Such was the conduct of the shepherds; as soon as they heard the message of the angel, they left all, their flocks and their rest, and "went with haste (to Bethlehem) and found . . . the Infant lying in a manger" (Lk 2:16). They were the first to find Jesus and to taste his peace.

St. Teresa of Jesus says, "Holy peace consists in a union with God's will, such a union that there is no division between him and the soul, but one same will. It is a union not based on words or desires alone, but a union proved by deeds. When the bride knows she is serving the bridegroom in something, there is so much love and desire to please him that she does not listen to the reasons the intellect will give her or to the fears it will propose. But she lets faith so work that she does not look for her own profit or rest" (Med 3:1). This is perfect "good will." Mary and Joseph are unsurpassable models of it. Despite the obscurity of the mystery and the great sacrifices it entailed, they clung to the divine plan in total abandonment, and had the supreme joy of receiving the King of heaven in their arms. To the greatest good will corresponds the greatest union with God, and the deepest peace and joy.

> *O eternal Deity, in you I see love that is priceless; and since through our misery and weakness we fall into the shamefulness of the sin of our first father's disobedience, I see that love constrains you, O our great eternal Father, to look with pity on our poor wretched souls; wherefore you sent the Word, your only-begotten Son, the Word made flesh, concealed in our poor flesh, clothed in our mortality.*
>
> *And you, Jesus Christ, the reconciler and reformer and redeemer, became also the mediator, the Word, love: you changed man's long warfare against God into a great peace...*
>
> *O eternal Godhead! I confess and I avow that you are a peaceful immensity, where the soul feeds and is nourished, and rests in you through affection, love and union in love; it conforms its will to your great eternal will, which has no other desire than our sanctification. Therefore the soul that observes this casts off its own will and clothes itself with yours.*
>
> St. Catherine of Siena, *Preghiere ed Elevazioni*

> *O Jesus you came to direct our steps into the way of peace. O peace, dear object of my affections! O Jesus, you are my peace, you put me in peace with God, with myself, with everyone; through this you make peace in heaven and earth; when will this come to pass, O Jesus? When will it happen that through faith in the remission of sins, through the peace of my conscience, through sweet trust in your favors and an absolute compliance... through conforming to your eternal will in every circumstance of life—when shall I possess this peace that is in you and comes from you and is itself you?*
>
> J. B. Bossuet, *Elevazioni a Dio sui misteri* 15:6

> *O eternal Word of the Father, Son of God and of Mary, renew once more in the secret depths of men's hearts the miracle of your birth! Re-clothe with immortality the children you have redeemed: make them aflame with charity, gather all together in the unity of your mystical Body so that your coming may bring real joy, sure peace and the true brotherhood of individuals and peoples. Amen, amen.*
>
> John XXIII, *Prayers and Devotions* p. 37

35 — SIGN OF CONTRADICTION

December 30

I thank you Lord, for my eyes have seen your salvation   (Lk 2:30)

1. The Gospel relates that forty days after the birth of Jesus, Mary and Joseph "brought him up to Jerusalem to present him to the Lord" (Lk 2:22). In the temple the Child was received by Simeon, who uttered the famous prophecy: "This child is set for the fall and rising of many in Israel and for a sign which shall be contradicted" (ib. 34).

The Son of man became man for all men: he brings and offers salvation to all, but many will not receive it. John says: "He was in the world, and the world was made through him yet the world knew him not. He came to his own home and his own people received him not" (Jn 1:10-11). Oh, what sadness in that observation! It is the great mystery of human freedom. God has made man intelligent and free; he offers him all the treasures of salvation and holiness contained in the infinite merits of Jesus Christ; man is free to accept or to refuse. This is our tremendous responsibility. Jesus came to save us, to offer himself for the good of each of us; he is ready to do it, he wants to do it, and yet he will not do it unless we *freely* accept his gift, unless we correspond to his loving solicitation with the *free* gift of our will. God "does not force our will, he takes what we give him, but he does not give himself wholly until we give ourselves wholly" (St. Teresa, *Way* 28:12).

If Jesus is the reason for the downfall of those who reject him, for those who open their minds and hearts to his message he is the cause of life, of a life so new that it could be called a resurrection. "To all who received him, who believed in his name, he gave power to become children of God" (Jn 1:12). Such is the power of faith inspired by love.

2. Among all those present when the Child Jesus was presented in the temple, there were only two who recognized him as the Savior: the aged Simeon and the prophetess Anna. Of Simeon it is said that "he was righteous and devout, looking for the consolation of Israel, and the Holy Spirit was upon him . . . Inspired by the Spirit he came into the temple;" and of Anna: "She did not depart from the temple, worshipping with fasting and prayer, night and day" (Lk 2:25,27,37).

These are the characteristics of souls well disposed to accept the redemptive work of Jesus: justice, or rather, rectitude of mind and will; sincere longing for God; diligence in his service; a life of prayer and mortification. The more profound these dispositions become, the more the soul opens itself to the divine action. The light of the Holy Spirit enables it to recognize in Jesus its

Redeemer and its Sanctifier; and Jesus can now wholly accomplish his work in it. Such souls find themselves in a special way under the influence of the Holy Spirit, who gives them an intuition of divine things, and guides them in providential ways, so that at the right moment they know how to find Jesus, grow in understanding his message and grasp the true meaning of his Gospel. If we want to recognize the Lord we must, like Simeon, be moved interiorly by the Spirit; now it is the "just" whom the Spirit moves, those who are "dear to God" and who live in longing for him. The spirit moves those who like Anna "serve God day and night" by doing his will, in continual prayer and a spirit of penance.

For such souls Jesus is in the fullest sense the cause of new life; these are the true children of God, who are "born not of blood, nor of the will of the flesh, nor of the will of man, but of God" (Jn 1:13). As St. Paul says: "All who are led by the Spirit of God, are sons of God" (Rom 8:14); they have died to sin and have risen to new life in Christ.

This world, created by God, but not knowing him, includes my soul. You made me, filled me with good things, permitted me to know you; but little by little I abandoned you and ended up by not knowing you or even believing in your any more. Please forgive me! You changed my heart, you sought for me as a good shepherd seeks for his wandering sheep. Strongly, and yet so sweetly you led me back, you loaded me with even greater graces than before, like the prodigal son who was treated better than his faithful brother, and in spite of it all, I still sin; and when I sin, my soul again no longer knows you, no longer loves you. Forgive me, please forgive me.
C. de Foucald, *Meditazioni sul Vangelo,* Op. sp.

O Christ Jesus, Our God and our Redeemer, Revelation of the Father, our elder Brother and our Friend, grant that we may know you! Purify the eyes of our heart so that we may contemplate you with joy; silence the noise of creatures that we may follow you unimpeded. Reveal yourself to our souls as you did to the disciples of Emmaus, while expounding to them the sacred pages which spoke of your mysteries, and we shall feel "our hearts burn within us" with the longing to love and attach ourselves to you!
C. Marmion, *Christ in His Mysteries,* I, III:7

December 31

Looking for the blessed hope and coming of our Savior Jesus Christ.
(Tit 2:13)

1. Time passes and does not return. God has assigned to each of us a definite time in which to fulfill his divine plan for our soul, the time of our life on earth. For each of us this is "the acceptable time . . . the day of salvation" (2 Cor 6:2), in which we must work diligently to cooperate with the grace given us for our sanctification; we have only this time and shall have no more. Time ill spent is lost forever. Our life is made up of this uninterrupted, continual flow of time, which never returns. In eternity, on the contrary, time will be no more; we shall be established forever in the degree of love which we have reached now, in time. If we have attained a high degree of love, we shall be fixed forever in that degree of love and glory; if we possess only a slight degree, that is all we shall have throughout eternity. No further progress will be possible when time has ended. St. Paul urges: "Let us not grow weary in well-doing, for in due season we shall reap if we do not lose heart. So then as we have opportunity, let us do good to all men" (Gal 6:9-10). Each passing year is a warning to treasure each present moment and to sanctify it with charity. "We must give each moment its full amount of love, and make each passing moment eternal, by giving it value in love." (Sr. Carmela of the Holy Spirit, O.C.D.).[1]

Charity sanctifies every action, even the most trivial and indifferent, and confers upon it a value for eternal life. In fact, "love urges us to live more intensely for him who died for us and rose again. We strive, therefore, to please the Lord in all things . . . Thus when we have finished the one and only course of our earthly life, we may merit to enter into the marriage feast with him and to be numbered among the blessed" (LG 48). By living in this manner we carry out the divine plan for our soul, and reach that level of love that God expects of us, and with which we shall love and glorify him for all eternity.

2. We have only the short day of this earthly life to grow in love and if we wish to derive from it the greatest possible benefit we must apply ourselves not only to doing good works, but to do-

---

[1]Sr. Carmela of the Holy Spirit, Discalced Carmelite, died July 23, 1949. In 1954 her biography was published, completed by some of her writings and some points of directions from Fr. Gabriel, who was her spiritual director at Carmel. *Suor Carmela dello Spirito Santo*, Carmelo S. Giuseppe, Roma 1954.

ing them with our whole heart, and with all the generosity of which we are capable, overcoming the inertia and pettiness which always make us inclined to the least effort. Then love will grow immeasurably and we shall be able to give the Lord the beautiful witness of St. Therese of the Child Jesus: "Your love . . . has grown with me and now it is an abyss, the depths of which I cannot fathom" (Auto. IX).

But what are these good works we must each accomplish? Those which are pointed out to us through the will of God; only these can sanctify. Jesus used to say: I "must work the works of him who sent me, while it is day. Night comes when no one can work" (Jn 9:4). This is why he became man: "I have come to do your will, O God" (Heb 10:7); this is why he lived: "Did you not know that I must be in my Father's house" (Lk 2:49). Life has one single purpose for Jesus, one single obligation: the will of his Father, the interests of his Father, the glory of his Father.

To be one of Jesus' followers means trying to relive his conduct fully, realizing that only one thing matters: "attending to the Father's business." Instead of this, how many times our lives are dispersed in all directions and in so many useless activities, in passing things that disappear with time and only reflect the vanity of the world. Only the time that is dedicated to God and to fulfilling his will will endure; being fixed in God makes man participate in his immutability. Then the passage of time will not cast a shadow of sadness on our lives, but rather fill our hearts with joy because it brings our eternal meeting with God the closer. May each passing year be a step forward toward our true home, and each day be marked with yearning for the Lord: "Come, Lord Jesus" (Rev 22:20).

> *Oh, how late have my desires been enkindled and how early, Lord, were you seeking and calling that I might be totally taken up with you. Do you perhaps, Lord, abandon the wretched or withdraw from the poor beggar when he wants to come to you? Do your grandeurs or your magnificent works, Lord, perhaps have a limit? O my God and my Mercy, how you can show them now in your servant! You are mighty, great God! Now it can be known whether my soul understands itself in being aware of the time it has lost and of how in a moment you, Lord, can win this time back. It seems foolish to me, since they usually say lost time cannot be recovered.*
>
> *May you be blessed, my God! O Lord, I confess your great power. If you are powerful, as you are, what is impossible for you who can do everything? . . .*
>
> *You know well, my God, that in the midst of all my miseries I never failed to acknowledge your great power and mercy. May that in which I have not offended you, Lord, help me. Recover, my God, the lost time by giving me grace in the present and future so that I may appear before you with wedding garments; for if you want to, you can do so.*
>
> St. Teresa of Jesus, *Soliloquies IV* 1-2

O my God, my whole life has been a course of mercies and bless-
ings shown to one who has been most unworthy of them. I require
no faith, for I have had long experience, as to your providence
towards me. Year after year, you have carried me on—removed
dangers from my path—recovered me, recruited me, refreshed me,
borne with me, directed me, sustained me. O forsake me not when
my strength fails me. And you will never forsake me. I may securely
repose upon you. Sinner as I am, nevertheless, while I am true to
you, you will still, and to the end, be superabundantly true to me. I
may rest upon your arm; I may go to sleep in your bosom. Only give
me, and increase in me, that true loyalty to you which is the bond of
the covenant between you and me, and the pledge in my own heart
and conscience that you, the Supreme God, will not forsake me, the
most miserable of your children.

J. H. Newman—*Meditations on Christian Doctrine* XIX:3

37 — SOLEMNITY OF THE HOLY MOTHER OF GOD

January 1

"Blessed are you among women, and blessed is the fruit of your
womb"   *(Lk 1:42)*

1. The Liturgy consecrates to the Mother of God the eighth
day of Christmas, which not only coincides with the beginning of
the calendar year, but, according to the Gospel, is the day on
which Jesus received his name. "At the end of eight days when he
was circumcised, he was called Jesus" (Lk 2:21).

The Lord's name, which is explicitly mentioned in today's
Gospel, is referred to in the first reading in the touching words of
the priestly blessing suggested by God himself: "Thus you shall
bless the people of Israel: you shall say to them: The Lord bless
you and keep you. The Lord make his face to shine upon you and
be gracious to you! ... So shall they put my name ... and I will
bless them" (Num 6:23-27). The Lord's blessing was once reserved
for the people of Israel, but is now extended to all the nations
through the mediation of Jesus. It is "in Christ Jesus" that God
blesses "with every spiritual blessing in the heavenly places"
(Ep 1:3) each of us who seeks him with a sincere heart; it is
because of Jesus that he "lifts up his countenance upon you and
gives you peace (Num 6:26). There is no better way to begin the
year than to call upon the name of God and receive from him the
precious gift of peace.

Today's Liturgy turns spontaneously to Mary, the Virgin
Mother, for the remembrance of the child of "eight days" canot be
separated from that of his mother; she is quietly present wherever
her divine Son is found. The Church gazes at him and asks her
motherly intercession for all the faithful: "O God ... grant that

we may experience the intercession of her through whom we were made worthy to welcome the Author of life, Jesus Christ, your Son." God's blessing takes on, so to speak, a maternal tone; we are blessed in Jesus through Mary's intercession, because only the purity and love of this humble Virgin make us "worthy to welcome the Author of life," Jesus, the Son of God.

The blessing of the Lord that was promised to Israel reaches out today to all men through Jesus and his Mother Mary, and brings grace and peace to every heart. "May God be gracious to us and bless us" (Ps 67:1).

2. Mary is continually present in the various liturgical texts, but always in a veiled manner that is perfectly in keeping with her characteristic humility and silence.

Paul mentions her in the second reading, though not by name; he only stresses the fact that Christ was born of a woman: God sent "his Son, born of a woman . . . that we might receive adoption as sons" (Gal 4:4-5). The incarnation of the Son of God is through a virgin birth, but in the normal way of human nature: he is born of a woman, Mary, and this inserts him as a true man among men. Precisely because he belongs to our race, because he is our brother in the flesh, Jesus is able to ransom us and make us his brothers in the spirit and therefore participants in his divine sonship. The grace of adoption reaches us through Mary who, since she is Christ's mother, is also the mother of those who become children of God in Christ. If "the Spirit of the . . . Son cries Abba, Father" (ib. 6) in the hearts of the faithful, this is also due to the maternal role of Mary, most holy, for God has so arranged it.

With like moderation the Gospel of today's Mass shows Mary carrying out her office of mother. Luke's account gives us a glimpse of her immediately after Jesus' birth: she welcomes the shepherds, and in her happiness shows him to them, she listens carefully to everything they relate of the great things announced by the angel. Then, as the shepherds depart, "glorifying and praising God for all they had heard and seen" (Lk 2:20). Mary remains with her Son and keeps "all these things, pondering them in her heart" (ib. 19).

Mary is Jesus' mother not only because she gave him flesh and blood, but also because she entered into his mystery and associated herself with him in the most intimate way: "she dedicated herself totally . . . to the person and to the work of her Son, with a function in the redemption, both dependent on him and with him" (LG 56). That is why Mary is our "mother in the order of grace" (ib. 61).

O most gracious Lord, you were born of a virgin for us . . . be not unmindful of those whom you formed with your own hand; show your love for us, O merciful One! Hearken to her who gave you birth, the Mother of God who intercedes for us, and save your afflicted people, O Savior!

Byzantine Rite: *Prayer to the Mother of God*

O maiden, ever virgin, the child you conceived has an eternal Father. O Daughter of earthly lineage, you carried the Creator in your holy maternal arms!...

You are truly more precious than all creation, because from you alone the Creator inherited the first fruits of our human nature. His flesh was formed from your flesh, his blood from yours; God was nourished with your milk, your lips touched the lips of God...

O most lovable Lady, thrice blessed! "You are blesed among women, and blessed is the fruit of your womb." O Lady, daughter of King David and Mother of God, the universal King! O holy and living masterpiece, in whom God the Creator takes delight, whose heart is guided by God and attentive to him only... For his sake you came into this life, with his grace you will be a means for universal salvation, so that through you God's long-standing plan will be accomplished—the incarnation of the Word and our sanctification.

St. John Damascene (attributed), Homilia in Nativitate BVM (6:7,9)

O Jesus, I see this new year as a blank page that your Father is giving me, upon which he will write day by day what he has arranged for me in his divine pleasure. With full confidence I am writing at the top of the page from now on: Lord, do with me what you will. And at the bottom I have already put my "amen" to every disposition of your divine will. Yes, O Lord, I say "yes" to all the joys, to all the sorrows, to all the graces, to all the hardships that you have prepared for me and which you will be revealing to me day by day. Let my "amen" be the Paschal amen, always followed by alleluia, uttered with all my heart in the joy of perfect giving. Give me your love and your grace and I shall be rich enough.

Sr. Carmela of the Holy Ghost, unpublished writings

38 — SECOND SUNDAY AFTER CHRISTMAS

"Glory to you, O Christ, preached among the nations, believed in throughout the world" (1 Tim 3:16)

1. "The Word became flesh and dwelt among us" (Jn 1:14); this verse from the fourth Gospel, repeated as a refrain in the responsorial psalm, synthesizes the Liturgy of the second Sunday after Christmas, which prolongs our reflection on the mystery of the incarnate Word.

The first reading (Sir 24:1-4; 8-12) introduces the theme by describing divine Wisdom, which has been present in the world from the beginning of creation, ordering all things, and which, by the will of the Most High, made its "dwelling in Jacob," that is, among the people of Israel: "I was established in Zion . . . I took root in an honored people, in the portion of the Lord who is their inheritance." In the Old Testament wisdom is especially considered a symbol of the presence of God in the midst of men.

But in the New Testament, it is placed on an immensely higher level. God's wisdom now appears as a divine Person, not allegorically, but in a most real and concrete manner: it is Christ Jesus, the Son of God, who embodies all the wisdom of the Father, for he is the "wisdom of God" (1 Cor 1:24). In Christ, divine wisdom takes human flesh and comes to live among us to reveal God's mysteries to us and to guide us more directly to him. We are not dealing with a revelation which is limited to the realm of knowledge, but one which aims at involving us in divine life itself, to the point of making us children of God. This is the theme St. Paul develops in the second reading: God has chosen us, "destining us to be his sons through Jesus Christ" (Eph. 1:4-5). Understanding this divine plan, which coincides with the history of salvation, must be the foundation of the formation of all who believe; this is why the Apostle prays that God may grant us the "spirit of wisdom and of revelation" and that he may "enlighten the eyes of our hearts so that we may know what is the hope to which he has called" us (ib. 17-18). Who else but Jesus, Wisdom and Word of God, can fully reveal these divine truths to us? By listening to Jesus and contemplating him, we discover God's wonderful design for our salvation, we discover to what hope we have been called.

2. Whereas St. Paul likes to show us Christ as "the wisdom of God" (1 Cor 1:24), the reflection "of his glory . . . and the very stamp of his nature" (Heb 1:3), the Evangelist John represents him as the Word, a term which at one and the same time expresses the thought of God and the spoken word of God. The same divine reality is presented with different shades of meaning; the Son of God is God, equal in all things to the Father: in him is all the wisdom, all the thought and all the word of the Father; he is the Word.

"In the beginning was the Word; the Word was with God, and the Word was God" (Jn 1:1). This is how St. John introduces the second Person of the most blessed Trinity, who presides with the Father and with the Holy Spirit over the creation of the universe; above all he reveals him as the life and light of men, who comes into the world to bring them life and to enlighten them. "The true light that enlightens every man was coming into the world . . . He came to his own home and his own people received him not. But to all who received him, he gave power to become children of God" (ib. 9:11-12). St. Paul expresses the same thought in his letter to the Ephesians: the Word, Son of God made flesh, comes into the world, and is called Christ Jesus, and those who accept him, that is, those who "believe in his name" (ib. 12), become in him and through him children of God.

John's sublime prologue culminates in contemplation of the incarnate Word' "the Word became flesh and dwelt among us . . . we have beheld his glory" (ib. 14). This is no longer wisdom as a symbol and sign of the presence of God who comes to pitch his tent among men, but Wisdom as the second Person of the most holy Trinity, the Word of God "made flesh," made true man. The evangelist speaks as an eyewitness: he saw him with his own eyes, touched him with his hands, heard him with his ears (1 Jn 1:1-3); he saw him living as a man in the midst of men, sharing their life; at the same time he was permitted to contemplate his glory: on Tabor, in the appearances after the Resurrection, at his Ascension into heaven. Every thing that the Evangelist saw and contemplated should inspire us who read his testimony, so that we may all believe in Christ, the Word made flesh, and welcome him and receive of his fullness "grace upon grace" (Jn 1:16), especially the grace to know God. "No one has ever seen God; the only Son who is in the bosom of the Father has made him known (ib. 18).

The Word became flesh and dwelt among us. Glorify the Lord, O Jerusalem, praise your God, O Zion . . . He has granted peace in your borders: with the best of wheat he fills you. He sends forth his Word to the earth, and swiftly runs his word.
Lectionary, *Responsorial Psalm,* 2nd Sunday after Christmas

O eternal Wisdom, full of goodness and infinitely loving, you made it your pleasure and your delight to be and converse with men. This was accomplished when you became man, when you took a human body and lived among us. Let me delight in you, O divine Word, the thought and wisdom of God. Let me listen to the words you speak to me in deep and admirable silence. Let me listen with the ears of my heart, saying to you like Samuel: "Speak, Lord, your servant is listening." Grant that by imposing silence on myself and on all that is not God, my heart may flow serenely toward the Word, toward eternal Wisdom . . . who became man and set up his dwelling in our midst.
cf. J.B. Bossuet, *Elevazioni a Dio sui misteri* 12:8

Jesus Christ, our Lord and our God, by the eternal will of the Father, you were born in the fullness of time of a Virgin who knew not man; you were subject to the law in order to ransom us from it, to free us from servitude to corruption and to bestow on us the dignity of sons . . .

My Lord, free us now from all folly, keep your promise and free us from the shame of sin by filling our hearts with your Holy Spirit, so that we may be able to say: Abba, Father.

Make us children of your Father, deliver us from all the evils of this world.
Early Christian Prayers, 218

39 — THE NAME THAT SAVES

January 2

O Lord, our God, how majestic is your name in all the earth!   (Ps 8:1)

1. "At the end of eight days when he was circumcised, he was called Jesus, the name given by the angel before he was conceived" (Lk 2:21). This name was not chosen on earth, but in heaven, and was made known, by God's will, to both Mary and Joseph. To Mary, the angel had said: "You will conceive ... and bear a son and you shall call his name Jesus" (ib. 1:31); and to Joseph: "He will save his people from their sins" (Mt 1:21). No name so expresses the deep reality of him who bears it as the name which was given to the Son of the Most High. Jesus, as his name declares, is by his nature the Lord who saves.

"There is no other name under heaven given among men by which we must be saved" (Acts 4:12), declares St. Peter after healing, in the name of Jesus, the cripple who sought alms at the gate of the temple. It is "by the name of Jesus Christ of Nazareth ... (that) this man is standing before you well—His name, by faith in his name, has made this man strong ... " (Acts 4:10; 3:16). Peter, the foundation stone of the Church, is the first to proclaim the saving powers of the name of Jesus: the Church is built upon Jesus in whose name we are baptized, redeemed from sin, made children of God and brought to eternal life. "There is salvation in no one else" (Acts 4:12).

Jesus himself said: "If you ask anything of the Father, he will give it to you in my name; ask and you will receive" (Jn 16:23-24). The Father never rejects anyone who prays to him in the name of his Son. It is not the name itself that is of special value, but what it stands for; the name of Jesus is all-powerful because it designates the mystery, the power and the mission of the Son of God who became man precisely in order to be the Savior of the world. To call upon his holy name with trust is to appeal to his incarnation, his passion and death, his resurrection; such a call is always heard because it rises up to God supported by the infinite merits of Jesus the Savior.

2. St. Paul indicates that the glory of the name of Jesus is a reward of his immense abasement: "He emptied himself, taking the form of a slave ... he humbled himself and became obedient unto death, even death on a cross. Therefore, God has highly exalted him and bestowed on him the name which is above every name; that at the name of Jesus every knee should bow, in heaven and on earth and under the earth" (Phil 2:2, 7-10). Here again the name represents the supreme dignity of Christ, infinitely superior to every created dignity, in whose presence all creatures must pay adoring homage, recognizing that "Jesus Christ is Lord" and

God. All in heaven and on earth, angels, men, and the entire universe are called to proclaim and adore together the divinity of Jesus, and to praise his holy name. The whole world seems to keep silence and stop for a moment in its course to hear and glorify that most holy Name in which is found the greatest glory of God and the greatest good of man: Let "every tongue confess that Jesus Christ is Lord to the glory of God the Father" (ib. 11).

"The Lord"—affirms the Council—"is the focal point of the longings of history and of civilization, the center of the human race, the joy of every heart, and the answer to all its yearnings" (GS 45). Mankind finds in Jesus all that it needs and all that it thirsts for: peace, pardon, love, liberty, joy, eternal salvation.

St. Bernard never tires of singing the glories of the name of Jesus: "it is light when it is preached, it is food in meditation, it is balm and healing when it is invoked for aid ... Is it not by the light of this name that God has called us into his marvelous light? ... Do you not feel strengthened as often as you recall it to mind? ... The name of Jesus is honey in the mouth, music in the ear, gladness in the heart. But it is also a remedy. Is any of you sad? Let Jesus come into the heart. Is anyone falling into sin? Or is he rushing in desperation into the snare of death? If he calls upon this life-giving name will he not straightway breathe again the breath of life?" (On the Cant. of Cant. 15:5-6).

Jesus, the very thought of thee with sweetness fills my breast; but sweeter far thy face to see, and in thy presence rest. Nor voice can sing nor heart can frame, nor can the memory find a sweeter sound than thy blest name, O Savior of mankind! O hope of every contrite heart, O joy of all the meek! To those who fall, how kind thou art; how good to those who seek! But what to those who find? Ah! this nor tongue nor pen can show: the love of Jesus, what it is none but his loved ones know. Jesus, may all confess thy name, thy wondrous love adore, and seeking thee, themselves inflame to seek thee more and more. Jesus, our only joy be thou as thou our prize wilt be; Jesus, be thou our glory now, and through eternity.
Roman Breviary, *Hymns*, Feast of Holy Name of Jesus

O my soul, hidden in the name of Jesus you have an admirable remedy, a beneficial cure that is effective against any malady from which you can suffer.

O Jesus, let your name be ever deep in my heart, ever in my hands, that all my thoughts, desires and actions may be directed by you and unto you as you urge me to do, saying: "put me as a seal upon your heart, as a seal upon your arm ... " In your name, O Jesus, I have the means of correcting my evil actions and perfecting those that are deficient, of guarding my affections from any defilement and of purifying those that are already stained.
St. Bernard: *On the Canticle of Canticles* 15:7

January 3

"I thank you, Christ Jesus our Lord that you came into the world to save sinners"   *(1 Tim 1:12,15)*

1. The Christmas feastdays center our gaze on Jesus. He reveals to us a little of the great "mystery hidden for ages in God" (Eph 3:9), the mystery we now wish to consider in synthesis in order to appreciate better its infinite richness.

"When the fullness of time had come, God sent his Son, the Word made flesh . . . the mediator between God and man; for his humanity united with the Person of the word was the instrument of our salvation. Thus, in Christ there came forth the perfect satisfaction needed for our reconciliation" (SC 5). The infinite distance, the impassable abyss between God and man that sin had caused, has finally been overcome. Jesus, the "only mediator between God and man, joins earth to heaven in a truly remarkable manner" (Myst. Corp.). In his office as mediator, he is really "at the center" between divinity and humanity; his mediation has all the qualifications for being perfectly pleasing to God, since he himself is true God, and all that is needed to make worthy satisfaction for the debt of sinful humanity, because he is also true man and as such represents the whole human race.

The divinity possessed by Jesus as the word is united in his Person with the humanity he possesses as man. The two natures are not merely in juxtaposition, but are united in one Person, the Person of the Incarnate Word, Jesus Christ, our Lord. In him and through him all mankind is readmitted to friendship with the heavenly Father; in him all find again the way to reach union with the Trinity.

The eternal Father deigned to reveal this wonderful mystery to St. Catherine of Siena: "It is my wish that you consider the bridge I have built in the Person of my only-begotten Son, and that you notice that it reaches from earth to heaven, because in him the majesty of the divinity is united with the lowliness of your human nature. It was necessary to construct this bridge in order to repair the road which had become impassable and to open a passage across the trails of this world to eternal life" (*Dialogue* 22).

2. "In him all the fullness of God was pleased to dwell and through him to reconcile to himself all things, whether on earth or in heaven, making peace by the blood of his cross" (Col 1:19-20). Jesus accomplished his work as Mediator on Calvary, where he shed all his Blood as the price of our redemption. But his work began at Bethlehem, where the Word took that ineffable "giant step" which brought him from heaven to earth. "Indeed the Word of God, by whom all things were made, was himself made flesh, so

that as perfect man, he might save all men and sum up all things in himself" (GS 45).

The terrible abyss which sin had produced between God and man has been filled up by the Child who rests in the arms of his Virgin Mother. All that sin had spoiled and destroyed is now, by God's will, saved and reestablished in Christ. Oh, how immense an admiration is joined to tenderness, how spontaneous is the need to praise and adore when we contemplate the Infant Jesus in this light!

The grace which Adam had received directly from God we now receive only through Jesus, our Mediator; all that is supernatural comes to us only through him, "through the riches of his grace" (Eph 1:7). If we wish to be united to God, we have no other means than to attach ourselves to Jesus, to pass through him, our Mediator, our bridge, our way. Jesus said: "I am the way and the truth and the life; no one comes to the Father but by me ... I am the door; if any one enters by me, he will be saved" (Jn 14:6; 10:9). Here then, is the only condition, the only way of salvation, of holiness.

O Lord, you are truly a pure and inexhaustible source of goodness. You rejected us, and again welcomed us with mercy. You hated us, and you made peace with us; you cursed us, and then you blessed us. You cast us out of paradise, but you have led us back; you took away the leaves with which we covered ourselves, to clothe us in a royal mantle. You opened the doors of prison to free the con-demned ... For us who had inherited sin, everything has been changed into shining joy, and we see the gates of paradise open up, even to heaven. Creation—earth and heaven—whose unity had been disrupted, now returns to its former friendship.

St. Gregory of Nyssa, from *Preghiere dei primi cristiani* 259

O God, I sought a way to obtain strength sufficient to enjoy you and found it not, until I embraced that mediator between God and man, the Man Christ Jesus, who is over all. God be blessed forever-more—he calls to us, saying: "I am the way and the truth and the life"—I was not yet humble enough to hold to my God, the humble Jesus, nor did I yet understand where his teaching would lead me. Your Word, eternal truth ... raises up to itself those who are humbled ... curing pride and nourishing love.

St. Augustine, *Confessions* VII 24

O Christ Jesus, I believe that you are true God and true man, that you are a divine way of infinite efficacy for making me bridge the gulf that separates me from God. I believe that your holy humanity is perfect and so powerful that in spite of my miseries, my shortcomings and weaknesses, it can bring me to where you are in the Father's bosom. Grant that I may listen to your words, that I may follow your example, and never be separated from you!

C. Marmion, *Christ in his mysteries* 20 p. 394-5

41 — THE FIRSTBORN OF ALL CREATURES

January 4

"Blessed be the God and Father of our Lord Jesus Christ, who has destined us in love to be his sons through Jesus Christ"(Eph 1:3,5)

1. Christ Jesus is "the image of the invisible God, the firstborn of all creation; for in him all things were created in heaven and on earth, visible and invisible . . . all things were created through him and for him. He is before all things, and in him all things hold together" (Col 1:15-17). Here St. Paul summarizes the infinite greatness of Jesus. As the Word, he is the substantial and most perfect image of the Father, having the same nature and proceeding from him by eternal generation. As the Word he is the firstborn of all creatures, begotten of the Father from all eternity, and therefore before all creation; furthermore he is the source of all life, as "all things were created through him," since they were present in him, eternal and infinite Wisdom. St. John of the Cross teaches: "God looked at all things in this image of his Son alone, giving them their natural being . . . making them vast and perfect, according to the words of Genesis (1:31): 'God saw everything that he had made, and behold, it was very good.' To look and behold that they were very good was to make them very good in the Word, his Son" (Sp C 5:4). The Word is not simply the firstborn of all creation, not simply its exemplary cause, but also its efficient cause; in fact, being God, he is, with the Father and the Holy Spirit, the Creator, the craftsman of the entire universe: all things "hold together in him" (Col 1:17), and "without him was not anything made" (Jn 1:3). All this greatness which by nature belongs to the Word becomes the splendor of Jesus, true God and true Man, by reason of his Incarnation and of his hypostatic union; in fact, St. Paul declares that in Christ "the whole fullness of Deity dwells bodily" (Col 2:9).

Although it pleased Jesus to conceal this infinite splendor of his divinity in the obscurity of the manger, our love and our faith incite us to acknowledge it and praise him.

2. Jesus is the firstborn of men, the source of their life, not only in the natural order, the order of creation, but also and especially in the supernatural order, the order of grace. In fact "with this image of his Son alone, God clothed his creatures in beauty, by imparting to them supernatural being. This he did when he became man, and elevated human nature in the beauty of God" (Sp C 5:4).

The Word became flesh precisely to permit us to participate in supernatural life; Jesus came into the world to make us children of God: he, God's only Son by nature, thus becomes "the firstborn among many brethren" (Rom 8:29), who in him through him are made children of God through grace. This is the wonderful and mysterious plan of our elevation to the supernatural state. "Blessed be God ... who has blessed us in Christ with every spiritual blessing in the heavenly places ... he destined us in love to be his sons through Christ Jesus, according to the purpose of his will ... " (Eph 1:3-6).

God the Father willed, from all eternity, to raise us to the dignity of sons; therefore he gave our first parents not only natural life, but also supernatural life, which they lost by sin. But God had foreknown their fall, and even permitted it, in view of a plan that was more wonderful than the first, a plan which would manifest in a most admirable manner his infinite charity and mercy: the Incarnation of his only begotten Son, that through him "we might receive adoption as sons" (Gal 4:5).

Two sublime mysteries are interwoven in this wonderful plan: Jesus the firstborn of every creature in the supernatural order and in that of man; and ourselves, the slaves of sin, who become, in him and through him, God's adopted children.

O Christ, you alone are visible, you reveal the image of your all-powerful Father, and so make us understand the greatness of the Father and of the Son. Just as the Father has power in the heavenly sphere, you, his Son are first in our universe ... the Lord of unlimited power ... you are our model, our organizer, our leader; you are our highway and the door which leads us to the light. You are the image of justice. You are our star and our light. We give you thanks and praise and blessing.

Trustingly we kneel before you and ask for all that is fitting. Grant that we may be steadfast in our faith ... Thus we shall sing to you in every circumstance without ceasing; we shall praise you because you are exalted everywhere, you are the immortal, the untiring, the eternal One. You are the model and the essence of our souls; you are our happy Father, our King, our God. If we look to you, O Lord, we shall not die. If we call upon your name, we run no risk of being lost. If we pray to you, we shall be heard.

A Christo Primogenito, da Preghiere dei primi cristiani 106

With the Word, we can say: "O Father, I am your son, I came out from you." The Word says it necessarily by right, being essentially God's own Son; we only say it by grace, as adopted sons;—the Word says it from all eternity; we say it in time, although the decree of this predestination is eternal ...

O Jesus you are the Son of God, the perfect, adequate image of your Father; you know your Father, you are wholly his, you behold his face; increase within me the grace of adoption which makes me the child of God; teach me to be, by your grace and by my virtues, like you and in you, a worthy child of the heavenly Father ... What we ought to ask and constantly seek after is that all our thoughts, all our aspirations, all our desires, all our activity, should tend, by the grace of our filiation and by love, to our heavenly Father.

C. Marmion, Christ in His Mysteries 3

January 5

"I will extol you, my God and my King, and bless your name for ever and ever"   *(Ps 145:1)*

1. In the Old Testament God showed himself to his people especially as the Lord and put his lordship before them as the foundation of the Decalogue: "I am the Lord your God . . . you shall have no other gods before me" (Ex 20:2-3). God's sovereignty permits no competitors and yet guarantees freedom to men. When Israel was faithful to its God, God freed it from slavery; it was a time of glory: "I brought you out of the land of Egypt, out of the house of bondage" (ib.). But Israel withdrew itself from God's sovereignty, it fell back into bondage; it was a time of sore distress (Judg 10:6-7).

However, Israel was only the figure of the messianic people into whom God had decreed beforehand to "gather all his children" after they wre scatttered. "It was for this reason that he sent his Son, whom he appointed heir of all things, that he might be Teacher, King and Priest of all, the Head of the new and unversal people of the sons of God" (LG 13). In reality, when the Son of God made man appeared on earth, he was commonly called "the Lord"; he himself acknowledged this title: "you call me 'Teacher' and 'Lord', and you are right, for so I am" (Jn 13:13), and he promised his disciples: "As my Father appointed a kingdom for me, so do I appoint for you" (Lk 22:29). Before the Roman authorities he openly proclaimed: "I am a king" (Jn 18:37), and before ascending into heaven, declared: "All authority in heaven and on earth has been given to me" (Mt 28:18).

Jesus is truly the universal King. As the eternal Word, he possesses all the power of the Trinity: he is Creator, Lord of the universe and of every creature. But also as man, through his hypostatic union, Jesus participates fully in this divine and absolute sovereignty. Christ is at the summit of creation: its beginning, its end, the King of every created thing: "I am the Alpha and the Omega, says the Lord God, who is and who was and who is to come, the Almighty" (Rev 1:8).

2. Jesus comes into this world as Lord and King to announce, diffuse and affirm the eternal lordship of God and to subject all creatures to it. The Liturgy gives us a most beautiful expression of this mission: "All-powerful and every-living God, you . . . have anointed your only Son, Jesus Christ, as eternal priest and universal King; by offering himself as the immaculate victim of peace on the altar of the Cross, he redeemed the human race; and bringing all creation under his power, he offers to your infinite Majesty an eternal and universal kingdom." (Pref. Christ King). With his

death Jesus destroyed sin, the enemy of God, in open rebellion against his rule; in this way he freed us from slavery to Satan and to our passions, and sweetly brought us back under his Father's rule, the only rule which does not enslave, but rather makes us free, since to serve God is to reign. And "when he had made purification for our sins, he sat down at the right hand of the Majesty on high" (Heb 1:3), as befitted his royal dignity as Son of God.

Christ, who has reconquered and reestablished God's kingdom on earth, was placed by his Father "far above all rule and authority . . . and above every name that is named, not only in this age but also in that which is to come. He has put all things under his feet and has made him the head over all things for the Church" (Eph 1:21-22). Jesus willed to reconquer as man the sovereignty that already belonged to him by right as God, and to purchase it at the cost of his blood in order to prove that his was a royalty of love. Because he loved us, that is, in order to save us, he was made one of us; for the same reason he died and was raised up for us (2 Cor 5:15): He reigns in the manger, he reigns from the cross, he reigns in glorious eternity in heaven. To glorify Jesus as our King means to acknowledge his sovereign rights over us, it means defending that liberty which he won for us at such a high price, it means living in docile submission to his gentle rule. For his glory and our salvation "he must reign" (1 Cor 15:25), "that in everything he might be preeminent" (Col 1:18).

> *Praise be to you, Lord Jesus, for you were slain and by your blood you ransomed men for God from every tribe and tongue and people and nation; and you have made them a kingdom and priests to our God.*
>
> *Worthy is the Lamb who was slain to receive power and wealth and wisdom and might and honor and glory and blessing (cf. Rev 5:9-12) . . .*
>
> *Great and wonderful are your deeds, O Lord God the almighty! Just and true are your ways, O King of the ages! Who shall not fear, and glorify your name, O Lord? For you alone are holy. All nations shall come and worship you, for your judgments have been revealed (Rev 15:3 -4).*
>
> *Revelations*

> *O King of glory and Lord of all kings your kingdom has no end! . . . I can speak with you as with a friend, even though you are Lord. You are not like lords here on earth, whose lordship all consists in artificial displays of authority . . . There is no need of intermediaries with you. Upon beholding your person one sees immediately that you alone . . . merit to be called Lord!*
>
> *O my Lord! O my King! Who now would know how to represent your majesty! It is impossible not to see that you in yourself are a great Emperor, for to behold your majesty is startling; and the more*

one beholds, along with this majesty, Lord, your humility and the love you show to someone like myself the more startling it becomes. Nevertheless, we can converse and speak with you as we like, once the first fright and fear in beholding your majesty passes; although the fear of offending you becomes greater. But the fear is not one of punishment, for this punishment is considered nothing in comparison with losing you.

St. Teresa: Life 37:5-6

43 — EPIPHANY OF THE LORD

January 6

"All kings fall down before him; all nations serve him"　　　(Ps 72:11)

1. "Rejoice in the Lord"—exclaims St. Leo the Great—"but a little while has elapsed since the solemnity of Christ's birth and, lo, the festival of his manifestation has begun to dawn on us. He whom the Virgin brought forth on Christmas, is acknowledged today by all the world" (St. Leo the Great, Ser. 2:1). Today Jesus manifests himself and is acknowledged as God.

The Mass brings us into this theme at once by presenting Jesus to us in the full majesty of his divinity: "Behold, the Lord is coming: the kingdom is his and government and power." The first reading (Is 60:1-6) breaks forth in a hymn of joy announcing the call of the nations to the faith; they too will acknowledge and adore Jesus as their God. "Arise, shine, O Jerusalem, for your light has come, and the glory of the Lord has risen upon you . . . Nations shall come to your light, and kings to the brightness of your rising . . . All those from Sheba shall come; they shall bring gold and frankincense, and shall proclaim the praise of the Lord." We no longer gaze upon the lowly scene of the shepherds gathered around Jesus; now we see the Magi who have come from the east to pay him homage; they represent all those who do not belong to his people. For in very truth, Jesus has not come only for the salvation of Israel, but for the salvation of all men of whatever race or country. He instituted "this new covenant in his blood by calling together a people made up of Jew and Gentile, making them one . . . so that they might be the new People of God" (LG 9). St. Paul also speaks of this magnificent mystery which it was his mission to announce to the world: "The gentiles are fellow-heirs, members of the same body, and partakers of the promise in Christ Jesus through the Gospel" (Eph 3:6).

The feast of the Epiphany, the first manifestation and realization of this mystery, urges each of us to share in the desires and labor of the Church, which "prays and labors, in order that the entire world may become the People of God, the Body of Christ and the Temple of the Holy Spirit" (LG 17). Epiphany, or Theophany, means precisely this "manifestation of God;" let us pray that the prayer and zeal of those who believe may hasten the time when every one on earth will be enlightened by faith, so that all may acknowledge "the unsearchable riches of Christ" (Eph 3:8) and adore him as their God.

2. "We have seen his star in the east and have come to adore the Lord;" the Alleluia of the Mass thus sums up the story of the Magi. When they saw the star they started out at once in search of it. They had no doubts: their faith was strong and sure and steadfast. They did not hesitate before the hardships of the long journey: their hearts were generous. Nor did they postpone their journey: their souls were ready.

Often enough a star appears on the horizon of our souls as a clear and intimate inspiration of God, inviting us to a generous act, to detachment, to a life of closer union with him. We must follow this "star" with the faith and generosity and prompt response of the Wise Men; then it will certainly lead us to a meeting with God and bring us to the One whom our hearts are seeking with sincere love.

The Wise Men persevered in their travel even though they did not know the exact place of Jesus' birth. In like manner each of us must persevere in doing good and in seeking God in spite of interior darkness, even when the light which shines on our path seems to grow dim. This darkness can only be overcome by an intense spirit of pure naked faith which trusts in God alone. I know that God wills it, I know he is calling, and this is enough for me. "I know him whom I have believed, and I am sure" (2 Tim 1:12); no matter what he permits or asks of me, I cannot doubt him. This is the best way to unite ourselves to the adoration of the Magi; "as they brought forth from among their treasures mystical gifts which they offered the Lord, let us also bring forth from our hearts something fit to offer him" (St. Leo the Great, Ser 2:4).

O God, who this day revealed your only Son to the nations, lead us too, who already know you by faith, to the contemplation of your glory.

Roman Missal, *Collect*

O Christ, in the Magi adoring you we recognize the first fruits of our calling and our faith. With exultant soul we celebrate the beginning of that blessed hope. From this day we begin to enter upon an eternal inheritance; from this day there lies open to us the hidden meaning of those Scriptures that refer to you. The truth which the Jews in their blindness rejected, sheds its light upon all nations. Therefore let this most holy day be honored among us, this day on which you manifest yourself as Author of our salvation; you, whom the Magi adored as an infant in the manger, we adore omnipotent in

*heaven. And as they brought forth from among their treasures
mystical gifts, we also desire to search our hearts for something fit
to offer you.*

St. Leo the Great, Sermon 2:4

*We adore you, O Lord, and with the Magi offer you the precious
gifts which we have received from your hands, for we have received
from you the gold of charity and the interior frankincense of our
hearts, laid open to you by prayer, and sweet and holy meditation on
your passion and death. It is evident, my Savior, the more I offer
you, the more I am your debtor. All I have is yours, and although
you need none of it, you gratefully accept whatever I give you,
because it was you who first gave it to me, and only what bears your
mark and comes from you is pleasing to you.*

J.B. Bossuet, Elevazioni a Dio sui misteri 17:9

44—MISSIONARY CHURCH[1]

*May your way be known upon earth; your saving power among all
nations.*   *(Ps 67:2)*

1. The feast of the Epiphany leads us to reflect again on the
missionary vocation of the Church. From the very beginning this
feast has been considered the first manifestation of Christ to the
world: "from the rising of the sun to its going down, the birth of
the true King is spread abroad. Through the Wise Men the
kingdoms of the Orient will learn the truth of the event, nor shall
it be hidden from the empire of the Romans" (St. Leo the Great,
Ser 2:1). It was the prelude to the universal announcement of the
good news, with which Christ charged his followers: "Go into all
the world and preach the gospel to the whole creation" (Mk 16:15).
The command is clear and obliges everyone who is baptized; no
one who has received the immense gift of faith may enjoy it
selfishly, but is bound by the duty of Christian love to share it
with others. "God chose to rely on men to be the bearers of his
gospel, the stewards of his grace, and the builders of his kingdom.
Who can claim that this is no concern of his? Since there is a variety of conditions of life, and consequently different ways of giving
a response, every member of the Church is reached by this call,
which is directed to each and every one. The whole Church is missionary, for her missionary activity is an essential part of her
vocation. To forget this or to carry it out carelessly would be, on
our part, a betrayal of our Master" (Paul VI, Disc. at
Sydney,—Oss. Rom. Dec. 17, 1970). We do not think about this
enough. Even fervent Christians often think they have done their
duty by a small donation to the missions. Jesus asks much more;

[1]For the Sunday after Epiphany take Meditation No. 50.

to all who have been baptized in his name, and so have already entered into the way of salvation, he repeats: "As the Father has sent me, even so I send you" (Jn 20:21). As the Father revealed his love to the world by sending his only-begotten Son to save it, and the Son immolated himself for the redemption of men, so we demonstrate that we have not received the Father's love and Christ's salvation in vain when we look for all kinds of ways to bring these blessings to our brothers.

2. "Missionary activity is nothing else and nothing less than a manifestation or epiphany of God's will and the fulfillment of that will in the world and in world history: in the course of this history, God ... plainly works out the history of salvation" (AG 9). God wanted man to collaborate in transmitting life and in providing for its necessities, not only at the physical, material level, but also at the spiritual level, by working out the history of salvation. Every baptized person constitutes a moment of this marvelous story; but he must not be satisfied with living it passively; he should become a leader and busy himself in urging on as many as possible of his brothers. God is indeed able to save us without the ordinary means of preaching and of the sacraments; nevertheless it remains true that Jesus has given us a clear command: "Go, therefore, and make disciples of all the nations" (Mt 28:19), and he added: "He who believes and is baptized will be saved, but he who does not believe will be condemned" (Mk 16:16). These words are both a goad and a grief for those who really love God and their neighbor. If the apostolic zeal of so many missionaries—like St. Francis Xavier, in action, or St. Therese of the Child Jesus, in desire—has contributed to hastening the salvation of innumerable souls, are not the apathy and lack of interest of so many of us perhaps responsible for the delay of that same salvation for the many of our brothers who are still awaiting it?

Certainly God continues to call his elect: "Go from your country and your kindred and your father's house to the land that I will show you" (Gen 12:1). May such souls know how to respond with generosity and promptness! But those who remain behind in their own land and in their own home must also have a missionary heart. They must support and assist those who are called, interest themselves in the life and problems of the missions, "spontaneously offer prayers and works of penance to God, that he may make the work of the missionaries fruitful by his grace" (AG 36). This is the teaching of the Council: "As members of the living Christ, all the faithful ... are duty-bound to cooperate in the expansion and growth of his Body, so that they can bring it to fullness as swiftly as possible" (ib.).

God, you sent your Son into the world to be its true light. Pour out the Spirit he promised us to sow the truth in men's hearts and awaken in them obedience to the faith. May all men be born again to life in baptism, and enter the fellowship of your one holy People.

Lord, look upon the face of Christ your Son who gave up his life to set all men free. Through him may your name be praised among all peoples from east to west, and everywhere may one single sacrifice be offered to give you glory.

Roman Missal, *Mass for Spread of the Gospel,* A

I feel the vocation of the warrior, the priest, the apostle, the doctor, the martyr; finally I feel the need and the desire of carrying out most heroic deeds for you, O Jesus . . .

O my Jesus, what is your answer to all my follies? Is there a soul more little, or more powerless than mine? . . . Charity gives me the key to my vocation. I understand that if the church has a body composed of various members, the most necessary and most noble of all cannot be lacking to it, and so I understand that the Church has a heart and that this heart is burning with love. I understand that it is love alone that makes the members act, that if love ever became extinct, apostles would not preach the gospel and martyrs would not shed their blood. I understand that love comprises all vocations, that love is everything, that it embraces all times and places . . . in a word, that it is eternal . . .

Well, I am a child of the Church and the Church is a Queen, since she is your spouse, O divine King of kings . . . Astounding works are forbidden to me, I cannot preach the gospel, or shed my blood, but what does it matter since my brothers work in my stead and I . . . stay very close to the throne . . . and I love in my brother's place, while they do the fighting.

St. Therese of the Child Jesus, *Autobiography B,* pp. 192-194, 196

45 — THE KINGDOM

Lord, may I hear the word of your kingdom and understand it; may the evil one not steal away what was sown in my heart. (Mt 13 :19)

1. "The Lord Jesus . . . inaugurated his Church by preaching the good news, that is, the coming of the kingdom of God, which had been promised for centuries in the Scriptures: 'The time is fulfilled and the kingdom of God is at hand!' " (LG 5). But what is this kingdom which the Old Testament announced and foreshadowed in the history of Israel, and which Jesus now proclaims is near? Above all, it concerns the lordship and universal power of God the Creator, Lord, King, and Father of every people, openly asserted through the preaching of Christ, and still more through the presence of God himself in the world in the person of his Son who, though become man, fully shares his divinity and his power. In the Old Testament God ruled his people and spoke to them through representatives who were simple men; now it is by means of his incarnate Word. There are no more intermediaries;

God comes in his Son to guide, enlighten and rule us. That is the reason Jesus said: "The kingdom of God is in the midst of you" (Lk 17:21). The time of waiting is over; his kingdom has come and is present in Christ who discloses the Father's plans for man's salvation and begins to carry them out in his works. At the same time, it is a mysterious and hidden kingdom which has nothing in common with the structure of earthly kingdoms; these are imposed with pomp and exterior power. "The kingdom of God is not coming with signs to be observed; nor will they say: 'Lo, here it is!' or 'There!' " (ib.). It is a spiritual kingdom, infinitely distant from everything of the senses, or of worldly success or political power; it encompasses the abiding values of the spirit, takes hold of a man from within, transforming him into a child of God, and hence, into a citizen of his kingdom. Even though God's kingdom in itself extends to the entire cosmos and to all created beings in heaven and on earth, we are not forced to enter it, but must do so freely. And when, through faith and obedience, we decide to do so, this kingdom begins to establish itself within us in a manner that is most intimate and secret, without causing any external change, yet changing everything within. Then, already born of flesh and of blood, we are born again in God by means of the Spirit (Jn 1:13, 3:5-6).

2. Among the parables that Jesus used to illustrate the various aspects of his kingdom, the one about the sower of seed stands out (Mt 13:1-9). Under the figure of a man sowing a plentiful measure of seed, which falls on most varied kinds of ground—a road, stony places, amid thorns, on good soil—he is pointing out, on the one hand, God's prodigality in planting his kingdom everywhere, and on the other indicating the necessary conditions for us to receive the seed, that is, "the word of the kingdom," and make it bear fruit in our hearts. The word of the kingdom is Jesus' teaching on the kingdom of heaven, it is his entire gospel; moreover, it is himself, eternal Word of the Father, sown in our humanity, so that becoming man like us, he translates God's word into human language, and therefore makes the precious seed of his kingdom fall into the hearts of all men. The seed—"the Word"—contains within itself the power to sprout and produce his kingdom in every man; but, like the seed in the field, it does not produce this effect unless it finds the soil ready and suitable for receiving it. First of all an attentive interior listening is needed, undistracted by the noises of the street; our hearts must be unencumbered by rocks or thorns, that is, by inordinate attachments to self or any other creature, by excessive preoccupation with worldly goods, or by the passions that snuff out every good resolution, that distract us from the good, and that make us weak and vacillating. We need to be that "good soil," like the heart of Mary who welcomed the Word of God within her; she was his mother, not only because she gave him birth in time, but even

more because she kept the word in her heart and expressed it in her life according to her Son's teaching: "My mother and my brethren are those who hear the word of God and do it" (Lk 8:21). Thus the seed sprouts, and being a divine seed has an immense capacity for growing even unto life eternal; it roots us in the kingdom of God here in time and for eternity. The seed "sown on good soil" is he who hears the word and understands it; he, indeed, bears fruit and yields, in one case a hundredfold, in another sixtyfold or in another, thirtyfold." (Mt 13:23).

O Jesus my Lord, I consecrate and abandon myself to your supreme sovereignty which is incommunicable to any creature, and to the excellent, absolute and specific power over everything created which your Humanity possesses by virtue of your wonderful, adorable Sonship.

I dedicate and consecrate myself completely to you ... and want you to have a special power over my soul and over my situation, over my life and my actions, as over something that belongs to you by a new and special right through the spontaneous act of my will, by which I intend to depend on your ... sovereignty always.

And since your power infinitely surpasses ours, I beg you, O Jesus, to deign to take from me whatever power I am not capable of giving to you. I beg you to accept me as your subject and slave, even though it be in a way that I do not understand, but which you know very well.

P. de Berulle, *Le Grandezze di Gesu* 2,6

O Father who sent into the world the eternal Word, your Word, begotten of you, so that he might be the seed of all your words ... I beg you, through this Word, your Son, to sow in my mind plentiful seed of holy thoughts, which may produce plentiful fruit of good works.

O eternal Word ... you came down from heaven to earth to sow the seed of your true teaching ... come, Lord, and plant in my intellect the abundant seed of divine enlightenment by which I may know you, and know myself, and know what I must believe and do in order to put it into practice.

O Holy Spirit, who breathe where you will, and will to breathe where your inspiration is needed, touch my will ... cast sparks of fervent desire upon it in order to kindle in my heart a burning fire of love ... and make sprout there the abundant fruits of the spirit that spring from such love. O Most blessed Trinity, I thank you for the bountifulness with which you plant your word in a land that is so base and despicable.

L. Da Ponte, *Meditazioni* III, 44:1

46 — GROWTH OF THE KINGDOM

"Our Father in heaven . . . your kingdom come"   *(Mt 6:9-10)*

1. The kingdom of God, says the Council, "is revealed to men in Christ's word, in his works and in his presence. The word of the Lord is like to a seed sown in a field: those, who hear the word with faith and become part of the little flock of Christ, have received the kingdom itself" (LG 5). Jesus made use of the example of the seed in various ways to explain the growth and the development of God's kingdom among men. The vitality and capacity for growth of the kingdom is like that of the seed which "sprouts and grows without the sower himself being aware of it" (Mk 4:27). The kingdom grows secretly, beyond the anticipation and expectation of those who sow the seed in the hearts of their brothers by their preaching, by their ministry, or by their educational work. Even when the ground seems altogether dry and infertile, and when every apostolic effort seems in vain, the seed of divine grace works silently in darkness, and suddenly, through God's secret intervention, it can stir up new energies and unexpected awakenings. Long-awaited hopes, failures, even the insurgence of evil—these things must not discourage us, neither make us desert the field of battle nor push us to rash zeal. Christ conquered the evil One and held up this victory as a sign of the coming of his kingdom: "If it is by the finger of God that I cast out demons, then the kingdom of God has come upon you" (Lk 11:20). But for us to make Christ's victory our own, and to belong to the kingdom, we must struggle. God allows the evil One to continue sowing his seed and does not want it to be uprooted ahead of time, "lest in gathering the weeds you root up the wheat along with them" (Mt 13:29). So we must persevere in doing good, lest the weeds choke out the wheat, and give it no chance to turn into wheat. Grace can accomplish these miracles in our hearts. And so through struggle and strife and apparent defeat, the kingdom grows, and through the strength of Christ's redemption, the tiny seed becomes a great tree, "with large branches so that the birds of the air can make nests in its shade" (Mk 4:32).

2. "The kingdom of heaven is like leaven which a woman took and hid in three measures of flour till it was all leavened" (Mt 13:33). This is the parable which perhaps best illustrates the internal dynamism of the kingdom, that is, its grace, its charity, and its faith. The little mustard seed which grows into the largest tree of the garden well depicts the external expansion of the kingdom and its diffusion in the world until it reaches all men. On the other hand, the yeast which is hidden in the lump of dough and leavens it entirely, seems rather to indicate the interior transformation of the individual and of society, which results from accepting the kingdom and from faith in Christ. This is a radical

transformation which aims at changing minds, consciences, and ways of judgment; it culminates in a profound change in conduct. Our values are turned upside down. For any one who enters the kingdom true good is no longer to be found in wealth, or honor, or success, or in earthly happiness; neither does it lie in strength or power or superiority over others; it is rather in poverty, tears, gentleness, mercy, purity, peace, and even persecution. This is the law of the kingdom which Jesus proclaimed in his beatitudes; the more the yeast of the gospel ferments in us, the more we spontaneously assume this new manner of feeling, of judging and, therefore, of acting. Not only that; we in our turn become leaven for the society in which we live; for the family, the school, the workplace. We do this not only through a prudent and timely word, but also by our simple presence which gives witness to an integral Christianity. The Council teaches that laymen themselves can be "powerful heralds" of the kingdom, "provided they steadfastly join to their profession of faith a life which springs from faith. This evangelization, this announcing of Christ, accomplished by a living testimony as well as by the spoken word, takes on a specific quality and a special force in that it is carried out in the ordinary surroundings of the world" (LG 35).

> *O sweetest Jesus, sower of every good seed, always waking and never sleeping, you see the weeds which your enemy is trying to sow in your field; do not allow him to plant anything in me which might turn me against you; and if I do fall asleep through carelessness, let your mercy be on the watch to awaken me so that I may resist the enemy before he takes hold of me.*
>
> L. Da Ponte, *Meditazioni* III 45:1

> *My Lord, my only God, my God and my All, let me never go after vanities. "Vanity of vanities; all is vanity!" (Eccles 1:2). All is vanity and shadow here below. Let me not give my heart to anything here. Let nothing allure me from you; O keep me, wholly and entirely. Keep this most frail heart and this most weak head in your divine keeping. Draw me to you morning, noon, and night for consolation. Be my own bright light, to which I look for guidance and for peace.*
>
> *Let me love you, O my Lord Jesus, with a pure affection and a fervent affection! Let me love you with the fervor, only greater, with which men of this earth love beings of this earth. Let me have that tenderness and constancy in loving you, which is so much praised among men, when the object is of the earth. Let me find and feel you to be my only joy, my only refuge, my only strength, my only comfort, my only hope, my only fear, my only love.*
>
> J.H. Newman, *Meditations on Christian Doctrine* III 2

47 — THE BASIC UNIT OF THE KINGDOM

May the Lord keep you in love with one another, so that the peace of
Christ may stay with you and be always in your home.
(Roman Missal, Mass of Matrimony, Solemn Blessing A)

1. The Council presents the Christian family, consecrated by
the sacrament of matrimony, as "an excellent school of the lay
apostolate, where Christianity pervades a whole way of life and
ever increasingly transforms it" (LG 35). The family is, in fact, the
primary cell, or better, the basic cell of God's kingdom on earth. In
it children are brought up "according to the faith they received in
baptism" (GE 3); from early childhood they learn to perceive
God's "sovereignty," to love and obey him as their first "Lord,"
their good Father who provides for all their needs, to whom they
owe everything. This primeval duty of the heads of families is
already found in the old law, where after stating the first commandment: "You shall love the Lord your God with all your heart,
with all your soul, and with all your strength," it adds: "These
words which I command you this day shall be upon your heart.
You shall teach them diligently to your children, and shall talk of
them when you sit in your house, and when you walk by the
way . . . write them on the doorposts of your house and on your
gates" (Dt 6:5-9). When faith in God, love for him, and respect for
his law are the foundation of family life, they govern the mutual
relations between husband and wife and of parents with their
children, and inspire the education given to these; the family is
then truly the "kingdom of God" where God is the first to be
loved, served, and obeyed. If the pious Israelite felt obligated to
make use of every means and circumstance to inculcate religious
principles in his children, how much more should Christian
parents be bound to do this? The grace of the sacrament of
matrimony confers on them a special gift for bringing up their
children in faith and piety, and for instructing them in the things
of God. In this way parents plant in their hearts "the message of
the kingdom" which in due time will bear fruit. If later, through
the vicissitudes of life, the faith received in the home grows weak
and sometimes even seems to be extinguished, it will have a better
chance of growing strong again precisely because it was absorbed
from early childhood.

2. "Husband and wife find their own vocation in the family in
being witness to one another and to their children of faith in
Christ and love for him" (LG 35). Through love, respect, and
mutual trust, with reciprocal help in the difficulties of life,
through a spirit of sacrifice for the right development of the
family—with all this made stronger by faith in God and attachment to his law—parents are the first witnesses of the gospel for
their children, "the first and foremost educators" (GE 3). Their

educational function is so decisive that scarcely anything can compensate for their failure in it" (ibid). The behavior of parents becomes the practical norm and living model of that of their children. "Parents only need be generous and give good example"—said John XXIII—"and their children will be obedient and willing" (Discourses IV). How many renowned Christians and great saints received their first impression right in the family! Such families are "the good soil" in which priestly and religious vocations or a calling to sanctity grow more easily; and at the same time such families become centers for spreading the gospel in the community around them. "The Christian family"—says the Council—"loudly proclaims both the present virtues of the kingdom of God and the hope of a blessed life to come. Thus, by its example and its witness, it accuses the world of sin and enlightens those who seek the truth" (LG 35). In today's society the family is more and more disintegrating, incapable of standing up against the rage of uncontrolled passions; even the human values of conjugal love, in the sense of the father's and the mother's roles, are being undermined to their very roots. Therefore the example of the Christian home, in which love develops calm and pure under God's eye, is vital. This is the most effective way to bring back so many poor wandering souls to the right path. And if even the Christian family can experience hours of anguish and storm, it will always find its saving anchor in faith in God and his law, as well as the strength to carry its cross while it waits patiently for the return of its lost ones. When the sacrament of matrimony is lived seriously it always confers on the married couple the grace to overcome any storm and to defend the family from every danger.

O Jesus, may peace and tranquility reign, may prayer and obedience to God's law—an obedience which is prompt and loving—be honored by all! . . . O Jesus, as you lived in Nazareth, so may you live in every Christian family, keep our families united in your love, in an everlasting bond, for every hour of time and for eternity. O Jesus, protect that domestic peace which alone can soothe the bitter sorrows of life.

John XXIII, *Prayers and Devotions #25*

Father, all-powerful and ever-living God, we do well always and everywhere to give you thanks. You created man in love to share your divine life. We see his high destiny in the love of husband and wife, which bears the imprint of your own divine love. Love is man's origin, love is his constant calling, love is his fulfillment in heaven. The love of man and woman is made holy in the sacrament of marriage, and becomes the mirror of your everlasting love. (Preface, Wedding Mass III)

Grant, O Lord, that they may share with each other the gifts of your love and become one in heart and mind as witnesses to your presence in their marriage. Help them to create a home together and give them children to be formed by the Gospel and to have a place in your family. (Nuptial Blessing B)

Roman Missal

48—WORKERS OF THE KINGDOM

May your favor be with us, O Lord; establish the work of your hands
(Ps 90:17)

1. "What will it profit a man, if he gains the whole world and forfeits his life?" (Mt 16:26). The kingdom of God is neither riches, nor honor, nor acquisition of worldly privilege; it is rather the opposite of all this. When the conquest of the world is understood as the possession of material goods and the search for comfort and pleasure, it is in open antithesis to the kingdom of heaven, where the first place is given to spiritual values and all else is subordinate to them. However, inasmuch as the world is a creature of God, it too must be conquered by the Christian, not from greed or ambition, but to subject all earthly realities to the service and glory of God. This is the task which the Council has identified as belonging in a special way to the laity, who, because of the circumstances of their lives are in continual and direct contact with earthly realities. "The laity must take on the renewal of the temporal order as their own special obligation. Led by the light of the gospel and the mind of the Church, and motivated by Christian love, let them act directly and definitively . . . Everywhere and in all things they must seek the justice characteristic of God's kingdom" (AA 7). Since they live in the earthly city, the laity can bring the spirit of the gospel to every situation: practicing a profession, doing business, carrying out any duty whatsoever with the honesty demanded by Christ.

When the tax collectors, the soldiers, and others who had received baptism from John, asked him what they ought to do, they were told to continue to follow their own occupations in justice and charity: "He who has two coats, let him share with him who has none, and he who has food, let him do likewise . . . Rob no one by violence or by false accusation, and be content with your wages" (Lk 3:11-14). Paul writes: "Slaves, obey in everything those who are your earthly masters. Masters, treat your slaves justly and fairly" (Col 3:22; 4:1). Whatever place we may occupy in society or in whatever activity we may be involved, we should behave in such a way that the light of the gospel and the charity of Christ are reflected in our conduct.

2. God who created man in his own image wanted him to collaborate in the work of creating and conserving the universe. This had been so from the very beginning, when God "took the man

and put him in the garden of Eden, to till it and keep it" (Gen 2:15). Everything had been created by God for man: for his support, his joy, his elevation, his perfection. When God entrusted all things to his industry, it was to make him use them for those ends so that by recognizing the goodness and providence of the Creator in these earthly goods man might be stimulated to love and glorify God. Sin upset this arrangement, and instead of man's work being a collaboration with the work of God, it degenerated into a frenzy for gain, a motive for pride, a provoker of passions and a means of satisfying them; at the same time, instead of earthly goods being a ladder for climbing up to God, they became occasions of sin and of estrangement from God.

It belongs to all of us who are redeemed by Christ, to redeem in our turn the work and the realities of the world from the falsifications of sin. This means we must work and deal with earthly goods in purity of heart and detachment, so that while seeking what is necessary for life, we do not lose sight of our duty to conform ourselves to the purposes and desires of God our Creator and Father. His works are unceasingly directed toward the good and salvation of men, and our labors, however material and humble, must aim at the temporal welfare and eternal good of ourselves and of all others. Just as God extends his providence to all men, we must make our industry of benefit not only to ourselves, but to our brothers also, using our abilities for their advantage, whether material, moral or spiritual. In this way Christians "can justly consider that by their labor they are unfolding the Creator's work, consulting the advantages of their brother men, and contributing by their personal industry to the realization in history of the divine plan" (GS 34). While building the earthly city, they are building and extending the kingdom of God, in which they are diligent and useful workers. While providing for their earthly needs, they spread throughout the world "that spirit by which are animated those poor, meek, and peacemaking souls whom the Lord in the gospel calls blessed" (LG 38).

O God, you have placed all the powers of nature under the control of man and his work. May we bring the spirit of Christ to all our efforts and work with our brothers and sisters at our common task, establishing true love and guiding your creation to perfect fulfillment. (Mass for the blessing of man's labor, B)

O Father, God of goodness, you give man the land to provide him with food. May the produce we harvest sustain our lives, and may we always use it for your glory and the good of all.
Mass after the harvest

O Lord, "give us this day our daily bread." Give us the means of sustaining our life here... so that when the time of our bondage is over, we may attain perfect liberty. Give us the bread we must eat in the sweat of our brow: this is our bondage... Each of us must toil *for our daily bread... But it is always you, O Lord, who give it to us, because it is you who bless our labors. So give it to us, each day. This petition expresses the completeness of our perpetual and irreparable poverty. Give it to us: we want it only from you and in the way you prescribe for us. Give us our bread. By this we mean all the things that you have made necessary for us. Grant us necessities, not luxuries. We ask for that upon which you willed our earthly existence should depend, for it was you who imposed this dependence upon us. Give us this day the bread which we need today, and shall need no less tomorrow. But I must be satisfied with having it today... "Sufficient for today are its troubles; let tomorrow take care of its own" (Mt 6:3 4).*

J.B. Bossuet, *Meditazioni sul Vangelo*, III:51 V.I.

49 . HIS KINGDOM WILL HAVE NO END

Lord, make these words of yours come true someday: "Come, O blessed of my Father, inherit the kingdom prepared for you from the foundation of the world" (Mt 25:34)

1. "The kingdom of God may be compared to a king who gave a marriage feast for his son, and sent his servants to call those who were invited to the marriage but they would not come" (Mt 22:2-3). God offers his kingdom to every man, he invites us all to the great wedding feast of his Son who espoused human nature when he came into the world; the wedding that opens the way of salvation to everyone, because Christ who is the Bridegroom through his incarnation will lead all back home to his Father's kingdom. Salvation is the great nuptial banquet prepared for the whole of mankind; the only condition for participation in it is to accept the invitation, which is as generous as it is absolutely free. However, like the invited guests of the parable, many close their ears to the invitation and reject it repeatedly. Salvation is a gift, and whoever does not accept it excludes himself from it by his own act; this is the meaning of eternal damnation, foreshadowed in the punishment inflicted on those who have disdained the wedding invitation. Others will be invited in their place and St. Luke specifies that these others are the "poor and maimed and blind and lame" (Lk 14:21); these hasten to the banquet; they represent those who, aware of their own poverty, are conscious of their need of salvation, and sense that only God can save them. Their very poverty makes them open to the divine gift.

Yet not all of those who accept the invitation are going to be finally approved. On earth, the kingdom of heaven—the Church —welcomes anyone who wishes to enter, somewhat like the field which accepts the seed of both wheat and weed, or like the fisherman's net cast into the sea, which gathers in both good fish and bad: at the end of time God himself will make the choice, and those who are taken by surprise "without a wedding garment" will be cast "into the outer darkness; these men will weep and gnash their teeth" (Mt 22:12-13).

The kingdom—eternal salvation—is the free gift of God's infinite love; but just because it is a gift of love it insists upon acceptance and a return of love. To refuse the gift is to refuse the love which offers it and therefore to put oneself deliberately outside God's kingdom which is a kingdom of love. But those who accept the invitation, who enter the Church and live a worthy life, will be approved and admitted to the eternal wedding-feast of the Son of God, to that kingdom that will have no end.

2. The kingdom of God will reach its full completeness only in the glory of heaven; here below, it goes on developing towards its totality as long as men are being born into the world, and continues to develop in each of us by establishing itself in us in an ever more permanent manner. Although the Son of God had consummated his marriage to mankind on the cross by ransoming it from sin and, by rising again, had caused it to be reborn to a new life and given the right to eternal glory, still as long as we live here on earth we live in hope, for "in this hope we were saved" (Rom 8:24). Hope does not deceive, because it is founded on the unfailing love of God who, to save the world, "did not spare his own Son, but gave him up for us all" (ib. 32). Hope, and therefore expectation, of future good is promised with certainty by God, yet it is still uncertain, because attaining it requires the free cooperation of each individual. This imparts a sense of precariousness to our present life, a feeling of expectation and of vigil. "We are truly called the sons of God and such we are"—states the Council, using the words of Holy Scripture—"but we have not yet appeared with Christ in the state of glory in which we shall be like to God, since we shall see him as he is. Therefore, 'while we are in the body, we are exiled from the Lord!' (and) we groan within ourselves and desire to be with Christ" (LG 48). Earthly life is not a stable, definitive value, but rather a trial, a road toward a precise goal: a blessed eternity. The Christian, therefore is not so concerned with settling down well here below, as he is with traveling without stopping toward the homeland which awaits him. If he makes proper use of worldly goods in this life, he will not become attached to them, because he does not want to stop in them; he wants to reach heaven. And if, in order to reach his goal, he has to renounce every worldly value, he does so willingly, knowing that "the kingdom of heaven is like a merchant who was seeking good pearls. When he found one pearl of great price, he went back and sold all that he had and bought it" (Mt 13:45-46). Yet, having done this, he would still feel convinced that he had done little, since all earthly kingdoms are as nothing compared to the kingdom of heaven.

O God, your eternal kingdom is as glorious and lofty as your majesty is sublime. Your royalty is not drawn from the kingdom; the kingdom proceeds from you. On your vesture and on your side, O King, is written: "King of kings and Lord of lords. Eternal is your power: your scepter will not be taken away, your kingdom not broken apart: tribes, peoples, and tongues will all serve you eternally; True King of peace, all heaven and earth will long to see you.

O how glorious is your kingdom, O most excellent King, where all the just reign with you, and whose laws are truth, peace, charity, life, and immortality!

St. Bonaventure, *The Tree of Life*, 45: Op. myst.

O God, may your kingdom come! When shall I be in your kingdom? My soul longs for you; it is languishing and panting to come into your eternal tabernacle, into that city which will never fall into ruin. All is passing, all is fleeting; when will I see him who will not pass away? When will I be confirmed in him, in such a way that I can no longer fear losing him? Oh that I could reach this kingdom right away! In the meantime rule in me, rule over all my desires, rule—you alone! One cannot serve two masters nor have two kings, nor can two objects dominate the heart. To serve them is to love them. This is what your Son teaches us, he who is Truth itself: that no man can serve two masters, since "he will hate one and love the other, or he will accept the one and despise the other." There is no middle way: one must either love or hate, accept or despise. Rule then, you alone!

J.B. Bossuet, *Meditazioni sul Vangelo* III, v. 1

50   BAPTISM OF THE LORD

Sunday after Epiphany

Ascribe to the Lord, you sons of God; ascribe to the Lord, glory and strength.   *(Ps 29:1-2)*

1. Today's feastday also is an "epiphany," a manifestation of the divinity of Jesus, made particularly solemn because of the direct intervention of heaven. Isaiah's prophecy of the "servant of God," the figure of the Messiah, is its prelude. The prophet presents it in the name of the Lord: "Behold my servant...my chosen, in whom my soul delights. I have put my spirit upon him" (Is 42:1). These are Christ's great characteristics: he is the "servant of God" par excellence, wholly dedicated to his glory and to his service, and his first words as he came into the world were: "Lo I have come to do your will, O God" (Heb 10:7); he is filled with the Holy Spirit, under whose influence his saving mission develops, and in him God is well pleased.

Isaiah's prophetic description is historically and completely realized in the gospel account of the baptism of Jesus. At that time "heaven was opened and the Holy Spirit descended upon him in bodily shape as a dove. A voice came from heaven: 'You are my beloved Son: with you I am well pleased' " (Lk 3:21-22). It is no longer the prophet who speaks in the name of God, but God himself in a most solemn manner. The whole Trinity intervenes in the great epiphany on the banks of the Jordan: the Father makes his voice heard, bearing witness to his Son, the Son is manifested in Jesus, and the Holy Spirit descends visibly upon him. The truth already announced by Isaiah in a veiled manner now shines forth in all its messianic meaning. The expression "my servant" is replaced by "my beloved Son," which indicates the divine nature of Christ more directly; the Holy Spirit, whom Jesus possesses fully, precisely because he is the Son of God, appears above him in visible form; also God speaks personally and publicly—all the people present hear his voice (ib. 21).

Jesus' baptism is like the official investiture of his mission as Savior; the Father and the Holy Spirit vouch for his identity as the Son of God and present him to the world so that the world may receive his message. Thus salvation history is worked out in Christ through the intervention of the entire Trinity. The Liturgy most opportunely invites us today to glorify God who has revealed himself to us with such liberality: "Render to the Lord, O children of God, render to the Lord the glory that befits his name; adore the Lord with holy splendor" (Resp. Ps).

2. St. Peter, an eyewitness of Jesus' baptism, presents it in his talk to Cornelius as the starting point of the Lord's apostolic life. "You know what happened...the baptism which John preached: how God anointed Jesus of Nazareth with the Holy Spirit and with power; how he went about doing good and healing all that were oppressed by the devil" (Acts 10:36-38). His words echo those of Isaiah and the gospel.

In every text Jesus is depicted as full of, and "anointed" by, the Holy Spirit. As his earthly life began through the work of the Holy Spirit, so his apostolic life also begins through a particular intervention of the same Holy Spirit: he is totally possessed by the Spirit and is guided by him in the fulfillment of his mission.

In an analogous way, the same thing happens with the Christian: by baptism he is born to life in Christ through the intervention of the Holy Spirit who justifies and renews him in his entire being, fashioning him into a child of God. And when grown to the age when he must embrace the duties of Christian life in a conscious and responsible manner, the Holy Spirit intervenes again with a fresh grace through Confirmation in order to strengthen his faith and make him a sturdy witness to Christ. The Christian's entire life develops under the influence of the Holy Spirit.

When the evangelist St. Matthew describes the baptism of Jesus, he makes it clear that the Baptist did not want to accept the commission: "I need to be baptized by you, and do you come to me?" (Mt 3:14). Obviously the Lord did not need to be baptized: nevertheless he goes to the Jordan, fraternizing with those who went there to seek the baptism of penance, and he insists upon it with John: "Let it be so now: for thus it is fitting for us to fulfill all righteousness" (ib. 15). The "righteousness" that Jesus wishes to accomplish is the perfect fulfillment of his Father's will; and almost as a reply to his humble gesture of putting himself on a part with sinners, his Father reveals to the world his dignity as Messiah, and the Holy Spirit descends upon him in a visible manner.

An indispensible condition for the Christian to make the grace of baptism bear fruit and for him to be led by the Holy Spirit is the humility which causes him to seek the will of God in everything, above any personal advantage.

You also, O Jesus, were immersed in the river Jordan, under the eyes of the crowd, although very few then were able to recognize you; and this mystery of tardy faith, or of indifference, prolonged through the centuries, is a source of grief for those who love you and have received the mission of making you known in the world.

Oh grant to the successors of your apostles and disciples and to all who call themselves after your name and your cross, to press on with the work of spreading the gospel, and to bear witness to it in prayer, suffering, and loving obedience to your will!

And since you, an innocent lamb, came before John in the attitude of a sinner, so draw us also to the waters of the Jordan. To the Jordan will we go to confess our sins and cleanse our souls. And as the skies open to announce the voice of your Father, expressing his pleasure in you, so, having successfully overcome our trial, when the day of your resurrection dawns may we hear once more in our innermost hearts, the same heavenly Father's voice, recognizing us as his children.

John XXIII, Prayers and Devotions — Jan 13

O Jesus! holy, innocent, undefiled, separated from sinners, you come forward as though guilty, asking baptism for the remission of sins! What is this mystery?...John refuses with all his might to confer the baptism of penance...and you reply: "Suffer it to be so now. For so it becomes us to fulfill all justice." What is this justice? It is the humiliation of your adorable humanity, which in rendering supreme homage to infinite holiness, constitutes the full payment of all our debts toward divine justice. You, the just and innocent one, take the place of all our sinful race...O Jesus, let me humble myself before you and acknowledge that I am a sinner, let me renew the renunciation of sin already made at my baptism.

C. Marmion, Christ in His Mysteries X:1

ORDINARY   TIME

WEEKS   1-8

NOTICE

The Meditations for "Ordinary Time" begin on the Monday which immediately follows the Feast of the Baptism of Jesus (Sunday after Epiphany: Meditation #50) and continue until the Tuesday preceding Ash Wednesday. Discontinue these of Ordinary Time for all of Lent and Paschal Time. Take them up again on the Monday after Pentecost and continue on until Advent; in this procedure, use the following schema:

When the weeks of Ordinary Time are 34, we begin on the Monday after Pentecost, with the week which immediately follows the week interrupted before Lent; e.g. if interrupted in the sixth week we begin with the seventh.

When the weeks of Ordinary Time are 33, one week is omitted: e.g. if interrupted by Lent in the seventh week, they are resumed after Pentecost with the ninth week.

For greater expediency consult the summary below:

Year	Weeks per year	Weeks interrupted before Lent	Weeks to be taken up after Pentecost
1983	33	eighth	tenth
1984	34	ninth	tenth
1985	33	sixth	eighth
1986	33	fifth	seventh
1987	33	eighth	tenth
1988	33	sixth	eighth
1989	34	fifth	sixth
1990	34	eighth	ninth
1991	33	fifth	seventh
1992	33	eighth	tenth

51 — JESUS THE TRUE VINE

O, that I may cleave to you, my Lord, for you are my life!
(Deut 3 0:20)

1. Jesus is the "one Mediator between God and men" (1 Tim 2:5); however, He did not will to effect the work of our redemption

independently of us, but used it as a means of strengthening the bond between himself and us. This is the wonderful mystery of our incorporation in Christ, the mystery which Our Lord himself revealed to his apostles the night before his Passion. "I am the true vine; and my Father is the vinedresser . . . Abide in me, and I in you. As the branch cannot bear fruit by itself, unless it abides in the vine, neither can you, unless you abide in me" (Jn 15:1,4).

Jesus strongly affirms that there is no redemption, no supernatural life, no grace-life for one who does not live in him, who is not grafted onto him. He points to the vine: the shoots will not live and bear fruit unless they remain attached to the trunk. Jesus wishes to actualize this close connection between himself and us, a connection which is necessary for our salvation and sanctification. We cannot receive the least degree of grace, except through Christ's mediation, even as the smallest drop of sap cannot reach a branch which is detached from the tree. "The true vine is Christ who gives life and fruitfulness to the branches, that is, to us. Through the Church we abide in Christ, without whom we can do nothing" (LG 6).

Moreover, Jesus declares that, if we abide in him, we shall not only have supernatural life, but we shall become the recipients of special attention from our heavenly Father, the "Husbandman" of the mystical vine. In fact, our heavenly Father acknowledges us as his adopted children, loves us as such, and takes care of us, precisely to the degree in which he sees in us Christ, his only begotten, his well-beloved Son. The grace of adoption then, is wholly dependent upon our union with Christ, a union so close that we form, as it were, a "living part" of him, as the branch forms a living part of the vine.

2. "Abide in me" (Jn 15:4). We can only abide in a place where we are already. Jesus tells us to "abide" in him because we have been grafted onto him. This spiritual engrafting, an accomplished fact, was made possible for all men by Christ's death on the cross, and it became effective for each one of us at the time of our baptism. Christ grafted us into himself at the cost of his precious Blood. Therefore we "are" in him, but he insists further that we "abide" in him and bring forth fruit.

Baptism is sufficient to graft us into Christ, and one degree of grace will permit us to abide in him like living branches, but we should not be content with this union only. We must show our gratitude for the immense gift we have received by endeavoring to become more and more firmly grafted into Christ. We must "live" this union with Christ, making him the center, the sun of our interior life. "Abide in me" is not a chance expression. Christ wished to show us that our life in him requires our personal collaboration with him, that we are to employ all our strength, our mind, our will, and our heart that we may live in him and by him. The more we try to abide in Christ, the deeper our little branch will grow into him, because it will be nourished more abundantly by the sap of grace.

"Abide in me and I in you." The more closely we are united to Christ by faith, charity, and good works done with the intention of pleasing God, the more intensely will he live in us and bestow on us continually a new life of grace. Thus we shall become, not merely living branches, but branches laden with fruit, the fruit of sanctity destined to bring joy to the heart of God, for Jesus has said: "By this is my Father glorified, that you bear much fruit" (Jn 15:8). This will be fruit not only of personal sanctity, but for the good of our brethren, and for all the Church, as befits a true disciple of Christ.

> O sweet, gentle grafting! O highest sweetness who deigned to unite yourself with our bitterness... you, the infinite one with us who are finite... Was your charity satisfied, having made this union? No, eternal Word, you watered this tree with your Blood. This Blood by its warmth makes it grow, if man with his free will grafts himself onto you, and units and binds his heart and affections to you, tying and binding this graft with the bond of charity and of following your doctrine... Because we must conform ourselves to you, O Christ, and engraft ourselves into you by the way of suffering, and of the cross and of holy desires. Thus through you, O Life, we bring forth fruits of life... So we see that you created us without us, but you do not will to save us without us. When we are grafted onto you, then the branches which you have given to our tree bear fruit."
>
> St. Catherine of Siena, *Preghiere ed Elevazioni*

> In your sight, O God, true glory is that in which you are glorified and not man... since it is you who give us strength to work well... You are glorified, O Father, when we bring forth much fruit and become disciples of Christ. For who makes us his disciples? You who gave us your mercy from the beginning, for we are in very fact, the work of your hands, created in Christ Jesus to accomplish good works.
>
> O Jesus, you say: As the Father has loved me, I also have loved you; abide in my love. This is where all our good works originate. From where else could they come if not from the faith that works through love? And how would it be possible for us to love if we had not first been loved?...
>
> When you say: just as the Father has loved me, so also I have loved you, you are presenting yourself precisely as Mediator, O Jesus. The Father indeed loves us also, but he loves us in you, for in this is the Father glorified: that we bring forth fruit in the vine, that is, in you his Son, and that we become your disciples.
>
> St. Augustine, *In John* 82:1-2

52 — THE MYSTICAL BODY OF CHRIST

Grant me, O holy Spirit, the riches of assured understanding, unto the knowledge of the mystery of Christ. (Col 2:2)

1. "I am the vine, you are the branches" (Jn 15:5). On these words of Jesus is founded the doctrine of the Mystical Body of Christ. Only the figure is changed: instead of the vine, we speak of the Body of which Christ is the Head and we are the members. In explaining this doctrine, St. Paul aptly paraphrases what Jesus had previously said: "Just as the body is one and has many members, and all the members of the body, though many, are one body, so it with Christ . . . Now you are the body of Christ, and individually members of it" (1 Cor 12:12,27).

The identity of thought is evident: as the branches are part of the vine on which they grow and from which they are nourished with one sap; as the parts of the human body form one body and have a single life; so we, being incorporated in Christ, make but one body with him and live of his life. This is the Mystical Body of Christ "which," St. Paul teaches, "is the Church" (Col 1:24).

Christ is the head of this Body. "Christ is the head of the Church his body . . . and is himself its head" (Eph 5:23). The Father "has made him head over all things for the Church, which is his body" (Eph 1:22,23). One Body, one life which comes to each of its members from the head. "Christ our Lord vivifies the Church with his own supernatural life; by his divine power he permeates the whole Body and nourishes and sustains each of the members . . . very much as the vine nourishes and makes fruitful the branches which are joined to it" (Mystical Corporis). The fact that every Christian has life in Christ and lives of the very life of Christ is reaffirmed in these words.

2. The union of the baptized with Christ, the head of the Mystical Body is certainly not to be understood as being identical with the union that exists between the various members of a physical body. In fact, although we are incorporated in him, each one of us preserves "intact his own personality" (ibid). But neither should we understand this union to be a mere moral union, such as exists, for example, among members of the same organization. No, it is something much more profound, it is a mysterious union, and in this sense is called *mystical,* but is no less *real* and *vital.* It is a union which comes from there being present in all the parts of the Body of the Church the Holy Spirit, who is "one and the same for all, fills and unifies the whole Church" (St. Thos., *De Ver.* 29,4). In fact Jesus "has shared with us his Spirit who, existing as one and the same being in the head and in the members, vivifies, unifies, and moves the whole body. This he does in such a way that his work could be compared by the holy Fathers with the function which the soul fulfills in the human body, whose principle of life the soul is" (LG) 7).

The Holy Spirit, "the soul of the Church" (Myst. Corp.) is the bond which intimately and really units and vivifies all the members of Christ, diffusing grace and charity in them. Therefore, it is not a question of a symbolical, metaphorical union, but of a real union, so real that it surpasses all the others "as grace surpasses nature, and immortal realities surpass perishable realities" (ibid). "By communicating his Spirit to his brothers, Christ made them mystically into his own body" (LG 7). It is a reality so great that it embraces not only our earthly life but, provided we preserve it, continues to be the source of our happiness for all eternity. Indeed, "grace is the seed of glory."

We are members of Christ. This is our greatness and our glory, infinitely surpassing all earthly dignity and glory.

"O my beloved Spouse and loving Word, you engender the Body of the holy Church in a way which you alone know and understand . . . By means of your blood, you make a well-organized, well-formed body of which you are the head. The angels delight in its beauty, the archangels admire it, the seraphim are enraptured by it, all the angelic spirits marvel at it, and all the souls of the blessed in heaven rejoice in it. The Blessed Trinity takes delight in it in a manner beyond our comprehension."
St. Mary Magdalen de Pazzi, *The Colloquies*, Op. v. 3

I aspire to you, O my Lord Jesus, and desire to share with you and in you in the grace of the mystery of your incarnation . . . I desire to be united to you, to exist in you and to live and bear fruit in you like the stump of a vine.

O my Lord Jesus, make me live and subsist in you as you live and subsist in one divine Person! Be my all and let me become part of your mystical body in the way that humanity is part of a divine compound subsisting in two different natures. Make me bone of your bone, flesh of your flesh, spirit of your Spirit; let me draw benefit from your holy prayer on the last day of your life before you set out for the cross, when, after exhorting your apostles, you prayed insistently to your eternal Father that we too might be one as you are one with him . . .

I see truly that because of your infinite dignity I am very far from you and from your sacred Humanity . . . and yet, O Jesus, deign to come near to me and unite me to you, incorporate yourself in me so that I may live and act in you and may be led and directed and possessed by you.
P. de Berulle, *Le Grandezze di Gesu* 2:3

53 — I AM THE LIFE

O Jesus, full of grace and truth, grant that from your fullness I may receive grace upon grace.   *(Jn 1:14,16)*

1. Jesus explained his mission in these words: "I came that they may have life, and have it more abundantly" (Jn 10:10). What is this life that he gives us? It is the life of grace, which is a participation in his divine nature (2 Pet 1:4).

Jesus in his divine nature as the Word possesses divine life in the same way and to the same degree that his Father possesses it. "As the Father has life in himself, so he has granted the son also to have life in himself" (Jn 5:26).

This plenitude of divine life reverberates in Christ's humanity by reason of the hypostatic union. His sacred humanity, placed in direct contact with his divinity, to which it is united in one Person, is inundated with divine life; that is, it receives the greatest possible participation in it through "such plenitude of grace that no greater amount can be imagined" (Myst. Corp.). The sanctifying grace which fills the humanity of Jesus is so superabundant that theologians do not hesitate to call it "infinite grace" which has been given to him without measure, as befits his dignity and his mission to sanctify all men (St. T., S.T. 3,7,11). "In him (Christ")—affirms St. Paul—"all the fullness of God was pleased to dwell" (Col 1:19), and St. John defines this as being "full of grace and truth" (Jn 1:14). But Jesus does not wish to keep all this immense wealth for himself alone; the Father has given him brothers with whom he can share it. For this reason he embraced his sorrowful passion; by dying on the cross, he merited for us his members that grace which he possesses in such great plenitude. This Christ becomes the one and only source of grace and supernatural life for us. He is so "full of grace and truth" that "from his fullness we have all received, grace upon grace" (ib. 16). Here, then, is how divine life comes to us: from the Father to the Word, from the Word to the humanity which he assumed in his incarnation, and from this humanity, which is the sacred humanity of Christ, to our souls.

2. Grace, like everything that exists, apart from God, is also created by God. Jesus as God, that is, as the Word, is, together with the Father and the Holy Spirit, the creator of grace. But as Redeemer, and therefore as man, he is the Mediator of grace, the one who merited grace and who bestows it upon us. He not only merited it for us once for always by his death on the cross, but is continually applying it to our souls. Thus grace is infused and made to grow in every baptized person by means of his living and ever-present action. In this way Jesus gives us life; he *is* life for us, the one source of the divine life in which we participate. From him, as the Council says, "as from their fountain and head issue every grace and the life of God's People itself" (LG 50).

Two precious, practical consequences follow from this. One who desires to possess grace and supernatural life must go to Christ, become incorporated in him and live in him. "He who has the Son has life; he who has not the Son of God, has not life" (1 Jn 5:12).

The grace which sanctifies our souls, is, in its essence, identically the same as that which adorns the sacred soul of Jesus (S.T. 3,8,5). Of course, they differ immensely in measure and perfection, but the nature of the grace is the very same. Thus it can sanctify us, making us live in union with God and for his glory. By giving us grace, Jesus has truly communicated his life to us; he has planted in us the seed of his sanctity, so that, provided we wish it, we can live a life similar to his own.

Father, all-powerful and ever-living God, in Christ our Lord you have renewed all things and given us a share in his fullness. Although he was God, he stripped himself of glory, and by shedding his blood on the cross he brought peace to the world. Therefore he was exalted above everything created and became the source of eternal life for all who obey him.

Roman Missal, *Common Preface* 1

O my God, let me never forget this truth—that you are not only my life, but my only life! You are "the way, the truth and the life." You are my life, and the life of all who live. All men, all I know, all I meet, all I see and hear of, live not unless they live by you. They live in you, or else they live not at all. No one can be saved out of you. Let me never forget this in the business of the day. O give me a true love of souls, of those souls for whom you died. Teach me to pray for their conversion, to do my part towards effecting it. However able they are, however amiable, however high and distinguished, they cannot be saved unless they have you.

O my all-sufficient Lord, you only suffice! Your blood is sufficient for the whole world. As you are sufficient for me, so you are sufficient for the entire race of Adam. O my Lord Jesus, let your cross be more than sufficient for them, let it be effectual! Let it be effectual for me more than all, lest I "have all and abound" (Phil 4:18), yet bring no fruit to perfection.

J.H. Newman, *Meditations on Christian Doctrine* VIII:3 (p. 367)

54 — THE INFLUENCE OF JESUS

From you, O Lord comes my salvation, from you comes my hope
(P 62:1,5)

1. "Power came forth from him and healed them all" (Lk 6:19), the Gospel says in speaking of Jesus and the astonishing miracles he worked. At the touch of his hand, the blind saw, the deaf heard,

the dumb spoke. The power which went forth from him was so great that the poor woman suffering from the issue of blood had only to touch the hem of his garment to feel herself instantly cured. It was just as easy for him to purify and sanctify souls and to forgive sins, as it was to heal bodies. "Which is easier, to say, 'Your sins are forgiven you,' or to say: 'Rise and walk?' but that you may know that the Son of man has authority on earth to forgive sins (he said to the man who was paralyzed), I say to you, rise, take up your bed and go home" (ib. 5:23-24). To remit sins is the prerogative of God alone. If, then, Jesus says of himself, who is visibly a man, that he has the power to forgive sins, he is affirming that he is God and that the divinity works in his humanity. "In fact—Vatican II teaches—the assumed nature inseparately united to the divine Word serves him as a living instrument of salvation" (LG 8). Indeed, his sacred humanity, full of grace and power, is precisely the instrument which his divinity uses to bestow all grace and life.

The sacred humanity of Jesus, now glorified in heaven, continues to impart the same power and virtue it once did in the districts of Palestine, and this power, being imparted to our souls, influences them from within, purifies, transforms and sanctifies them. "The interior influence from which grace comes to our souls belongs . . . to Christ, whose humanity, because it is united to his divinity, has the power to justify" (S.T. 3,8,6).

2. "In the human nature which he united to himself, the Son of God redeemed man and transformed him into a new creation by overcoming death through his own death and resurrection" (LG 7). We can distinguish two closely joined, indeed inseparable, phases in Christ's work of redemption. The first phase is his sorrowful life which began with the incarnation and ended with his death on the cross; the second is his glorious life which began at his resurrection and still continues, since Jesus, risen and glorious, is always bestowing upon our souls the grace he merited for us once for always on Calvary. "But grace was given to each of us according to the measure of Christ's gift" (Eph 4:7). Jesus distributes grace to each of us who are baptized, according to his will and his divine plan, gradually transforming us into a "new creature." We all live continually under his influence: "As the head rules the members," says the Council of Trent, "as the vine sends its sap through all its branches, so does Jesus Christ exert his influence at every moment over all the just. This influence precedes, accompanies, and crowns their good works, and makes them pleasing to God and meritorious in his sight" (Sess VI, Can 16).

Jesus is "able for all time to save those who draw near to God through him, since he always lives to make intercession for them" (Heb 7:25). He is living in the most holy Sacrament of the Altar, and he is living in heaven, where, seated in glory at the right hand of his Father, he shows him the reddened wounds of his passion, thereby making continual intercession for us. In addition, "He is himself choosing, determining, and distributing graces to each one according to the measure of his gift" (Myst. Corp.). Christ is then—in the fullest sense, in the most actual sense—the source of all our life. "Christ is our life" (cf. Col 3:4).

O Lord of my soul and my Good, Jesus Christ crucified... Where have all my blessings come from but from you?... What a pity it was for me to have left you, my Lord, under the pretext of serving you more!... When I was offending you, I did not know you, but how, once knowing you, did I think I could gain more by this path! Oh, what a bad road I was following, Lord! Now it seems to me I was walking on no path until you brought me back, for in seeing you at my side I saw all blessings...

Whoever lives in the presence of so good a friend and excellent a leader, who went ahead of us to be the first to suffer, can endure all things. The Lord helps us, strengthens us, and never fails; he is a true friend...

I see clearly, and I saw afterward, that God desires that if we are going to please him and receive his great favors, we must do so through the most sacred humanity of Christ, in whom he takes his delight. Many, many times have I perceived this truth through experience. The Lord has told it to me. I have definitely seen that we must enter by this gate if we desire his sovereign Majesty to show us great secrets...

This Lord of ours is the one through whom all blessings come to us... In beholding his life we find that he is the best example. What more do we desire than to have such a good friend at our side, who will not abandon us in our labors and tribulations, as friends in the world do? Blessed is he who truly loves him and always keeps him at his side!

St. Teresa of Jesus, *Life* 22:3-7.

O Lord Jesus Christ, who are at the same time God, the savior of men, and a man all-powerful with God, I invoke you, I praise you, I pray to you. Be near me with your indulgence and compassion and forgiveness. Fill my heart with desires only you can satisfy; put on my lips prayers only you can answer, and into my behavior acts which only you can bless.

Prayer of the Mozarabic Mass PL 85, 187

55 — JESUS AND THE HOLY SPIRIT

Take not your holy Spirit from me, O Lord.   *(Ps 51:11)*

1. Although grace was created equally by the three Persons of the Blessed Trinity, without any difference or distinction, its diffusion in souls is usually attributed especially to the Third Person,

the Holy Spirit, to whom everything that concerns the work of sanctification is referred by appropriation. In this sense the tremendous gift of grace which filled the humanity of Jesus must be attributed to the work of the Holy Spirit. The soul of Jesus possesses every supernatural gift because "the Holy Spirit dwells in Christ with such plenitude of grace that no greater plenitude can be imagined" (Myst. Corp.). This plenitude of grace, which is a created gift, corresponds to the plenitude of the Holy Spirit, who is the uncreated Gift. Jesus, the only one who "received this Spirit in an unlimited degree" (ibid), has received from him the immense capital of grace which permits him to merit it for all of us.

The soul of Jesus is uniquely beautiful, holy, intimately united to the divinity, so that the Holy Spirit "takes delight in abiding in it as in his chosen temple" (ibid). He dwells in it with such plenitude and sovereignty that he inspires, directs, and guides all the actions of Jesus, and that is why the Holy Spirit "is correctly called the Spirit of Christ or the Spirit of the Son" (ibid). The gospel tells us several times that Jesus, "filled with the Holy Spirit," was "led by the Spirit" (Lk 4:1); this happened not only in some special circumstance, but always. Jesus himself affirmed it at the beginning of his ministry in the synagogue of Nazareth: "The Spirit of the Lord is upon me, because he has anointed me to preach good news to the poor" (ivi 18). Jesus was not moved by any other impulse, by any spirit other than the Holy Spirit.

2. "When the work which the Father had given the Son to do on earth was accomplished, the Holy Spirit was sent on the day of Pentecost in order that he might forever sanctify the Church, and thus all believers would have access to the Father through Christ in the one Spirit" (LG 4). Jesus, by his death and resurrection, merited for us, not only grace, but the very Author of grace, the Holy Spirit, whom he had promised to the apostles and whom, after his ascent into heaven, he had sent to them at Pentecost. We too receive the Holy Spirit through Jesus; it is always he who, together with the Father, sends us the Holy Spirit. This divine Spirit "is bestowed from the fullness of Christ himself according to the measure of the giving of Christ" (Myst. Corp.). We receive the Holy Spirit according to the measure of our union with Christ; the Holy Spirit, in turn, unites us to Christ. "Any one"—says St. Paul—"who does not have the Spirit of Christ does not belong to him. But if Christ is in you . . . your spirits are alive, because of righteousness" (Rom 8:9,10). To possess the Holy Spirit is to be united to Christ; and he who lives in Christ has the Holy Spirit who justifies him. Christ cannot dwell in us without the Holy Spirit being also with us.

To live in Christ is to live in the Holy Spirit, it is to be a member of his Mystical Body, to be a temple of his Spirit: "Do you not know that you are God's temple, and that God's Spirit dwells in you?" (1 Cor 3:16) The grace merited for us by Christ and dispensed to us by him is not diffused in us save by the intervention of the Holy Spirit. Each increase of grace is caused simultaneously by the creative action of the Holy Spirit and the mediation of Christ. "Christ is in us by his spirit whom he communicates to us and by means of whom he acts in us in such a way that it may be said that everything that is divine is accomplished in us by the Holy Spirit and also by Christ" (Myst. Corp.).

O power of the eternal Father, come to my aid! Wisdom of the Son, illumine the eye of my intellect! Sweet clemency of the Holy Spirit, inflame my heart and unite it to yourself! I confess, O sweet, eternal Goodness of God, that the mercy of the Holy Spirit and your burning charity are trying to inflame my heart and unite it to you, together with the hearts of all rational creatures ... Burn with the fire of your Spirit, consume and destroy, down to the very roots, all love and affection of the flesh, in the hearts of the new plants which you have deigned to graft onto the Mystical Body of holy Church. Deign, O God, to carry us away from worldly affection into the garden of your love, and create in us a new heart and clear understanding of your will, so that, despising the world, ourselves, and our pride, and filled with the true fervor of your love ... we may follow you for yourself alone, in chaste purity and fervent charity! ...

St. Catherine of Siena, *Preghiere ed Elevazioni*

O Jesus, dearest Beloved of my heart, it is most true that no spiritual fruit can be borne without being watered by the dew of your Spirit and ripened by the heat of your love. Have pity on me, then, take me into the arms of your love, and warm my whole being by your Spirit! ...

Come, Holy Spirit, come O Lord who are love, fill my heart, for alas! it is empty of anything good. Set me on fire, that I may love you. Enlighten me, that I may know you. Attract me, that I may delight in you. Arouse me, that I may experience the fruition of you ...

O holy and almighty Paraclete, in that love whereby you have sealed me for yourself ... grant that I may love you with my whole heart, cleave unto you with my whole soul, expend all my strength in loving and serving you, live according to your heart, and, at the hour of my death, enter immaculate upon the divine nuptials you have made ready.

St. Gertrude, *Exercise 2*, (p. 19-21)

O Lord, strengthen our participation in the divine life of him who willed to take upon himself our human nature. **(RM)**

1. "Truly, truly I say to you, unless one is born anew of water and the Holy Spirit, he cannot see the kingdom of God" (Jn 3:5). We can attain to God and his kingdom only through Christ, through our incorporation in him. This was effected in us by "water and the Holy Spirit" on the blessed day of our baptism. Jesus said to Nicodemus: "You must be born anew" (ib. 7); and this means truly a new birth, because in baptism we receive the seed of a new life, a participation in divine life. "By the sacrament of baptism . . . a man becomes truly incorporated into the crucified and glorified Christ, and is reborn to a sharing of the divine life" (UR 22). Before we receive this sacrament, we have only a human life; afterwards we participate in divine life, in the life of Christ. "For as many of you as were baptized into Christ—writes St. Paul—have put on Christ" (Gal 3:27). There is no question here of a reclothing, but of something interior, of a divine reality which becomes part of a man's intimate being and transforms him so profoundly that he is changed, in Christ, into a "new creature" (2 Cor 5:17), born not of flesh, but of the Spirit, "not of blood . . . nor of the will of man, but of God" (Jn 1:13).

"Do you not know that all of us, who have been baptized into Christ Jesus, were baptized into his death? We were buried therefore with him by baptism into death; so that as Christ was raised from the dead . . . we too might walk in newness of life" (Rom 6:3-4). Born again in Christ, we must live a new life in him, one like his own. For as Christ "died to sin, once for all," that is, by his death destroyed men's sins, "so you also must consider yourselves dead to sin and alive to God in Christ Jesus." To live in Christ Jesus demands absolute death to sin. "For sin will have no dominion over you" (ib. 10-14).

2. "May the mingling of this water and wine be a sign of our sharing in the divinity of Christ who willed to share in our humanity!" (cf. RM) These words said by the priest in every Mass express the wonderful reality which springs from baptism, whereby every baptized person is made a partaker in Christ's divinity. However, this gift, bestowed on us without any merit on our part, requires our cooperation. "Recognize your dignity, O Christian," St. Leo exclaims, "and having become a sharer in the divine nature, beware lest you return to your former baseness by unworthy conduct. Remember the Head and Body to which you belong" (Ser. 21:3).

Every sin, fault, or voluntary negligence dishonors Christ, our Head, and grieves the Holy Spirit who dwells in us. A genuine Christian, however, cannot remain content with merely avoiding sin; we must also strive to make Christ's life increase in us. In fact, baptism is "wholly directed toward the acquiring of fullness of life in Christ" (UR 22). It is not enough to live in Christ; this life must be full and exuberant. In the life of nature, we grow without the help of our wills; but this is not true of the life of grace. Without our cooperation, it is possible for this life to remain stationary in us for twenty, thirty, fifty years after our baptism, after hundreds of confessions and Holy Communions. What a tremendous disproportion! We may be adults or even aged in years, but children according to grace!

We must grow in Christ, and He must increase in us. The words of St. John the Baptist form our program: "He must increase, but I must decrease" (Jn 3:30). See what the development of grace in us exacts—the death of self, "the old man" with his bad habits, faults and imperfections, so that the Christ-life in us may grow to perfection, to "the measure of the stature of the fullness of Christ" (Eph 4:13).

O Jesus, fountain of life, come, give me to drink a cup of the living water which flows from you, that once I have tasted you, I may nevermore thirst save for you. Immerse my whole being in the depths of your mercy. Baptize me in the spotlessness of your precious death. Renew me in your blood wherewith you have redeemed me. In the water from your holy side, wash away every stain wherewith I have ever sullied my baptismal innocence. Fill me with your Spirit and take possession of my whole being in purity both of body and soul.

St. Gertrude, *Exercise I* (p. 10)

O my Jesus, grant me mercy!... Grant that I may remain united to you by grace and good works, so that I may bear fruit worthy of you. Grant that I may not become, through my sins, a dead branch, good for nothing but to be gathered up and cast into the fire (cf. Jn 15:6).

Dom C. Marmion, *Christ in his Mysteries*, 14:viii

O my Lord and my God! When you have raised up a soul and it has understood how miserably it has ruined itself to gain some brief pleasure and is determined ever to please you and you help it with your favor (for you never forsake those who love you nor fail to answer those who call upon you), what help is there, Lord, for such a soul, to enable it to live, instead of dying with the remembrance of having lost all the good that it would have were it in the state of baptismal innocence? The best life that that soul can live is a life which sorrow for its sin turns into death... My Lord! I seem to have forgotten your wonders and your mercies, and how you came into the world for sinners, and purchased us at so great a price, and paid for our false pleasures by suffering such cruel tortures and scourgings!...

*May this self of mine die, and may another, greater than myself
and better for me than myself, live in me, so that I may serve him.
May he live and give me life; may he reign and may I be his captive,
for my soul desires no other freedom.*
                    St. Teresa of Jesus *Soliloquies* 3:2-3; 17:3

57 — SECOND SUNDAY OF ORDINARY TIME

YEAR A

*O God who sanctifies us in Christ Jesus, give us your grace and
peace   (1 Cor 1:2-3)*

1. In the spirit of Epiphany, today's readings continue to
show forth Christ's divinity and his mission. In place of the
Father's testimony declaring: "This is my beloved Son with whom
I am well pleased" (Mt 3:17), we are given that of St. John the
Baptist, who proclaims: "Behold the Lamb of God, who takes
away the sin of the world" (Jn 1:29). Jesus, whom the father had
presented as his beloved Son, is now shown to us as the innocent
lamb who will be sacrificed in expiation for sin. Thus we are not
dealing with a political messiah, come to bring earthly power and
glory to Israel, but with "the servant of Yahweh" announced by
Isaiah, who takes upon himself the iniquity of mankind and
atones for it by his death. Through his sacrifice he becomes the
light and salvation, not of Israel only, but of all men; in him the
glory of God is made manifest: "You are my servant, Israel, in
whom I will be glorified . . . I will give you as a light to the nations,
that my salvation may reach to the end of the earth" (Is 49:3-6).
When Isaiah's prophecy is read by Christian eyes, it becomes very
clear. He whom God designated by the mouth of his prophet as
"his servant" is the very one whom now, in the fullness of time, he
points out to the world as "his Son" in whom is all his pleasure.
Christ's divinity shines forth: the Only-Begotten of the Father, he
is God like the Father; when he took human nature his divinity
was not diminished. Yet he hid it, almost as if annihilating it,
when he took the form of a servant and abased himself to the state
of a lamb offered in holocaust. But precisely by means of this
sacrifice, which opens into the resurrection, he recovers his full
glory as Son of God, and gains the power of sharing it with all
men, redeeming them from sin and presenting them to the Father
as sons.
    Confronted with the greatness of Christ, John observes his
own littleness and confesses: "This is he of whom I said, 'After me
comes a man who ranks before me, because he was before me' "
(Jn 1:30). Enlightened from above, he recognizes the absolute
primacy of Christ and of his mission; he is "God's chosen one"
who has come to baptize, not with water, but "with the Holy

Spirit" (ib. 33-34). In comparison, with Christ every apostle is nothing, or rather has value, and is able to act, only insofar as he depends humbly and entirely on him.

O Word! O Jesus! How beautiful you are! How great! Who will ever succeed in knowing you? Who will be able to understand you? O Jesus, deign to make me know you and love you.

You who are the light, let a ray of light shine upon my poor soul, so that I may see you and comprehend you. Let me turn my gaze on you, infinite beauty. Open my ears so I may hear your voice and meditate upon your divine teachings. Open also my mind and my intellect so that your word may reach even to my heart, let me savor and understand it. Conceal a little of the splendor of your glory so that I may be able to contemplate and look at your divine perfections.

Awaken in me a great faith in you so that your every word may be light that illuminates me and attracts me to you and persuades me to follow you in all the ways of justice and truth.

O Jesus, O Word, you are my Lord, my one and only teacher: speak, I want to listen to you and put your word into practice. I want to listen to your word because I know it comes from heaven. I desire to listen to it, to meditate upon it and put it into practice, because in your word is life and joy and peace and happiness.

Speak, you are my Lord and my teacher; I desire to hear no one but you.

A. Chevrier, *Il vero discepolo* p. XVIII

YEAR B

"Speak, Lord, for your servant hears"   *(1 Sam 3:10)*

Like the boy Samuel of whom we read in the Bible, the Christian must always be ready for any kind of call from God. But it is nonetheless true, that it is not always easy to recognize the Lord's voice. Samuel recognized it only after he had sought out the priest Eli who enlightened him, and suggested his course of action: "Pay attention: if he calls you, you shall say, 'Speak, Lord, for your servant hears'" (1 Sam 3:9). Even when God calls individuals directly, he wants them to have recourse to the Church for enlightenment as to the meaning of his call; it is the Church's duty to recognize and interpret divine inspiration. This being supposed, the basic disposition needed to welcome God's call is one of promptness and availability, coupled with the desire to know and to follow the Lord.

The Gospel offers a typical example of this in the vocation of John and Andrew. They are not called directly by God but through an intermediary, their teacher John the Baptist, who says to them: "Behold the lamb of God" (Jn 1:36); they recognize these words as the announcement of the long-awaited Messiah and they immediately follow Jesus. They want to become acquainted with him that day" (ib. 39). John's honesty and unselfish disinterestedness are striking. His only interest in making converts is to announce the Messiah to them, and to direct them to him, completely faithful to his mission as the "voice" who makes ready the way of the Lord (ib. 23); then quietly he disappears. Likewise the immediacy with which John and Andrew leave their old teacher is striking. Once they had learned Jesus was the Messiah, all that mattered was to follow him and to try to attract others to him also, as Andrew does immediately by calling his brother Simon.

Every Christian is called—in a manner suited to his state in life—to walk in Christ's footsteps to holiness, to an apostolate. "Do you not know that your bodies are members of Christ?" (1 Cor 6:15). Precisely because he belongs to the Mystical Body of Christ, the Christian must be holy and a follower of Christ. Just as an unwholesome member dishonors the head and injures the whole body, a holy member honors Christ, helps to sanctify the body and works together with Christ himself for the salvation of his brothers.

> How good you are, my Lord Jesus, to be willing to be called the Lamb of God, which means that like a lamb you are a victim, and as meek as a lamb ... and that you belong to God, so that whatever you do, you do for God!
>
> Following your example, we too are victims, O beloved Jesus; we are victims on accont of your love, holocausts that burn in your honor through mortification and prayer, pouring ourselves out in absolute renunciation of self for you alone, utterly forgetting ourselves and dedicating every moment to trying to please you as much as possible.
>
> Like you we must be "victims for the redemption of many," uniting our prayers and sufferings to your example in order to help effectively in your redemptive work, since suffering is the indispensable condition for doing good to our neighbor: "Unless a grain of wheat falls into the earth and dies, it remains alone ... "
>
> O Jesus, your first word to your disciples is: "Come and see," that is to say "follow and observe" which means "copy and contemplate" ... Your last word is "Follow me" ... How tender and sweet and beneficial and loving is this word! "Follow me" ..., that is "imitate me!" ... What can be sweeter to hear for one who loves? What more salutary, from the moment that imitation is thus intimately joined to love?
>
> C. De Foucauld, Meditazioni sul Vangelo, Op. sp.

YEAR C

Sing to the Lord a new song! . . . tell of his salvation day after day
(Ps 96:1-2)

To express God's love for his people, so strong and tender, so jealous and merciful, the prophets could find no more meaningful image than that of nuptial love. So it was from this viewpoint that they pictured the relationship of alliance and friendship that God wished to establish with Israel and the work of salvation that he wanted to accomplish in Jerusalem's benefit. "As a young man marries a virgin, so shall your maker marry you, and as the bridegroom rejoices over the bride, so shall your God rejoice over you" (Is 62:5). The New Testament takes up the allegory again, giving it a deeper and more concrete meaning. By becoming man, the Son of God is wedded to human nature, and joins it to himself in a personal and indissoluble way. This is why, when speaking of the kingdom of heaven, Jesus so often compares it to a wedding feast, and phrases the invitation to it as if to a wedding. It is his wedding which is celebrated in the Incarnation and then consummated on the cross.

In the context, Jesus' first miracle, which was performed during a wedding celebration, recalls the inexpressible reality of the relation of love, intimacy and communion which the incarnate Son of God came to establish with men. Not only Israel or Jerusalem, but the whole of mankind is called to participate in this nuptial union with God. The price of this privilege will be paid for by Jesus on the cross at the time ordained by the Father.

When Jesus went with his disciples and his Mother to Cana, his time had not yet come (Jn 2:4); yet through Mary's intercession he anticipates it with a "sign" that foreshadows salvation and redemption. Water is changed into an abundance of the best wine, as if to indicate the deep change that will be worked in men by the death and resurrection of Christ, making grace abound where sin used to abound, changing the cold, tasteless water of human selfishness into the strong, noble wine of charity. All this is realized because man—each one of us—is invited to take part in this wedding of the Word with humanity, and thereby to enjoy his love and his intimacy as a spouse.

The presence and intervention of Mary at the wedding in Cana is a strong reason for confidence; we feel ourselves unworthy of communion with Christ, but if we put our trust in his Mother, she will prepare us and usher us to him, even hastening the time.

O unfathomable depth and height of charity, how much you love this bride of the human race! O life through whom all things live! You drew her from the hands of the devil who was possessing her as his own . . . and then at the end, made payment with your whole bleeding body.

O priceless love and charity! Who showed us such burning desire; who ran as if blind and intoxicated to the infamy of the cross. The blind cannot see, nor the inebriated; so you seem as lost to yourself—almost, as if you were dead—to be, as it were, blind and inebriated over our salvation. Neither our ignorance, nor our ingratitude or our over-weening self-love could hold you back.

O Jesus, my sweetest love, you have let yourself be blinded by love so that you cannot see our sinfulness; you have lost your feeling about it. O sweet Lord, it seems to me that sin had wanted to punish your most sweet body, giving you over to the torments of the cross; and that you remain on the cross as a lover to demonstrate that you do not love us for your own advantage, but for our sanctification.

St. Catherine of Siena, *Epistolario* 221,225

58 — I AM THE TRUTH

"In your light, O Lord, we shall see light"   *(Ps 36:9)*

1. Jesus came to give us life, and to show us the way which leads to it. He, the source of life, is also the teacher of life.

At the beginning of Jesus' apostolate, the heavenly Father presented him to the world as its divine teacher. The Holy Spirit, descending upon Jesus in the form of a dove immediately after his baptism, and the voice from heaven saying: "This is my beloved Son, with whom I am well pleased" (Mt 3:17), are, as it were, the divine credentials guaranteeing his teaching and giving the basic reasons for it. Who could refuse to believe his doctrine if he is the Son of God and the Holy Spirit is with him? Two years later on Mr. Tabor, the same presentation is renewed; the same voice, the same words: "This is my beloved Son with whom I am well-pleased," but this time an explicit mandate is given us: "Listen to him!" (ib. 17:5). By these words an even greater light is cast upon the teaching mission of Christ.

Jesus revealed himself as teacher, as the one and only teacher: "you call me teacher . . . and you are right, for so I am" (Jn 13:13). "Neither be called masters, for you have one master" (Mt 23:10). When Jesus affirmed that he was the life, he also stated that he was "the truth;" later, when Pilate was questioning him about his origin and his mission, he declared: "For this was I born, and for this I have come into the world, to bear witness to the truth" (Jn 18:37). Those who hear and practice his word hear and know the truth. "If you continue in my word, you are truly my disciples, and you will know the truth" (Jn 8:31-32).

2. A man may or may not be a teacher; in either case he remains a man. Jesus, on the other hand, is teacher by nature, because he is the incarnate Word. God is truth, absolute truth; all the truth which is in the Father is communicated to the Word and comes to us through Christ. God "sent his Son, the eternal Word,

who enlightens all men, so that he might dwell among men, and tell them the innermost realities about God. Jesus Christ, therefore, the Word made flesh, sent as a man to men, speaks the words of God" (DV 4).

Jesus is teacher because he is the Word, the substantial Word of the Father, and, as such, he possesses and manifests all truth, all wisdom, all knowledge; indeed, he himself is the truth, the wisdom, the splendor, the light of the Father. It is because of this that Jesus could say that he was the one and only Master. Other teachers know only a part of the truth; Jesus not only knows all truth, but because he is the Word, he *is* the Truth. Other teachers set forth truths which are superior to them, truths which exist outside themselves, and of which they can have but an imperfect knowledge. Jesus, on the contrary, teaches the truth which he himself *is* by nature. His teaching, therefore is supreme, unique and infallible. This is why he said: "I have come as light into the world" (Jn 12:46); and even more explicitly: "I am the light of the world; he who follows me will not walk in darkness, but will have the light of life" (Jn 8:12). Jesus alone could call himself the light of the world, because the Word alone is the light and the spoken word of God.

The teaching of Jesus does not consist then in mere human words, however sublime and elevated they may be, but is the revelation of God himself. This is the Word to which he invites us to open our minds and hearts.

O Father, most high God, point out to me the form and manner and way by which I can know you and attain to you through love. You show us this way and this teaching in your beloved Son ... Therefore the soul that aspires to find divine light must study, meditate, and read continually in the book of life which is the whole life of Christ on earth.

Bl. Angela of Foligno, Il libro della B. Angela II

I adore you, O my God, as the true and only light! From eternity to eternity, before any creature was, when you were alone, alone but not solitary, for you have ever been Three in One, you were the infinite light. There was none to see you but yourself. The Father saw that light in the Son, and the Son in the Father.

Such as you were in the beginning, such you are now ... in this your uncreated brightness, most glorious, most beautiful ... O most gracious God, who shall approach you, being so glorious, yet how can I keep from you?

How can I keep from you? For you, who are the light of angels, are the only light of my soul. You enlighten every man that comes into this world. I am utterly dark, as dark as hell, without you. I droop and shrink when you are away. I revive only in proportion as you dawn upon me.

You come and go at your will. O my God, I cannot keep you! I can only beg of you to stay. "Stay with us, Lord, for it is toward evening." Remain till morning, and then go not without giving me a blessing. Remain with me till death in this dark valley, when the darkness will end.

Remain, O light of my soul, "for it is toward evening." The gloom, which is not yours falls over me ... I am disconsolate and sad. I want something, I know not what. It is you that I want.

J. H. Newman, *Meditations on Christian Doctrine* p. 363-5

59 — THE DOCTRINE OF JESUS

O Jesus, Master, you alone "have the words of eternal life" (Jn 6:68)

1. The truths Jesus taught are so important and essential that, to know them or not, to believe them or not, is a matter of life and death. His doctrine is not optional; rather, it is so essential that we cannot attain eternal life without it. "Whoever believes in him ... (will) have eternal life ... he who does not believe is condemned already, because he has not believed in the name of the only Son of God" (Jn 3:16,18). Compared to the truths taught by Jesus, all others are insufficient.

Because the doctrine of Jesus is absolutely indispensable, he proved its truth by miracles in order to help our weak faith to adhere to it. To the blindly obstinate Jews who refused to believe in him, he said: "These very works which I am doing, bear me witness that the Father has sent me" (Jn 5:36); on another occasion he added: "even though you do not believe me, believe the works." When the disciples of John the Baptist asked him if he were the Messiah in whom they were to believe, he answered simply: "Go and tell John what you hear and see: the blind receive their sight and the lame walk, lepers are cleansed and the deaf hear, and the dead are raised up" (Mt 11:4-5). The Gospel almost always concludes a recital of the wonders performed by Jesus with such words as: "and his disciples believed in him," or, "many believed in him" (Jn 2:11; 11:45), "they were all amazed and glorified God" (Mk 2:12). Jesus is the only teacher who can guarantee with miraclels the truth of his doctrine: "Through his words and deeds, his signs and wonders, ... he confirmed with divine testimony what revelation proclaimed" (DV 4).

2. Jesus wants everyone, even the simple and the ignorant, to understand his doctrine; he often said that he had come "to preach good news to the poor" (Lk 4:18). Jesus is not a teacher seeking glory and praise; he seeks only the good of his disciples. He uses simple language which can be understood by all, and he illustrates the most sublime truths by very ordinary things. Thus, for example, he uses the water in the well to represent the living water of

grace, and the vine of the field to explain the mystery of our union with him, the true vine. Further, Jesus does not wait for us to seek him; he is the Master who goes himself in search of his disciples, and he seeks them everywhere—in the tax collectors' office, in the homes and haunts of the publicans, in the streets and squares, in the country. He teaches in the synagogues and from the porch of the Temple as well as in Peter's boat or on the grassy slopes of the hillsides. He welcomes Nicodemus by night and stops at the well of Sichem to wait for the Samaritan woman.

Jesus explains his doctrine in a manner which is adapted, not only to the mentality and needs of the people of Palestine, but also to that of all future generations. His words are always living and timely, suited to the needs of every age and every people.

His hearers were divided into two groups: the proud, obstinate hearts who refused to believe, even when they saw the most astounding miracles, and of whom Jesus said: "If I had not come and spoken to them, they would not have sin; but now they have no excuse for their sin" (Jn 15:22); and the upright hearts, sincerely eager for the truth, who accepted his words with faith and love. Jesus rejoiced because of them, saying: "I thank thee, Father, Lord of heaven and earth, that thou hast hidden these things from the wise and understanding and revealed them to babes" (Mt 11:25).

O Jesus, you are that gentle Master who taught us the doctrine of truth, and if we follow it, we cannot fall into darkness.

You are the way by which we make progress in your school, that is, the way we follow by imitating your actions; for you said: "I am the way and the truth and the life." This is indeed so, because whoever follows you, O divine Word... in true holy poverty, humbly and meekly bearing every insult and injury, in genuine patience, learning from you, sweet Teacher, who are our way ... such a one returns good for evil to everyone—for such is your teaching.

O gentle Master, you have instructed us well in your way and your doctrine and you told the truth when you said that you are the way and the truth and the life. Therefore whoever follows your way and your teaching will never die, but will receive everlasting life, and neither demon nor any creature, nor injury received will be able to take this from us, unless we ourselves desire it.

St. Catherine of Siena, *Epistolario 101*, v.2

O Lord, my God, how you possess the words of eternal life, where all mortals will find what they desire if they want to seek it! But what a strange thing, my God, that we forget your words in the madness and sickness our evil deeds cause!... What is this, O Lord?... Oh, what great blindness that we seek rest where it is impossible to find it! Have mercy, Creator, on these your creatures. Behold, we don't understand or know what we desire, nor do we obtain what we ask for. Lord, give us light; behold, the need is greater than with the man born blind, for he wanted to see the light and could not. Now, Lord, there is no desire to see...

You alone, O Lord, teach us the truth, and show us the way of salvation. Oh, how unfortunate we are, my Lord! For we believe in everlasting joy and know the truth well; but with so pronounced a habit of failing to reflect on these truths, they have already become so foreign to our souls that these souls neither know about them nor desire to know about them.

Grant, O Lord, that your words may be indelibly inscribed upon my heart.

St. Teresa of Jesus, *Soliloquies VIII* 1-2; *XIII* 2

60 — JESUS REVEALS HIS FATHER

Lord, show us the Father, and we shall be satisfied (Jn 14:8)

1. "This is eternal life, that they know you, the only true God" (Jn 17:3), declared Jesus. And John the Evangelist notes: "No one has ever seen God; the only Son, who is in the bosom of the Father, he has made him known" (1:18). Only Jesus, the Son of God, can give us knowledge of the Father: he alone, as God's Word, is by nature the revealer of God.

Our words express our thoughts; likewise, the Word, the substantial utterance of the Father, expresses the Father and reveals the nature of God. When the Word was made flesh, he continued to be what he was, the Word, the splendor of God, the revealer of God. Becoming incarnate, he made himself known to men, and accessible to our human capacity, but that implied no lessening of his divine nature. Even when Jesus does not speak, his very Person and actions reveal God to us. He often remarked sadly, in the face of misunderstanding, "If you knew me, you would know my Father also" (ib. 8:19). To Philip who, at the Last Supper, asked him to show them the Father, he replied in a tone of gentle reproach, "Have I been with you so long, and yet you do not know me, Philip, He who has seen me, has seen the Father ... Do you not believe that I am in the Father, and the Father in me?" (ib. 14:9-10).

Jesus is the "image of the invisible God" (Col 1:15); it is sufficient to look upon him with faith and love in order to know God. From no other master, through no other way can we acquire such knowledge, indispensable for eternal life. "No one knows the Father except the Son and any one to whom the Son chooses to reveal him" (Mt 11:27). The revelation of the Father is the great gift of Jesus to mankind.

2. When by reason we trace creatures back to their first cause, we are able to know that God exists, that he is the creator and ruler of the universe.

There are other truths, however, which cannot be reached by the human intellect alone, for example, the Trinity of God, the Incarnation of the Word, the universal fatherhood of God, our incorporation in Christ, and our elevation to the supernatural state. We would never be able to arrive at these profound truths, which disclose so many things about God and his intimate life, and which at the same time are concerned with our supreme destiny, if Jesus had not come to reveal them to us. "The deepest truth about God and the salvation of man—states Vatican Council II—is made clear to us in Christ, who is the mediator and at the same time the fullness of all revelation" (DV 2).

Jesus opens the treasure of revelation to us with the greatest authority: "We speak of what we know, and bear witness to what we have seen . . . I speak of what I have seen with my Father . . . Him you do not know. I know him for I come from him" (Jn 3:11; 8:38; 7:28-29). Jesus made use of the parables of the prodigal son and the lost sheep to describe in touching words the goodness of his heavenly Father, "who makes his sun rise on the evil and on the good" (Mt 5:45) and who feeds the birds of the air and clothes the lilies of the field (cf. Mt 6:26,28), thus revealing God's infinite mercy toward us, and his fatherly providence, which provides for us as his children. The revelation of these great truths is further clarified by the works of Jesus: his concern for material and spiritual misery, his love which keeps him continually seeking souls to be saved, even to giving his life for them. The good tidings that Jesus brought to the world consist above all in this revelation of God as infinite charity, of God as our loving Father; the whole New Testament and the whole Christian life are based entirely on this revelation.

O Father, I do not know you because I have never seen you, but I accept all that your divine Son, your Word, reveals to me about you.

O Jesus, by your mysteries, show us your Father, his perfections, his rights, his will; reveal to us what he is for you, what he is for us, so that we may love him and he love us—and we shall ask nothing more. Show us your Father and we shall be satisfied.

C. Marmion, *Christ in His Mysteries III*, 2 (p. 43)

Jesus, teach me to delight in the infinitude of the Father! Speak to me of the Father! Treat me as a child and talk to me of him in the way that earthly fathers talk with their children; treat me as your friend so you can speak to me of him as you did to Lazarus in his home in Bethany; treat me as an apostle of your word and converse with me about him as you did with John; draw me close to your Mother the way you drew your twelve close to her in the cenacle . . . full of hope that the spirit you promised may speak to me again of him, and teach me how to speak of him to my brothers, with the simplicity of a dove and the splendor of a flame.

G. Canovai, *Suscipe Domine*

Lord Jesus, you are the mediator between God and man; not like a diaphragm, but as a channel; not an obstacle, but a roadway; not one wiseman among many, but as the one Master; not just any prophet, but the only one, the indispensable interpreter of religious mystery, the unique One who joins God to man and man to God. No one can know the Father, you have said, except the Son and he to whom the Son (that is yourself), O Christ, Son of the living God, has wished to reveal him (Mt 11:27; Jn 1:18). You are the true revealer, the bridge between the kingdom on earth and the one in heaven. Without you we can do nothing (Jn 15:5).

Paul VI, *Insegnamenti* v. 6

61 — BE PERFECT

Good Teacher, teach me the way that leads to life (Mk 10:17; Mt 7:14)

1. The knowledge of God in which eternal life consists, as Jesus has said, is not the kind of knowledge which stops at the enlightenment of our intellects, but a knowledge which stirs up our wills to love the God whom we know, and which regulates our whole life so that it will be pleasing to him. Consequently, once Jesus has brought us to the knowledge of the Father, he teaches us what we must do to please him: "You, therefore, must be perfect, as your heavenly Father is perfect" (Mt 5:48). In this brief formula, the divine Teacher reveals two great truths: God is the model of sanctity, because he alone is the fullness of perfection, free from every shadow of fault or failing; secondly, God's will in our regard is that we also be perfect, which we shall be according to the degree in which we try to imitate God's perfection.

Yet how can a mere creature imitate divine perfection? Jesus came to us to give us this possibility. The grace which Jesus merited for us and which he is continually giving us, together with the infused virtues and the gifts of the Holy Spirit, raises us from the human level to the supernatural, divine level; we are made sharers in the divine nature, the divine life. Faith also makes us sharers in God's truth and in the knowledge which he has of himself and of all things. Charity gives us a participation in the infinite love with which God loves himself and his creatures.

However, we cannot see God's perfection and holiness, because he "dwells in unapproachable light, whom no man has ever seen or can see" (1 Tim 6:16). But Jesus reveals God to us: he manifests him to us in himself, his works, and his words. Hence, Jesus is the perfect teacher of holiness. He teaches us that God wants us to be holy, shows us God as the supreme, infinite ideal of holiness, and enables us to start out toward this sublime ideal.

2. When Jesus says to us: "Be perfect as your heavenly Father is perfect," he gives us a model of perfection that we can

never exhaust. The perfection of the very greatest saints when compared with God's perfection is nothing. Jesus teaches us, then, not to rest complacently in the degree of perfection we have attained, nor to be satisfied with our progress or even with our efforts. Compared with the lofty ideal he sets before us, we are nothing. This is why he tells us never to stop on the road of holiness, never to say: "This is enough." No matter how much progress we make, we never advance far enough. Who, indeed, can become as just, as merciful as God? As long as we are on earth, our holiness will always consist in a continual striving toward divine perfection. "Strive for it untiringly and uninterruptedly"—says St. Augustine—"no one, as long as he lives, can ever say he has arrived" (In Ps. 83,4).

Among the infinite perfections of God which Jesus has revealed, charity has first place. Precisely because "God is love" (Jn 4:16), Jesus teaches that "the great and first commandment" is the love of God, and the second, like to it, is the love of neighbor (Mt 22:36-39). The commandment of love, like that of striving for perfection, has no limits: however much we love God we shall never succeed in loving him as much as he is capable of being loved, that is, as much as he deserves; and however much we love our neighbor, we shall never love him as God loves him.

The ideal of holiness proposed by Jesus is so sublime that it exacts unceasing progress, a continuous ascent toward ever higher goals. In this sense St. Paul, who had already been raised to the third heaven, writes humbly: "Brothers, I do not consider that I have made (perfection) my own; but one thing I do, forgetting what lies behind and straining forward to what lies ahead, I press on toward the goal." He concludes: "Let those of us who are mature be thus minded . . . only let us hold true to what we have attained" (Phil 3:13-16).

My God, what you ask, more than anything else, is that we imitate you, according to Christ's words: "Be perfect as your heavenly Father is perfect". . . Therefore I wish to give myself to you with a great desire of imitating you in your holiness, and in your purity and charity, in your mercy and patience, your prudence, your gentleness, and in all your other perfections. For this reason I beg you to choose to imprint on my soul a perfect image and likeness of the holiness of your life and of your virtues.

St. John Eudes, *Miseria dell'uomo e grandezza del cristiano* II:8

O Lord, you cannot inspire unrealizable desires. I can, then, in spite of my littleness aspire to holiness. It is impossible for me to grow up, and so I must bear with myself such as I am with all my imperfections. But I want to seek out a means of going to heaven by a little way, a way that is very straight, very short, and totally new. We are living now in an age of inventions, and we no longer have to take the trouble of climbing stairs, for . . . an elevator has replaced these very successfully. I wanted to find an elevator which would raise me to Jesus, for I am too small to climb the rough stairway of perfection. I searched, then, in the Scriptures for some sign of this elevator, the object of my desires, and I read these words coming from the mouth of eternal Wisdom: "Whoever is a little one, let him come to me." And so I succeeded. I felt I had found what I was looking for ... The elevator which must raise me to heaven is your arms, O Jesus! And for this I had no need to grow up, but rather I had to remain little and become this more and more. O my God, you surpassed all my expectation. I want only to sing of your mercies.

St. Teresa of the Child Jesus, *Autobiography,* Ms. C, pp.207-8

62 — WHAT JESUS' TEACHING EXACTS

Lord, I have laid up your word in my heart, that I may not sin against you   *(Ps 119:11)*

1. In calling us to imitate the holiness of his heavenly Father, Jesus summons us to an unrelenting war against sin, which is in direct opposition to God's infinite perfection and is the greatest offense against him. In all his teachings he tries to inculcate in us a deep hatred of sin, especially of pride, hypocrisy, and obstinate willful malice, all of which constitute a state of complete opposition to God. Jesus, who shows such great mercy toward sinners, has scathing words for the Pharisees: "Woe to you, scribes and Pharisees, hypocrites! for you are like whitewashed tombs ... You serpents, you brood of vipers, how are you to escape being sentenced to hell?" (Mt 23:27,33). Again, he describes the ugliness of sin and its disastrous effect on man, lowering him to a state of complete moral degradation, such as that of the prodigal son who, because he had left his father's house, was reduced to "feeding swine" (Lk 15:15).

"Everyone who commits sin is a slave to sin" (Jn 8:34); a slave of sin cannot be a servant of God; hence the Master insists: "No one can serve two masters; for either he will hate the one and love the other, or he will be devoted to the one and despise the other" (Mt 6:24).

Jesus, our Savior, came to destroy sin by his death; it is precisely by his death that he shows us most clearly the terrible malice of sin. Sin is so great an enemy of God and has such destructive power that it brought about the death of the divine Master.

2. "By himself and by his own power, no one is freed from sin or raised above himself, or completely rid of his sickness ... or his servitude. All stand in need of Christ, their Model, their Mentor, their Liberator, their Savior, their Source of life" (AG 8). And

Jesus, who died to destroy sin, continues to grant every soul of good will the sufficient grace to fight it in all its forms.

Only mortal sin is completely opposed to God; this opposition is so great that it separates the soul from God. However, every sin, even venial sin, and every fault and imperfection, is in opposition to God's infinite holiness. Therefore Jesus offers the perfection of his heavenly Father as a norm for our Christian life, and engages us in an intense struggle against sin in order to destroy in us its deepest roots and even its slightest traces. This is what Jesus teaches in these few short words: "deny yourself." We must deny "self" with all its imperfect habits and inclinations; and we must do so continually. Such a task is fatiguing and painful, but it is indispensable if we wish to attain sanctity. Jesus says: "The gate is narrow and the way is hard that leads to life, and those who find it are few" (Mt 7:14). In echo of Jesus, all the masters of the spiritual life insist strongly on detachment and self-renunciation as the indispensable foundation of the spiritual life. St. John of the Cross offers a soul who is desirous of attaining union with God the harsh way of the "nothing."

But first and foremost, it is Jesus, the divine Teacher, who has pointed out to us the absolute necessity of passing through this way: "If any man would come after me, let him deny himself" (ib. 16:24).

Forgive me, my God, oh forgive me the offenses of my childhood, and those of my youth, so many horrible sins, the offenses of my adult years and those of my religious life and all that I have committed up to this very minute ... O my God, there is not a day nor an hour, nor an instant for which I do not owe you immeasurable gratitude; and likewise there is not a day, nor perhaps an hour or even an instant for which I do not need to beg forgiveness a thousand times over! Forgive me, oh! forgive me all my sins and offenses and infidelities ... everything in which I have offended and displeased you, from my birth to the present moment.

Help, O God, make the old man in me die, that part of me which is vile, lukewarm, ungrateful, unfaithful, weak, indecisive and languishing; and "create a new heart within me," warm and brave, grateful, faithful, strong, decided and energetic ... I consecrate to you every moment of the second part of my life ... Make my future the complete opposite of the past, deign to redeem it, make it fully occupied in doing your will, so that every moment may glorify you in the measure of your desire.

C. de Foucauld, *Sulle feste dell'anno,* Op. sp. (It. p. 313)

O Lord, I cry to you like a slave that has been sold listen to me, O you who redeemed me! Under the power of evil I sold myself and received but the wretched enjoyment of the forbidden tree. Here is my cry: Straighten my way which I made crooked, and guide my

steps in conformity with your word ... I am all upside-down under
the weight of iniquity, but your word is the rule of truth; so since I
am crooked by my own fault, set me straight by your yardstick ... I
sold myself by my own will, you redeem me with your blood: put
pride to shame in me, and glorify grace in you, for you resist the pro-
ud and give grace to the humble.

St. Augustine, *Sermon* 30:2

63 — THE INTERIOR TEACHER

O Lord, incline my heart to your testimonies; lead me in the path of
your commandments   *(Ps 119:36,35)*

1. Jesus not only imparts truth to us, he also helps us to accept it. This is the task of any teacher, but he can work only from
the exterior, trying to clear his pupil's mind of the errors which
obscure it and to present the truth in a clear and convincing manner. Jesus, however, does much more than this; his activity is far
more intimate and profound. He is the only teacher capable of acting directly on the souls, the minds, and the wills of his pupils.

Jesus moves our souls *interiorly* to accept his teachings and
to put them into practice. The truths Jesus teaches are divine
mysteries; therefore, we cannot master them by the art of human
reasoning. To accept them, our minds must be equipped with a
new supernatural light and power, the light and power of faith.
Faith comes to us through Jesus as a fruit of his redemptive work:
he is the "author and perfecter of faith" (Heb 12:2), and since he
has merited it, he therefore infuses it in us. Thus, while Jesus is
revealing eternal truths to us, he is also filling our souls with this
divine light, until he produces in us a profound, mysterious
knowledge, giving us an intuition, a *sense* of divine things; he acts
on our wills in the same way by the virtue of charity, drawing us to
love him, our Savior, and our heavenly Father and all our brothers,
impelling us to put his teachings into practice. While Jesus is
teaching us, he is kindling in us the fire of divine love just as he
did in the two disciples from Emmaus, who said to each other:
"Did not our hearts burn within us while he talked to us on the
road, while he opened to us the Scriptures?" (Lk 24:32).

2. "Jesus"—writes St. Teresa of the Child Jesus—"has no
need of books or teachers to instruct souls; he teaches without the
noise of words. Never have I heard him speak, but I feel that he is
within me at each moment; he is guiding and inspiring me with
what I must say and do. I find just when I need them certain
lights which I had not seen until then" (Auto. Ms A., p. 179). Jesus
interiorly teaches souls who know how to listen to him, and he
teaches them above all by his Spirit, the Holy Spirit, according to

what he had promised the apostles: "the Holy Spirit, whom the Father will send in my name, he will teach you all things, and bring to your remembrance all that I have said to you" (Jn 14:26).

Jesus and the Father are always sending the Holy Spirit from heaven into our souls; this divine Spirit makes us understand the profound meaning of our Lord's teaching and suggests practical applications for our daily life.

Jesus teaches us through the authority of the Church, to which he has entrusted the task of preserving his doctrine and transmitting it unchanged to all the faithful.

When we accept Jesus as our Teacher, we must also accept all his teachings: the written words of the Gospel, the living word of the Church, and the mysterious, secret word by which he teaches our souls individually. If his word is to be truly a treasure, it is not enough for us merely to hear it; we must sound the word of Jesus to its depths. "The disciple is bound by a grave obligation toward Christ his Master ever more adequately to understand the truth received from him" (DH 14); an understanding that is acquired by study, but which is deepened through prayer and meditation, imitating Our Lady who "kept all these things in her heart," (Lk 2:19) meditating on everything her divine Son said and did.

O Love, O Master, O my Lord, who are higher than the heavens and deeper than the abyss, the vision of whose marvelous wisdom is the beatitude of all your creatures! ... who look down upon the lowly in this vale of tears and gather the little children to instruct them in the ways of salvation; come, refuse not your lessons to me in my meanness, but refresh me, I beseech you, with your lifegiving doctrine ... Begin at once to teach me; separate me from myself for the ministry of your living charity and affection, and possess, sanctify and utterly fill my spirit.

I am your handmaid, O Jesus most loving! Give me understanding, that I may learn your commandments ... Open straightway unto me the school of chaste love; let me hear your precious teachings, and through you let my soul attain unto holiness and perfection in truth; immerse my spirit so deeply in your charity, that through you I may become a child gifted with understanding, and you yourself may be in truth my Father, Teacher, and Master ...

O Love, O God, how present you are unto them that seek you! How kind, how lovable unto them that find you! If you would but explain to me now the rudiments of your science, that my heart may have one lesson therein from you! ... Let me not be the only one ever left behind in your school of charity, like a tiny chick that cannot profit by your care because it has not yet been hatched; but in you, and through you, or rather with you, let me grow into maturity day by day and advance from strength to strength, daily bringing forth fruit unto you, my Beloved, in the new path of your love.

St. Gertrude, *Exercise* V:4

Divine Master, let me be established in faith, in such faith that it keeps me wide-awake under your eye, and entirely recollected under your creative word...

O eternal Word, expression of my God, may I spend my life in listening to you; may I become completely docile that I may learn everything from you. Then, through all the nights and voids, in all my times of helplessness, may I ever cling to you and dwell in your great light. O my beloved Star, so enchant me that I can never turn from your radiance.

Sr. Elizabeth of the Trinity, *2 Retreat 13*   *Sp. Writings, Philipon*
p. 62

64 — THIRD SUNDAY OF ORDINARY TIME

YEAR A

The Lord is my light and my salvation (Ps 27:1)

Matthew, who is always careful to compare the facts of the life of Jesus with what the prophets had foretold of the Messiah, begins his account of Jesus' apostolic labors by referring to the prophecy of Isaiah about "the land of Zebulun and Naphtali" where the Master was then living: "The people who sat in darkness have seen a great light ... For those who sat in the region and shadow of death, light has dawned" (Mt 4:16). Matthew has seen this prophecy become a reality before his own eyes. The light that illumines Galilee and spreads from there throughout the world is Christ; Matthew has recognized him, followed him and listened to him, and wants to transmit the good news to the whole world. "Jesus began to preach, saying: 'Repent, for the kingdom of heaven is at hand'" (ib. 17). The message is urgent; it is urgent to spread it abroad because the kingdom that Christ has come to establish is offered to all men and is close at hand. The preaching of Jesus, which is completely directed toward conversion and salvation, witnesses to this, as likewise do the miracles that he performs, "healing every disease and every infirmity" (ib. 23), for physical cures are a "sign" of that deeper healing he desires to work in souls. It is also attested to by the choice and calling of the first disciples whom Jesus wished to be coworkers in his ministry of salvation. Matthew points out four of them: Simon and Andrew, James and John. Two of these had already met the Master when the Baptist pointed him out on the banks of the Jordan, and they had immediately gone with him. Now Jesus himself invites them as they are fishing on the lake each with his brother: "Follow me and I will make you fishers of men. Immediately they left their nets and followed him" (ib.

19-20). God does not call us only once in our lifetime; his calls to us are repeated and become ever more pressing and compelling. Now, it is not only a matter of following Jesus, but of becoming "fishers of men" by following him. Their response is as immediate as it was the first time, but enriched now by the generous abandonment of their nets, their boat and, for James and John, even of their father, whom they leave behind on the lake. This is how God's calls should be received, no matter what the way in which they are revealed: both important calls and likewise the most humble ones which come to us through the concrete circumstances of daily life, or in the form of an interior impulse to greater generosity, self-denial and sacrifice.

> *Shine on me, O fire ever burning and never failing (cf. Ex 3:2), and then I shall begin, through and in your light, to see light, and to recognize you truly as the source of light.*
> *Stay, sweet Jesus, stay for ever. In this decay of nature, give more grace. Stay with me and then I shall begin to shine as you shine: so to shine as to be a light to others. The light, O Jesus, will be all from you. None of it will be mine. No merit to me. It will be you who shine through me upon others. O let me thus praise you, in the way which you love best, by shining on all those around me. Give light to them as well as to me; light them with me, through me. Teach me to show forth your praise, your truth, your will. Make me preach you without preaching—not by words, but by my example and by the catching force, the sympathetic influence, of what I do—by my visible resemblance to your saints, and the evident fullness of the love which my heart bears to you.*
> J. H. Newman, *Meditations on Christian Doctrine* p. 365

YEAR B

"Make me to know your ways, O Lord" (Ps 25:4)

"Jesus came into Galilee preaching the gospel of God and saying, 'The time is fulfilled and the kingdom of God is at hand! Repent and believe in the Gospel!' " (Mk 1:14-15). Mark's way of presenting the beginning of Jesus' apostolic ministry does not differ much from that of Matthew, yet it has some significant details which are full of meaning: first of all, the statement: "The time is fulfilled." Now the time of promises and of waiting is over; the Messiah has come and is beginning his ministry. It is his presence which gives fullness to the times and makes them a vehicle of God's mercy and the history of salvation. That is why "the kingdom of heaven is at hand;" so close at hand that the Son of God is among men to teach and open to them the way that leads to it. The kingdom is "at hand," but is not yet a full reality, although in a stage of fulfillment; nearness will become actual presence and personal possession when, by accepting Jesus' invitation, we carry out within ourselves the necessary conditions for entry.

The first condition is conversion, the profound change in our life which requires, above all, a struggle against sin, the denial of everything that makes us deviate from the love and the law of God. This is a conversion like that which God had called for at Ninevah through Jonah and which the Ninevites had carried out, for "they turned from their evil way" (Jon 3:10). But abstaining from sin is only the first phase of the conversion preached by Jesus; a second condition is also required which is clearly expressed in Mark's "believe in the Gospel." The Christian must adhere to the Gospel in a positive way with faith made alive by love which is not satisfied with accepting the Gospel only in theory, but translates it into life, and puts it into practice. It therefore behooves us to put aside that worldly mentality by which we live and act solely in view of our temporal interests and happiness. "The form of this world is passing away," warns St. Paul (1 Cor 7:31); it is not Christian to be attached to it like oysters to a reef. We must develop an evangelical mentality capable of producing desires, intentions, habits, and behavior entirely in accordance with the Gospel of Christ. This is all the more urgent since "time has grown very short" (ib. 29), is, in fact, determined by the coming of Christ, so that now there remains only the one phase of history which separates today from his final coming. Henceforth time has only one purpose: to get man, individually and collectively, into step on his journey toward eternity.

O wicked and perverse love, which bound and drove me, an unhappy sinner, to reject and despise true love and instead to embrace with my whole heart evil love, to desire it, hold it close, and make use of it with all my energies ...

O most merciful Lord Jesus Christ, who alone are worthy of being loved, what can I do, sinner that I am ... I cannot save myself by myself, but I dare not resort to you, because I have not loved you ... Yet I do have recourse to your great tenderness, O Love, by which you lead the wayward back to salvation; O you who are so full of compassion and mercy and want no one to perish, but save those who hope in you. Come then to my aid and pardon my sins; give me the grace never again to look only at myself, but only at you, or else at myself in you.

R. Giordano, *Contemplazioni sull'amore divino* 33

Lord, you alone have the words of eternal life ... We truly believe that you are the divine Word, come down on our earth in order to teach us; you are truly God, speaking to our souls; for God "in these days has spoken to us by his Son" ... We believe in you, O Christ, we accept all that you tell us of the divine secrets, and because we accept your words, we give ourselves to you in order to live by your Gospel. Lead us, O indefectible Light, for in you we have the most invincible hope. You will not reject us; we come to you that we may be brought to the Father.

C. Marmion, *Christ, the Ideal of the Monk* 2

YEAR C

Your words, Lord, are spirit and life (Jn 6:63)

Today, the Liturgy gives special prominence to commemorating the word of God. The first reading presents the solemn proclamation of the divine law which was made at Jerusalem before the entire people gathered in the public square after their return from Babylon. The reading opens with the "blessing" of the priest to which the people answered: "and they bowed their heads and worshipped the Lord with their faces to the ground" (Neh 8:6); he continued reading "from early morning until midday ... and the ears of all the people were attentive" (ib. 3). The details of the people's lament are interesting: first, an expression of repentance for their own offenses, evidenced by their attentive listening to the law; and, at the end, the joyful proclamation: "This day is holy to the Lord, and do not be grieved, for the joy of the Lord is your strength" (ib. 10). Every disposition that is required for heeding God's word is briefly indicated: Respect, attention, comparison of one's own conduct with the holy text, repentance for sin, joy at having once more discovered God's will as expressed in his law.

The Gospel gives us another proclamation of the word, more modest in its external form, but in reality infinitely more solemn. In the synagogue at Nazareth Jesus opened the book of Isaiah and read—certainly not by chance—the passage that concerned his mission: "The spirit of the Lord is upon me, because he has anointed me to preach good news to the poor ... " (Lk 4:18). Only he can read it in the first person, applying directly to himself the prophecy that until now had been read with the soul reaching out toward the mysterious personage that was being foretold, only he can say after finishing the reading: "Today this scripture is fulfilled in your hearing" (ib. 21) ... It is not the Evangelist who makes the connection—Luke simply relates it—but Christ himself; he, the object of the prophecy, is present in person, full of the Holy Spirit, come to proclaim salvation to the poor, the little, the humble. He is the "fulfillment" of the word just read; he, the eternal Word of the Father.

Although not with this same immediacy, Christ is always present in Scripture: the Old Testament but announces and prepares for his coming; the New simply attests to it and spreads his message abroad. Whoever listens to the sacred word in a spirit of faith will always encounter Jesus of Nazareth, and each such meeting signals a new stage of his salvation.

Father of the only Son, full of goodness and mercy, and of love for men . . . you overwhelm with blessings all those who turn to you: look favorably upon our prayer, give us knowledge, faith, piety and holiness . . . We kneel before you, O uncreated Father; through your only Son amend our minds and make them prompt to serve you; grant that we may seek you and love you, that we may search into and plumb the depths of your divine words; stretch out your hand and set us on our feet again; raise us up, O God of mercy, help us to look upward, open our eyes, reassure us, grant we may not have to blush, nor experience shame and condemnation; destroy the contract drawn up against us; write our names in the book of life, put us among your prophets and apostles through your only Son, Jesus Christ.

St. Serapion, *Early Christian Prayers* 190

O Father of Christ, with whom nothing passes unnoticed, hear my prayer today. Let your servant hear your wonderful song. Guide my steps along your ways, O God of ours, through him who knows you because he was born of you: Christ, the king who has freed men from all their miseries.

St. Gregory Nazianzen, *Early Christian Prayers* 248

65 — I AM THE WAY

O Jesus, you left us an example; grant that I may follow in your footsteps. (1 Pet 2:21)

1. Jesus is not only the Master who teaches us how to attain to the perfection of his heavenly Father, but he is also the living model of that perfection. Men, on the other hand, however holy they may be, are by their very nature so limited and imperfect that they can never serve as perfect models for us. At the same time, we cannot see God, who is holiness itself. But the Son of God, his living image, by becoming man, has made infinite perfection incarnate in himself: "in Christ Jesus . . . God perfectly manifested himself and his ways" (DH 11). In Jesus we see, we know, we touch, so to speak, the sanctity of God. The divine perfections, which were beyond our grasp and inaccessible to our senses, we find as a living, concrete, tangible reality in Christ our Lord. The Father has presented him to the world as his beloved Son in whom he is well pleased, because he sees in him his own perfect image and all his own infinite perfections. The Father gives Christ to us, not only as our Master, but as our model, since

from all eternity he predestinated us "to be conformed to the image of his Son" (Rom 8:29).

Jesus himself has told us: "I am the way . . . No one comes to the Father but by me" (Jn 14:6). By his example he shows us how we can approach God's perfection in order to come to him. He says very definitely that we must imitate him: "for I have given you an example, that you also should do as I have done to you" (Jn 13:15); "learn from me, for I am gentle and lowly of heart" (Mt 11:29). When we imitate Jesus, we are imitating our heavenly Father; when we endeavor to practice the virtues as he did, we are drawing nearer to God's infinite perfection. When we become conformable to the image of Christ, we become conformable to the image of the Father; man "is being renewed after the image of his Creator" (Col 3:10).

2. In the Acts of the Apostles we are told that Jesus "began to do and teach" (1:1). All his acts and words are the model for our own. All the virtues which he recommended to his disciples, he himself practiced first, perfectly and in the highest degree. He then told them to do as he had done. His doctrine shows us exactly what our conduct should be in order to resemble his. Therefore all Christian tradition declares that the way to attain sanctity is to imitate Christ, who—as Vatican Council II teaches—"gave us an example that we might follow in his footsteps" (GS 22).

St. John of the Cross writes: "First, have a habitual desire to imitate Christ in all your deeds by bringing your life into conformity with his. You must then study his life in order to know how to imitate him and behave in all events as he would" (Asc I, 13:3). This must not be a merely exterior and material imitation of Jesus' acts; we must endeavor to enter into the interior dispositions of his soul, so as to make these dispositions our own, according to the counsel of St. Paul: "Have this mind among you which was in Christ Jesus" (Phil 2:5). In this way, the imitation of Jesus is based on that is most profound and vital, that is, on his intimate dispositions, which constitute the interior principle of all his actions. This putting on the "mind" of Christ is within the reach of all, whatever our state or condition of life, whereas the exterior imitation of the life of Jesus can never be complete, since it always varies according to the circumstances in which each one finds himself.

Thus, every Christian "with unveiled face, beholding the glory of the Lord," that is reflecting the splendor of Christ's life in his own conduct, will be "changed into his likeness" (2 Cor 3:18).

O Christ, eternal truth, what is your doctrine? And by what path do you direct us to the Father? I can find no way but the one which you have marked out in virtue of the fire of your charity. The path, O eternal Word, which you marked with your blood is the way.

Therefore our fault consists in loving what you hated and in hating what you loved. I confess, eternal God, that I have always loved what you hated and hated what you loved. But I cry out today to your mercy, that you give me strength to follow your truth with an open heart. (Preghiere ed Elevazioni)

Those who follow this road are the sons of the truth, because they follow the truth, and pass through the door of the truth and find themselves united to you, O eternal Father, through the door and the road of your Son, eternal Truth, who is eternal peace. (Dialogue 27:3)
St. Catherine of Siena

You, O Lord, are "the way, the truth, and the life," (Jn 14:6). Earth will never lead me to heaven. You alone are the way; you alone. My God, shall I for one moment doubt where my path lies? Shall I not at once take you for my portion? To whom should I go? You have the words of eternal life. You came down for the very purpose of doing that which no one here below could do for me. None but he who is in heaven can bring me to heaven. What strength have I to scale the high mountain? . . . Though I filled my station well, did good to my fellows, had a fair name or a wide reputation, though I did great deeds and was celebrated, though I had the praise of history, how would all this bring me to heaven? I choose you, then, for my one portion, because you live and do not die. I cast away all idols. I give myself to you.

I pray you to teach me, guide me, enable me, and receive me to you.
J. H. Newman *Meditations on Christian Doctrine XIII,* (2)

66 — I AM IN THE FATHER

May my life be hidden with Christ in God (Col 3:3)

1. The intimate dispositions of Jesus toward God and his relations with him are of the utmost importance to us. Jesus is the Son of God, herein lies all his greatness and holiness. By his very nature, he is the only Son of God; but we, who are made to his image through his mediation, are sons of God by grace, since the Father had "predestined us . . . to be his adopted sons in Jesus Christ" (Eph 1:5). Jesus has shared with us that divine sonship which belongs to him by nature; hence, like him, all our greatness and holiness consists in our living as true children of God. Therefore as far as is consistent with our human nature, we should try to reproduce in ourselves the interior attitude of Jesus toward his heavenly Father.

"The Father is in me, and I am in the Father" (Jn 10:38), says Jesus, revealing his intimate union with him. Jesus, the eternal Word, is united to the Father in a substantial way by his nature;

this is an incommunicable union, which no one can ever imitate. But Jesus, the man, also lives in intimate union with the Father: all his love is concentrated on the Father; all his mind is directed toward him; all his will is fixed on the will of the Father which he fulfills in everything. This union of Jesus with his heavenly Father is the model for our union, because in Christ also it is the fruit of grace. The grace that Jesus possesses is limitless; it has a fullness and a perfection not to be found in any other creature; therefore the union with God that results from it is the most perfect that can be imagined. Yet even the grace given us enables us, at least to a certain point, to keep our souls directed toward the Father, and our will and affection centered on him. Jesus gives us the example himself, and asks for us a close union with the Father, similar to his own: "As you, Father, are in me, and I in you, that they also may be in us" (Jn 17:21). Our Lord could not have asked anything more for those who love him, and the fact that he did ask this in his supreme prayer to his Father is an invitation and encouragement to strive toward this lofty goal.

2. The soul of Jesus is completely immersed in the Blessed Trinity. His human intellect enjoys the beatific vision, in which he sees God, whose nature he possesses; he knows the Person of the Word as the subject of all his human activity, He sees the Father and knows that he is his Son; he sees the Holy Spirit who dwells within him, His heart is filled with created charity, as infinite as the grace which adorns his soul. This charity continually ascends toward his heavenly Father with a very rapid movement, thence to pour itself out upon our souls. Whether Jesus is busy in the workshop at Nazareth, walking the roads of Palestine, preaching, teaching, debating with the Pharisees, healing the sick, or talking with the multitudes—while giving himself to all, he never interrupts that life of wonderful union with the three divine Persons which goes on in the depths of his soul: "He who sent me is with me" (Jn 8;16), "the Spirit of the Lord is upon me" (Lk 4:18).

By means of grace, our souls have become the temples of the Blessed Trinity. The three divine Persons are really present within us, continually offering and giving themselves to us, so that we, even here on earth, may begin to know, love, and possess them. It is by faith that we can know them, by charity that we can love and live in union with them. It was to enable us to possess this life of close union with God that Jesus merited for us the grace and charity which he is continually bestowing upon us. This grace and charity are identically the same as that which fills the soul of Jesus, although given to us in a lesser degree and with far less perfection. Jesus sees God face to face, in the beatific vision; we "see" him through the obscure, yet certain, knowledge of faith.

In this way we, too, can have a share in Christ's interior life which is completely immersed in the Blessed Trinity. Did not St.

Paul say, "Your life is hidden with Christ in God" (Col 3:3)? And can we not aspire to "emulate, by faith, insofar as it is possible for a creature, the hidden, interior life and activity of the intellect and will of the sacred humanity of Jesus Christ, hypostatically united to the Word" (St. Teresa Margaret, *Spirituality*).

O my soul: Consider the great delight and great love the Father has in knowing his Son and the Son in knowing his Father; and the enkindling love with which the Holy Spirit is joined with them; and how no one of them is able to be separate from this love and knowledge, because they are one. These sovereign Persons know each other, love each other, and delight in each other. Well, what need is there for my love? Why do you want it, my God, or what do you gain? . . .

Be joyful, my soul, for there is someone who loves your God as he deserves. Be joyful, for there is someone who knows his goodness and value. Give thanks to him, for he has given us on earth, someone who thus knows him, as his only Son. Under this protection you can approach and petition him, for then his Majesty takes delight in you. Don't let any earthly thing be enough to separate you from your delight, and rejoice in the grandeur of God; in how he deserves to be loved and praised; that he helps you to play some small role in the blessing of his name.

St. Teresa of Jesus, *Soliloquies* VII 2,3

Our Father, you know what is needful for us; if you call us, you likewise give us the grace to come to you. You give us your Son in order that he may be our way, that he may bring us truth, and communicate life to us.

In uniting ourselves with you, O Jesus, we incorporate ourselves with you; you are in us, and we are in you; we stand in the presence of the Father, We do not behold him, but by faith we know ourselves to be with you in the bosom of the Father, in the sanctuary of the divinity . . . In spite of our miseries and our weaknesses, never let us fear to approach God; by your grace, O Savior, and with you, we can be for ever in the bosom of our heavenly Father.

C. Marmion, *Christ in His Mysteries*, 3, p. 55; 16, p. 320-321

67 — THE PRAYER OF JESUS

Through Christ, with Christ, and in Christ, may my prayer give you glory, O Father (RM)

1. Although Jesus was always indissolubly united to his Father by the beatific vision and the plenitude of charity, he willed to consecrate to him exclusively a part of his human activity: the time of prayer. The long years spent at Nazareth and the forty

days in the desert were especially consecrated to prayer, and during his apostolic life Jesus usually prayed during the whole or part of the night.

The Gospel clearly notes this prayer of Christ at the more solemn moments of his life: before he chose the twelve apostles, Jesus "went out into the hills to pray; and all night he continued in prayer to God" (Lk 6:12). He prayed before Peter's confession, before the Transfiguration, at the Last Supper, in Gethsemane, on Calvary, and at many other times. Morever, he frequently interrupted his apostolic activity, desiring to "withdraw to the wilderness and pray" (Lk 5:16); and often, before performing a miracle, he would raise his eyes to heaven and call upon his Father; also, when evening had come, "after he had dismissed the crowds, he went up into the hills by himself to pray" (Mt 14:23).

We cannot imagine a more intimate and profound prayer than the prayer of Jesus. Only in heaven, where it will be given us also to see God face to face, shall we be able to understand it and really participate in it. But even here on earth we can imitate the conduct of Jesus by readily interrupting any activity, even apostolic work, in order to devote to prayer the time assigned to it, leaving everything else to focus our attention on God alone.

2. Only the prayer of Jesus is perfect praise and adoration of the Trinity, perfect thanksgiving and always efficacious supplication. He alone can offer infinite homage to the Trinity. But in his prayer, by which God is perfectly glorified ... Christ always associates the Church with himself; "she is his beloved bride, who ... through him offers worship to the eternal Father" (SC 7). Our prayer has value only insofar as it is united to that of Jesus and is an echo and extension of his.

The prayer of Jesus was completed in sacrifice; sacrifice was its logical accompaniment as well as its culmination; the sacrifice of nights spent in vigil; the sacrifice of fasting and of penance which for forty days accompanied his prayer in the desert; the sacrifice of a laborious life, without having even a place to lay his hand. This rhythm of sacrifice progressively increased, until it reached its maximum in his agony in the garden and on the Cross. At this point, the prayer of Jesus became the total sacrifice of his life for the glory of the Father and the salvation of souls. Our prayer must also be substantiated with sacrifice, with a generous offering of our whole being with Christ, until we become, with him and in him, a sacrifice of praise and propitiation.

While we are on earth, prayer, even contemplation itself, cannot consist solely in the enjoyment of God; it must always be united with sacrifice—only thus is it true. Authentic prayer and contemplation incite the soul to generosity, disposing it to accept for God any labor or toil, and to give itself entirely to him. On this earth, the gift of self is always realized in sacrifice. St. Teresa of

Jesus says that the purpose of the graces of contemplation is precisely to "strengthen our weakness so that we may be able to imitate the Lord in his great sufferings" (IC VII, 4:4).

O Jesus, you withdraw to the mountain to pray alone in order to teach us by your example that, if we want to pray to God with a pure heart and great affection, we too must separate ourselves from the disorder and confusion of the crowd... In this way the prayer that you addressed to your Father on behalf of your disciples will be fulfilled in us: "that the love with which you have loved me may be in them, and I in them" (Jn 17;26)... This will take place when all our love, our every desire, effort, inquiry and thought—everything by which we live and speak and breathe—will be only you, O God; when the unity that reigns between you, Father, and your Son... is transfused into our hearts and souls, when by imitating the pure and indissoluble love with which you love us, we in our turn shall love you with an everlasting and inseparable love, and be so united to you that every breath we take, every thought and every word of ours will bear your mark.

cf G. Cassiano, *Conferenza X* 6,7

The prayer of Christ! It is the greatest and most beautiful mystery of the great mystery of the Incarnation: God-man talking with God... yet the prayer of Christ the man is a true human prayer: he is the son of man who addresses his Father...

O Lord!... if only I too in my infinitely tiny way could pray like that! For you have also established with me a sweet and indescribable union... through communion with your physical body you have made me part of your mystical body, so that I literally live by you and by the effusion of your grace: you have established me in a mysterious oneness... like to that of the Father with you... though that your humanity had with your person is unique... for it was the humanity lived by your divine person, but in which we were all united to you, since we were to participate in your divine nature. If I knew how to keep alive within me the remembrance of the mystery you created within me, my prayer could be a distant shadow of yours... born of continual union with you.

G. Canovai, *Suscipe Domine*

68 — THE WILL OF THE FATHER

I have come to do your will, O God   (Heb 10:7)

1. "When Christ came into the world, he said: 'Sacrifices and offerings you have not desired, but a body have you prepared for me'... Then he said... 'I have come to do your will, O God'" (Heb 10:5-7). These words reveal the constant interior disposition of Jesus with regard to his Father's will. When the apostles begged him to take a little food, he answered: "I have food to eat of

which you do not know ... My food is to do the will of him who sent me and to accomplish his work" (Jn 4:32,34). The only desire of Jesus and the source of his strength is the fulfillment of his Father's will; his gaze is fixed upon it and he never acts save in conformity with it.

The human will of Jesus is so perfectly transformed and so completely lost in the will of God, that he acts only under the influence of this will. "I have come down from heaven not to do my own will, but the will of him who sent me ... because I seek not my own will, but the will of him who sent me" (Jn 6:38; 5:30). This is the refrain that marks his life, the norm that governs his whole behavior, the underlying motive of all his actions. Jesus accomplishes the will of his Father not through necessity, but with absolute sovereign freedom, prompted by his great filial love. His absolute submission to the Father is the characteristic expression of his love and the reason for the Father's own love for him: "The Father loves me because I lay down my life ... No one takes it from me, but I lay it down of my own accord ... This charge I have received from my Father" (Jn 10:17-18). Thus his life, which began with the cry, "I have come to do your will," ends with another which overcomes, through love, all his natural repugnance to his greatest suffering: "Father ... not my will, but yours be done" (Lk 22:42).

2. For us also, the adopted children of God, the way to sanctity, the rule of our actions, must be our heavenly Father's will. Like Jesus we must be nourished by this holy, sanctifying will; we must feed on it at every moment, we must seek it and desire to live by it alone, making it the one great motive for all our actions. We must fully conform our will to God's, so that, as St. John of the Cross teaches, in our thoughts and actions "there is nothing contrary to the will of God" (Asc. I 11:2).

Conformity to God's will and the growth of love in us are the two constituent elements of sanctity and of a life of union with God. These two elements are inseparable, for one depends upon the other. Our increase in love corresponds to our degree of conformity to God's will. Jesus said: "If a man loves me, he will keep my word, and my Father will love him; we will come to him and make our dwelling place with him" (Jn 14:23). "Keeping his word," that is obeying God's will, is the condition for living and growing in love and in grace and, hence, for enjoying the presence of the Blessed Trinity in our soul. The more complete our conformity to God's will becomes, embracing not only the grave precepts, but also the smallest details of the divine law, so as to exclude not only mortal sins, but even venial sins and the slightest voluntary imperfection, and the more we try to seek God's good pleasure in everything and accept all the circumstances of our lives as his will, the more we grow in love and in grace. The three divine Persons, on their part, give themselves more and more to our souls, establishing their in-dwelling ever more fully and profoundly, thus drawing us to greater union with themselves.

Jesus has told us: The Father "is with me, he has not left me alone, for I always do what is pleasing to him" (Jn 8:29).

O eternal Lord, grant that your will may be done always, never mine. We are not in this world to do our own will, but to accomplish the desires of the infinite Goodness which has created us. Of you it was written, O Savior of my soul, that you should do the will of your eternal Father, and at the moment of your conception, with the first human desire of your soul, you lovingly embraced this ordinance of the divine will and set it within your heart, so that it might rule and govern you for ever. Oh, who but you will get for my soul the grace to have no other will than the will of God?

St. Francis de Sales, *On the Love of God VII*, 6

O good Master, you know that nothing is of more profit to us than to consecrate our will to your eternal Father... But, O good Jesus, how little it is that you offer in our name compared to what you ask for us! What we give is in itself nothing at all by comparison with all that has been given to us by so great a Lord. But in truth in offering you this nothing, we are giving all that we can—I mean if we give in the spirit of these words; "Thy will be done on earth as it is in heaven."

If we truly burn with love, let not the prayers we make to so great a lord be words of mere politeness, but let us brace ourselves to suffer with generosity what you desire... it would certainly not be right to mock you so often—for it is by no means seldom that we say the Our Father. O Lord, grant that we may give you once and for all the jewel, which is our will... For the truth is that you give it to us first so that we may give it back to you.

O my Father, your Son gave you this will of mine in the name of us all and it is not right that I for my part should fail. Grant me the grace of bestowing on me your kingdom so that I may do your will, since he has asked this of me. Dispose of me as of that which is your own, in accordance with your will.

St. Teresa of Jesus, *Way* 32:9,1,7-10 (E. Allison Peers)

69 — THE WORKS OF THE FATHER

O Jesus, may I work with you the works which the Father has entrusted to me   *(Jn 9:4)*

1. "The works which the Father has granted me to accomplish, these very works ... I am doing ... We must work the works of him who sent me" (Jn 5:36;9:4). Jesus has no other aim than to accomplish the mission entrusted to him by the Father, and to accomplish this mission for the glory of the Father himself

and for the redemption of mankind. Burning with desire to perform this work perfectly, he goes to face his passion and to embrace the cross. "I have earnestly desired to eat this passover with you" (Lk 22:15), he will say on the evening of the last Supper, knowing that that passover would be the prelude to his supreme sacrifice.

We are all called to share in the great redemptive work of Jesus, and consecrated souls are especially invited to cooperate in his work: "they"—the Council teaches—"impelled by a love which the Holy Spirit has poured into their hearts . . . spend themselves ever increasingly for Christ and for his Body the Church" (PC 1). Above all, we must cooperate with grace, so that the fruits of the redemption can be fully applied to our souls. This is the work of our own personal sanctification. It is not limited to this one aspect, however . . . We are called to sanctify ourselves in order to be able to bring others to salvation, and growth to the Church. We must collaborate with Christ in extending his kingdom and in gathering into his fold the "children of God who are scattered abroad" (Jn 11:52) in order to bring the fruits of the redemption to as many as possible. This work is entrusted to us by the heavenly Father and we must apply ourselves to it with the interior disposition of Christ: a total, generous, exclusive dedication, a love capable to making even the greatest sacrifices. All actions are of value only insofar as they help toward the accomplishment of this work.

Let us repeat with Jesus: "I must work the works of him who sent me."

2. "I am not alone for the Father is with me—My Father is working still and I am working—As I hear (from the Father) I judge—I do nothing on my own authority, but speak thus as the Father has taught me" (Jn 16:32; 5:17,30; 8:28).

Jesus not only devoted himself completely to the mission entrusted to him by the Father, but in accomplishing this mission, and in every detail of it, he always acted in union with the Father and in perfect harmony with him, always depending upon him and regulating his whole life according to what he heard and saw in him. His acts were but the human, tangible expression of the unceasing, invisible work of the Father: "The Son can do nothing of his own accord, but only what he sees the Father doing. For whatever he does, the Son does likewise. For the Father loves the Son and shows him all that he himself is doing" (Jn 5:19-20). Jesus could not manifest more clearly the absolute accord of his life and actions with the Father, which stems from the infinite love which units them in most intimate and perfect communion.

Although in a much more modest form and only by analogy, yet for all that in a real way, every soul in the state of grace can say, "I am not alone, for the Trinity is in me: the Father, Son and

Holy Spirit." Our attitude should mirror the attitude of Jesus: we must work in continual dependence upon God present within us, listening to his voice, to the interior motion of grace, and acting in accordance with it. We must conform our judgment to God's will, trying to see everything in his light, and working in such a way that our actions will always be in harmony with his views, designs, and good pleasure. In all our actions we, too, should be able to say, "I do nothing by myself, I act according to God's inspiration, in order to do what is most pleasing to him."

Any work, no matter how exalted, which deviates from this line of conduct is, from a supernatural point of view, vain and sterile.

Father, Son and Holy Spirit, O burning and creating Trinity, who lead all creatures in the universe toward their eternal destiny with strength and sweetness, join me to the fecundity of your action, give me a soul like Christ, a soul like the Redeemer.

Let my whole life unroll on the plane of redemption, with full awareness that your eternal plans are realized through the smallest details of human existence. By the light of your inspiration and with the help of your grace, may I choose to be redeemer and collaborator in the wonderfully fruitful action of your Trinity in the world . . .

Grant me invincible strength of heart. Make my love for you stronger than death. Never let my will bend in the face of duty, nor anything succeed in diminishing my ardor in your service. Instill in me the courage to undertake great things and give me the strength to accomplish them, even to martyrdom, if that is necessary, for the greater glory of your name.

M.M. Philipon, *Consecration to the Holy Trinity*

O Jesus, if only I could imitate you by making the salvation of men the work of my life to the point where the word "Savior" would perfectly express what I am, as it does indicate perfectly what you are. For the sake of this I want to become everything to everyone with the one only desire of my heart being that of giving you to souls . . .

Lord, light within me a passionate desire to save souls; let me know how to prepare and do everything in view of that, and know how to put the good of souls before everything else; help me to be always zealous in making use of the means you give us for converting and saving unbelievers: the offering of the holy Sacrifice, adoration of the most holy Sacrament, kindness, prayer, penance, good example and personal sanctification. "As the pastor, so the flock;" "the good that a soul does is in direct proportion to its interior spirit."

cf, C. de Fouauld, Retraite a Beni-Abbes, *Spir. Writings*

70 — FOR THE GLORY OF THE FATHER

To you alone, O Father, be glory for evermore through Jesus Christ
(Rom 16:27)

1. "I honor my Father . . . I do not seek my own glory—I do not receive glory from men" (Jn 8:49-50; 5:41).

It is evident that Jesus ever sought only his Father's glory, and to this end chose for himself utter humiliation, even to becoming "scorned by men, despised by the people" (Ps 22:7). Bethlehem, Nazareth, Calvary—these wre the great stages of the humble, hidden life of Jesus, in which he veiled his glory as the Son of God. Even during his public life, when his divinity was more openly manifested, Jesus tried to flee as much as possible from human glory. Many times after performing a miracle, he imposed silence on those who had witnessed it. "See that no one knows it" (Mt 9:30), he says to the two blind men whose eyes he had opened with a single gesture. He commands Peter, James, and John, the witnesses of his transfiguration, "to tell no one what they had seen, until the Son of man should have risen from the dead" (Mk 9:9); and following the first multiplication of the loaves, "perceiving that they were about to come and take him by force to make him king, he withdrew again to the hills by himself" (Jn 6:15).

The glory of Jesus lies in the fact that he is the Son of God: he desires no other glory. It is as though he would relinquish this essential glory if he accepted any other. Therefore he said: "If I glorify myself, my glory is nothing; it is my Father who glorifies me" (Jn 8:54). Just as the Father finds all his pleasure in his beloved Son, so the Son takes delight only in his Father, and in the glory his Father gives him; and, besides, he accepts this not so much for himself, but because it redounds to the glory of the Father himself. Jesus knows that after his death he will rise again to be glorified and acknowledged as the Son of God and Savior of the world, but he desires even this glory to be the glorification of his Father: "Father, the hour has come; glorify your Son that the Son may glorify you" (Jn 17:1).

2. If a Christian wants to live in imitation of Jesus, he must seek only God's glory, and for himself no other glory than that of a child of God, a brother of Jesus Christ, and a member of his mystical Body.

We must always be on our guard against that tendency of pride which inclines us to seek a little satisfaction, praise and personal glory even in our most spiritual actions. If we seek glory for ourselves, though it be only in insignificant matters, this glory is of no value; it elevates us in the eyes of men, but lowers us in God's eyes; it lessens and may even endanger our glory as children of God.

Seeking human glory and taking pleasure in it hinder and blind us on our way to perfection. Jesus said to the proud, haughty Pharisees, "How can you believe, who receive glory from one another and do not seek the glory that comes from the only God?" (Jn 5:44). More often than we perhaps think certain crises of faith have their root in pride.

Only profound humility, joined to great uprightness of intention, will enable us to overcome the snares and deceptions of pride, and to put resolutely aside the pretenses of self, to silence the interior voices of self-esteem and vain complacency, and to act without concern for the opinion of others, seeking always and in everything only the glory of God. St. John of the Cross urges us to fix our eyes on the interior dispositions of Jesus and to renounce everything that "is not purely for the honor and glory of God . . . for the love of Jesus Christ, who in this life, had no other gratification, nor desired any other, than the fulfillment of his Father's will" (Asc I 13:4).

> *O Jesus, like a giant, you rejoice to run the way of your mission in pursuit of the glory of the Father. This is your primal disposition. You tell us clearly: "I seek not my own will, but the will of him who sent me . . . I seek not my own glory, but that of him who sent me" . . . You seek it to such a degree that you have no solicitude for your own. You have ever these words upon your lips: "My Father" . . . For you all is summed up in seeking the will and glory of your Father.*
>
> *And what constancy in this search! You yourself declare that you never deviated from it: "I do always the things that please him" . . . The primary and habitual sentiment of your soul is this: I live for my Father, I love my Father, and because I love him I give myself up to all he wills.*
>
> *So to please our heavenly Father, in order that he be glorified, that his kingdom be established within us and his will be done by us totally and steadfastly—that, O Jesus, is the perfection you teach me.*
>
> C. Marmion, *The Trinity in our Spiritual Life* 13

> *Grant me, O Christ, a habitual desire to imitate you in all your actions, bringing my life into conformity with yours. Help me, then, to renounce everything that is not purely for the honor and glory of God, and out of love for you, O Jesus, who in this life neither had, nor wished to have, any other gratification than to do the Father's will, which you called your meat and food (Asc I 13:3-4).*
>
> *Grant that I may serve you with a pure and entire love without any interest in joy, pleasure, comfort and praise—that I may serve you with no other interest or satisfaction than your honor and glory (Asc III 27:5).*
>
> St. John of the Cross

YEAR A

Save us, O Lord our God ... that we may give thanks to your holy name

(Ps 106:47)

After announcing God's punishment to sinning Israel, Zephaniah gives a word of hope: "Seek the Lord, all you humble of the land" (2:3). Salvation is offered to the humble; God will scatter the proud and the rebellious, and only a "remnant" will remain of Israel, a "remnant" made up of the humble and the poor. "I will leave in the midst of you a people humble and lowly, who shall seek refuge in the name of the Lord" (Zeph 3:12).

Jesus has come to bring salvation to this "remnant," to these "poor and lowly ones;" so it is not surprising that the sermon on the mount opens with the joyous message: "Blessed are the poor in spirit: for theirs is the kingdom of heaven" (Mt 5:3). However, we quickly note an important specification. It is not material poverty that he calls blessed, but that spiritual disposition—that being "poor in spirit"—by which we base our trust, not on ourselves nor on worldly goods, but upon God. Material poverty is blessed only to the extent that it leads to this interior attitude. The other beatitudes are to be understood in the same way. "Blessed are those who mourn," that is, those who accept the trials of life, recognizing that God has the right to try them through suffering, without in any way doubting his fatherly love. "Blessed are the meek," who although poor and afflicted, are not rebellious nor tempted to procure a better situation for themselves through violent means or by trying to overcome others. "Blessed are they who hunger and thirst for righteousness," not because they want to claim what is theirs, but rather because they aspire to a justice that is a virtue, a greater holiness. "Blessed are the merciful," since, aware of their own need of God's mercy, they know how to compassionate and sympathetically excuse the faults of others. "Blessed are the pure in heart," for their souls are not darkened by passion and sin, and thus they are capable of understanding the things of God. "Blessed are the peacemakers," who, since they are at peace with God and with themselves, sow the seed of peace wherever they go. "Blessed are those who are persecuted for righteousness' sake," who suffer for a just cause, for their faith, for the Gospel. All these categories of persons have an essential attitude in common, which makes them apt for the kingdom of heaven and open to God. Rather than trust in their own material or moral resources these put their trust in God; rather than seek their satisfaction in the goods of earth, they live in expectation of those of heaven. To these are promised God, his kingdom and his mercy, the vision of the Godhead and everlasting happiness. To be numbered among these "blessed," we must have the right dispositions, without which one cannot be a disciple of Christ, nor be saved by him.

O Jesus, you proclaim blessed the poor in spirit, not only those poor who have left all to follow you—those to whom you promised the hundredfold in this life and eternal life in the next, but also those whose spirit is detached from earthly goods, those who really live in poverty without murmuring or becoming impatient; those whose hearts are not attached to riches ... nor dominated by pride or injustice or the insatiable greed which takes everything for self ... Since on this earth poverty makes a person contemptible, weak and powerless, O Lord, you promise the poor happiness ... in the highest degree in the form of a kingdom ... What would we not be prepared to suffer for a kingdom and, what is more, for a heavenly kingdom? ...

O Lord, I give you everything, I abandon everything in order to belong to this kingdom! Oh that with such a hope to sustain me, I may be able to rid myself of everything as is necessary! I am stripping myself in heart and soul, and if it pleases you to despoil me altogether, I submit to it from this moment.

J.B. Bossuet, *Meditazioni sul Vangelo* I 2,v.1

Far be it, Lord, far be it from the heart of your servant who here confesses unto you, far be it, that, be the joy what it may, I should therefore think myself happy. For there is a joy which is not given to the ungodly, but to those who love you for your own sake, whose joy you yourself are. And this is the happy life: to rejoice, united to you, of you, for you; and outside this, there is no other. For they who think there is another, pursue some other and not the true joy.

St. Augustine, *Confessions X*, 32

YEAR B

O Lord, that I may hearken to your voice, and harden not my heart
(Ps 95:7-8)

"The Lord your God will raise up for you a prophet like me ... him you shall heed! ... I will put my words in his mouth; and he shall speak to them all that I command him" (Deut 18:15, 18). Thus God promised Moses; and an uninterrupted series of prophets followed him, announcing the word of God to the world. The line ended with him who was not just one of the prophets, but the Prophet: Christ Jesus. He not only has God's word on his lips, he is his incarnate Word; "by the very fact of his presence and by his revelation of himself" (DV 4), he reveals God with his entire life and works. He makes known to men all that the Father commands him; all that he has heard from his Father (Jn 15:15).

Mark relates that when Jesus went into the synagogue at Capharnaum and began to teach, "those who were listening were amazed, because he taught like one having authority." Even the evil spirit present in a poor possessed man avoided him and, while shouting to Jesus to keep quiet, could not but recognize in him "the Holy One of God." Then, when the Lord had expelled the demon, thus freeing the man who had been possessed by it, the amazement of those present changed to fear: "What is this? A new teaching—with authority! He commands even the unclean spirits and they obey him!" (Mk 1:21-28) Jesus is teaching a new doctrine: consider for example the beatitudes, the commandment to love, the counsels of the gospel; he manifests a new power: he drives out demons without restoring to exorcism, by a mere command only, with an immediate effect. He is the new man who renews the world precisely because he is the God-Man. In him the revelation of God and the communion of God with men reach their summit.

This new fullness of God's gift requires a new fullness of response on man's part. How can we dispute God's right to first place in our hearts and lives, when he offers himself so freely to us? Although this is the inescapable duty of all the faithful, still there are various degrees of it. St. Paul notes that married people, who are occupied by family obligations, are unable to give themselves to the service of God as fully as those who are consecrated; he praises and recommends virginity, which permits a person to be concerned with the things of the Lord with undivided heart and devotion (cf. 1 Cor 7:35). Consecrated virginity is a special type of the new response owed to God by the followers of Christ, and at the same time serves to remind all of us that God must always be given first place.

After having spoken to our forefathers in many and various ways by the prophets, in these last days, O God, you have spoken to us by your Son, your Word; by his word the heavens were made, and by the breath of his mouth all their host (Ps 33:6). Speaking through your Son, you have revealed for all to see, how much and in what way you have loved us. You did not spare your Son, but for our sake gave him who loved us and offered himself for us in sacrifice.

He is your Word, O Lord, the omnipotent Word that you speak to us. While silence enveloped all things—the deep silence of error—he came down from his kingly throne (Wis 18:14-15) to battle against the darkness of sin and to bring us love. In everything he did, in everything he said on earth, even to the insults he endured and the being spat upon and slapped, even to the cross and death, you desired to speak to us in your Son in order to arouse and awaken our love for you by your love for us.

William of St. Thierry, *Tract on contemplating God*
6:12-13

YEAR C

You are my hope, O Lord, my trust from my youth (Ps 71:5)

Jesus' first sermon in the synagogue of Nazareth scored a success similar to that which he had achieved in the synagogue of Capharnaum (Mk 1:22,27). "All spoke well of him and wondered at the gracious words wich proceeded out of his mouth" (Lk 4:22). But the Nazarenes soon let themselves be swept away by considerations that were too human: perhaps Christ was just a man like themselves, the son of Joseph? For if he really was the Messiah, why did he not perform in his own country the miracles he did elsewhere? Did his own countrymen not have a more special claim to them?

Jesus intuitively senses these complaints and answers: "No prophet is acceptable in his own country" (ib. 24). But he does not alter his course; in fact, to show that man cannot dictate to God, and that God is free to distribute his gifts to whom he wishes, he reminds them of the case of the widow of Sarepta, to whom, in place of all the widows of Israel, the prophet Elias was sent, and that of the stranger Naaman, the only leper whom Elisha healed. Jesus wants his fellow-countrymen to understand that he came to bring salvation not to one city or one people in particular, but to all men, and that divine grace is not bound to country or race or personal merit, but rather is completely gratuitous. The Nazarenes reacted violently; blinded by their human spirit and angered at not having gotten what they expected, "they put him out of the city, and led him to the brow of the hill . . . that they might throw him down headlong" (ib. 29).

It is the fate the world has in store for those who, like Christ, have the mission of proclaiming the truth. The Biblical account of Jeremiah's calling records it and parallels the passage of Luke we are now considering. God had chosen Jeremiah to be a prophet, even before his birth, but when, as a young man, he became aware of this choice, he trembled, and foreseeing the dangers of such a life, was about to refuse. But God encouraged him: "Be not afraid of them, for I am with you to deliver you" (Jer 1:8). One who is chosen by God to be his spokesman can count on divine grace, which has already prepared him and will be with him in every situation. He will not lack contradiction, danger and risk, just as the prophets and Jesus himself did not lack them, but God will repeat to him as to Jeremiah: "They will fight against you, but they shall not prevail against you, for I am with you . . . to deliver you" (ib. 19). If prophets and apostles have the obligation to face every danger with courage, the faithful have that of heeding them and following them in a spirit of faith without permitting themselves to be led astray by human considerations.

*In you, O Lord, do I take refuge; let me never be put to shame.
In your justice deliver me and rescue me . . . Be to me a rock of
refuge, a strong fortress to save me, for you are my rock and my fortress. Rescue me, O my God, from the hand of the wicked . . . For
you, O Lord, are my hope, my trust, O Lord, from my youth. Upon
you I have leaned from my birth; you are he who took me from my
mother's womb. My praise is continually of you.*

Psalm 71:1-6

*We pray with all our heart, O Lord, that you may enable us to
fight to the end for truth with all the strength of our soul and body.
If the time comes for our faith to be tested—since as gold is tried in
the furnace, so our faith will be tested through danger and persecutions—if a persecution breaks out, grant that we may be prepared so
that our house may not collapse in winter, and our dwelling not be
destroyed by storms as if built upon sand.*

*And when the winds of the devil blow, that is, of the worst of the
spirits, may our works stand firm, as they have done up to today if
they are not undermined from within; and grant that, prepared for
any trial, we manifest the love we have for you, O God, to whom
belongs the glory and the power for ever.*

Origen, from *Early Christian Prayers* 61

72 — JESUS AND MANKIND

*Grant me, O God, to live in harmony with my brothers in accord
with Christ Jesus.* *(Rom 15:5)*

1. Jesus always remains in closest union with the Blessed
Trinity and therefore in the most profound contemplation, yet he
is ever mindful of the needs of mankind. It was for men Jesus
came—to save them and bring them to the Father; and he gives
himself to them with the utmost solicitude and love. The same
charity which unites Jesus to his Father descends upon the men
created by the Father's love. Jesus wills to redeem them all
because they belong to the Father, to whose image and likeness
they were created.

In a most touching manner Jesus expresses his tender love for
men, comparing himself to the Good Shepherd: "I am the good
Shepherd. I know my own and my own know me as the Father
knows me and I know the Father; and I lay down my life for the
sheep" (Jn 10:14-15). Jesus likens his union with us to the union he
enjoys with his Father, the terms of comparison being knowledge
and love. Certainly it is only a simple similitude and yet Jesus
delights to speak of it, to show how much he loves every man. He
sees and knows the Father in the splendor of his glory, but he also
sees and knows each one of us as an individual, in the reality of our
poverty, sorrows and longings. He loves the Father and gives

himself totally for his glory, and at the same time he loves each one of us and gives himself wholly for our salvation; or rather Jesus sees and knows us only in the Father and in relation to him. This is the very reason for his love for all humanity and for each individual creature; his infinite love for the Father has made him the good Shepherd who gives his life for his sheep. At the hour of his passion Jesus will say: "I do as the Father has commanded me, so that the world may know that I love the Father. Come then! Rise, let us go hence" (Jn 14:31). It is precisely because he so loves the Father, that Jesus loves men and goes willingly to face death on the cross for their salvation.

2. Our love and contemplation of God, our desire for intimate union with him, should not make us strangers to our brethren, should not lessen our sensitivity to their needs and sufferings; it should not prevent us from giving ourselves to them with true supernatural charity, as far as our state in life permits. No state of life, even the most contemplative, can exclude us from the duty and necessity of caring for our neighbor: if external works are reduced to a minimum, we must devote ourselves to our neighbor by prayer and apostolic immolation. The Council affirms in this perspective that those who are consecrated to God do not thereby become "strangers to their fellowmen or useless citizens of this earthly city. For even though in some instances religious do not directly mingle with their contemporaries, yet in a more profound sense these same religious are united with them in the heart of Christ" (LG 46). When love for God is genuine and intense, it does not confine the soul within itself, but leads it to open itself, with all "the tenderness of Christ" to the needs of the neighbor, seeing them as brothers, as God's creatures, his children and the object of his love.

Although Jesus was God, he did not hold himself aloof from men. He willed to feel and experience all their needs, even their temptations, "yet without sinning" (Heb 4:15); he shared with them a life of privation, fatigue, poverty and suffering. Therefore if we wish to attain to an effective fraternal charity, we must feel the sorrows, the poverty, and the material and spiritual needs of our neighbor; we must feel these in order to sympathize with him, help him, and even share in his trials. We must sacrifice ourselves, our ease and comfort, in order to give ourselves to others. We shall be able to do this only if our love resembles the love of Jesus, that is, if it springs from our love of God.

"God grant you to live in harmony with one another in accord with Christ Jesus" (Rom 15:5) writes St. Paul. Only one who loves as Jesus loves, who loves in and for God, is capable of a generous, persevering fraternal love that extends to all and never fails.

> O sweet and kind Lord Jesus Christ, source of true love, you loved us with sweet tenderness . . . when you humbly put on our mortal flesh . . . impelled only by your loving affection . . .

O Lord Jesus Christ, you have been our life, our kindly friend, our prudent adviser and our strong support . . . and just as, through your excessive goodness, you once appeared visibly on our earth in order to accomplish our salvation, so now, through your immense love for our souls, you come invisibly every day to save us, and enlighten our minds with your invisible and powerful grace.

If I were to consider your infinite goodness, O most merciful Lord Jesus Christ, I would have no need to cross the ocean or penetrate the clouds or scale mountains, since I need no long journey to arrive at loving you. I only need to watch myself, to bestir myself to compunction of heart and to confession . . . in order to reach you through grace and love.

R. Giordano, *Contemplazioni sull'amore divino* 3

O my Jesus, how great is the love you bear the children of men, for the greatest service one can render you is to leave you for their sake and their benefit—and then you are possessed more completely. For although the will is not so satisfied through enjoyment, the soul rejoices because it is pleasing you. And it sees that while we live this mortal life, earthly joys are uncertain, even when they seem to be given by you, if they are not accompanied by love of neighbor. Whoever fails to love his neighbor, fails to love you, my Lord, since we see you showed the very great love you have for the children of Adam by shedding so much blood.

St. Teresa of Jesus, *Soliloquies* 2:2

73 — LIVING CHRIST

O Lord, may your life be manifested in our mortal flesh (2 Cor 4:11)

1. The imitation of Christ should not be limited to some particular aspect of his life; it means living Christ and becoming completely assimilated to him, and living his life as far as it is possible to us. The life-giving principle of participation in his life is grace, always joined to charity; the more we grow in grace and charity, the more we are ready to live Christ. In fact, the grace received in baptism renders us like to him: "In this holy rite"—the Council declares—"a union with Christ's death and resurrection is both symbolized and brought about" (LG 7). In death, because through baptism we are buried in Christ's death, which destroys sin in us; in the resurrection, because baptism confers grace upon us and so associates us with the life of the Lord, now risen and living in glory. Day by day we must live what baptism accomplishes and signifies: it is up to us faithfully to keep sin dead in us, and therefore to struggle generously against our passions and any inclination which could lead us toward evil. Sin is a contradiction and something abnormal for those who are baptized: "You must consider yourselves dead to sin"—St. Paul exhorts—"do not let

sin reign in your mortal body" (Rom 6:11-12). Dead to sin, we must live in Christ, in the fullness of the grace which makes us share in his resurrection while still here on earth. "If we have been united with him in a death like his, we shall certainly be united with him in a resurrection like his" (ib. 5). Christian perfection consists essentially in this participation in the mystery of the death and resurrection of Christ: in dying with him in order to live a new life with him, his own life.

"For me to live is Christ," exclaims the Apostle (Phil 1:21), who so fully lived in him that he could say: "It is no longer I who live, but Christ who lives in me" (Gal 2:20).

2. "This life—writes St. John of the Cross—"is not good if it is not an imitation of his life" (Let 23). The life of a Christian must be a prolongation of the life of Christ, and is of value only in the measure that it mirrors his life. This is the great testimony that the world expects of us who believe, and it is the most efficacious and convincing of testimonies. St. Paul never tires of impressing it on us: "Let the life of Jesus be manifested in our mortal flesh" (2 Cor 4:11). Faced with this duty we understand still better that all sin, and not only mortal sin, is in absolute antithesis to Christian life, which ought to shine with the holiness of Christ the Lord.

To live the holiness of Jesus means to spend our lives, as he did, for the glory of the Father and the salvation of men. We can no longer live for ourselves or for our own selfish interests; we belong to him who redeemed us with his blood and animated our life with his own life. Therefore he has the right to see that his redeeming work and his sanctifying grace do not come to naught in us. When Jesus looks upon the redeemed, he must be able to recognize them as living branches of his vine, worthy members of his Mystical Body in which there is nothing contradictory to his holiness.

"The love of Christ urges us"—cries St. Paul—"for we are convinced that one has died for all . . . that those who live might live no longer for themselves, but for him who for their sake died and was raised" (2 Cor 5:14-15). One who is really struck by the thought that Jesus died for our salvation will want to return his love by wearing out his whole life for him, living it for him, offering it to him to be of whatever use he wishes, just as Jesus had spent himself each day of his mortal life for the glory of the Father and for the world's salvation. This was the great desire of Sr. Elizabeth of the Trinity who aspired to be for Christ "another humanity in which he might renew all his mystery" (Elevation).

O my beloved Christ, crucified by love, may I be a bride after your own heart; may I cover you with glory and love you unto death! Yet I realize my weakness and beg you to clothe me with yourself, to identify my soul with all the movements of your own; I beg you to envelop me, to surge up within me; to substitute yourself for me, that my life may be but a radiance of your own. Come and dwell in me as Adorer, as Restorer and as Savior...

O consuming Fire, Spirit of love, descend upon me and effect in my soul as it were an incarnation of the Word, that I may be to him another humanity wherein he renews all his mystery. And, O Father, incline yourself toward your poor little creature, and overshadow her, seeing in her only your beloved Son in whom you are well pleased.

Elizabeth of the Trinity, *Spiritual Writings* (Philipon) 50

O Lord Jesus! May we live in you and for you, as you live in your Father and for your Father. May our soul be pure capacity for receiving you, and be completely filled by you, just as your Humanity is total capacity for receiving God and is filled by God in all fullness. Just as the fullness of the Godhead rests happily in you, may you be our everything, our sufficiency, our fullness. Grant, by your grace, that living and established in you who are our life and foundation, we may always say in all truth... who can separate us from the love of Christ?

O Jesus, my Lord, you are the true life, the model of our life, the pattern that was shown us upon the mountain... and to which we are commanded to conform our life. Then grant that, deep within us, we may be occupied in contemplating, adoring, and imitating your interior life! May our own spiritual life ever consider and imitate the practices and occupations of your divine soul and most holy life. Following your example, may we all contemplate and adore with you the same divine object, your Father!

P. de Berulle, *Le Grandezze di Gesu* 5:8, 3:4

74 — CHRIST OUR ALL

Blessed be you, O Father, who have blessed us in Christ with every spiritual blessing　　　　　　　　　　　　　　　　　*(Eph 1:3)*

1. Jesus, the incarnate Word, is both true God and true Man. As Man, he is our *Way:* he came to take us by the hand and lead us back to our Father's house. He is the source of our life because he merited grace for us and still continues to dispense it to us; he is the Master who shows us the way to go to God; the Model who, by his example, teaches us how we should live as children of God. Having merited our participation in the divine life, which he as Word possesses in its full plenitude, Jesus has made us worthy to be readmitted to the intimacy of the family of God. "This means that you are no longer strangers and sojourners"—St. Paul affirms—"but you are fellow citizens of the saints and members of the household of God" (Eph 2:19).

In his last prayer, as if summing up his work as Redeemer, Jesus said to the Father: "The glory which you have given me I have given to them" (Jn 17:22). Jesus shares with men his glory as

Son of God, making them through grace children of God. He treats them as such: he loves them as brothers and brings them to the intimacy of the Father so that the love of the Father may be poured out upon them also. "I have called you friends for all that I have heard from my Father I have made known to you" (Jn 15:15); the whole purpose of his friendship and of these confidences was to make them share in the love of the Father: "Righteous Father . . . I made known to them your name, and I will make it known that the love with which you have loved me may be in them" (Jn 17:26).

Jesus shares everything he possesses with us: his glory as Son of God, his divine life, the Father's secrets, and even the love with which the Father loves him. In him we find everything we can desire, everything we need for our salvation and for our sanctification, for our life of union with God. Truly all mankind can repeat with the apostle: "Blessed be God . . . who has blessed us in Christ with every spiritual blessing" (Eph 1:3).

2. Jesus is also our *end*. He is the incarnate Word and, as the Word, he is in all things equal to the Father and the Holy Spirit. Equally with the Father and the Holy Spirit he is our beginning, the Creator of everything in the natural and supernatural order. He is also our last end, the end toward which we must move in this life with faith, generosity and perseverance, in expectation of the joy of eternal union with him and the Father and the Holy Spirit in heaven. Jesus, as Man, merited grace for us; as the Word he bestows it on us. He creates it in union with the other two Persons of the Blessed Trinity. If, as Man, Jesus merited the coming of the Holy Spirit, as the Word, He, together with the Father, is continually sending the Spirit into our souls, because the Holy Spirit proceeds from him as well as from the Father.

In Jesus, therefore, we find our Mediator and our God. When as Mediator he guides us, he is also drawing us to himself as God; and when we are united to Christ the Man we are also united to Christ as Mediator. Whether, according to our own interior attraction, we prefer to fix our gaze on the humanity of Jesus or on his divinity, we may never separate the one from the other; they are so closely joined together as to form only one person, Jesus the incarnate Word, our Savior, and in this one single person must they be considered.

To go to Jesus is to go to the Word; and to go to the Word, is to go also to the Father, to the Holy Spirit: to the Trinity. That is why St. Teresa insists so strongly that we must never separate ourselves from Christ: "We must enter by this gate (Jesus) . . . let us desire no other path, (for) on this road we walk safely. This Lord of ours is the one through whom all blessings come to us" (Life 22:6,7).

O Lord, do you not say that you are the Way? Do you not also say that you are light and that no one can come to the Father save by you? If we lose our guide, good Jesus, we shall be unable to find our way (cf. IC VI 7:6).

What am I, Lord, without you? And what am I worth if I am not near you? And if once I stray from you, be it ever so little, where shall I find myself?

O my Lord, my mercy and my good! What more do I want in this life than to be so near you that there is no division between you and me? In such company, what can become difficult? What can one not undertake for your sake with yourself so near? . . . Never, with your help and favor, will I turn my back on you.

I see, O my Spouse, that you are mine; I cannot deny it. For my sake you came to the world; for my sake you endured these scourgings; for my sake you have remained with us in the most holy Sacrament . . .

What can I do for my Spouse? . . . What can a person do for you who has contrived such evil things as I? I can only lose the favors you have granted me. And even if, by your favor, I should accomplish something, consider how little a miserable worm can do. How can a powerful God have need of it? Only love lets us dare think that you, my true Lover, my Spouse and my Good, have need of us . . .

If you come to me, O Lord, how can I doubt that I can render you great services? Henceforth, Lord, I would forget myself and look solely at the ways in which I can serve you and have no will save your own. But my will is powerless, my God; it is you who are powerful. All I can do is to resolve to serve you, and this resolve I make and will henceforth carry into action (cf. Med IV 8-12).

St. Teresa of Jesus

75 — THE CHURCH

O Christ, you loved the Church and gave yourself up for her, make me love you with the heart of a son   (Eph 5:25)

1. When Jesus took leave of his own before he ascended into heaven, he said: "Lo, I am with you always until the end of the world" (Mt 28:20). In truth, he abides with us in the Blessed Sacrament as the companion and viaticum of our earthly pilgrimage, and he has remained invisibly but truly present in the Church as our guide, our shepherd, and our teacher. After having formed the first nucleus of the Church by his preaching and by choosing and instructing the apostles, he gave her life by dying on the cross. "The Church is the spouse"—says Vatican II—"whom Christ loved, and for whom he delivered himself up that he might sanctify her (cf. Eph 5:26), whom he unites to himself by an unbreakable covenant" (LG 6), making her his collaborator, the one who continues his work of saving men. Christ no longer lives on earth in his *physical body,* which is gloriously enthroned in

heaven, but in his *mystical Body,* the Church, his bride and our mother. Christ is the living head of the Church; it is always he who rules her invisibly by his Spirit; he sustains and vivifies her unceasingly, for it is he who gives her life, who asks graces from the eternal Father and dispenses them to each of her members "according to the measure of Christ's gift" (Eph 4:7). The Church lives by Christ alone, she is holy through the holiness he shares with her, she is the mother of souls through the powers and fecundity she receives from her union with him. This union is so intimate and vital that the Church may be considered a prolongation of Christ. "By an excellent analogy . . . (the Church) is compared to the mystery of the incarnate Word. Just as the assumed nature inseparably united to the divine Word serves him as a living instrument of salvation, so, in a similar way, does the communal structure of the Church serve Christ's Spirit, who vivifies her by way of building up the body" (LG 8).

Therefore, whoever wishes to find Jesus, to live by his grace, be nourished by his teachings and be guided and ruled by him, must embrace the Church. "He filled her with heavenly gifts for all eternity" and through him "she communicates truth and grace to all" (ib. 6,8).

2. "Whoever does not have the Church as his mother cannot have God as his Father" says St. Cyprian (*De cathol. eccl. unitate* 6). Jesus came to save and sanctify the world, but under ordinary circumstances he does this by means of the Church. He gave his life and shed his blood for us; he put his most precious merits at our disposal; he gave us the sacraments and the heritage of his doctrine; but he wished the Church to be the sole depository and dispenser of these benefits. Christ, says the Council, established the Church "as the universal sacrament of salvation" (LG 48), or "the sign and instrument" of the sanctification of men and of their "intimate union with God" (ib. 1). Indeed the Church spreads the faith by preaching the word of God and, by administering the sacraments, communicates and nourishes the life of grace through which we are engrafted into Christ as living members of his mystical Body. In this manner each of us becomes in turn the "Church", that is, a living cell of this great family which, uniting us with God, also unites us with each other like children of the same Father and the same mother, like brothers bound by ties of reciprocal love.

Because we are living members of the Church, we cannot be satisfied with enjoying the benefits which come from this, but must feel bound to share in her life, her anxieties and her sufferings, and to contribute to her growth, exactly as a child takes an active part in the life of his own family and shares its vicissitudes.

To feel and live with the Church is to feel and live with Christ, who is continually living and acting within her; he saves and sanctifies, uniting us to him and to each other so that we may attain to eternal life. To go to the Church is to go to Jesus; to love and serve the Church is to love and serve Christ her head. And just as he loved the Church so much that he gave her life "with his own blood" (Acts 20:28), so we must love her with filial obedience and devotion, with full dedication to her cause.

O Christ, our Lord, you have transmitted to your Church the sovereign power which you have received. By virtue of your dignity, you have made her queen and spouse. You have given her supreme power over the entire universe. You have commanded all men to submit to her judgment. She is the mother of all the living, and her dignity increases with the number of her children.

Every day she gives birth to new children by the operation of the Holy Spirit. As a vine, her branches cover the whole world. Her boughs are upheld by the wood of the Cross and they reach up to the kingdom of heaven.

Your Church, O Christ, is a strong city built on a mountain, visible to all and enlightening all. You are her founder and foremost citizen, O Jesus Christ, Son of God and our Lord.

Ambrosian Preface,
Cons. Cathedral from Early Christian Prayers 330

O Divine Redeemer, who loved the Church and gave yourself up for her in order to make her holy . . . and to make her resplendent in glory before you, let your holy Face shine upon her! May your Church, one in your love, holy in sharing your very holiness, still be, for the world today, the vessel of salvation for men, the center of unity for all hearts, inspiring holy resolutions for a general and stirring renewal. May her children, no longer divided, and forsaking all unworthiness, do her honor always and every where, so that those who do not yet belong to her, may consider her and find you, the way, the truth and the life, and in you be brought back to the Father in the unity of the Holy Spirit!

Paul VI, *Insegnamenti* v.1

76 — THE MINISTERIAL PRIESTHOOD

Pray the Lord of the harvest to send out laborers into his harvest   *(Mt 9:38)*

1. The Church, the Mystical Body of Christ, is not to be regarded merely as a spiritual institution; it is a concrete organism which is visible in its members, the faithful, who are joined together under the leadership of their pastors. And "as in one body we have many members, and all the members do not have the same function" (Rom 12:4), so in the Church there are members of diverse importance, having various functions: there are the faithful and there are pastors. "For the nurturing and con-

stant growth of the People of God Christ the Lord instituted in his Church a variety of ministries, which work for the good of the whole Body. For those ministers, who are endowed with sacred power, are servants of their brethren, so that all . . . may arrive at salvation" (LG 18). Christ has placed all the powers given to his Church in the hands of the priests under the authority of the Bishops and the Pope. To these are addressed the great words: "As the Father has sent me, so I send you.—He who hears you hears me, and he who rejects you rejects me" (Jn 20:21; Lk 10:16). The whole of the priestly dignity and power depend upon this investiture by Christ. Priests must be thoroughly aware of the great dignity of their call if they wish to live at the height of their vocation. "They can and must pursue perfection, since . . . they have been consecrated to God in a new way by the reception of orders and have become living instruments of Christ the eternal Priest, so that . . . they can accomplish his wonderful work on earth" (P.O. 12). The faithful must be aware of this also, so that they may see and venerate Christ himself in his priests.

"So we are ambassadors for Christ, God making his appeal through us" (2 Cor 5:20), writes St. Paul, giving us the exact meaning of priestly power and dignity. And St. Catherine of Siena cautioned her disciples to see priests only as "the dispensers of the blood of the humble, immaculate Lamb", and to overlook the faults which they might notice in them (Dial. 110). Priests are always fallible men, capable of making mistakes, but this does not prevent them from being the Anointed of the Lord, "consecrated to preach the gospel, shepherd the faithful and celebrate divine worship" (LG 28).

2. Without the priesthood, the gospel would not be preached, the Church would not have the Holy Eucharist, sinners would never have the indescribable consolation of hearing said to them in the name of Christ: "Take heart, my son, your sins are forgiven" (Mt 9:2); there would be no nuptial blessing for newlyweds, the dying would be deprived of final consolation; all men would become totally immersed in misery, with no one to raise them up and lead them to God, with no one to pray to him in their name and for their welfare. But Jesus, the sole mediator between God and man, willed to institute the priesthood to perpetuate among us, in a visible manner, his work of mediation, salvation and sanctification. The priest accompanies us at every step of our life. Soon after our birth, he welcomes us at the baptismal font; he administers the sacraments to us, he helps us to understand divine truths, he shows us how to lead a good life, blesses our efforts, sustains our footsteps, and strengthens us in our last agony. He often works unseen and unknown, misunderstood, never sufficiently appreciated; yet his apostolic work is priceless, indispensable. Every Christian ought to be grateful for the gift of the priesthood: in the first place, we should be grateful to Jesus who

instituted it, and then to those who perform its sublime duties. We should express this gratitude, not only by showing reverent respect and filial docility to God's ministers, but also by assiduously offering our prayers and good works for priestly vocations. Jesus himself instructs us to "pray the Lord of the harvest to send laborers into his harvest" (Mt 9:38). "What prayer", comments Pius XI, "can be more pleasing to the Sacred Heart of the Redeemer? . . . Ask, and it shall be given to you: ask for good, holy priests, and the Lord will not refuse to send them to his Church" (Ad Cath. sacerd.). To fervent prayer we must add, as the Council exhorts us, "a fully Christian life" and also "penance", remembering that "the task of fostering vocations devolves on the whole Christian community" (OT 2). Blessed are the families that have had the honor of giving a priest to God; blessed are all those who by their prayers, sacrifices, and good works help in the formation of holy priests!

O Lord, by your Holy Spirit you anointed your only Son High Priest of the new and eternal covenant. With wisdom and love you have planned that this one priesthood should continue in the Church.

Christ gives the dignity of a royal priesthood to the people he has made his own. From these, with a brother's love, he chooses men to share his sacred ministry by the laying on of hands. He appoints them to renew in his name the sacrifice of our redemption as they set before your family his paschal meal. He calls them to lead your holy people in love, nourish them by your word, and strengthen them through the sacraments.

They are to give their lives in your service and for the salvation of your people, and honor you by their courageous witness of faith and love.

Roman Missal, Preface of Chrism Mass of Holy Thursday

O Lord, punish my sins; purify me, O eternal Goodness, ineffable Deity! Hear your servant, and do not consider my many iniquities. I beg you to draw to you the hearts and wills of the ministers of your holy Church, your Bride, that they may follow you, O bleeding Lamb, a poor man, humble and meek, along the way of your holy Cross—in your way, not theirs. Oh, that they may be angelic creatures, earthly angels, for it is their office to administer the Blood and Body of your only begotten Son, the spotless Lamb . . . Unite them, O divine compassion, and bathe them in the tranquil sea of your kindness so that they may not wait longer, losing what they have through what they do not have.

St. Catherine of Siena, *Preghiere ed Elevazioni*

77 — THE SACRAMENTS

O God, you have saved us through grace; grant that it may prepare us for good works   *(cf. Eph 2:5,10)*

1. The Church is "the universal sacrament of salvation" (LG 48) through which men find God, and was made by Christ the depository of the sacraments, through which we are made participants in the life of Christ himself.

The sacraments are at the same time the work of Christ, who is their author and who gives them life, and the work of the Church, their depository and administrator. They have two causes: one, invisible, is the action of Christ who is "present (by his power) in the sacraments, so that when a man baptizes it is really Christ himself who baptizes" (SC 7); the other is visible, the external action, with which the Church, through the priest, administers the sacrament, fulfilling the rite. Christ's action is the essential element; without it the sacraments could neither produce nor communicate grace. When we approach them, we should be fully aware of the invisible reality of which they are efficacious signs. By means of the sacraments Jesus works within us, infusing his life in us and increasing it in us. "In that body (the Mystical Body) the life of Christ is poured into the believers, who, through the sacraments, are united in a hidden and real way to Christ" (LG 7). But the action of the Church is also indispensable, since Jesus wished his intervention in our lives to be linked to the sacraments in such a way that the manner of their administration would clearly evidence his invisible action. This shows the deep, inseparable union between Jesus and his Church; he wills to make use of her exterior acts in sanctifying souls, but he reserves for himself the power to vivify these acts and make them effective. This explains why, when blessing the baptismal water, the Church prays: "O God, through the sacramental signs, you perform the wonders of salvation with unseen power" (Easter Vigil).

2. When God called us to salvation, he wished, in his ineffable kindness and understanding, to respect our nature. Man is not pure spirit. We need sensible, visible signs to signify divine realities which are beyond the reach of our senses. Considered in this light, Christ is truly the sacrament of God, a wonderful and infinite sign of his love for us; the Church is the sacrament of Christ always present and active in the world; the sacraments are the last link of that sacramentality that characterizes the whole mystery of our relations with God. We must look at the sacraments in this light, as an integral part of the universal plan of salvation, as living and lifegiving elements, because they are vehicles of God's action, efficacious signs of grace, communicated to us through Christ with the help of the ministry of the Church.

In the ordinary course of events God has disposed that the mystery of redemption should reach us and be realized in us through the sacraments, which derive their efficacy from the paschal mysteries of the Passion, Death and Resurrection of Christ (SC 61), whose infinite merits are applied to every Christian. When one of the faithful receives a sacrament, he is not only freed from sin and sanctified by grace, but freed and sanctified in Christ, immersed in his mystery, renewed in his life, and united "in a hidden and real way to the suffering and glorified Christ" (LG 7).

The sacraments cannot be considered exercises in piety; they are vital acts which place us in a vital relationship with Christ: dead with him and living with him (2 Tim 2:11); buried with Christ and raised from the dead with him, and glorified in heaven with him (Rom 6:4-5; Eph 2:6), that, as St. Paul concludes: "he might show the immeasurable riches of his grace in kindness toward us in Christ Jesus (ib. 7).

O God, the supreme Father of all the faithful, you multiply the children of your promise all over the world by the grace of your adoption ... grant that they may respond worthily to the grace of your call.

O God of unchanging power and light, look with mercy on your entire Church. Bring lasting salvation to mankind, so that the world may see the fallen lifted up, the old made new, and all things brought to perfection, through him who is the beginning of all things, Jesus christ our Lord.

Roman Missal, Easter Vigil Prayer

What greater thing can we do than proclaim your power, O Lord? You broke down the gates of hell and carried off to heaven the souls who had fallen through the devil's envy ...

The blessed spring that gushed from your side swept away our heaped up sins, and from your holy altars you distribute to reborn souls the food they need for eternal life.

Gelasian Sacramentary, (from Liturgia—CAL 30)

O good, sweet Jesus! Father of lights, from whom every perfect gift proceeds, look upon us with mercy, upon us who know you; you truly understand that we can do nothing without you. You gave yourself as the price of our redemption. Although we are unworthy of such a precious gift, grant that we may correspond with your grace entirely, perfectly, and in all things, so that, being conformed to the likeness of your Passion, we may recover what we have lost by sin, the likeness of your divinity.

St. Bonaventure, *La vite mistica* 24:2

YEAR A

O Lord, light rises in the darkness for the upright   *(Ps 112:4)*

After Jesus finished his sermon on the beatitudes, he described the greatness of his disciples: "You are the salt of the earth . . . you are the light of the world" (Mt 5:13-14). This presupposes a condition: that they really be those poor and meek, merciful and pure, peaceful and serene, joyful even in persecution, of whom the Lord has just spoken. Only to the extent that they make the spirit of the beatitudes their own and live in conformity with it, do the disciples acquire that supernatural wisdom which makes them "the salt of the earth." They are called to transform a world which is insipid and foolish, because it is based on vain, transitory things, into a wise, prudent world founded on eternal values. But there is also another side of the coin: if the disciple does not have the spirit of the gospel, he is not "salt," he is "no longer good for anything except to be thrown out" (ib. 13).

But when he is "salt," he is also "light," a still more imposing comparison. The light of the world, "the true light that enlightens every man" (Jn 1:9) is Christ alone, the Son of God, the glory of the Father; but he shares his brilliance with those who live according to the gospel. Thus every disciple, every authentic Christian becomes a bearer of the light of Christ, and his conduct must be so pure that it will permit the brightness of Christ and his teaching to shine through. "Let your light so shine before men that they may see your good works and give glory to your Father who is in heaven" (Mt 5:16). Works performed in the truth and charity of Christ are the lighted candle placed in the candlestick which gives light to "all in the house" and attracts them to faith and love. The Old Testament also presented works of charity as messengers of light: "If you pour yourself out for the hungry and satisfy the desire of the afflicted, then shall your light rise in the darkness" (Is 58:10). Charity dispels the darkness of sin and also illuminates those who are very far from the faith. Besides, the charity of the Christian is a reflection of Christ's own love, it is a prolongation of his love which stoops down to suffering humanity.

The apostle Paul is a splendid prototype of a disciple of Christ as salt and light of the world. The success of his apostolate does not lie in "lofty words or wisdom" but in a life totally inspired by the gospel and conformed to Christ crucified. "I decided to know nothing except Jesus Christ and him crucified." (1 Cor 2:1-2). It is only in this way that we become the salt that transforms the world to its depths and the light that illuminates it fully.

O sweet Jesus, make me salt of the earth, even if I must go through fire and water to become so; do not permit me to give scan-

dal rather than savor, or be like soil sown with salt become sterile through my own fault, thus changing the work you gave me for your service into uselessness.

O sun of justice, from whom the stars of the Church receive light, make me like one of these stars, free from all darkness, so that from wherever you have put me I may come running quickly at your voice and joyously light up the world you created for your glory. You who so desire the glory of your eternal Father, grant me such brightness of life that through it his glory may increase here on earch, and spread out among men, and he may be glorified by all.

O Redeemer of the world, you made Paul, your chosen vessel, experience how much he would have to suffer for your sake, and at the same time gave him joy in suffering; choose me also as your vessel into which you can pour an abundance of labors with the richness of the consolation of suffering for your love.

L. DaPonte, *Meditazioni* III 12:1-2; V 31:5

YEAR B

Praise the Lord for he is good . . . he heals the brokenhearted and binds up their wounds   *(Ps 147:1,3)*

Job laments under the torment of his tribulations: "Has not man a hard service upon earth? . . . Like a slave who longs for the shadow . . . so I am allotted months of emptiness, and nights of misery are apportioned to me" (Job 7:1-3). Job is the symbol of oppressed humanity, grieving under an excess of physical and moral ills. His suffering reaches a paroxysm, and borders on desperation, yet he believes in God and calls upon him: "Remember that my life is like a breath" (ib. 7). This lament, a glimmer of hope in a sea of woe, is not in vain. God will stoop down to man and send him a Savior to alleviate his suffering and to open his heart to greater hope.

It is in this context that the Gospel presents Jesus, surrounded by a multitude of suffering: "They brought to him all who were sick or possessed with demons. And the whole city was gathered together about the door, and he healed many who were sick with various diseases, and cast out many devils" (Mk 1:32-34). To raise mankind from the condition of physical and moral suffering in which it was floundering, Christ preaches and heals. By his preaching he enlightens minds, reveals God's love, leads to faith, gives meaning to affliction, and shows the way to salvation. By his miracles he heals aching bodies and expels demons. Christ wants to save the whole man, body and soul; in fact, he heals the flesh so it may become a sign and means of salvation to the soul. When he does not take suffering away, he teaches us how to bear it with hope and love, so that it may bear the fruit of eternal life.

The work of salvation begun by Christ is in process right now; since it must continue on until the end of time, he left his mandate to the Church and, in the Church, to every one of the faithful. The apostle Paul, who was most sensitive to this duty, and pledged to it with all his energies, could say to the Corinthians: "If I preach the gospel, that gives me no ground for boasting. For necessity is laid upon me, and woe is me if I do not preach the gospel" (1 Cor 9:16). Every one who has been privileged to receive the gospel must feel a sense of responsibility toward those who have not had this favor, and must do everything possible to make them share in it. Whoever lives within salvation's orbit cannot look with indifference upon those who are afar off; it is incumbent upon us to draw in as large a number of our brothers as possible.

Glory to you, O Christ, light of truth and sun of justice, you came to make your abode in your Church, and she has been enlightened by you; you came to your own creation and your presence shines through it everywhere. Sinners have approached you and been purified. Fugitives and exiles have met each other again. The blind have seen you and had their eyes opened; souls in darkness have drawn near the light. The dead have heard your voice and been raised up; prisoners and slaves are freed, scattered peoples reunited. You are the light that never sets; the radiant morning that never sees the evening. Open the eyes of our hearts to your light, and let the appearance of your morning be for us the beginning of every good. Let our souls be bound by your love; and since, through your mercy, you have made us worthy of escaping from the shadows of the night and of drawing near to morning, grant that through your living and all-powerful word all the afflictions that assail us may dissipate like smoke. Through the wisdom that comes to us from you, make us triumph over all the wiles of our enemy the devil, who tries to appear as an angel of light. Protect us, O Lord, keep us from being tempted to acts of darkness and of death; let our gaze never stray from your dazzling light, so that we may be guided by your precepts in all our actions.

Oriental Liturgy, from *I giorni del Signore*

YEAR C

Though the Lord is high, he regards the lowly; but the haughty he knows from afar. (Ps 138:6)

The Liturgy of the Word today relates the vocations of three men: Isaiah, Peter and Paul. In each case the divine call is preceded by a manifestation of the Divinity: before entrusting a special mission to a man, God reveals himself, so as to be known. Marvelous was the revelation granted to Isaiah: "I saw the Lord sitting upon a throne, and lifted up" (Is 6:1); around him the

Seraphim kneeled in adoration, singing: "Holy, holy, holy is the Lord of hosts" (ib. 3). Isaiah trembles before such holiness; he feels himself more than ever impure and unworthy to stand in God's presence. But when he hears the Lord's voice, addressing him, "Whom shall I send? Who will go for us?" he does not hesitate for a moment and answers: "Here am I! Send me!" (ib. 8). Man cannot, by his own decision, assume the mission of collaborating with God, but if God calls him, his unworthiness cannot be an excuse for holding back.

The circumstances of Peter's call to be a "fisher of men" were completely different. It took place, not in the temple as with Isaiah, but on the lake in a very simple human context that was in keeping with God made man, who had come to share the life of men. After preaching from Peter's boat, Jesus ordered him to lower the nets. "Master, we toiled all night and took nothing, but at your word I will let down the nets" (Lk 5:5). His tractability and trust are rewarded for they caught so many fish that the nets broke, and their catch filled two boats "so that they began to sink" (ib. 7). The unexpected miracle revealed who Jesus was, and Peter, frightened like Isaiah, fell to his knees, saying: "Depart from me, for I am a sinful man, O Lord" (ib. 8). Faced with God's revelation of himself, man becomes aware of the contrast of his wretchedness and nothingness, and feels a deep need to humble himself. God's great call follows this act of humility. "Do not be afraid; henceforth you will be catching men." Here again, the answer is immediate—not only Peter's but that of his companions also: "And when they had brought their boats to land, they left everything, and followed him" (ib. 10-11).

In the second reading St. Paul speaks to us of his vocation to be herald of the mystery of Christ. Christ had revealed himself to him on the road to Damascus, and Paul was so overwhelmed that for the rest of his life he considered himself not only the last of the apostles, but as "one born out of due time" (1 Cor 15:8). Again the correspondence with the divine call was complete; Paul bears witness that God's grace in him was not in vain.

Three different vocations, these, but all characterized by the same attitude of humility and availability, which is the foundation of every response to God's call.

> God has created me to do him some definite service; he has committed some work to me which he has not committed to another... Somehow I am necessary for his purposes... if, indeed, I fail, he can raise another, as he could make the stones children of Abraham. Yet I have a part in this great work; I am a link in a chain, a bond of connection between persons. He has not created me for naught. I shall do good, I shall do his work; I shall be an angel of peace, a preacher of truth in my own place, while not intending it, if I do but keep his commandments and serve him in my calling.
>
> J.H. Newman, *Meditations on Christian Doctrine* I:2

"Master, we have toiled all night and have caught nothing, but at your word, I will let down the nets." I, too, Lord, know that is like night for me when you do not speak . . . I have sent out my voice like a dart . . . and have not yet captured anyone. I have called out all day; now I await your order: at your word I will cast my net. O empty presumption, O fruitful humility! Those who formerly caught nothing, Lord, now catch huge quantities of fish. This is not the fruit of human eloquence, but the result of a call from heaven.

St. Ambrose, *Commentary on Gospel of St. Luke* IV, 76

79 — SACRAMENTAL LIFE

Lord, now that we have been set free from sin and have become slaves of God, let our fruit be sanctification. (Rom 6:22)

1. In instituting the sacraments, Our Lord organized them in such a way that they accompany us in each important stage of our life. By baptism we are born into the life of grace; by confirmation we grow; we are nourished by the Holy Eucharist; healed by penance; by the social sacraments—holy orders and matrimony—we become supernaturally and naturally fruitful; and by the anointing of the sick we are comforted in sickness and helped on the way to eternal life. In this manner the whole of Christian life is structured and substantiated by the sacraments, which, by infusing grace, make us share in God's life and, therefore, in his sanctity. "By God's gifts we must hold on to and complete in our lives, the holiness which we have received" (LG 40). Only God is holy and only God can make holy. The initiative for man's sanctification comes from God, and in actuality is carried out precisely through the sacraments. Spiritual life and our straining toward holiness are not simply moral obligations by which we seek to imitate the perfection of our divine model in an external way, but are based on a supernatural reality that God himself has infused into the life of a Christian, changing and transforming us from within so radically as to make us a new creation in Christ (2 Cor 5:17), "who is being renewed after the image of his Creator" (Col 3:10). God is the unique source, the primordial cause of our holiness.

St. John says: "We love because he first loved us" (1 Jn 4:19). We may say, by way of analogy: we can become a saint because God has first of all shared his own life with us, and has called us to communion with him.

2. Sacramental life consists of receiving, assimilating, and living the sacraments in such a way that we derive from them all the fruits of holiness and communion with God for which they are ordained.

When the sacraments are conferred on persons capable of receiving them, they have of themselves unfailing effectiveness because God himself operates in them. Nevertheless, the grace and holiness that they impart do not reach their full fruitfulness unless we add our collaboration. Therefore, although God's initiative is the first step of our sanctification, we must voluntarily collaborate with him and assimilate and live the holiness we have received from him. "Yield yourselves to God as men who have been brought from death to life," says St. Paul to those who have been reborn through baptism, "and yield your members to God as instruments of righteousness" (Rom 6:13).

The fact that certain sacraments, like penance and the Eucharist can be received frequently does not mean that our receiving them should become a simple habit. Habits are inert, static situations, while receiving the sacraments should always be a living act, ever more alive, so that our sacramental life is characterized by progress and development. This development does not necessarily consist in multiplying sacramental acts, but in intensifying and fulfilling these acts with greater perfection. This means we need to concern ourselves with approaching the sacraments with ever better dispositions, so that our own limitations may not stand in the way of the flow of grace, and that we may always participate more fully in the life of Christ in the Church.

Our responsibility in regard to the sacraments lies in our making ourselves fit to receive them, in expanding our receptivity and making ourselves better disposed, and in being fully open to the gift that is being offered. The more we tend toward holiness and union with God, the more we ourselves must be involved in taking full advantage of the sacraments. Sacramental life is the essential and substantial reality of Christian life.

O Father most holy, who through your Son, our Lord Jesus Christ, caused me to be born again of water and of the Holy Spirit, grant me today the full remission of all my sins, and deign to anoint me with the chrism of your Spirit unto eternal life.

O Jesus, Son of Justice, come, let me clothe myself in you, that I may live as you would have me live... O Jesus, light that shall never fail, come, enkindle in me the burning lamp of your unfailing charity and teach me to keep my baptism without blame; that when I am summoned unto your marriage feast, being found ready, I may deserve to enter upon the delights of eternal life, beholding you, the true light, and the glorious face of your Godhead. O Jesus Christ, my Lord, may your adorable Body and your precious Blood keep my body and my soul unto eternal life...

O Jesus, my dearest Beloved, sweetest guest of my soul, may your gracious presence within me be unto me today the remission of all my sins; may it atone for all my shortcomings and regain all the losses of my poor life. May it be my eternal salvation, the restora-

tion of my soul and body, the enkindling of my love, the renewal of my virtues, and the everlasting ending of my life in you. May it be unto me liberty of spirit, soundness of life, and purity of manners. May it be unto me a shield of patience, a badge of humility, a staff of trust, a solace in sadness, and help unto perseverance. May it be unto me the armor of faith, the strength of hope, the perfection of charity, the fulfillment of your commandments, renewal of spirit, sanctification in truth ... May it be unto me the source of virtues, the end of vices, the increase of all gifts, and the deathless covenant of your love.

St. Gertrude, *Exercises I* (pp. 11-13)

80 — BAPTISM

We pray to you, O Lord, to revive in us the grace of baptism (RR)

1. On the day of baptism when a Christian is reborn in the name of the Father and of the Son and of the Holy Spirit, he receives grace, that is, a participation in the life of Christ, and becomes an adopted child of God; he is inserted into the mysterious reality of the Mystical Body of Christ the Lord, and becomes a member of the whole Christ. The sacrament of baptism is like the gate which introduces us to Christian life; it is the fundamental and radical qualification for receiving all the other sacraments in order to arrive at the state of "mature manhood, to the measure of the stature of the fullness of Christ" (Eph 4:13). Indeed, as the Council explains, "Baptism of itself is only a beginning, a point of departure, for it is wholly directed toward the acquiring of fullness of life in Christ" (UR 22; cf. GE 2). To permit baptism to produce all its fruit, we must adapt our life to the grace of adoption, which is the characteristic and fundamental grace of this sacrament. "You have received the spirit of sonship"—attests St. Paul—"when we cry out 'Abba,' Father, it is the Spirit himself bearing witness with our spirit that we are children of God" (Rom 15-16). Having been made a child of God, one who is baptized can no longer live a purely human life, but must conform his life to that of the only Son, Christ the Lord. The Apostle never tires of repeating: "You were buried with him in baptism in which you were also raised with him ... If then you have been raised with Christ, seek the things that are above ... Set your minds on things that are above, not on things that are on earth" (Col 2:12; 3:1-2). Our thoughts and affections must stretch out toward eternal values, to eternal life, and must not linger over earthly matters. We must make progress on this path every day until we reach "the fullness of life in Christ."

2. Baptism imprints upon us the character of children of God, a character which nothing—not even the most serious sins we

could commit—can destroy: we are "marked" for all eternity.

This point is brought out very clearly in the prayers used during the rite of baptism. As he blesses the water, the priest prays: "Come with your power, O Father, and bless this water, so that through it our sins may be washed away, and we may be reborn to a new life as your sons. Bless this water so that, baptized in the death and resurrection of Christ, we may be conformed to the image of your Son." And in order to assure the newly baptized a life in keeping with their status as children of God and brothers of Christ, the Church reminds parents and godparents of their responsibility to educate them in the faith and in love and obedience to God, according to the spirit of the baptismal promise, (which is the reason for renewing them each Easter). After he has administered the sacrament, the minister says as he hands over the symbolic white robe: "May this white robe be a sign of your new dignity; helped by the words and example of your dear ones, may you wear it without blemish until you come to life everlasting." Then he says to the parents, handing them a lit candle: "Take care that your children, enlightened by Christ, always live as children of the light; and persevering in the faith, go to meet the Lord, who is coming" (New baptismal rite). The rite and the prayers sum up what manner of life the new children of God should lead. Both the baptismal rite itself and its accompanying prayers should be indelibly engraved on the mind and heart of each one of us, so as to be the enduring norm of our life. As the years go by and worries, duties and obligations of all kinds pile up on our shoulders, our first duty must always be that of preserving intact the grace of our baptism. In vain will be acts of piety, without fruit our Holy Communions and the other sacraments, futile our apostolate, our consecration to God, or the sacred ministry itself, if we do not take care to maintain the full splendor of our baptismal grace, and keep the light of faith burning brightly. Each of us must keep alive the consciousness of our baptismal vows, remembering that at the holy font we were each solemnly consecrated a temple of the glory of God, a dwelling of the Holy Spirit, and a member of the Mystical Body of Christ (ib.).

Almighty and eternal God, look with favor upon this your servant whom you have called to the faith; take from me all blindness of heart; free me from the snares of Satan which until now have held me; open to me, O Lord, the gate of your mercy. Relieve me of the corruption of evil desires and let me find pleasure in keeping your commandments; give me the happiness of serving you in your Church and make progress from day to day in the way of perfection.

Make me always fervent in spirit, joyful in hope, and zealous in your service.

O Lord, holy Father, I beg for your never-ending and most holy mercy. O fount of light, may it please you to grant me the light of your own wisdom; cleanse me and make me holy; give me true

knowledge so that I may be worthy to come to the grace of your baptism; maintain in me firm hope, sound judgment, and holy doctrine.
cf. *Former Rite of Baptism*

I beseech you, keep my faith pure and grant that, until my last sigh, I may feel the testimony of a good conscience. Grant that I, who have been baptized in the name of the Father, and of the Son, and of the Holy Spirit, may always believe what I professed in the sacrament of my regeneration. Let me adore you, my Father, and your Son with you; let me be worthy of the Holy Spirit who proceeds from you and your only-begotten Son. Truly I have a worthy pledge of faith to guarantee what I believe, and it is he who said, 'Father, all that is mine is yours, and all that is yours is mine,' Jesus Christ, my Lord, who lives in you and who, remaining God, proceeds from you, and is always near you, and is blessed forever and ever.
St. Hilary of Poitiers, *De Trinitate XII* 57

81 — CONFIRMATION

O Lord, that I may receive power from the Holy Spirit to be your witness (Acts 1:8)

1. Baptism is the first step in Christian initiation, confirmation is the second. The sacrament of *confirmation confirms* us in our faith, and strengthens us in the Christian life which baptism first generated in us. Baptism is the act of being born to Christian life, confirmation the act of passage to adult Christian life. The Christian is "incorporated into Christ's Mystical Body through baptism, and strengthened by the power of the Holy Spirit through confirmation" (AA 3). By means of baptism man is consecrated a child of God, a temple of the Holy Spirit; in confirmation, this divine Spirit intervenes to consecrate him a perfect Christian and soldier of Christ. Moreover, confirmation gives him the fullness of the Holy Spirit which strengthens him spiritually, as befits maturity, by conferring upon him the capacity to function as an adult and to face spiritual battle with the enemies of his faith (St T 3,72,2).

Jesus said to his followers: "I will pray the Father and he will give you another Paraclete, to be with you for ever: the Spirit of truth" (Jn 14:16). Jesus' promise was fulfilled on the day of Pentecost with the coming of the Holy Spirit, who infused new vigor into the apostles and made them capable of preaching the gospel freely and courageously: "With great power the Apostles gave their testimony to the resurrection of the Lord Jesus" (Acts 4:33). The sacrament of confirmation is somewhat like a Pentecost for each of us; strengthened by the Holy Spirit, we must henceforth act as a mature Christian with the courage and steadiness of an adult. In this way, says St. Paul, we can "attain to the measure of the fullness of the stature of Christ, so that we may no longer be children, tossed to and fro and carried about by every wind of doctrine . . . but rather speaking the truth in love, we are to grow up in every way into him who is the head, into Christ" (Eph 4:13-15).

2. Like baptism and holy orders, confirmation stamps us with a special character to which St. Paul refers when he says: "It is God who establishes us . . . in Christ, and has commissioned us; he has put his seal upon us, and given us his Spirit in our hearts as a guarantee" (2 Cor 21-22). The character imprinted by confirmation is that of a militant Christian, a soldier of Christ; it is a character which gives us the right to receive, at the opportune moment, the graces necessary to remain faithful to God in spite of all the struggles and wiles and seductions of the evil one. We can virtually say that confirmation is the sacrament which consecrates the heroes of the faith and of duty, that it consecrates the martyrs. The prospect of martyrdom cannot and must not be excluded from the horizon of Christian life; Vatican Council II expressly speaks of it: "From the earliest times . . . some Christians have been called upon—and some will always be called upon—to give the supreme testimony of love to all men but especially to their persecutors . . . Though few are presented with such an opportunity, nevertheless all must be prepared to confess Christ before men, and to follow him along the way of the cross through the persecutions which the Church will never fail to suffer" (LG 42). This takes on particular importance at this present time, when, in the face of constant opposition to the Church, much strength is needed to remain firm in the faith and in Christian morality; not infrequently this demands serious sacrifices, sometimes even to giving up life itself.

When pusillanimity threatens to overcome us, let us remember that in confirmation God stamped "his seal" upon our hearts, and that he has given us "the pledge of the Holy Spirit" to support us from within with his omnipotent power. "You shall receive power when the Holy Spirit has come upon you"—said Jesus to his apostles, and through them to all the faithful—"and you shall be my witnesses" (Acts 1:8). Jesus' promise is infallible. Faith in the efficacy of the sacrament we have received, and in the fullness of the action of the Holy Spirit, makes the grace of confirmation operative, and confers upon the Christian the strength to bear witness to Christ in everything he does.

Almighty and eternal God, who in your kindness gave me a new birth through water and the Holy Spirit, and granted me remission of all my sins, send forth upon me from heaven your sevenfold Spirit, the holy Consoler. Infuse into me the Spirit of wisdom and understanding; the Spirit of counsel and fortitude; the Spirit of knowledge and piety, and also the Spirit of your fear.

O God, you gave the Holy Spirit to your apostles, and willed that through them and their successors he be given to the rest of the faithful; look with favor on this your servant who has been anointed with holy chrism and signed with the sign of the holy cross. May the Holy Spirit who has come down upon me, deign to dwell always in my heart and renew my consecration as a temple of your glory.

Old Rite of confirmation

O Christ, you died for me, a sinner. When I was God's enemy, I was reconciled with him through your death. This is why I deem yours the greatest love because you gave your life for me, when I was not your friend but an enemy. What great love you have for me, and what tender affection! You loved me, a sinner, even to giving your life for love of me...

Grant that I may believe this, and, for the sake of my salvation, not blush to confess it. Indeed to obtain justification we believe with the heart; to have salvation we profess our faith with our mouth. Then that I might not hesitate nor be ashamed when I embrace the faith, you placed your seal on my forehead... Help me raise up my head so that others may not be afraid to speak. You yourself say: if anyone is ashamed of me before men, the Son of Man will be ashamed of him before the angels of God. Therefore, let me not be ashamed of the ignominy of the cross which you, O Lord, did not hesitate to embrace for me, and make me repeat with the Apostle: far be it from me to glory in anything but the cross of our Lord Jesus Christ.

St. Augustine *Sermon* 215:5

82 — THE PEOPLE OF GOD

O God who has called us out of darkness into your marvellous light, make us declare your wonderful deeds   *(1 Pet 2:9)*

1. Baptism and confirmation likewise are not simply the personal concern of those who receive these sacraments and are thereby reborn and perfected in the Christian life; these are ecclesial events that interest the entire Church, both because they are carried out through her ministry, and because the sacraments not only join man to God, but also to other men. "For by one spirit we were all baptized into one body" (1 Cor 12:13), the Mystical Body of Christ, which is the Church. The Church is formed, grows and develops precisely through the new children she begets through the sacraments.

Our Lord, "in explicit terms, affirmed the necessity of faith and baptism, and thereby affirmed also the necessity of the Church, for through baptism, as through a door, men enter the Church" (LG 14). That same sacrament which makes man a child of God, makes him a member of the Church; and the very sacrament which makes him a perfect Christian, enrolls him in the Church's militia. "When in the womb of the baptismal font, the Holy Spirit begets to a new life those who believe in Christ, he gathers them into the one people of God" (AG 15). This is not an accessory reality of secondary importance, but a part of God's own plan for the salvation of mankind, since "it has pleased God to make men holy and save them, not merely as individuals without any bond between men, but by making them into a single people, a people which acknowledges him in truth and serves him in holiness" (LG 9). With that purpose in mind, God chose the people of Israel from the very beginning, and sanctified and bound them to himself with a special covenant; yet this was only a symbol of the new messianic people whom the Lord Jesus would redeem with his blood, and whose head he would become. Thus, all who are baptized in Christ make up the people saved by him: the people of God who have received mercy (cf. 1 Pet 2:10). This privilege, which we owe directly to divine mercy, should find a generous response in us. "All the sons of the Church should remember that their exalted status is to be attributed not to their own merits, but to the special grace of Christ," to which they must respond "in thought, word and deed" (LG 14).

2. The mystery of salvation is simultaneously carried out on a vertical plane in what unites man with God, and on a horizontal one in what unites man with other men. To grasp the deep meaning of this, we must be mindful that for human solidarity to be Christian, it must be based essentially on God, that is upon the union of each individual with God and that of all of us with God. There is no question here of forming a solely earthly people, but of the People of God, sanctified by his grace and directed by his Spirit and his laws. Its heritage is "the dignity and freedom of the sons of God, in whose hearts the Holy Spirit dwells as in his temple. Its law is the new commandment to love as Christ loved us" (LG 9).

Since the faithful form one single people, they cannot remain disinterested in each other; the welfare and holiness of each individual should be ordered to the well-being and sanctification of all; the intensity of the Christian life and of the sacramental life of each of the faithful is the patrimony of the Christian community. Each one should be conscious of the fact that in praying and in receiving the sacraments he is not enriching and sanctifying himself alone, but the entire People of God as well. This is a powerful stimulus to increasing our own receptivity and opening to grace, so that it may be poured out upon all our brothers. Nor is it enough to stop here: there are also other men to be reached. Although God's People is still "a little flock," it is "used by Christ . . . as an instrument for the redemption of all, and is sent forth into the whole world as the light of the world and the salt of the earth" (ib.). This is the foundation of the apostolic vocation of every Christian. By the simple fact of having been baptized, we each have the duty to be an apostle, and to live accordingly, so that our whole life may express the Lord's gospel in word and deed.

Glory to you, O Lord, merciful Father! You have made our new life as your children issue from the baptismal font. With water and the Holy Spirit, you make all the baptized into a single people of Christ. You send the Spirit of your love into our hearts to give us freedom and peace. You call upon the baptized to proclaim with joy Christ's gospel to the whole world.

Hear us, O Lord, and grant that all who have been anointed with the sign of the cross may openly profess their faith in every circumstance of life . . . Keep in one same faith and love all those whom you have joined by baptism into a single family.

Rite of baptism for children

What love for you, O holy Church of God, does this thought enkindle in my heart, "I am one of your members: I am a member of Christ!" What love it gives me for all Christians, since they are my brothers and we form one in Christ!

Nothing that has to do with you can leave me indifferent. Sad, when I see you persecuted, I rejoice at the story of your conquests and your triumphs.

O holy Church of God, I wish, as far as it depends on me, that you may be more beautiful, more holy, and more numerous, since the splendor of your whole body results from the perfection of each of your children, based on that close fellowship which was the main thought of the prayer of our Lord after the Last Supper and the true testament of his heart. "That they may be one . . . that they may be made perfect in one."

G.B. Chautard, *The Soul of the Apostolate* V (p. 225)

83 — THE PRIESTHOOD OF THE FAITHFUL

O Jesus, who made us priests to your Father, to you be glory and power for ever and ever (Rev 1:6)

1. "You are a chosen race, a royal priesthood, a holy nation, God's own people, that you may declare the wonderful deeds of him who called you out of darkness into his marvelous light" (1 Pet 2:9). These well-known words of St. Peter give us the meaning of the common priesthood of all the faithful; by virtue of the sacraments, particularly baptism and confirmation, we are consecrated to the service and worship of God, and are delegated to be his heralds among men. The priesthood of the faithful is essentially distinguished from the ministerial priesthood which is derived from the sacrament of holy orders; in fact the faithful have

no power to consecrate the Eucharist, to forgive sins, or to administer the other sacraments—except baptism in particular cases—not even that of preaching the word of God with authority. Yet, even the simple faithful are called to an effective participation in the universal priesthood of Christ. St. Thomas explains that this is a result of the sacramental character of baptism and of confirmation, a character which consists precisely in a participation in the priesthood of Christ, through which the faithful are appointed to the worship of God (St. Thos. 3,63,2-3). Besides, St. Peter has already said: "Come to him (Christ) . . . Like living stones, by yourselves built into a spiritual house, to be a holy priesthood, to offer spiritual sacrifices acceptable to God through Jesus Christ" (1 Pet 2:4-5). The life of grace leads us to such a dignity, for, being itself a participation in the life of Christ, it makes us also participate in his priesthood. This is a truth heavy with meaning and obligates us as Christians to make sure that our whole life takes on a priestly character; which means that every one of our actions should be worthy of being offered to God as an act of worship, as a "spiritual sacrifice," destined to render him honor and to acknowledge his sovereign majesty, and all of this not in our own name only, but in the name of all men, in union with the priesthood of Christ.

2. The faithful exercise their royal priesthood 'by receiving the sacraments, by prayer and thanksgiving, by their witness of a holy life, and by self-denial and active charity" (LG 10). Thus our whole life is placed at the service of our priestly function; still certain particular acts stand out, the sacramental acts.

Sacramental life is the foundation of the priesthood of the faithful, and is at the same time its highest exercise. It is especially the foundation: "Incorporated into the Church by baptism, the faithful are consecrated by the baptismal character to Christian religious worship; as sons of God they must profess before men the faith they have received from God through the Church" (ib. 11). Baptism is a true consecration; through it we are dedicated to God's service and to his worship. This is why, before administering the sacrament, the Church asks for the express renunciation of Satan, and a formal profession of faith, a renunciation and profession which the Christian must express in his daily life, everywhere bearing witness to God. All this is completed and confirmed by the sacrament of confirmation: "By the sacrament of confirmation (the faithful) are more perfectly bound to the Church, and are endowed with the special strength of the Holy Spirit. Hence as true witnesses of Christ they are more strictly obliged to spread and defend the faith by word and deed" (ibid). These two sacraments, then, are not only the basis of the life of grace, but also of the priesthood of the faithful; a priesthood that is not superimposed, but by its nature included in the life of grace itself—a fact of which we need to become increasingly aware. The more we force ourselves to live fully the grace of baptism and confirmation, the more we shall be exercising our priesthood, and becoming able to offer ourselves, with all our activities, "as a living sacrifice, holy and acceptable to God" (Rom 12:1) in intimate union with Christ, priest and victim, for the glory of the Father and the salvation of mankind.

Father, all-powerful and ever-living God, we do well always and everywhere to give you thanks through Jesus Christ our Lord. Through his cross and resurrection he freed us from sin and death and called us to the glory that has made us a chosen race, a royal priesthood, a holy nation, a people set apart. Everywhere we proclaim your mighty works, for you have called us out of darkness into your own wonderful light.
Roman Sacramentary, Sundays in Ordinary Time I

O incredible mystery of Christian priesthood: man, of himself, is at the same time victim and priest. I no longer have to seek outside myself for what I desire to sacrifice to you, O Lord, since I carry with me and in me what I wish to sacrifice to you for my own good. It is an extraordinary sacrifice in which the body is offered up without being destroyed, and blood is given without being shed.
This sacrifice is like yours, O Christ, who, while yet alive, immolated your body for the life of the world: you made your body a living victim, since, although slain, you live. Therefore I may not refuse to be God's sacrifice and his priest. But may I put on the robe of sanctity, gird myself with the belt of chastity; and may you, O Christ, be like a veil upon my head, and let your cross rest as a protection upon my brow. Let me always burn like the sweet incense of prayer, brandish the sword of the spirit, and make my heart an altar, so that secure in your protection I may conduct my body to the sacrifice. O God you desire faith, not death; you thirst for a right intention rather than blood; you are appeased by holy desires rather than by the sacrifice of life. You dealt thus with the holy patriarch Abraham, when you commanded him to offer up his son, but did not permit him to slay him ... My body is immolated, yet at the same time lives every time I put my bad habits to death and sacrifice my life to you, O God, through the practice of virtue.
cf. St. Peter Chrysologus, *Sermon 108,* PL 52, 488 C-501A

84 — THE EUCHARIST

May all of us who share in the Body and Blood of Christ be brought together in unity by the Holy Spirit   (Eucharistic Prayer II)

1. "The other sacraments ... are linked with the holy Eucharist and are directed toward it. For the most blessed Eucharist contains the Church's entire spiritual wealth, that is,

Christ himself, our Passover and living bread. Through his very flesh, made vital and vitalizing by the Holy Spirit, he offers life to men" (P.O. 5).

Christian initiation begins with baptism and confirmation and is completed by the Eucharist. This divine food, which nourishes and increases the life of grace in the faithful, raises them to a living, intimate, personal communion with Christ. "I am the living bread which came down from heaven"—Jesus said—"If anyone eats of this bread he will live forever; and the bread which I shall give for the life of the world is my flesh . . . He who eats my flesh and drinks my blood abides in me and I in him" (Jn 6:51,56). The words with which the Lord announced and promised the Eucharist were literally realized on the evening of the last Supper, when he "took bread, and blessed, and broke it, and gave it to his disciples and said: 'Take, eat; this is my body' " (Mt 26:26). There is no question here of a symbol, but of a reality as true and concrete as it is mysterious: the substance of the bread and of the wine is changed into the substance of the Body and Blood of Christ. St. Ignatius the Martyr wrote to the early Christians: "The Eucharist is the flesh of our Savior, Jesus Christ; the flesh which suffered for our sins, but which the Father in his goodness raised again" (Smirn. 7).

Just as our natural life has its proper food for the growth and sustenance of the body, so the life of grace has its divine food: Jesus, the living bread, "the strength of our life's journey" (GS 38), which nourishes and perfects it until it is one day transfigured in eternal life. "O holy banquet"—sings the Liturgy—"in which Christ is received, the memory of his passion is renewed, the soul is filled with grace, and there is given to us a pledge of future glory" (RR).

2. "The faithful, already marked with the sacred seal of baptism and confirmation, are, through the reception of the Eucharist, fully joined to the Body of Christ" (PO 5). Like baptism and confirmation, the Eucharist also has an ecclesial dimension, for, while it intimately unites to Christ the faithful soul in whom it feeds and nourishes the life of grace, at the same time it perfects and accomplishes his full insertion into the Mystical Body of Christ. The two effects are simultaneous and indivisible: one necessarily calls forth the other. While the first, directly personal, is ordained for the sanctification of the individual and to his intimate communion with Christ, the second, which springs from the first, is directed toward his communion with the Church and with his fellow men. Communion with Christ cannot but be communion with those who are his members. Vatican Council II spells this out clearly: "Truly partaking of the Body of the Lord we are taken up into communion with him and with one another; 'Because the bread is one, we though many, are one body, all of us who partake of the one bread' (1 Cor 10:17). In this way all of us are made members of his Body" (LG 7).

Just as the individual Christian lives and grows supernaturally by eating the Eucharistic bread, so also "the Church constantly lives and grows from this bread" (LG 26). The Eucharist is the nourishment and viaticum of the individual, and by this very fact that of the People of God; just as it strengthens and nourishes union with Christ, so does it strengthen and nourish union between Christians. "In the sacrament of the Eucharistic bread, the unity of all believers who form one body in Christ is both expressed and brought about" (LG 3). Union with our Lord and union among the faithful is the characteristic grace of the Eucharist, which we should prepare ourselves to receive fully; hence we should behave in such a way that it will be operative in our lives, translating into practice our communion with Christ and with our brothers.

Our Father, as this broken bread was scattered over the hills and then, when gathered, became one mass, so may your Church be gathered from the ends of the earth into your kingdom. For yours is the glory and the power through Jesus Christ forevermore . . .

We give you thanks, O holy Father, for your holy name which you have enshrined in our hearts, and for the knowledge and faith and immortality which you have made known to us through Jesus, your Servant . . .

You, Lord Almighty, have created all things for the sake of your name and have given food and drink for men to enjoy, that they may give thanks to you; but to us you have vouchsafed spiritual food and drink and eternal life through the work of Jesus, your Servant . . .

Remember, O Lord your Church: deliver her from all evil, perfect her in your love, and from the four winds assemble her, the sanctified, in your kingdom which you have prepared for her.

Didache 9, 10

We are one bread, one body, even though we are many.

Oh, great mystery of love! Great symbol of unity! Great bond of charity! Whoever desires to live, has a place to live in, and what he needs in order to live. Believing, I will draw near, I will become part of him in order to be vivified by him. Let me not avoid union with the other members, nor be myself a corrupt member that deserves to be cut off, nor a deformed one of which the body is ashamed; rather, let me be a beautiful, modest, healthy living member, joined to the body and alive in and for you, O God; I will toil now in order to reign in heaven.

O Lord, let me be inebriated with the riches of your house, and give me to drink at the torrent of your delights, for in you is the source of life. Not outside of you, but within, in you is the spring of life. Here would I enter in order to live. I ought not believe that I am sufficient myself, for I would perish; I do not believe that I can be satisfied by myself alone, for then I would die of starvation; I must put my lips to that fountain whose water never fails.

St. Augustine, *In Io* 26:13; 25:17

YEAR A

Blessed are they who walk in the law of the Lord   (Ps 119:1)

Fidelity to the law of God is one of the central themes of the Old Testament, and it is interesting to see how the sacred author stresses man's responsibility in the face of this obligation. "If you will, you can keep the commandments; and to act faithfully is a matter of your own choice ... Before a man are life and death, and whichever he chooses will be given to him" (Sir 15:15,17). This is like saying that whoever follows the divine law will have life, and whoever turns his back upon it will meet death; eternal life as well as eternal death are but the consequence of his choices. Man is free, and therefore he is responsible for his actions; the evil he commits is to be blamed only on himself. God "has not commanded any one to be ungodly, and he has not given any one permission to sin" (ib. 20).

Love and faithfulness to the law constituted the entire justice and holiness of the people of Israel. However, the law was not yet perfect and men had made it too materialistic. Jesus comes and says "Think not that I have come to abolish the law and the prophets. I have come not to abolish them, but to fulfill them" (Mt 5:17). Jesus is teaching that fidelity to the material, external law is not enough; a deeper and more interior fidelity is demanded, one which engages mind and heart. "You have heard that it was said to the men of old ... but I say to you ... "; with this sentence, repeated six times, St. Matthew indicates the chief substance of the completion Jesus gave the law. For instance, it is not enough not to kill; we must guard against even simple words that express dislike or scorn or resentment against our neighbor. When we harbor anger or a grudge toward our brother we are, as it were, killing him in our heart; he is dead to our love, excluded from our good will and concern. It is not enough to abstain from actual actions against the law, we must also eliminate evil thoughts and desires, because he who consents to these has already sinned "in his heart" (ib. 28): he has killed his brother or has committed adultery, whatever the case may be. The work of excelling and completing the old law consists precisely in a careful attention to interior purity and to justice, not only in external behavior which is visible to all, but in the deep stirrings of heart and mind as well, which can be seen only by God. The prophets in the Old Testament had already spoken many times in this vein, but only Jesus, eternal Wisdom, could give the law its final perfection. For the Christian to be able to understand and live on such a level, he must let himself be penetrated with the wisdom of the gospel, which is not the wisdom of this world, but "a secret and hidden wisdom" (1 Cor 2:7): the mystery of Christ's cross which each of us must relive by dying to the wisdom of the world and of the flesh.

> *With my whole heart I seek you; let me not wander from your commandments! I have laid up your word in my heart, that I might not sin against you. Blessed be you, O Lord; teach me your statutes! (10-12).*
> *Open my eyes, that I may behold wondrous things out of your law . . . My soul is consumed with longing for your ordinances at all times (18-20).*
> *I have chosen the way of faithfulness, I set your ordinances before me. I cleave to your testimonies, O Lord; let me not be put to shame! I will run in the way of your commandments when you enlarge my understanding! (30-32).*
> *Your word is a lamp to my feet and a light to my path. I have sworn an oath and confirmed it, to observe your righteous ordinances (105-106).*
> *My tongue will sing of your word, for all your commandments are right . . . I long for your salvation, O Lord, and your law is my delight (172, 174).*
>
> *Psalm 119*

> *Oh, how sweet and desirable is the yoke of the law you impose on us, O Lord, who love us so much and are worthy of our love! . . . The heart that loves you loves your commandments, and the more difficult they are, the more sweetness and delight it finds in them, as an added opportunity to please you more perfectly and to render you greater honor. So it is when you teach your commandments, the heart of a lover pours forth hymns of gladness . . . and finds more comfort and refreshment in the weight of your precepts than in anything else in this mortal life.*
>
> St. Francis de Sales, *Love of God VIII* 5, v.2

YEAR B

Blessed is he whose transgression is forgiven, whose sin is covered (Ps 32:1)

The law of Moses prescribed: "The leper shall dwell alone in a habitation outside the camp" (Lev 13:46). This hard law is explained by the anxiety to avoid contagion, and by the concept that the Jews had regarding leprosy, which they saw as God's punishment for sinners. As a result the leper was avoided by everyone, and considered "unclean" and "smitten" by God, a cursed person.

Jesus, who had come to redeem man from sin and its consequences, had the right to go beyond the old law, and does so with the deliberate action of one who had full powers. "A leper came to

Divine Intimacy

him beseeching him and kneeling said to him: 'If you will, you can make me clean' " (Mk 1:40). What great faith! The poor fellow, abandoned by men and considered to be abandoned even by God, has more faith than many who are following in Christ's footsteps. Real faith does not get lost in subtle reasoning, but goes by a very simple logic: God can do all he wishes, he has only to will it. To his bold request expressing limitless trust, Jesus responds with an action that was unheard of among a people who were forbidden to have any contact whatever with lepers: "he stretched out his hand and touched him." God is master of the law, and can break it. "I will, be clean," he says, as if to emphasize the leper's words (ib. 41).

By welcoming and touching the leper, Jesus infringes the law; then he fulfills it, saying: "Go, show yourself to the priest, and offer for your cleansing what Moses commanded" (ib. 44). Charity can make legitimate the infringement of specific commandments, but it never condones the attitude of those who, under pretext of greater freedom for practicing love, would like to do away with all laws. Certainly the first law is love, but love is not authentic if it is not ordered according to God, and if it does not place God and his will above all things.

Mark makes it clear that Jesus performed the miracle "moved with pity" (ib. 41), a phrase we often meet in the gospel. Jesus has compassion on the leprosy that tortures bodies, but even more on that which tortures souls. By curing the one, he demonstrates his desire and ability to cure the other; his mission as Savior becomes visible; it will be carried out fully when, taking upon himself the leprosy of sin, he too will appear "despised and rejected by men . . . stricken, smitten by God, and afflicted" (Is 5:3-4).

Blessed is he whose transgression is forgiven, whose sin is covered. Blessed is the man to whom the Lord imputes no iniquity and in whose spirit there is no deceit . . . I acknowledged my sin to you, and I did not hide my iniquity; I said: 'I will confess my transgressions to the Lord,' then you forgave the guilt of my sin.
Psalm 32:1-2,5
Benefactor of all who turn to you, light of those in darkness, creator and principle of all life, gardener of all spiritual growth, have pity on me, Lord, and make of me a spotless temple. Do not consider my sins; if you pay attention to my faults I will not be able to stand your presence; but with your immense mercy and your infinite compassion cancel out my stains through our Lord Jesus Christ, your only most holy Son, the physician of our souls.
Early Christian Prayers, 89

Blessed is the man who trusts in the Lord   *(Jer 17:7)*

The Christian does not found his hope on himself, nor on other men, nor on worldly goods. His hope is rooted in Christ who died and rose again for him. St. Paul says: "If for this life only we have hoped in Christ, we are of all men most to be pitied" (1 Cor 15:19). Christian hope goes well beyond the limits of earthly life and reaches to eternal life precisely because of Christ, who rising again gave us the right to share one day in his resurrection.

The beatitudes proclaimed by the Lord are to be understood in this spirit, for, being anchored in the eternal, they go beyond every expectation of security and happiness in this world. With his beatitudes Jesus brought about a shift in the values of things: these are no longer to be considered in relation to the immediate and transitory suffering or joy they contain, but according to their future and eternal worth. Only one who believes in Christ, and, trusting in him, lives in expectation of the kingdom of God, can comprehend this very simple and essential line of reasoning: "Blessed are you poor ... Blessed are you that hunger now ... Blessed are you that weep now ... Blessed are you when men hate you" (Lk 6:20-22). Obviously it is not poverty, hunger, grief, or persecution as such that makes us blessed, nor do they give us entry to the kingdom of God; rather, it is through our acceptance of these privations and sufferings, sustained by trust in our heavenly Father. The more we open ourselves to trust in God when we are deprived of earthly security and happiness, the more we shall find our support and salvation in him. "Blessed is the man who trusts in the Lord, whose trust is the Lord" (Jer 17:7). On the other hand, the rich, those who are satiated, those who laugh now—these hear themselves threatened with painful "woes" (Lk 6:24-26), not so much because of the comforts they possess as because their great attachment to these things makes them put all their heart and all their hope in them. One who is satisfied with goals that are attainable on this earth is menaced by the worst of dangers: that of being shipwrecked through his own self-sufficiency without realizing the precariousness of his situation or feeling his urgent need to be saved from it. The kingdom of this world so satisfies him that the kingdom of God means nothing to him. That is why the prophet says: "Cursed is the man who trusts in man, and makes flesh his arm, whose heart turns away from the Lord" (Jer 17:5). The Lord's beatitudes are offered to everyone, but only those who are detached from self and from worldly goods are in a position to attain them.

Now, as long as I am in the body, I am far from you, Lord, since I go forward through faith and not through sight. The time will come when I shall see what I now believe without seeing, and when

I see what I now believe, I shall be happy ... Then the reality of what I now hope for will come ... Now I lament, as I go about searching for a secure refuge where I can be safe; now, seeing myself sick, I have recourse to the doctor ... Now in the time of hope, of tears, in the time of humility, sorrow and sickness ... I have become an object of wonder for many ... because I believe what I do not see. In fact, those who are happy in what they see take their delight in drink and in pleasure ... in greed and wealth and rapine and worldly honors ... they delight in these things. But I walk by a different path, paying no heed to present reality and fearing success in this life. I find security in nothing except in your promises, O my God (In Ps 70,8-9).

I live happily in my hope, because you, Lord, are true to your promises; yet since I do not yet possess you, I groan under the sting of desire. Make me persevere in this desire until what you have promised comes: then will my lamentation cease and only praise will ring out (In Ps 148:1).

St. Augustine

86 — THE EUCHARISTIC SACRIFICE

In union with the Eucharistic offering accept, O Father, the offering of myself as a living sacrifice, holy and acceptable to you (Rom 12:1)

1. The Eucharist is not only a sacrament, it is also a sacrifice; indeed, the sacrament is completed through the sacrifice: "At the last Supper, on the night he was betrayed, our Savior instituted the Eucharistic sacrifice of his Body and Blood. He did this in order to perpetuate the sacrifice of the cross throughout the centuries, until he should come again, and thus he entrusted to his beloved spouse, the Church, a memorial of his death and resurrection: a sacrament of love, a sign of unity, a bond of charity, a paschal banquet in which Christ is consumed" (SC 47). After blessing and distributing the bread Jesus said: "This is my body which is given for you;" and then added: "Do this in remembrance of me" (Lk 22:19). The Eucharistic Sacrifice perpetuates and renews upon our altars the sacrifice of the cross for the glory of the most blessed Trinity, in reparation for our sins, and at the same time, it prepares the sacrament of the Lord's Body, which is the food of our souls. Thus the Eucharistic Mystery is at once a sacrifice and a sacrament, an oblation and a banquet. It is "the center and culmination ... of all Christian life" (CD 30; cf. LG 11); above all, of the worship that must be rendered to God, and also of the sanctification of the faithful, of their union with Christ, and with one another. The Eucharistic Sacrifice is "the one sacrifice of the New Testament" (LG 28), and each time "it is celebrated on an altar, the work of our redemption is renewed" (ib. 3). Faced with so sublime a mystery in which is gathered together all God's action

for the sanctification of the world, and all the worship that men render God, one can understand the Church's deep concern that the faithful should take part in it not "as strangers or silent spectators, but . . . that they participate knowingly, devoutly and actively" (SC 48), and identify themselves through their prayer and interior dispositions with what is taking place on the altar.

2. Vatican II affirms: "The faithful join in the offering of the Eucharist by virtue of their royal priesthood . . . Taking part in the Eucharistic Sacrifice, which is the fount and apex of Christian life, they offer the divine Victim to God, and offer themselves along with it. Thus both by the act of oblation and through Holy Communion, all perform their proper part in this liturgical service" (LG 10-11). This is the highest actualization of the priesthood of the faithful, the one which most intimately links them to Jesus the Priest, who in a special way is "present in the Sacrifice of the Mass, not only in the person of his minister . . . but especially under the Eucharistic species" (SC 7). By participating in the Mass we join in the prayer of praise, of thanksgiving, of entreaty and of reparation which Christ, the eternal high Priest, offers to the Father; moreover we are associated in his sacrificial offering, not only by word, but much more by our interior attitude. The action that the minister performs at the altar in virtue of Holy Orders when he offers to God "this holy and perfect sacrifice" (Euch. Pr. I) is also fulfilled by the faithful in virtue of their spiritual priesthood; they accomplish it in the depths of their hearts, accompanied by the offering of themselves. The Council specifically exhorts them that "by offering the immaculate victim, not only through the hands of the priest, but also with him, they should learn to offer themselves" (SC 48). This offering should be so concrete that it embraces all the varied aspects of life: prayer, work, duties of our state of life, sufferings, contradictions, so that all things "become spiritual sacrifices . . . During the celebration of the Eucharist, these sacrifices are most lovingly offered to the Father along with the Lord's Body" (LG 34). Our entire life is thus taken up into the Eucharistic Sacrifice and consecrated in it. This is completed and perfected by our participation at the holy table by which we are most intimately assimilated to Jesus, priest and victim, "since the partaking of the Body and Blood of Christ does nothing other than transform us into that which we consume" (LG 26).

In all things and through all things, we sing to you, we bless you, we offer you thanks, O Lord, and declare you to be our God.
For this, most holy Teacher, we also who have been deemed worthy to serve at your holy altar, not through our merit, for we have done nothing good on earth, but through your goodness and your superabundant mercy, we dare to approach your altar and to offer the sacrament of the holy Body and Blood of your Christ . . .

*May all of us who share in the one bread and the one chalice be
united with each other in communion with the one Holy Spirit, and
may none of us participate in the holy Body and Blood of Christ for
our judgment and condemnation; but may we rather find compassion and grace with all the saints who have been pleasing to you
from the beginning.*

St. Basil, from *Early Christian Prayers* 306

*O God, look with love upon this victim which you yourself have
given to your Church: by your Holy Spirit gather all who eat of this
one bread and drink of this one chalice into the one body of Christ,
that they may become in Christ a living sacrifice of praise.*

Roman Sacramentary, Eucharistic Prayer IV

*During the Consecration and Communion, I will offer myself to
you with great love, my Lord, and with deep reverence tell you from my
heart that, just as you offer yourself to the Father for me and for my
welfare, so do I desire to offer myself entirely to his divine Majesty
and to dedicate myself with all my strength to the service of his
kingdom. Lord, break me like the bread of your sacrament, bend me,
twist me if necessary in the coils of your will, but let me be united to
the Host broken over the chalice, my only source of peace.*

G. Canovai, *Suscipe Domine*

87 — PENANCE

*O Lord, turn away your face from my sins, and blot out all my
iniquities*   *(Ps 51:9)*

1. The grace conferred by baptism, strengthened by confirmation and nourished by the Eucharist, does not make man impec-
cable. Although it contains in itself an unfailing power of sanctification, it does not compel us to be good. We are always free to
correspond, or not to correspond, with the divine gift; we always
have the unhappy possibility of resisting grace by acceding to
evil. Although we are called to be saints, in reality "we all make
many mistakes" (Jas 3:2), "we all need God's mercy
continuously" (LG 40). The mystery of salvation was specifically
instituted by divine mercy to save man the sinner. "I came not to
call the righteous, but sinners" (Mt 9:13), said Jesus, and it was
for the remission of sins that he instituted the sacrament of
penance: "If you forgive the sins of any, they are forgiven, if you
retain the sins of any, they are retained" (Jn 20:23).

The sacrament of penance presupposes interior repentance on
the part of the penitent, that is to say, conversion, for without it
the sacrament itself would have no effect. Jesus began his public
life by preaching this repentance: "Repent and believe in the
gospel!" (Mk 1:15). Sin, of whatever degree, always brings with it

a refusal—more or less serious—of the love of God, and is therefore an estrangement from him, from his law, and from the gospel; only God can forgive this, but such forgiveness requires an internal change which will cause man to reverse his direction. "I will arise"—said the prodigal son who by leaving home had rejected his father's love—"and go to my father, and I will say to him: 'Father, I have sinned against heaven and before you'" (Lk 15:18). The Christian who approaches the sacrament of penance by confessing his sins with this attitude will receive pardon; a forgiveness so copious and generous that it will confer an increase of grace upon him, or if this has been lost—restore it intact as on the day of his baptism.

2. In speaking of the woman who was a sinner, Jesus said: "Her sins which are many are forgiven, for she loved much" (Lk 7:47). The more repentance for sins is accompanied, indeed even generated, by love, the more it disposes us for a full generous forgiveness. "Love covers a multitude of sins" (1 Pet 4:8), so that an act of perfect contrition, that is, one motivated by love for God, can obtain justification for us, quite apart from the sacrament. However, this does not mean that the sacrament is superfluous, or that it can be neglected, since it is God's will that all serious sins be subject to it. Moreover, as St. Thomas teaches, there cannot be true contrition without at least the implicit intention of confessing. (cf. Quod libet 4,10,3). On the other hand, who can be certain of having perfect contrition for his sins and, hence, of having obtained their pardon? But the sacrament helps the penitent to perfect his repentance and also makes him sure of God's forgiveness and of his being re-established in his friendship. Herein lies the great value of the sacrament of penance, in which Christ works to convert the sinner and vivify him through his grace.

The Council urges the faithful "to submit their sins with a contrite heart to the Church in the sacrament of penance . . . (so they) will be drawn ever closer to the Lord each day" (PO 5). In virtue of their priesthood the faithful are not just passive subjects of the sacraments; they take a vital part in them in the sense that they cooperate in their actualization. In regard to confession, their cooperation consists precisely in "submitting their sins with a contrite heart to the Church" which means they are supplying the material for the sacrament. This is accomplished not only by the confession of grave sins, as is required, but also through what is optional, but still very much to be recommended, the confession of venial sins. In every case we must be conscious of our own responsibility in regard to the sacrament, and approach it with a truly contrite heart; only in this way will it help us "to draw closer to the Lord each day"; then each confession will be a step forward on the road to total conversion.

My soul, if you have sinned and are still wounded, here is your God, here is your physician ready to heal you. His omnipotence permits him to remit all your sins in one moment, his goodness and his mercy impel him to forgive you. Perhaps you are frightened because he is your judge; but have confidence, my soul, because if he is your judge, he is also your defender to excuse you and justify you if you are sorry; he is your judge not to condemn but to save you, if only you humble yourself. His mercy is infinitely greater than all your iniquity. I am telling you this, not because, by remaining in your sin, you make yourself unworthy of his mercy, but because, if you cast off evil, you have no longer any cause to despair of his mercy and pardon.

Bl. Ludovicus Blosius, *Paradise of the Faithful Soul* I, 1

O most loving Lord Jesus Christ ... you overflow with such great and inexpressible goodness that your love for us is always anticipating ours; you show yourself and run to meet those who are seeking you; you love, and your immense charity extends even to enemies. You reject no one, nor do you scorn anyone, but call everyone to you and receive them as your friends, except those who are stubbornly rebellious and, on account of their sin, and in spite of and contrary to your will, draw away from you. Even then your mercy is so overflowing and infinite that you wait for the repentance of those who are miserably wallowing in sin, and sometimes, even when rebellious, you constrain them to come back to you.

O deign to help me, most merciful Lord Jesus Christ, the fire and light of love; inflame and enlighten my stubborn heart which is so rebellious to your love. Grant that, with your help, I may be sorry for my sins and all my sinfulness, and do worthy penance. Help me to perform with a pure, humble and loving heart works of zeal that will please you, so that preceded, aided, and accompanied by your grace, I may live here in your love, and when my life is over, may through your mercy obtain eternal life in order to love you in glory.

R. Giordano, *Contemplazioni sull' amore divino* 6

88 — THE ECCLESIAL VALUE OF PENANCE

O Jesus, who love the Church as your bride, and gave yourself up for her to make her holy, do not let me defile your work with sin   *(Eph 5:25-26)*

1. The Council wishes to "impress on the minds of the faithful, not only the social consequences of sin, but also the fact that the real essence of the virtue of penance is hatred for sin as an offense

against God" (SC 109). The primary motive for repentance of sin is the injury done to God, that is the resistance to his love, the rejection or low esteem of his friendship, ingratitude for his benefits, scorn or indifference to his will as expressed in the law. Obviously God cannot be harmed by the sins of men, but still, when they directly harm the neighbor, they always wound God who loves each of his creatures, and desires and safeguards the welfare of each. Therefore sin can be forgiven only by God, and is to be detested above all as an offense against his infinite goodness. But we need to remember that every sin also brings with it more or less serious social consequences that are more or less evident according to their nature. In the Church of the early centuries there was a very lively sense of the social aspect of sin; public penances were imposed on public sinners, and only when they had atoned for their wrong doings were they readmitted to the community. Time has changed this practice but not its spirit; today also, anyone who has sinned gravely is excluded from the Eucharistic Communion until he has been reconciled with God and with the Church in the sacrament of penance.

"Those who approach the sacrament of penance"—teaches the Council—"obtain pardon from the mercy of God for offenses committed against him. At the same time they are reconciled with the Church which they have wounded by their sins and which by charity, example and prayer seeks their conversion" (LG 11). Although confession is a secret and strictly private act, the fact that God's pardon reaches the penitent through the medium of the priest, expresses not only the Church's presence, but also reconciliation with the Church. Therefore while the sacrament of penance has intimate and personal value for him who receives it, it also has an ecclesial value. It reestablishes and strengthens our relationship of friendship with God and with the Church; it purifies the individual and at the same time heals the wound our sins have inflicted on the Church.

2. St. Paul expresses it: "We, though many, are one body in Christ, and individually members one of another" (Rom 12:5). Through the solidarity that unites all those who believe in Christ, to the point of forming one single body in him, the good as well as the evil of each one is the good or evil of all. Sin wounds Christ, the head of the Mystical Body, because it is an offence against God, and it wounds the members of that same Body because it spiritually or materially injures our brethren. Even the most secret and personal sin has harmful consequences in the community because it diminishes the level of grace, of virtue and of holiness, and increases the weight of misery that obstructs the road to God. Just as a single act of charity increases love throughout the Church, so love is diminished by a single act of aversion. Besides, sin very often injures our neighbor more directly, as with wrongs against justice. sincerity, charity and respect

for the person and the goods of others. This calls for just reparation, and the sacrament of penance provides for this whether the priest, who is at one and the same time the representative of God and of the Church, forgives sins in the name of God and of the Church, and therefore of the community as well, or whether, by imposing sacramental penance, he points out to the penitent how he must compensate for the harm done to his neighbor.

In every case, the penitent must approach the sacrament conscious of both the Church and the community, that is, not only for his own personal conversion, progress and salvation, but also, in view of the welfare of his brothers, with a desire to make up for the harm his sins have done to them, and to put himself in a position to bring to society and to the Church that contribution of holiness he has acquired through baptism. The Church shines before men and attracts them to God in the measure of her holiness. But she is more or less holy according to the holiness of her children, and more or less in need of purification, according to their faults and deficiencies. Each of the faithful must be concerned not to increase by his sins what can be censured in the Church; therefore he must not cease to "do penance and renew himself" (LG 8) so that, as far as depends on him, the Church may be as Christ wants her to be, "holy and immaculate, without stain or wrinkle" (Eph 5:27).

We confess to you, O God, lover of men, and we offer you our weakness, begging you to be our strength. Pardon our past sins, remit the faults of a period, make new men of us. Make us, your servants, pure and spotless. We consecrate ourselves to you: accept us, O God of truth, accept your people and wipe out all our stains; make us live in uprightness and innocence. Make us such that we may be counted among the angels, all of us elect and holy.
Early Christian Prayers, 183

Now I beg you, Father, to be merciful to the world and to your holy Church. I pray you to accomplish what you have caused me to ask of you. Alas! what a wretched and sorrowful soul is mine, the cause of all these evils. Do not put off any longer your merciful designs towards the world, but descend and fulfill the desire of your servants . . .
O eternal Father, your servants cry out to your mercy; do you then reply. I know well that mercy is your own attribute, wherefore you cannot destroy it or refuse it to him who asks for it. Your servants knock at the door of your truth . . . your only begotten Son . . .
Wherefore open, unlock, and break the hardened hearts of your creatures, not for their sakes who do not knock, but on account of your infinite goodness, and for love of your servants who knock at you for their sakes . . . For what do they

pray? For the blood of Christ, your door and your Truth; with this blood you have washed away our iniquities and destroyed the stain of Adam's sin. This blood is ours, for you have made it our bath, wherefore you cannot deny it to anyone who truly asks for it. Give, then, the fruit of your blood to your creatures. Place in the balance the price of the blood of your Son, so that the infernal devils may not carry off your lambs. You are the good Shepherd who, to fulfill your obedience, laid down his life for your lambs, and made for us a bath of his blood. That blood is what your hungry servants beg of you, begging you through it to do mercy to the world and to cause your holy Church to bloom with the fragrant flowers of good and holy pastors.

St. Catherine of Siena, *Dialogue* 134

89 — PENANCE AS A VIRTUE

Lord, let me crucify my flesh with its passions and desires (Gal 5:24)

1. "Penance" is the sacrament that remits sins, it is the repentance and interior conversion from which flows a change in one's manner of life; it is also the virtue which induces a man to make amends for his sins by personal acts of atonement. First among these is the "penance" that the confessor imposes on the penitent; although it is generally a small act, still it has a quite special value because it is linked to the sacrament and therefore shares in the infinite atoning merits of Christ. But sacramental penance does not exhaust our obligation to make reparation for our sins; in fact the Church used to remind us of this in the prayer of the priest that followed: "May ... whatever good you do and evil you endure be cause for the remission of your sins ..." The grace of forgiveness harmonizes with the duty of either fleeing sin or atoning for it. It is not simply a question of interior spiritual penance, but must also include one that is external and corporal. This is repentance in the full sense that Jesus preached, and of which he himself gave an example. "Christ, is indeed the supreme model of penitents: he wished to undergo punishment for sins that were not his, but those of others" (Paul VI, Paen. 5). Christ's passion and death give concrete evidence that penance cannot be only spiritual, but must also be corporal and physical; it must embrace the whole man. Since it is the whole man who sins, it is the whole man who must do penance. All the more so because on account of the disorder caused by original sin, the flesh always tends to rebel against the spirit, and to impede its doing good. St. Paul admits it: "I see in my members another law at war with the law of my mind" (Rom 7:23). To reestablish order, to subject the flesh to the spirit, we must mortify the flesh. This "does not imply con-

demnation of the flesh, which the Son of God deigned to assume; as a matter of fact, mortification aims at man's liberation, for on account of his concupiscence he often finds himself as if shackled to the sense part of his nature" (Paen. 8). Penance frees man from the weight of sin so that he can run swiftly in the service of God.

2. The Church "insists above all that we practice the virtue of penance by persevering faithfully in the duties of our state of life, by accepting the difficulties which arise from our work and from human society, and by patiently putting up with the trials of earthly life and with the deep insecurity that pervades it" (Paen. 10). This is the most important and sanctifying penance, because it does not depend upon our personal choice, but upon the will of God, who disposes and measures out what is best suited to each individual for the atonement of his sins and for reaching sanctity. The life of each of us contains a sufficient measure of suffering to make a saint of us, if only we will accept it with a humble and obedient heart.

In addition, the Church "invites all Christians, indiscriminately, to respond to the divine precept of penance with some voluntary act besides the renunciations caused by the weight of daily life" (ib. 11). These voluntary acts demonstrate good will on our part, our sincere desire for conversion, our awareness that we must compensate for the injury done to God by a generous active love that overcomes all resistance to his infinite love. If we then add to this a deeper love for God and our neighbor—one which impels us to do penance also for the sins of others, we become like Christ who took it upon himself to atone in his innocent flesh for the sins of all mankind. If we follow the Master in this way, we shall no longer be living for self, but for him who loved us and gave his life for us, and we too shall live "for the brethren, completing 'in our body what is lacking in the sufferings of Christ . . . for the good of his body which is the Church' " (Paen. 6). In this way, the penance which began with a humble act of repentance and atonement for our own sins, ends in an act of intense love that likens us to the crucified Christ, and intimately unites us to him in suffering that is willingly embraced for the salvation of our brothers.

Penance thus becomes an excellent apostolic work which has an irreplaceable value, for there are certain victories which are not won save by paying a personal price. "Unless the grain of wheat falls to the earth and dies, it remains alone; but if it dies, it produces much fruit" (Jn 12:24).

Lord, if you had desired sacrifice, I would certainly have offered it to you. But you are not pleased with holocausts. But then, shall I offer you nothing? Shall I come to you like this? How can I placate you? I will offer—certainly there is something in me to offer. I shall not prepare any gift from outside myself. . . . I shall not seek outside myself for an animal to sacrifice; I have within me a victim for the sacrifice. O God, my sacrifice to you is a contrite and humbled heart ... I know that you are most high; if I raise myself up, you will withdraw from me; but if I humble myself, you will draw near.

When the whole animal was placed on the altar to be consumed by fire, it was called a holocaust. Let your divine fire take complete hold of me, O Lord, and possess me entirely. Let not only my soul be seized by the fire of your wisdom, but my body also, so that I may become worthy of eternity.

St. Augustine, *In Ps.* 50:21-23

My Lord and my God, I am so worthless; how much need there is for you to make me love penance, by showing me how indissolubly it is tied to your love!

It should suffice for me to know that you practiced it all your life, secretly and publicly, that you fasted during Lent and died on the cross. Oh! let your example be enough to make me practice penance with all my might, with no other motive than pure love and the simple need of imitating you, to be like you, to share in your life and especially in your sufferings! And if I love you so little that your example is not enough, perhaps your words will help me: "Do penance ... when the bridegroom has gone, they will fast."

O my God, grant that I may offer you in a spirit of sacrifice and in your honor all the thoughts, words and actions of each day, my activity, my very being. I beg that it may all be a sacrifice that will please you, and so make me a perpetual victim of a sacrifice that will be present in every moment of the day.

cf. C. de Foucauld, *Retreat at Nazareth,*
(Meditations of a Hermit, p. 88)

90 — THE ANOINTING OF THE SICK

May the Lord forgive you by this holy anointing and his most loving mercy whatever sins you have committed. (RR)

1. St. James writes: "Is there any among you sick? Let him call for the elders of the Church, and let them pray over him anointing him with oil in the name of the Lord" (5:14). These words make known to us the sacrament of the sick, whose function has been clarified by Vatican Council II: "The anointing of the sick is not a sacrament for those only who are at the point of death. Hence as soon as any of the faithful begins to be in danger of death from sickness or old age, the appropriate time for him to receive this sacrament has certainly already arrived" (SC 73). This is an important clarification, because ignorance about this sacra-

ment and the fear of upsetting the sick have often led to the custom of confining its administration to the last moment when the sick person is by then unconscious and is incapable of receiving it with all its fruit. We need, therefore, to remember that the anointing of the sick is ordered not only for the salvation of the soul, but also for the benefit of the body, so as to alleviate and sanctify physical and moral sufferings. In administering the holy rite, the Church prays: "Cure the illness of this sick person, we implore you, O our Savior . . . and drive away from him all pains of mind and body. In your mercy give him health so that he may be able to take up his usual work" (RR). Jesus cured many sick people during his earthly life and does so still through this sacrament in which he himself continues to work with his omnipotent power. We must not conclude from this that the holy anointing will always restore health; this will happen only when God so disposes it for the greater spiritual good of the sick person. Still, if it were received with lively faith, this effect of the sacrament would certainly be less rare. "The prayer of *faith*"—says St. James—"will save the sick man and the Lord will raise him up" (5:15). However, the most suitable disposition for receiving the grace of this sacrament is, together with faith, *devotion* (St. Thos. *Supp.* 29:4) in the Latin sense of the word, i.e. the interior offering of the person who gives himself, who consecrates himself to God without reservation, leaving himself completely in his hands as regards both the welfare of his soul and that of his body.

2. "By the anointing of the sick and the prayer of her priests, the whole Church commends those who are ill to the suffering and glorified Lord, asking that he may lighten their sufferings and save them. She exhorts them, however . . . to associate themselves freely with the passion and death of Christ" (LG 11). The Church is concerned for her sick children with a mother's solicitude, and when administering extreme unction prays for their salvation and, indeed, for their "*full* spiritual health" (RR). St. Thomas teaches that the anointing of the sick is like the "consummation"—the perfection—of the soul's purification, by which it is made ready to enter into glory (*IV contra Gentes* 73; St. Thos. *Supp.* 29:1,2). Its particular effect is precisely "the grace of the Holy Spirit whose anointing takes away the residue of sin, and animates and revives courage in the sick person, arousing great trust in God's mercy, so that the soul bears the sufferings of illness more calmly and resists more easily the temptations of the devil" (Conc. Trent DZ-SCH 1696). Without doubt, the anointing has the power also to "cancel the venial sins which the sick person, although he has attrition, may not be able to confess" (*Catech.* St. Pius X); however this is not its characteristic grace, which is rather the effect proper to the sacrament of penance. Nevertheless, it destroys the last consequences of sin, healing the soul of the lassitude and the weakness which are the natural effects of sins already forgiven by

confession, whose punishment has been remitted. Just as confirmation perfects the effects of baptism, so the anointing of the sick perfects those of penance. Thus he who receives this sacrament with a lively faith finds himself ready, when God calls him, to go directly from this earthly exile to eternal glory, without having to stop in purgatory. This is a most precious consequence for the soul that yearns eagerly for the supreme meeting, and is due to the great mercy of Jesus our Savior. Then, if the illness is prolonged, the sick one will be helped by the grace of the sacrament to endure his sufferings with greater resignation, so as to "contribute to the welfare of the whole People of God by associating himself freely with the passion and death of Christ" (LG 11). The holy anointing makes the sick person like the suffering Jesus, in whose passion it makes him share for his own sanctification and for the good of the whole Church.

You have softened the terrors of death for us, Lord; you have made the end of our life the beginning of true life. You make our body rest for a short time, but only for a short time. Then you will awaken us with the sound of the last trumpet. You commit us to the earth which you have made, that it may preserve us; some day you will restore our mortal remains and make them beautiful for ever.

For us you became malediction and sin to save us from the curse of sin. You prepared our resurrection when you burst the gates of hell and destroyed by your death the one who had empire over death.

You have given to the fearful the sign of the cross to destroy their enemies; and you have assured us that we will have life, O eternal God, to whom I was offered as a babe and whom I have loved with all my strength.

O Master, send me an angel of light to conduct me to that place of refreshment, whence flows the spring that quenches our thirst.

You gave paradise to the man who was crucified with you, and the fear of your judgment has pierced my flesh. Grant that the abyss may not separate me from your elect! Remember not my sins. If, because of the weakness of my nature, I have failed in thought, word, or deed, pardon me, for you have the power to forgive sins. May my soul be found without guilt when I lay aside the garment of my body. At that moment, deign to receive it without spot or blemish into your hands as an offering pleasing to you.

St. Macrina, from *Early Christian Prayers* 258

91 — OUR BLESSED HOPE

O Lord, teach us to live sober, upright and godly lives in this world, awaiting our blessed hope   *(Tit 2:12-13)*

1. According to Pauline thought, we must live, "awaiting our blessed hope, the appearing of the glory of our great God and Savior Jesus Christ" (Tit 2:13). The living faith of the early Church was expressed in a deep yearning for eternal life; St. Paul's letters document this: "Here indeed we groan and long to put on our heavenly dwelling" because "while we are at home in the body we are away from the Lord" (2 Cor 5:2,6) and therefore our "desire is to depart and be with Christ" (Phil 1:23).

Nevertheless for the "blessed hope" of returning to God to be realized, we must pass through the dark reality of death. Death always awakens a feeling of repulsion and of horror. This is natural, indeed the Church declares that man judges "rightly . . . when he abhors and repudiates the absolute ruin and total disappearance of his own person. Man rebels against death, for he bears in himself an eternal seed" (GS 18). Man was in fact created for live in the fullest sense: eternal life in God. "Because God did not make death";—warns Scripture—"ungodly men by their words and deeds summoned death" (Wis 1:13,16).

Death, the consequence and the punishment of sin, does violence to our nature; it is opposed to our vocation to eternity. Only faith, a lively faith in Christ the Savior can make us accept death serenely, as a passage that leads to our eternal meeting with God. In reality, when the Son of God redeemed us from sin, he also redeemed us from death; by taking death upon himself, he conquered death itself, and snatched away its prey, and by rising again made us share in his eternal life. Regarding death, there is always the bitter reality that it dissolves the body; but it cannot damage the soul: through the bitterness of our physical destruction, we depart from this exile "to be with Christ" and the day will come when our body also will "put on the imperishable" (1 Cor 15:54), and will share in his glory. Thus the Christian finds again, in Christ the Savior, his destiny for eternal life; death is not an irremediable end but the beginning of true life "in an endless sharing of a divine life beyond all corruption" (GS 18).

2. "My desire is to depart and to be with Christ" (Phil 1:23). Faith and love are so strong in the saints that when they consider death they are much more struck by the joy of meeting Christ than by the fear of dissolution of the body, to the point where they even desire the latter so that they may obtain the former. "Tear through the veil of this sweet encounter," sings St. John of the Cross, and he explains that persons who have reached transforming love are so possessed by the desire to be reunited with God that although "the death of other people is caused by sickness or

old age, the death of these persons is not so induced: in spite of their being sick or old, their soul is not wrested from them unless by some impetus and encounter of love ... (capable of) tearing through this veil and carrying off the jewel, which is the soul" (LF 1:30). This is a "death of love," a precious and blessed death, a true nuptial meeting of the soul with God, which introduces it directly to the beatific vision of heaven.

Jesus also, when speaking of death, compared it to an encounter with the bridegroom. "At midnight there was a cry: Behold the bridegroom! Come out to meet him!" But while the wise virgins who had been waiting with ready lamps, were ushered into the wedding, the foolish virgins who had fallen asleep, unprepared, were left outside; the parable ends with the warning: "Watch, therefore, for you know neither the day nor the hour" (Mt 25:1-13). We must be so vigilant that at whatever moment the Lord calls, death may not take us by surprise, but may find us ready, like those faithful servants who wait for their master, "so that they may open to him at once, when he comes and knocks" (Lk 12:36). Then there will be no regrets, no fears or anxieties, for anyone who has always lived in expectation of the Lord does not fear his coming, but, as soon as he comes, runs to meet him, lovingly saying to him: "Behold, I come" (Ps 40:8). Thus death becomes the final and most meritorious act of our adherence to the will of God. Just as the divine will must place its mark on the entire life of a Christian, so it must also countersign our last step. When death is accepted with loving adherence to God's will, it is truly a death of love, even though stripped of eagerness and accompanied by natural repugnance.

Lord ... I have loved you with my whole soul and all my life. I will be happy in seeing you and you will give me rest, and henceforth I shall live no more in this world ... I shall receive that life that knows no suffering, nor worry, nor anguish, neither persecutor nor persecution, neither oppressor nor oppression, neither tyrant nor victim ... My wounded feet will find healing in you, O way of all pilgrims; my tired limbs will find their rest in you, O Christ, the chrism of our anointing. In you, the chalice of our salvation, the sadness of my heart will disappear, and in you, our consolation and our joy, all my tears will be wiped away.
St. Simeon of Seleucia, from Early Christian Prayers 83

O my delight, Lord of all created things and my God! How long must I wait to see you? What remedy do you provide for one who finds so little on earth that might give some rest apart from you? O long life! O painful life! Oh, what lonely solitude; how incurable! Well, when, Lord, when? How long? What shall I do, my God, what shall I do? Should I, perhaps, desire not to desire you? O my God and my Creator, you wound and you do not supply the medecine; you wound and the sore is not seen; you kill, leaving one with more life! ...

Divine Intimacy

The soul, so imprisoned, wants its freedom, while desiring not to depart one iota from what you want. Desire, my Glory, that its pain increase; or cure it completely. O death, death, I don't know who fears you, since life lies in you! But who will not fear after having wasted a part of life in not loving God? And since I am one of these, what do I ask for, and what do I desire? Perhaps the punishment so well deserved for my faults? Don't permit it, my Good, for my ransom cost you a great deal.

St. Teresa of Jesus, *Soliloquies* 6:1-2

92 — SEVENTH SUNDAY IN ORDINARY TIME

YEAR A

The Lord is merciful and gracious, slow to anger and abounding in steadfast love   *(Ps 103:8)*

The law of Moses said: "You shall not hate your brother in your heart . . . You shall not take vengeance or bear any grudge against the sons of your own people, but you shall love your neighbor as yourself" (Lev 19:17-18); it is a beautiful passage, a true pearl of the Old Testament, in which the spirit of the New is already included. However, whether it was due to the way the law was formulated or to the tendency to interpret it in a restricted sense, what happened in practice was that love of one's neighbor was restricted to one's fellow-countrymen.

Jesus broke down the barriers and gave the precept of brotherly love a universal dimension. "You have heard it said, 'You shall love your neighbor and hate your enemy.' But I say to you, 'Love your enemies and pray for those who persecute you'" (Mt 5:43-44). Actually, no passage of the Bible prescribed hatred of one's enemies; it was the practical result of a mutilation of the law becoming the norm of life. Jesus confronts and totally condemns it; he had come to perfect the law, and does so in a special way in regard to charity, which man through selfishness is so much inclined to wound and adulterate. The terms Christ used are so clear that they admit no arbitrary interpretation; a Christian must love friend and enemy without exception. The motive is the same for both: both are children of God, therefore all men are brothers—neighbors. Seen in this light, there is no reason for distinctions between one people and another, between one race and another. There are not even distinctions based on love or hatred, good or evil, kindness or injury, or insults or injustices suffered. Nor is it permissible, for any reason, to hate one's brother, the son of the same Father, the object of the same paternal love. Upon the acceptance or the rejection of this duty by the individual depends his being or not being recognized by God as his child. "Love . . . so that you may be sons of your Father who is in heaven; for he makes his sun rise on the evil and on the good, and sends rain on the just and on the unjust" (ib. 44-45). Just as a son reflects the features of his father, so in his relations with his equals a Christian must reflect God's love for all men.

The world considers it foolishness to return love for hate, good for evil, and forgiveness for insults; but St. Paul warns that if we want to follow Christ we must make ourselves foolish, "for the wisdom of this world is folly with God" (1 Cor 3:19), Christians are not to be preoccupied with the world because they are "Christ's and Christ is God's" (ib. 23); being Christ's, they follow only his teaching, and with him and in him want to belong to God, emulating his infinite perfection and his limitless love.

> *Nothing in nature more resembles you, O most sweet Jesus Christ, than one who is merciful toward malicious and injurious enemies; since he who loves his enemy imitates you who loved us when we were still your enemies; and you not only loved us, but you even chose to die an ignominious death for us, and you prayed for those who crucified you.*
>
> *You commanded us to love our enemies, saying: "Love your enemies, and do good to those who hate you;" and you promise this reward: "that you may be children of your Father who is in heaven."*
>
> *O Lord Jesus Christ, who by nature are always inclined to mercy and to forgiveness, there is only one absolute proof of real charity: to love those who are against us and who impede our good works ... I will confess to you with my heart and with my mouth that I have lived wickedly, and because of my malice and wickedness, I am deprived of true charity. Among other thoughts and actions, Lord, which I despicably conceived and executed, is that of having hated my enemy. I harbored resentment toward many, and gave full vent to such a sentiment, both in my heart and in my will ...*
>
> *Help me, O loving Lord Jesus Christ; through your blessed and merciful love, grant me forgiveness so that I may amend my wretched life and love you and others for your sake, so that this love may never grow less, but may last for ever in eternal life.*
>
> R. Giordano, *Contemplazione sull'amore divino*, 32

YEAR B

O Lord, be gracious to me; heal me, for I have sinned against you
(Ps 41,4)

God calls Israel to judgment: Israel, the object of his predilection and of his favors, yet always ready to betray him, to neglect his love and his worship. "Yet you did not call upon me, O Jacob; but you have been weary of me, O Israel ... You have burdened me with your sins, and have wearied me with your iniquities" (Is 43:22,24). Yet God, faithful to his covenant with his people, is still disposed to forgive: "I am he who blots out your transgressions, and I will not remember your sins" (ib. 25).

If man is inexhaustible in sin, God is even more so in pardon. The incarnation of his only Son and the work of redemption are the clearest proof of that. In a thousand ways Christ showed how much God loves to forgive; how he even anticipates forgiveness before it is asked for. There is the case of the paralyzed man of Capharnaum who was let down through the roof upon his mat in front of Jesus, who was hemmed in by the crowd that had rushed into the house to hear him. The poor sick man, who, in hope of recovery, had let himself be transported in such a manner, heard unexpected words directed to him: "My son, your sins are forgiven" (Mk 2:5). Probably, at that moment, it was not his sins that were worrying him but his illness. Nevertheless, the first miracle that Christ performed for him was to free him from the weight of the sins that hindered his soul more than the paralysis that immobilized his limbs. To make it understood that this was not an arbitrary act, the Lord added authoritatively: "that you may know that the Son of Man has authority on earth to forgive sins, I say to you" (addressing the paralyzed man): "Rise, take up your pallet and go home" (ib. 10-11). The healing of the body testifies to the remission of sins; it is an external sign for all to see of the pardon granted, and at the same time shows the generosity of God's pardon; he not only destroys the man's sins, but blesses him in a wonderful way.

Forgiveness of sins originates in God's infinite mercy, which seeks every way of saving man, the creature of his love. God is faithful; he desired the salvation of mankind and achieved it in Christ; in him the promises have become reality, "have become the 'yes' " of which St. Paul speaks (2 Cor 1:20). Hence it is urgent that man decide to respond with fidelity to God's fidelity, with his "yes" to God's "yes." And just as in liturgical prayer our "Amen" goes up to God through Christ Jesus (ib.), so the "yes" of our repentance and of our love ought also to go to God through him.

Bless the Lord, O my soul! . . . He forgives all your iniquity, he heals all your diseases. He redeems your life from the pit, he crowns you with steadfast love and mercy. He satisfies you with good as long as you live so that your youth is renewed like the eagle's.

As a father pities his children, so the Lord pities those who fear him. For he knows our frame, he remembers that we are dust.
Psalm 103: 1,3-5,13-14

A sinner, I turn to you, O God, source of mercy, because I am full of stains, and you can purify me.

O Sun of justice, enlighten a blind man. Eternal physician, heal one who is wounded. O King of kings, cover one who is naked; O Mediator between God and men, reconcile a culprit. O good Shepherd, lead a wanderer back to the flock. O God, grant mercy to a wretch, forgiveness to a sinner, life to a corpse, justification to an impious man, and the unction of your grace to a heart grown hard.

O gentle God, call back a runaway, attract a stubborn soul, raise up one who has fallen, support one who is standing, guide him who is on the way.

Forget not him who has forgotten you, nor abandon him who has abandoned you, nor scorn a sinner. I have offended you by sinning, my God, I have harmed my neighbor and have not even spared myself.

St. Thomas Aquinas, *Preghiere*

YEAR C

Merciful and gracious is the Lord, he forgives all your iniquity
(Ps 103:8,3)

The Old Testament presents to us in David an exceptional example of generosity towards one's enemy. The young man, who was the object of deadly persecution by Saul, came to the enemy's camp one night; the king lay there asleep, his lance at his side, and all around him everyone was asleep. It was an opportune chance and his friend Abishai proposed killing the king. But David forbade it and fled, taking Saul's spear away with him; then holding it up shouted to him from afar: "The Lord gave you into my hand today, and I would not put forth my hand against the Lord's anointed" (1 Sam 26:23). A Christian might perhaps not be capable of so much!

Yet David's generous action, which was an exception in the time when the rule of 'an eye for an eye' was in force, is a rule that should be strictly observed by those who follow Christ. "Love your enemies; do good to those who hate you. Bless those who curse you, and pray for those who abuse you (Lk 6:27-28). Jesus understands the human heart that has been wounded by sin; he knows that in the face of insults, injustice, and violence, the instinct for revenge surges up almost overwhelmingly; nevertheless he presents forgiveness not as an heroic act reserved for saints, but as the simple duty of every Christian. This requires a profound conversion, a real interior upside-down upheaval of thoughts and feelings, but this is exactly what Jesus asks of his disciples: "If you love those who love you, what credit is that to you? For even sinners love those who love them" (ib. 32). The Christian cannot act with the mentality of sinners or of those who have not yet been touched by the light of the gospel; he should stand out from them particularly in the fields of charity and forgiveness. For this reason the Lord is insistent with his upsetting proposals: "To the man who strikes you on the cheek, offer the other also ... Give to everyone who begs from you ... " (ib. 29-30). If these words are not always to be applied literally, still they must not be put to one side; we must grasp their full meaning: we must refrain from returning an injury, be ready to help anybody, give back more than is strictly just if we can, renounce our own rights rather than contend with our brother. In short, we are dealing with a "higher holiness" (Mt 5:20), inspired by a love which goes beyond bounds, the love that Jesus came to teach and which he was the first to practice, spending his whole life for a rebellious and ungrateful people, and dying for us "while we were yet sinners" (Rom 5:8).

Natural man, the son of Adam, can neither understand nor live this doctrine; to be capable of that he must be reborn in Christ and, in him, become a spiritual man. St. Paul expresses it: "Just as we have borne the image of the man of dust, we shall also bear the image of the man of heaven" (1 Cor 15:49). This will fully come to be only in glory, but it begins in this world through baptism, which gives us life through grace and through the Spirit of Christ. Precisely through this we become capable of loving in the way Christ loved and taught.

How great is your patience, my God! . . . You make the day to dawn, and the sun to rise upon the good and upon the wicked; you water the earth with your rain, and exclude no one from your benefits, for the water falls without distinction on the just and the unjust. We see you acting with equal patience toward the guilty and the innocent, toward those who acknowledge you and those who deny you, toward those who know how to thank you and to the ungrateful . . . Insults are heaped upon you often, indeed constantly; yet you give no vent to indignation, and wait patiently for the appointed day of judgment. Vengeance is in your power, yet you prefer to remain patient for a long time—you even prefer in your clemency to postpone it, in the hope that man's obstinate malice may finally undergo a change . . . Indeed you yourself say: "I have no pleasure in the death of the wicked, but that . . . he may live" (Ezek 33:11), and again: "Return to me" (Mal 3:7), "Return to the Lord your God, he is gracious and merciful, slow to anger, and abounding in steadfast love, and he repents of evil" (Joel 2:13).

O Father, we reach full perfection only when your patience dwells within us, when our resemblance to you, which was lost with Adam's sin, is revealed and shines out in our actions.

St. Cyprian, *On the advantages of patience,* 4-5

93 — PROPHETIC FUNCTION OF THE FAITHFUL

God who have made us share in the consecration of your only begotten Son, help us be witnesses in the world to his work of salvation
(RM Chrism Mass)

1. "O Lord, let the faithful, who are invested with a dignity that is at once royal and prophetic by virtue of the sacrament (of baptism) which you instituted, be enveloped by the gift of your in-

corruptible grace" (Mass of Chrism). This prayer of the former Roman Missal very aptly summarizes the prerogatives of the common priesthood of the faithful. In addition to having a priestly dignity which qualifies them for divine worship and especially for the sacramental acts and for participation in the Eucharistic Sacrifice, they also have a prophetic and royal dignity and function, a kind of reflection of the grace of Christ—priest, prophet and king—in which they have been reborn and taken over.

"Christ, the great Prophet, who proclaimed the kingdom of his Father by the testimony of his life and the power of his words, continually fulfills his prophetic office, not only through the hierarchy, but also through the laity. For that very purpose he made these his witnesses and gave them understanding of the faith and the grace of speech (cf. Acts 2:17-18; Apoc 19:10), so that the power of the gospel might shine forth in their daily social and family life" (LG 35). Since all the faithful share in Christ's prophetic capacity, they are thereby invited and even expected to spread the gospel and to carry its spirit, faith and authentic practice into their own ambit of life.

The task of the prophet does not consist so much in announcing future events as in keeping a sense of religion alive among men as the prophets of the Old Testament did: they never ceased reminding the people of Israel of the existence of the true God and of the worship due him. This continues to be necessary and urgent in modern society, which is so distracted, indifferent, and often hostile regarding God and religion. It belongs to the laity who live in the midst of today's society to be concerned with the delicate duty of bringing the gospel to every locality, every sector and level of social life in which they must serve as yeast in the dough. "Laymen are called by God to burn with the spirit of Christ, and to exercise their apostolate in the world as a kind of leaven" (AA 2).

2. The official preaching of the gospel is directly entrusted to priests, missionaries, and religious, but its gradual spread is the special work of the laity, who, being part and parcel of society, are in a position to approach men one by one, house by house, on the job, as also in various meeting-places. St. Peter urged the early Christians: "Always be prepared to make a defense to anyone who calls you to account for the hope that is in you" (1 Pet 3:15); and in the Acts we read that the faithful "continued to speak God's word with confidence" (4:31), that is, with a holy boldness without human respect. At the same time he continues his exhortation with the recommendation that they do this "with gentleness and reverence" (ib. 15); the announcement of the gospel must always unite love of truth and the gospel virtues of mildness and humility. Words should be accompanied by a living example, or rather, this latter should take first place; there is always need to "keep your conscience clear, so that when you are abused"—the Apostle

continues—"your good behavior in Christ may put to shame those who revile you" (ib. 16). Our behavior must never belie in action what we preach in word.

We need to overcome that individualistic way of thinking which considers faith, salvation and holiness as only personal matters, so that we believe we are on the right track when we try to attain these virtues inside ourselves. But on the contrary, we are not fully Christian if we do not live the grace of Christ in all its totality, and this grace includes the obligation of spreading the gospel. The Council specifies: "The law of love which is the Lord's greatest commandment impels all the faithful to promote God's glory through the spread of his kingdom and to obtain eternal life for all men . . . On all Christians, therefore, is laid the burden of working to make the divine message of salvation known and accepted by all men throughout the world" (AA 3).

Sovereign Lord, who made heaven and earth and the sea and everything in them, who said by the Holy Spirit:—"Why did the gentiles rage and the peoples imagine vain things?"—. . . But now, Lord, look upon their threats and grant to your servants to speak your word with all boldness . . . in the name of your holy servant, Jesus.

Acts 4:24,25,29

O Lord, the idea of bearing witness occupies and absorbs my whole interior life. To live in such a way that I can bear witness to you at every moment, O Christ, that every fragment of my time, like the fragments of bread that you multiplied, may be witness to your omnipotence which performed the miracle, and of the sweet mercy which inspired it. Let our life also bear witness through its peace, its goodness and unbroken serenity, its continual union with you, and its unceasing gift of love . . .

To take into the midst of the world and of society, a soul that is holy, really holy with the most consummate earthly lovableness and the most perfect celestial holiness! What an ideal! To bear perfect witness to you in the world, O Christ! And yet if I were holy, I could do it. Oh, the anguish of not being holy! Oh, to know how to love with God's fullness and to make love felt in every word! To make love for God vibrate in each external movement, a love so powerful, so deep, so absolute, that it obtains grace for everyone. This is holiness! Lord, give it to me, make me holy: I beg you with every drop of my blood; do whatever you want with me, but make me holy, absolutely, entirely; grant me a will of steel, because only a strong soul can receive this great grace.

G. Canovai, *Suscipe Domine*

94 — KINGLY FUNCTION

Glory and power to you, O Christ, who made us a kingdom and priests to God, your Father   *(Rev 1:6)*

1. Jesus Christ "has freed us from our sins by his own blood, and made us a kingdom, priests to his God and Father" (Rev 1:5-6). Jesus, the universal king, to whom all creatures are subject, that he might subject all to his Father, has not only made his faithful a priestly people, but also a kingdom which shares in his sovereignty. "He communicated (this royal power) to his disciples that they might be established in royal freedom, and that, by their self-denial and a holy life, they might conquer the reign of sin in themselves" (LG 36). There can be no kingdom of God without first overcoming the reign of evil. Jesus himself reached the glory of his kingdom only after destroying sin by his death: "he humbled himself"—says St. Paul—"and became obedient unto death, even death on a cross! Therefore God has highly exalted him" (Phil 2:8). "Was it not necessary that the Christ should suffer . . . and so enter into his glory?" (Lk 24:26). This is the road that every one of us must travel to reach the royal freedom of God's children; only "self-denial" will make us master of our passions, and will give us control over the evil and the sin which constantly try to reduce us to slavery; only thus will the "kingdom" of God come, where all is completely submissive to him; in such a kingdom we shall find the only true freedom.

After mastering ourselves and submitting to God, we must then try to bring all men back to him: "that, serving Christ in our fellow men, we may through humility and patience lead our brothermen to the King, to serve whom is to reign" (LG 36). Just as the Savior rescued us from the slavery of sin and led us to his Father's kingdom, humbling himself and making himself our servant to the point of giving his life for us, so shall we win over our brothers to God's kingdom through humble and patient service, accompanied by a generous, unselfish dedication.

2. Man was not created to be a slave to things, to be unduly attached to creatures and enslaved by them, but rather to be their master and ruler, and through such mastery to subject and consecrate all creatures to God. "Whether the present or the future, all are yours"—says St. Paul—"and you are Christ's and Christ is God's" (1 Cor 3:22-23). Therefore, recognizing "the deepest meaning and value of all creation, and how to relate it to the praise of God" (LG 36), we must behave like a sovereign who uses everything without becoming enslaved by any creature; we make use of everything, but without subjugating ourselves to anybody or anything; in this way we help creation to attain its purpose, which is to serve man so that he may adore and glorify God. Freed and saved by Christ, the Christian must in his turn free and save

his brothers, and all creation as well, so as to lead every creature to its final end. To attain this goal we are called upon to "assist one another to live holier lives, even in our daily occupations. In this way the world is permeated by the spirit of Christ, and more effectively achieves its purpose in justice, charity and peace" (ib.). In the practice of his profession, in family and social life, the Christian ought to bring the spirit of the gospel to heal what sin has damaged and give a Christian spirit to that which lack of religion has alienated from God; this must hold true in all areas: in the world of work, of techniques, culture, politics, and in every other activity. The faithful will attain these aims "by remembering that in every temporal affair they must be guided by a Christian conscience. For even in secular affairs there is no human activity which can be withdrawn from God's dominion" (ib.). The task of parents and teachers is particularly important: these have it in their power to transform the family and the school into real arenas of Christian life where children and pupils are guided toward God by their example and their teaching.

In this way the faithful all work together to build Christ's kingdom and, "as worshippers whose every deed is holy, . . . consecrate the world itself to God" (LG 34).

O Christ, by divine anointing you are king, pontifif and prophet. And by sharing in your anointing we are made kings and priests: a royal priesthood. Then give us royal courage so that we may not allow ourselves to be subjected to our passions, and cause us to nurture only great thoughts, and not become slaves of the world's way of thinking.

Grant, that as kings we may be magnanimous, aspiring to what is noblest; and as spiritual priests, let us aspire to what is holiest. We are no longer unholy people; we are those to whom your Father said: "Be holy because I am holy."

You made us prophets, too; so teach us how to act by a kind of heavenly instinct, going beyond the limits of present things, filling ourselves with things of the future, breathing only eternity. We cannot content ourselves with building on this earth. O Lord, help us to raise ourselves, to think of that country where we shall reign with you who said: "Fear not, little flock, for it is your Father's good pleasure to give you the kingdom" (Lk 12:32).

cf. J.B. Bossuet, *Elevazioni a Dio sui misteri* 13:3

O Jesus, that I may set about establishing everything in you. I must begin with myself; make me more Christian. So that the world may become good again, help me to become better; in order that it may become more Christian, help me to become a better Christian.

Give me a deeper sense of being Catholic; make me more charitable, more penetrated by the incalculable consequences of my actions and of my omissions.

*Make my Christianity deeper, more heartfelt, more radiant,
more worthy of you, adored Master, my beloved Savior.*
cf. R. Plus, Christ in our Brothers

95 — GOD CALLS

*Blessed is he whom you choose and bring near to dwell in your
courts*

(Ps 65:4)

1. "The kingdom of heaven is like a householder who went out early in the morning to hire laborers for his vineyard" (Mt 20:1). This householder is a symbol of God who is continually calling men to "the kingdom of heaven," that is, to salvation. God calls everyone, at all times, without discrimination: "You go along into my vineyard too" (ib. 4). It is the universal call to the Christian life, to holiness. The divine call is not a simple external stimulus, for when God calls, he himself enables men to answer his call, by offering them the gift of grace. "It is evident then . . . that all the faithful of whatever rank or status are called to the fullness of Christian life and to the perfection of charity" (LG 40); to attain it they have but to live fully the grace they have received in baptism.

However, within the framework of this universal call to holiness—single in its substance because it is based on "one faith, one baptism" (Eph 4:5) "the same grace and the same charity—not all proceed by the same path" (LG 32). God, like the householder of the parable, is free to call us how and when he chooses, charging us with various duties and offices, and lavishing the same grace in different measure and in a different manner; that is, he "apportions to each one individually as he wills" (1 Cor 12:11). Therefore, beside the laity who are called to fulfill their calling to holiness in the midst of family and social life, there are "consecrated souls" who are called to a more direct and exclusive service of God. The universal vocation to holiness—says Vatican Council II—"shines out in a particularly appropriate way in the practice of the evangelical counsels. This practice . . . undertaken by many Christians under the influence of the Holy Spirit . . . produces in the world, as produce it should, a shining witness and model of (the) holiness" of the Church (LG 39).

2. The Christian is already consecrated to God by his baptism, is appointed to his service and to his worship. But that does not prevent him—when called by God through a divine and mysterious choice—from deepening this initial consecration by carrying it to its utmost consequence: that of freely embracing, for the love of God, the evangelical counsels of poverty, chastity and obedience. "The faithful can bind themselves to the three previously mentioned counsels either by vows, or by other sacred bonds which are like vows in their purpose. Through such a bond a

person is totally dedicated to God by an act of supreme love and is committed to the honor and service of God under a new and special title" (LG 44). Thus one enters into a special state in life: the state of perfection, whose essential characteristic is a more intimate and total following of Christ: poor, chaste and obedient, entirely consecrated to the glory of the Father and the salvation of men. In other words, the evangelical counsels of poverty, chastity and obedience are accepted as a particular, lifelong obligation in order to become more perfectly like Our Lord and to express his life more faithfully. "The religious state imitates with particular accuracy and perpetually exemplifies in the Church that form of life which he, the Son of God, accepted in entering the world to do the will of his Father, and which he also proposed to his disciples" (LG 44).

The religious state does not constitute a different holiness from that proposed for all the baptized, but rather a different route, which, headed more directly toward Christ, more easily overcomes the obstacles that stand in the way of attaining holiness. The faithful, teaches the Council, "in order to derive more abundant fruit from the baptismal grace, intends, by profession of the evangelical counsels in the Church, to free himself from the obstacles which might draw him away from the fervor of charity" (ib.). The call to the state of perfection is therefore a grace that is immensely precious, not only for individual holiness, but for the holiness of the whole Church, since it is ordered to a more faithful incarnation of the mystery and life of Christ, so that all men may be drawn to him.

My Lord, who came into this world to do your Father's will, not your own, give me a most absolute and simple submission to the will of Father and Son. I believe, O my Savior, that you know just what is best for me. I believe that you love me better than I love myself, that you are all-wise in your providence, and all-powerful in your protection. I am as ignorant as Peter was what is to happen to me in time to come (Jn 21:22); but I resign myself entirely to my ignorance, and thank you with all my heart that you have taken me out of my own keeping, and, instead of putting such a serious charge upon me, have bidden me put myself into your hands. I can ask nothing better than this, to be your care, not my own.

I protest, O my Lord, that, through your grace, I will follow you withersoever you go, and will not lead the way. I will wait for your guidance, and, on obtaining it, I will act upon it in simplicity and without fear. And I promise that I will not be impatient, if at any time I am kept by you in darkness and perplexity; nor will I ever complain or fret if I come into any mishap or anxiety.
J.H. Newman, *Meditations on Christian Doctrine* XII:2

I come, O most loving Jesus, I come unto you whom I have loved, whom I have desired. Drawn by your kindness, your compassion, and your charity, I follow because you have called me...

Let me have all things in you, whom I am eager to love above all things, and let me keep the vows of which I have made profession . . . O you who search hearts, let me seek to be pleasing to you rather in heart than in body . . .

Come, O Jesus, my brother, my bridegroom, you great king who are God, you who are the lamb! Put such a mark upon the face of my soul that I may choose nothing under the sun, desire nothing, love nothing other than yourself. And do you yourself, who are dearest of all things dear, deign so to take me unto yourself in the bonds of mystical marriage, that I may be made your true bride and your true betrothed, by an indissoluble love stronger than death.

St. Gertrude, *Exercises III*

96 — DIVINE GIFT

O Lord, who call to yourself those whom you desire, grant that I may follow you   *(Mk 3:13)*

1. To the young man who asked what he must do to gain eternal life, Jesus answered: "Keep the commandments." But when the young man replied: "All these I have observed; what do I still lack?", Jesus added: "If you would be perfect, go, sell what you possess . . . and come, follow me" (Mt 19:17-21). The Lord was not saying by this that there are two distinct kinds of holiness; an obligatory one of keeping the commandments, and an optional one of choosing the counsels. The substance of holiness is always, and for everyone, the commandments, of which the greatest is charity. The counsels, on the other hand, are means for observing the commandments themselves with greater perfection. Jesus said: "If you would *be perfect,*" thus subordinating the counsels to an ideal of perfection.

The counsels of the gospel are not imposed, but proposed as a loving, divine invitation. As the Council states: "They are a divine gift which the Church has received from her Lord which she ever preserves with the help of his grace" (LG 43). Jesus gave them to his bride, the Church, so that through them there might continue to shine in her his example of a poor, chaste, and obedient life. The Church is the depositary of this, and has the mission of preserving this great gift intact, in order to transmit it to those who are called by God himself to live it. The vocation comes from God alone: "If you will . . . come, follow me." It is a call of predilection that depends entirely on God's plans; he is always the head of the house who calls when, how, and whom he wishes. "Not all can receive this precept"—said Jesus on the subject of perfect chastity—"but only those to whom it is given" (Mt 19:11). The grace of a vocation consists in an interior light, in a movement of the will by which the faithful soul is led to understand God's gift, and is impelled to desire it and to choose it in preference to anything else.

2. All men belong to God in that they are his creatures; the baptized belong to him in a special way by reason of the grace that makes them his adopted children; those who are called to the state of perfection are his "by a new and special title" because they give themselves totally to him in that same "manner of virginal and humble life that Christ the Lord elected for himself, and that his Virgin Mother also chose" (LG 46). All the faithful, without exception, are called to live the grace of Christ in their state of life, whatever it may be; but the "consecrated" are called to live it in the same situation that Christ chose here on earth: in perfect chastity, in voluntary poverty, in total dependence on the Father. Jesus was the first great religious of the Father, consecrated to his worship and to his glory, even to his total sacrifice of self upon the cross. He invites countless men and women to follow him, who are called "religious" just because, like himself, "they consecrate themselves entirely to the divine service, offering themselves in holocaust to God" (St. Thos 2-2; 186-1). Thus, religious consecration carries to its highest fulfillment the baptismal consecration which remains the foundation, the indispensable substantial premise.

Whoever embraces the state of the evangelical counsels chooses God in preference to any creature, to any human tie however good and holy; "he gives himself totally to God who is supremely loved" says the Council (LG 44). But he would not be able to make this choice or accomplish this gift, unless God himself had invited him: "You did not choose me, but I chose you" (Jn 15-16). The love with which one gives himself totally to God is but a free response which has been foreknown by God and provoked by his infinite love: "I have loved you with an everlasting love; therefore I have continued my faithfulness to you" (Jer 31:3). Confronted with the mystery of this divine predilection, which is always gratuitous and therefore independent of any personal merit, the most beautiful attitude is that of the Virgin Mary: "Let it be to me according to your word . . . My soul magnifies the Lord . . . for he has regarded the low estate of his handmaiden" (Lk 1:38, 46-48).

> O Lord, you command us to follow you, not because you need our service, but only to give us salvation. Indeed, to follow you, O savior, is to share in salvation, to follow your light is to enjoy the light . . . Our service adds nothing to you, because you do not need our service; rather, you give life and immortality and eternal glory to those who follow and serve you . . . If you require service for men, it is because you are good and merciful and desire to confer benefits on those who persevere in your service. In proportion to your need of nothing, is our need for communion with you; indeed, this is our glory: to persevere and remain steadfast in your service. For this reason, Lord, you told your disciples: "You did not choose me, but I

chose you" (Jn 15:16); you meant that we did not glorify you by following you, but in following you we were glorified by you.

St. Irenaeus, *Adversus haereses IV,* 13;4; 14:1

O Jesus, O Love, in your fair love prepare for me the way which will lead me unto you; may I in chaste charity follow you eternally whithersoever you go, in the love of your nuptial alliance with me, where you reign and rule in the infinite fullness of your divine Majesty! There, in incomparable union with your living love and in the living affection of your fiery Godhead, you lead after you the ranks of thousands upon thousands of virgins, clothed in white garments and jubilantly singing the sweet canticles of your eternal espousals. Come then, O Jesus, Love, keep me during this wretched life under the shadow of your charity; and after this exile bring me, spotlessly pure, into your sanctuary amid that virginal band. There may the fountain of your divine love be my sole refreshment and the enjoyment of yourself my sole satisfaction.

St. Gertrude *Exercise 3*

97 — PURIFICATION

O Lord, be gracious to me; heal me (Ps 41:4)

1. The more strongly we are called to a life of intimate communion with God, and the more closely we approach him, the sharper is the contrast we see between our wretchedness and the infinite holiness of him who is drawing us to himself. Peter's cry rises spontaneously: "Depart from me for I am a sinful man, O Lord" (Lk 5:8). It could be said that the splendor of God's holiness is penetrating us and searching out our soul's very depths, and that it brings to light, by contrast, all our opaquenes: our sins, our faults, our evil tendencies and bad habits. God is not doing this to torment a soul that has resolved to follow him more closely, but to purify and prepare it for more intimate communion with him. Nevertheless, this purification is painful. "My son"—warns the Holy Spirit—"if you come forward to serve the Lord, prepare yourself for temptation ... For gold is tested in the fire, and acceptable men in the furnace of humiliation" (Sir 2:1,5). It is painful to undergo temptations and to discover unsuspected tendencies and passions within us; it is hard to pass through the crucible of trial; but it is indispensable, whether for our purification or for progress in the ways of God. For this reason it is necessary not only to accept such trials, but, as far as possible, to collaborate with them willingly. We shall accomplish this especially by humbling ourselves deeply before the discovery of our wretchedness, and by imploring divine help to free us from it. Then we shall try to second God's action by mortifying our disorderly inclinations. "Those who belong to Christ Jesus have crucified the flesh with its passions and desires" (Gal 5:24); the austere course of action

that St. Paul did not hesitate to propose for the early Christians was fully accepted by St. John of the Cross, who translated it into very practical counsels. "All objects living in the soul—whether they be many or few, large or small—must die, in order that the soul enter into divine union, and it must bear no desire for them but remain detached as though they were nonexistent to it, and it to them" (Ascent I 11:8). Recognizing these "objects" is a great grace, and is the fruit of divine light, which penetrates the spirit; to further this, the soul must pursue a generous renunciation "out of love for Jesus Christ. In his life, he had no other gratification, nor desired any other, than the fulfillment of his Father's will" (ib. 13:4).

2. "On a dark night,—fired with love's urgent longings,—ah! the sheer grace,—I went out unseen, my house being now all still-ed" (Asc I-1). In this way, St. John of the Cross shows us the soul, which has experienced the weight of its limitations and the hindrance of its passions, as well as the insufficiency of creatures to satisfy its thirst for freedom, for love, and for the infinite; now, with a resolute movement, it escapes from itself and flings itself into the search for God. This escape takes place in the night, a night which comes from "the mortification of the appetites' disordered tendencies and the denial of pleasure in all things" (ib. 4:1). The Saint notes that one could not resolve on this total deprivation unless led to it by God and by his love, "unless enkindled with love" (ib. 1:4). But sustained by charity and sensing that the good he is seeking—union with God in love—will repay it with high interest for every renunciation, he does not hesitate to leave his senses "deprived of all pleasure in things"—thus left empty and in the dark as in a dark night. His decision is so efficacious that he perseveres in this conduct even when the needs or circumstances of life force him to seek some relief—food, rest, or proper recreation—endeavoring to conduct himself then with freedom of spirit, without lingering to savor the pleasure selfishly. Such is the Apostle's directive: "So whether you eat or drink, or whatever you do, do all to the glory of God" (1 Cor 10:31).

Entering into the night of this privation and total dispossession is "a happy fortune," a great grace. And although man can prepare for it by freely practicing renunciation, only God can lead him into the depth of the night and thereby bring his purification to a successful conclusion through trials in which he can do nothing but accept what God permits, humbly bowing his head under his almighty hand. But one who loves does not retreat, for he knows that only through this painful torment can he arrive at "the sweet and delightful life of love with God" (Dk N 1:1).

Lord, I am not worthy . . . You alone understand in their fullness the words which I use. You see how unworthy a sinner is to receive the one holy God, whom the seraphim adore with trembling. You see, not only the stains and scars of past sins, but the mutilations, the deep cavities, the chronic disorders which they have left in my soul. You see the innumerable living sins, which clothe me, though they be not mortal, living in their power and presence, their guilt, and their penalties. You see all my bad habits, all my mean principles, all my wayward lawless thoughts, my multitude of infirmities and miseries, yet you come. You see most perfectly how little I really feel what I am now saying, yet you come. O my God, left to myself should I not perish under the awful splendor and the consuming fire of your Majesty. Enable me to bear you, lest I have to say with Peter, "Depart from me, for I am a sinful man, O Lord! (Lk 5:8).

My God, enable me to bear you, for you alone can. Cleanse my heart and mind from all that is past. Wipe out clean all my recollections of evil. Rid me from all languor, sickliness, irritability, feebleness of soul. Give me a true perception of things unseen, and make me truly, practically, and in the details of life, prefer you to anything on earth, and the future world to the present. Give me courage, a true instinct determining between right and wrong, humility in all things, and a tender longing love of you.

J.H. Newman, *Meditations on Christian Doctrine XV 2:2*

98 — ALL FOR THE ALL

O Lord, grant that, forgetting what lies behind, and straining forward to what lies ahead, I press on toward the goal   *(Phil 3:13-14)*

1. "The kingdom of heaven is like treasure hidden in a field, which a man found and covered up; then in his joy he goes and sells all that he has and buys that field" (Mt 13:44). One who by the light of faith has finally discovered that "the kingdom of heaven"—God, his love, his friendship—is the greatest of treasures, finds it quite natural to leave all the rest, "to sell all"—property, satisfactions, earthly joys—in order to possess it. And this action is all the more spontaneous and full of impetus, the more a man, through his faith and love, has sensed the supreme goodness and infinite love of God. Once he has made this discovery, whatever renunciation is necessary in order to obtain this divine treasure becomes possible. Then Jesus' words do not seem excessive: "If your right eye causes you to sin, pluck it out and throw it away" (Mt 5:29), and we understand that even if what is dearest to us becomes an obstacle to the attainment of God, it must be taken and thrown away. It is worth the pain of sacrificing all—an earthly "all," fleeting and transitory—in order to gain the eternal All. "I have suffered the loss of all things, and count them as refuse"—says St. Paul—"in order that I may gain Christ and be found in him" (Phil 3:8-9).

In this spirit, St. John of the Cross teaches us to take the swift sure road of total despoliation. It is not a matter of renouncing this thing or that, but of everything that binds us, more or less strongly, to worldly possessions, detaining our heart and our will in them, and so hindering us from throwing ourselves on God and from loving him with all our strength. The root of these attachments or inordinate affections—which the Saint calls "appetites"—is not in created things but in ourselves, for, if we are not purified and in control of our passions, we seek creatures and stop in them to satisfy self. For that reason the rule is: "to reach perfect union with God through the will and love, one must obviously first be freed from every appetite however slight" (Asc I 11:3). There can be no reservations; even some small attachment, some small satisfaction of self that is voluntarily sought, and which the soul "never really desires to overcome" (ib. 4) is an obstacle to achieving the treasure of union with God. Once again, we must sell everything because "to possess God in everything, we should not possess anything in everything" (St. J.C., Letter 17).

2. To be detached from creature does not mean despising them: in fact they are good because they come from the hand of God (Gen 1:31). Instead, it means to learn to use them with interior freedom, without being fascinated by their presence or our possession of them, and without letting ourselves be upset by their absence or our privation of them. Only by "making use of and enjoying God's creation in poverty and freedom of spirit does man come to the threshold of true possession of the world" (GS 37). Detachment, the product of self-denial and renunciation, is indeed the means for attaining freedom of spirit.

Detachment from creatures does not even mean separation or actual aloofness from them: this is not always possible, nor ever the case in an absolute sense. On the other hand, the measure of practical detachment expected of the religious who must leave all to give himself to the exclusive service of God is different from that required of the layman, who is called to sanctify himself in family life and in society. Still, interior detachment, that of the heart, is required of all and is indispensable for union with God. However in practice it will be impossible to effect this interior detachment from self and all creatures unless actual material detachment is also practiced, at least to some degree. If we cannot renounce superfluous things, things which are purely for our own convenience and satisfaction, we shall never achieve interior detachment. And those who, on consecrating themselves to God, have already given up persons and things dear to them, must stay on the alert to keep themselves interiorly free of every attachment. In short, in every station in life, one must tend toward the substance of detachment, which is detachment of the heart and mind. This is St. Paul's teaching: "Let those who have wives live as though they had none; those who buy as though they had no goods; and those who deal with the world as though they had no dealings with it, for the form of this world is passing away" (1 Cor 7:29-31).

O my soul, leave all and you will find all: leave all things for Christ and in Christ you will possess all things, because when you have him, he will give you all and when you are poor on his account, you will be much happier than if you were very rich.

O Christ, leaving all ... myself included, I renounce being mine and begin to be yours, finding pleasure only in thinking of you, speaking of you, and pleasing you in everything. O God of true love, grant me this excess of love. O all-powerful love, carry off my heart, take it where you are, so that I may always remain united with you in love, and that you may live in me, supporting me with love.

L. Da Ponte, *Meditazioni,* V 31:1; 32:2

Good Jesus, tender Shepherd, my sweet Teacher, King of eternal glory, when shall I appear before you without stain and truly humble? When, for love of you, shall I thoroughly disdain all the goods of this world? When shall I be wholly detached from myself and from all things? For if I were truly free of all attachments, I should no longer have a will of my own; I should no longer groan under the yoke of passions and disordered affections, nor any longer seek myself in anything. The lack of this absolutely total abadonment is the only real obstacle between you and me that holds me back from casting myself upon you. Ah! when shall I be divested of everything? When shall I abandon myself to your divine will without any reservation? Or serve you with a pure, humble, calm, serene spirit? Or love you perfectly? As I receive you into my breast, when will my soul be joyfully united with its beloved? When shall I cast myself upon you with a tender and burning desire? When will my tepidity and imperfections be absorbed in the immensity of your love?

Bl. Ludovicus Blosius Paradise of the Faithful Soul

99 — EIGHTH SUNDAY OF THE YEAR

YEAR A

For God alone my soul waits in silence; for my hope is from him (Ps 62:5)

In a time of trial Israel had said: "The Lord has forsaken me; my Lord has forgotten me" (Is 49:14); but God replied through the mouth of the prophet: "Can a mother forget her infant, that she should have no compassion on the son of her womb? Even if she should forget, yet will I not forget you" (ib. 15). It would be un-thinkable for God to abandon the creature he had created in an act of love. Yet, especially when trials press us hard, we are prone enough to doubt God's love and his fatherly help. Jesus, who revealed God to us as Father, often dwelled on this point: "Do not be anxious about your life, what you shall eat, or what you shall drink ... nor what you shall put on" (Mt 6:25). We are full of anx-ieties and distress when we depend too much on our own resources and put more confidence in our own initiatives than in God's help. Thus we become engrossed in business, so eager in the search for money that we no longer have either the time or the heart to pay attention to God. Jesus introduced his discourse on trust in Pro-vidence by saying: "No one can serve two masters" (ib. 24). Money is the worst of masters, it tyrannizes over a man and takes away his freedom to serve and love God and his brethren. God, on the other hand, the one supreme Master, is so good that when we put ourselves at his service and trustfully abandon ourselves to him, he frees us from the worries of life and, by giving us the security of his providence, makes us generous with others: "If God so clothes the grass of the field, which today is alive and tomorrow is thrown into the oven, will he not much more clothe you, O men of little faith!" (ib. 30).

In reality, it is scantiness of faith that makes us so unsure of God and so preoccupied with self. Jesus considers this kind of behavior suited to pagans: one who has faith should not behave as if providence did not exist. It is easy for even Christians to let themselves be so carried away by a purely worldly mentality as to see no further than earthly horizons and to believe only in what they have in their hands. We need to "be converted" and to ac-quire an evangelical mentality: not in order to be dispensed from work and from the duties of our state in life, but, while attending to these duties with care, not to neglect "the one thing necessary" (Lk 10:41), and to believe that, when we come to the end of our abilities, the providence of the heavenly Father takes over. "Seek first his kingdom and his righteousness, and all these things shall be yours as well" (Mt 6:33).

O Lord my God, you are very great! ... The earth is satisfied with the fruit of your work. You cause the grass to grow for the cattle, and plants for man to cultivate that he may bring forth food from the earth, and wine to gladden the heart of man, oil to make his face shine, and bread to strengthen man's heart. The trees of the Lord are watered abundantly, the cedars of Lebanon which he planted. In them the birds build their nests ...

O Lord, how manifold are your works! In wisdom you have made them all; the earth is full of your creatures. Yonder is the sea, great and wide, which teems with things in-numerable, living things both small and great ... These all look to you, to give them their food in due season. When you give to them, they gather it up; when you open your hand, they are filled with good things. When you hide your face, they are dismayed; when you take away their breath, they die and return to their dust. When you send forth your Spirit, they are created; and you renew the face of the earth.

Psalm 104: 1, 13-17, 24-30

O Lord, my God, O Lord our God, since we may come to you, make us happy with you. Away with gold and silver and power; we do not want any part of these worldly things which are so vain and which pass with the passing of life. Let no vanity be on our lips. Make us happy with you, let us never again lose you. When we shall possess you, let us never again lose you nor wander away from you. Make us happy with you, for blessed are the people who have the Lord for their God.

St. Augustine, *Sermon* 113:6

YEAR B

Bless the Lord, O my soul, and foret not all his benefits (Ps 103:2)

Even in the Old Testament, which is generally considered a time when fear prevailed over love, God revealed his love for men with expressions that were increasingly tender and human. For instance, when he assured Israel that even if a mother should abandon her child, he would never abandon his people (Is 49:15); or when, after Israel had been unfaithful and punished, he called his people back to him and renewed his covenant of love, declaring: "I will betroth you to me for ever; I will betroth you to me in righteousness and in justice, in steadfast love and in mercy; I will betroth you to me in faithfulness" (Hos 2:19-20). God has always used every possible means to make his love for mankind understood, and he did not disdain to express it in the ways most familiar to man, such as those of maternal and conjugal love.

Jesus followed the same pattern, and when the Pharisees criticized him because his disciples did not fast, he replied: "Can the wedding guests fast while the bridegroom is with them?" (Mk 2:19). Jesus ascribed to himself the title of bridegroom which, in the prophets, God had reserved for himself. Jesus is God in very truth, come down among his people, for in becoming man and being born of a Virgin, he had espoused human nature with an indissoluble bond: "I will betroth you to me for ever". The prophecy of Hosea was fulfilled in him; the salvation foretold in nuptial terms between God and mankind is realized in Christ. This is why his residence among men is the wedding time, a time of festival in which fasting is out of place.

Divine Intimacy

Jesus had no intention, by his answer, of disapproving of fasting, which he had already affirmed (Mt 6:16-18); what he wanted to make clear was the presence of a bridegroom who had come to bring joy and salvation, and also that such a presence would not last long: "The days will come when the bridegroom will be taken away from them; and in that day they will fast" (Mk 2:20). There is a veiled hint here of his passion and death, when he will be violently taken away from his friends. Then it will be time for fasting and tears. In this we have a glimpse of the life of the Church—the faithful bride—who, amid tribulation, mourns the absence of her spouse in penance and prayer, and prepares for her last meeting with him: "Come, Lord Jesus!" (Apoc 22:20).

Jesus did not come to put "a piece of unshrunken cloth on an old garment", nor "new wine into old wineskins" (Mk 2:21-22), but to renew the whole human race from its roots. His insertion into time and into human life and history gives the world a new appearance and a new meaning; the old mentality of the Pharisees was not able to accept this "new thing"; this required a new mentality built upon the word of Christ. He had not come to restore the synagogue, but to found his Church, a "new thing" born of his sacrifice; and only to her will he give the "new wine" of his blood and of his doctrine, to sustain her life and to nourish all her children in a nuptial banquet that begins here on earth, but is fully completed only in heaven.

> *Our souls are not hungry: the hungry ones are those who are not with you, O Christ, and who have no provision of good works stored up. On the other hand, those who rejoice in virtue and who receive you into their dwellings, offer you a great supper, that is, the spiritual banquet of good works, from which the rich are barred while the poor have their fill. This is why you say that the children of the bridegroom cannot fast as long as the bridegroom is with them.*
>
> *You are the good groom, O Lord Jesus. With your birth you inaugurated a new life, which espoused to you, is freed from the corruption of the flesh ... It has shown us that there is no true beauty in anything disfigured by sin.*
>
> *But you, O divine Spouse, are surrounded by light whose beauty can never perish. Let me bear you in my soul, that I may adore you in its temple, let me bear you in my body as it is written: "Bear the Lord in your body". Grant that I may enter your new nuptial chamber to contemplate your marvelous beauty and be reclothed in you and gaze at you as you sit at the right hand of the Father, and to rejoice in having such a spouse. Then you will cover me with blessings so that the scars of sin may cause me no distress.*
>
> St. Ambrose, *Commentary on St. Luke's Gospel*
> V 19, 24

Lord, give your angels charge of me to guard me in all my ways (Ps 91:11)

In St. Luke's gospel the discourse on charity is followed by some practical applications which delineate the characteristic features of Christ's disciples, who, in St. Matthew's words, must be "the light of the world" (5:14).

First of all, it is impossible to bring light to others if we are without light ourselves. "Can a blind man lead a blind man?" (Lk 6:39). A disciple's light does not come from his own acuteness of discernment, but from the teachings of Christ which he has obediently accepted and followed, because "a disciple is not above his teacher" (ib. 40). Only to the extent in which we assimilate and express the teaching and example of the Master in our own lives, can we be beacons of light for our brothers and attract them to Christ. This is a work to engage us for a lifetime in a continuous effort to become ever more like Christ; and one that requires a clear introspection which will enable us to recognize and correct our faults so that we do not fall into that absurd situation which Our Lord denounced: "Why do you see the speck that is in your brother's eye, but do not notice the log that is in your own eye?" (Lk 6:41).

It must never happen that a disciple of Jesus should exact from others what he does not do himself, or that he should presume to correct in his neighbor what he tolerates in himself, perhaps in a more serious form. To fight evil in others, and not to fight it in our own heart is hypocrisy, against which the Lord flung himself with uncompromising energy. The criterion for recognizing the authentic disciple from the hypocrite is given by works, "each tree is known by its own fruit" (ib. 44). The Old Testament put it in this way: "The fruit discloses the cultivation of a tree; so the expression of a thought discloses the cultivation of a man's mind" (Sir 27:6). Jesus repeats this comparison which was already familiar to his listeners, and develops it, stressing that the most important thing is always a man's interior, where all his behavior originates. Just as the fruit makes known the quality of a tree, so do a man's works reveal the goodness or wickedness of his heart. "The good man out of the treasure of his heart produces good, and the evil man out of his evil treasure produces evil" (Lk 6:45). The hypocrite can disguise himself as much as he wants, but sooner or later the good or evil in his heart overflows and makes itself known: "Out of the abundance of the heart his mouth speaks" (ib.). Here then is the main point: to guard the "treasure of one's heart" carefully, rooting out every trace of wickedness, and cultivating every kind of goodness, especially uprightness, purity and good sincere intentions.

Yet it is clear that a naturally good and honest heart is not enough for a disciple of Christ: he needs a heart that has been renewed and formed according to Christ's teachings, a heart that is totally converted to the gospel. The obligation is an arduous one, because sin and temptation are always lying in wait, even in the heart of a disciple. St. Paul reminds us by way of encouragement that Christ has conquered sin, and his victory is a guarantee of ours. "But thanks be to God who gives us the victory through our Lord Jesus Christ" (1 Cor 15:57).

O Jesus, you have enkindled the light so that it may continue to burn. Grant that we may be watchful and full of zeal, not just for ourselves, but also for those who ... have been brought to the truth... Grant that our lives may be worthy of the grace and truth which we have received: and since this is being preached everywhere, at the same time make our own lives keep in step.

You have said: let your light shine, that is, let your virtue be great, your flame bright, and your light beyond words to express. And in fact, when virtue reaches this height of perfection, it is impossible for it to remain hidden... Nothing makes man so luminous as the brightness born of virtue, even though he may desire to remain completely unknown.

St. John Chrysostom, *Commento Vang. S. Matteo* 15:7-8

Mountains do not water themselves, neither do they illuminate themselves ... By your light, O Lord, I shall see light. If then we shall see the light by your light, he for whom you are not the light will fall down far from you, the light. If I seek to be my own lamp, I shall fall far from you who are lighting up my way. Therefore, since I know that the only ones who fall are those who want to be their own lamp, when all around them is darkness ... I beg you not to let pride set foot in me nor let me be dragged down by the example of sinners ... so that I may not fall far away from you.

St. Augustine, *In Ps.* 120:5

100 — EVANGELICAL POVERTY

O Lord, let me use the things of this world, as though I were not using them (1 Cor 7:31)

1. When Jesus was explaining the parable of the sower, he said: "The seed is the word of God ... as for what fell among the thorns, they are those who hear, but as they go on their way, they are choked by the cares and riches and pleasures of life, and their fruit does not mature" (Lk 8:11, 14). The fertile seed of the word of God cannot reach maturity in those whose hearts are busy and preoccupied with earthly goods. We see this in the story of the

rich young man who heard Jesus say to him: " 'If you would be perfect, go, sell what you possess and give to the poor' ... The young man went away sorrowful, for he had great possessions" (Mt 19:21-22). He was a good young man; from his youth he had kept the commandments and he sincerely longed for eternal life, so much so that Jesus "looking upon him loved him" (Mk 10:21). Besides, the word of God had been sown in his heart, not through intermediaries, but by God himself, and yet it did not take root, but was suffocated by his love for wealth. Commenting on this fact, Jesus turned to his apostles and said: "How hard it is for those who have riches to enter the kingdom of God ... It is easier for a camel to go through the eye of a needle than for a rich man to enter the kingdom of God" (ib. 23,25). The difficulty is not that earthly goods are bad in themselves, but that too often man, in his greed, allows himself to be fascinated by them and becomes so much their slave that he prefers them to God. Moreover it is clear that Jesus' words must not only be applied to those who are "rich" because they have great possessions, but more especially to those who are "rich" because they are "attached" to what they possess, whether it be much or little. Here the exhortation of Vatican II is very appropriate: "Let all see that they guide their affections rightly. Otherwise they will be thwarted in the search for perfect charity by the way they use earthly possessions, and by a fondness for riches which goes against the gospel spirit of poverty" (LG 42).

2. One day a scribe approached Jesus and said: "Teacher, I will follow you wherever you go", and Jesus answered: "Foxes have holes, and birds of the air have nests, but the Son of Man has nowhere to lay his head" (Mt 8:19-20). To those who want to follow him, Jesus does not promise honor or wealth, but presents a picture of his life, a life that is extremely poor and without the smallest comfort, because anyone who has not the courage to share his earthly poverty—at least to some degree—can have no part in his eternal wealth. All the faithful—in different ways, according to their state in life—are called to follow "the humble, cross-bearing Christ, in order to be worthy of being partakers of his glory" (LG 41).

Poverty liberates a man from the excessive attachment to riches which is denounced by the Lord as a serious obstacle to eternal salvation: "No one can serve two masters ... you cannot serve God and mammon" (Mt 6:24). However it is not material poverty in itself that saves man. That kind of poverty is not sufficient to free him from the slavery of mammon unless it is accompanied and completed by spiritual poverty, that is, by poverty of affections, of desires, of anxiety for earthly possessions. St. John of the Cross teaches that only this poverty frees the soul from such attachments. "The mere lack of things ... will not divest the soul if it craves for all these objects; we are dealing with the renunciation of the soul's appetites and gratifications ... this is what leaves it free of all things, even though it possesses them" Asc. I; 3:4). Material poverty is a means for attaining spiritual poverty, without which privation and austerity would mean very little. In fact if after renouncing something one continues to nourish a desire or regret for it, he will always have his heart bound. "It is not the things of this world that occupy and harm the soul, because they do not penetrate it, but rather the desire for them which resides within it" (ibid).

O gentle Lord Jesus Christ, most rich in love, experience has taught me that there is nothing in life more wearisome than to burn with earthly desires, for the love of riches is an insatiable hunger which so tortures the soul by the ardor of desire that it does not find solace even when it obtains what it covets.

The acquisition of wealth causes great fatigue; the possession of it brings great fear; its loss occasions great sorrow. One who loves riches, cannot love you, O Lord, but perishes with the things that are perishable, and he who relies on them with affection, vanishes with them in sadness. He who finds them, loses his peace; when he lies awake at night, he tries to think of ways to add to them; if he sleeps, he dreams of thieves; during the day he is anxious and troubled; at night his fears increse, and thus he is always miserable.

R. Giordano, *Contemplazioni sull' amore divino* 35

O my Lord Jesus, how quickly any one who loves you with all his heart will become poor, for he will not be able to endure being richer than his Beloved ...

O my Lord Jesus, how quickly he will become poor, for when he thinks that all that is done for one of these little ones is done to you, and that what is not done to them is not done to you, he will relieve all the misery that is within his reach ...

How soon he will become poor if he receives your words with faith: "If you would be perfect, sell what you have, and give it to the poor ... Blest are the poor ... Whoever has left all his possessions for my name's sake will receive a hundredfold in this time and in the age to come eternal life" ...

O my God, I do not see how it is possible for some souls to see you poor and willingly remain rich ... and not want to be like you in everything ... Yes, I think they love you, O my God, but still I think something is lacking in their love ... I cannot conceive of love without a dire need to conform and to be like and most of all to share in all the hardships, troubles, difficulties and the bitterness of life ...

C. de Foucauld, *Retreat at Nazareth,
Meditations of a Hermit,* p. 81

101 — THE SPIRIT OF POVERTY

O Lord, let me not be anxious for worldly possessions, let me seek first your kingdom (Lk 12:22,31)

1. The Council points out as a particular fault of our days, the fact that many, even among Christians, "have fallen into an idolatry of temporal things, and have become their slaves, rather than their masters" (AA 7); and as a remedy, the Council proposes a sincere return to the spirit of poverty proposed by Christ to all his followers: "Blessed are the poor in spirit, for theirs is the kingdom of heaven . . . Do not lay up for yourselves treasures on earth where moth and rust consume and where thieves break in and steal, but lay up for yourselves treasures in heaven . . . for where your treasure is, there will your heart be also" (Mt 5:3; 6:19-21). These words are not reserved for a chosen group, but are directed to the crowd, to all who want the teaching of Jesus; and it is interesting to observe that the Sermon on the Mount opens precisely with the preaching of the beatitude of poverty. Man is, in fact, so greedy for earthly goods, so concerned with possessing and accumulating them, and finds himself so enslaved by their yoke, that only when he succeeds in disengaging himself from their snares can he commence his journey toward holiness, and toward the kingdom of heaven. "What will it profit a man if he gains the whole world and forfeits his life?" (Mt 16:26). Obviously, not everyone is called to make the vow of poverty, but everyone is expected to live according to the spirit of evangelical poverty. On the other hand, for such a spirit not to remain a utopia, we have to practice renunciation and privation, at least in things that are not strictly necessary, and so much the more in those that are superfluous. One who can never deny himself in anything must not delude himself into thinking that he has the spirit of poverty. For this reason, John of the Cross suggests to those who want to aim at perfection, that they should endeavor to be always inclined "not to go about looking for the best of temporal things, but for the worst, and to desire to enter into complete nudity, emptiness, and poverty in everything in this world, for the love of Jesus Christ" (Asc.I 13:6).

2. The gospel does not condemn the ordered use of earthly goods, nor even the labor involved in acquiring them honestly, according to one's particular condition and need. Jesus himself chose the life of a workingman and wished to earn his bread by the sweat of his brow; in fact he was commonly called "the carpenter's son" (Mt 13:55). The father and the mother of a family have the duty to provide for the needs of their children and to make sure that they have suitable means of subsistence. But they must avoid becoming so engulfed in worldly matters that they never have enough time or sufficient freedom to attend to the things of

the spirit, and to the worship and service of God. The laity, rather, are called to "live in the world, that is, in each and in all of the secular professions and occupations" and are called "to seek the kingdom of God by engaging in temporal affairs and by ordering them according to the plan of God"; they should use their professions and their positions for this purpose, and in practicing them be "led by the gospel spirit" of poverty and detachment. In this way they will contribute "to the sanctification of the world from within in the manner of leaven" (LG 31).

Another aspect of the spirit of poverty which our Lord insisted upon is the duty to give alms. Jesus asked the rich young man not only to sell his possessions, but also to give to the poor what he received from the sale; he suggested the same to all his followers: "Sell your possessions and give alms" (Lk 12:33). The concept of evengelical poverty includes not only detachment from temporal goods, but also depriving oneself of these in favor of the needy. Selfishness and greed are diametrically opposed to the spirit of poverty, which is authentic only when it leads to charity toward our brothers. The Council is emphatic on this point, recalling that: "the greater part of the world is still suffering from so much poverty that it is as if Christ himself were crying out in these poor to beg the charity of his disciples" (GS 88); on the other hand all "men are obliged to come to the relief of the poor, and to do so not merely out of their superfluous goods" (ib. 69).

> O Lord, help me find you, the true poor man . . . who, from being rich made yourself poor for love of me . . . I contemplate you in your richness: every thing has been created through you. I contemplate you in your poverty: the Word became flesh and dwelt among us . . .
>
> O poverty of my Lord! You are born in a wretched hovel, and wrapped in bits of cloth, you are laid in a manger. Then, O Lord of heaven and earth, Creator of the angels, author and ordainer of everything visible and invisible, you are nursed by your mother, you wail, you are brought up by your parents, you grow, you endure the weaknesses of your age, and you hide your majesty . . . O poverty! (Ser. 14:9)
>
> Transitory goods do not satisfy me, O my God, nor temporal goods; give me what is eternal, grant me something eternal. Give me your Wisdom, give me your Word, God unto God, and you, O God the Father and the Son and the Holy Spirit.
>
> Like a beggar I stand before your door: O Lord whom I invoke, do not sleep . . . for in truth you are most anxious to give, but you only give to those who ask, so as not to give to those who will not know how to receive . . . You do not sleep, do not let my faith sleep. My soul, so yearns to be satisfied by some lofty, ineffable good . . . but feels itself impeded by the weight of the body; understanding that it cannot be satisfied

in this life, it says to you: I have discovered the good that I desire, I know what can satisfy me; I recognize it in Philip's desire: Show us the Father and that will be enough ... I know what I want, but when shall I be satisfied? (In Ps 102:10).

O Lord, as long as we live in the body, we are exiles, far from you ... One who finds exile sweet does not love his country; now I sense the sweetness of my homeland and the bitterness of exile ... Nothing I have here apart from you is sweet to me. I want nothing of all that you have given me except yourself, the giver of all things. Be not deaf to this prayer of mine; listen to the voice of my pleading. (In Ps 85:11).

St. Augustine

102 – VOLUNTARY POVERTY

O Lord who have become poor, although you were rich, let me become rich through your poverty (2 Cor 8:9)

1. "Mother Church rejoices at finding within her bosom men and women who more closely follow and more clearly demonstrate the Saviour's self-giving by embracing poverty with the free choice of God's sons" (LG 42). Voluntary poverty professed by means of a vow or some special promise, is the badge of those, who by consecrating themselves totally to God in a state of perfection, wish to share "the poverty of Christ, who became poor for our sake when before he had been rich, that we might be enriched by his poverty" (PC 13). Voluntary poverty is thus embraced out of love; in fact, one who loves yearns to become like the one loved, to share his life and his lot in life, as well as to follow his counsels as fully as possible. The vow of poverty is thus seen as the most complete fulfillment of Christ's teaching on evangelical poverty. Any one who makes such a vow or equivalent promise, is not considering a poor life a burden or an economic necessity, but an ideal; an ideal is something loved, not something submitted to; it is sought, not avoided, it is lived and defended at all cost.

A religious has chosen to be poor, not for a day or a year, but for all the days of his life: in health and in sickness, in youth and in old age. He has no desire to get rich: a religious works and toils like the poor because Jesus so worked and toiled, but not—as a lay person may legitimately do—to better his condition in life. He offers himself to the service of God and of his neighbor with the utmost disinterestedness, and, precisely because there is nothing to hold him back in his dedication, he has chosen to live here on earth as "poor, exiled, orphaned, thirsty, without a road and without anything, hoping for everything in heaven" (St. J C Letters 19). "God wishes"—says St. John of the Cross—"a religious to be a religious in such a way that he be done with all, and that all be done to him, because God himself wishes to be the riches, comfort and delightful glory of the religious" (Letters 8).

2. Vatican Council II declares that especially today "poverty voluntarily embraced in imitation of Christ provides a witness which is highly esteemed" (PC 13). In fact, even though modern society is dominated by economic values and is wholly taken up by the quest for well-being and the pleasures of life, it is particularly sensitive and exacting in regard to the poverty of "church people". The lived example of detachment, of unselfishness and of an austere life has a special fascination for men of today, and, perhaps more than any other factor, has the power to bring them back to eternal values. The Council speaks of it in this sense: "The religious state by giving its members greater freedom from earthly cares more adequately manifests to all believers the presence of heavenly goods already possessed here below . . . and witnesses to the fact of a new and eternal life . . . (LG 44). Religious, conscious of their responsibility, feel more than ever obligated to this function of witness. For this it is not enough for them to be subject to their Superiors in "the use of the world's possessions, but they ought . . . to be poor in both fact and spirit" (PC 13). To be poor in name by reason of the vow of poverty and not to be poor in everyday concrete life is hypocrisy and a scandal, besides being a betrayal of the ideal embraced. If superiors—according to the rules of the Constitutions of the various institutes and the needs of individuals—may authorize the use of specified goods, and allow certain aids and allieviations, they can never dispense either themselves or their subjects from the substantial renunciation which is intimately connected with a life of voluntary poverty. In every circumstance, religious, whether individually or collectively, must always behave in such a way as to be shining examples of genuine evangelical poverty, animated by personal unselfishness and by charity for their fellowman; therefore, far from accumulating the proceeds of their labor, they will be liberal in providing for the "needs of the Church and the support of the poor, whom religious should love with the tenderness of Christ" (ib.). Only in this way does the religious state achieve that "splendid and striking" testimony "to the spirit of poverty and of charity [that] are the glory and authentication of the Church of Christ" (LG 31; GS 88).

> Poverty of spirit is a good that includes within itself all the good things of the world. In it lies great dominion. I say that it gives once again to one who does not care for the world's good things dominion over them all. What do kings and lords matter to me, if I don't want their riches, or don't care to please them if in order to do so I would have to displease God in even the smallest thing? Nor what do I care about their honors if I have understood that the greatest honor of a poor person lies in the fact of his being truly poor?
> . . .

True poverty brings with it overwhelming honor. Poverty that is chosen for you alone, O Lord, has no need of pleasing anyone but you ...

Holy poverty is our insignia ... O Lord, grant that poverty's insignia be on our coat of arms, for we must desire to observe it everywhere in houses, clothing, words, and most of all in thought ...

Let us in some manner resemble you, our King, who had no house but the stable in Bethlehem, where you were born, and the cross where you died. These were houses where there was little room for delight!

St. Teresa of Jesus, *Way* 2:5-9

Poverty is the hidden treasure of the field of the gospel; to purchase it, one must sell all that he has. Anyone who aspires to reach the heights of holy poverty renounces human wisdom, despoils himself of every possession, and throws himself, naked, into your arms, O crucified Christ.

O Lord, you took delight in poverty, and I hold it a royal dignity and a signal nobility to follow you who, being rich, make yourself poor for our sake. Just in order to possess false riches, I have no desire to give up this regal dignity with which you clothed yourself for our sake in order to enrich us with your poverty and to make us, who are truly poor in spirit, kings and heirs of the kingdom of heaven.

cf St. Francis of Assisi, *Detti*

103 — CHASTITY A BAPTISMAL REQUIREMENT

O God, who gave me new life in water and in the Holy Spirit, may your Spirit teach me to overcome the desires of the flesh (Gal 5:16)

1. The thorns that choke the seed of God's word and of his grace are not only riches, but are also—as Jesus himself pointed out—"the pleasures of life" (Lk 8:14). Like attachment to worldly goods, the inordinate search for the pleasures of the flesh smothers the precious seed of the Christian vocation, making us deaf to God's word and distracted from his service.

While baptismal grace frees us from slavery to Satan and makes us the dwelling place of the Holy Spirit, the sin of impurity produces the opposite effect and drives God from the Christian who has been already consecrated as his temple. "Do you not know"—cries St. Paul—"that your body is a temple of the Holy Spirit within you which you have from God? You are not your own; you were bought with a price! So glorify God in your body" (1 Cor 6:19-20). The whole man, redeemed by the blood of Christ, is reborn in us through baptism, and hence the body comes to be sanctified and must be used to glorify God; it must be pure and worthy of him who said: "Be holy, as I am holy" (Lev 11:45). On the contrary, unchastity degrades the body and makes the members of Christ "the members of a prostitute" (1 Cor 6:15). Paul's strong language very expressively crystallizes the gospel teaching on chastity, an indispensable virtue for every Christian, although in different ways according to each one's particular state. In fact, outside of marriage, absolute continence is required of all, that is, abstention from every sensual pleasure; and marriage itself requires conjugal continence. The renunciation connected with continence comes into the picture again in that renunciation of the works of the devil already promised at baptism, whose purpose is to ensure the effect of the sacrament in the Christian, which is his death to sin, so as to live "to God in Christ Jesus" (Rom 6:11).

2. "My brothers"—says St. Paul—"remember that you were called to freedom, only do not use your freedom as an opportunity for the flesh" (Gal 5:13). Baptism, which frees us from the slavery of the senses, has given us, through grace, the capability of being masters of our body and of our instincts so as to live in the freedom of the children of God. But all this has been given, not as an already accomplished reality, but as a seed, a potentiality; as long as we are on this earth, freedom from sin is not a victory achieved once and for all, but one that must be pursued day after day with fidelity to grace, which always enables us to be faithful to renunciation. "The desires of the flesh are against the spirit and the desires of the spirit are against the flesh; for these are opposed to each other to prevent you from doing what you would" (ib. 17). The sacrament of regeneration has not exempted us from this struggle, but has given us the weapons to win the battle: grace with all the infused virtues. Besides, what is infinitely more, God himself, dwelling in the baptized, is in us to englighten us, guide us, and sustain us with his spirit, the Holy Spirit, the Spirit of Christ. The Apostle can therefore say: "Walk by the Spirit, and do not gratify the desires of the flesh" (ib. 16). Victory is assured to those who let themselves be led by the Spirit and who submit to him.

In this perspective, we understand that chastity, like the other Christian virtues, is not only something physical, dealing with bodily integrity, but is above all a spiritual, interior matter which embraces the whole of us, and therefore also the mind and the heart. "What comes out of the .. heart"—said Jesus—"this defiles a man. For out of the heart come evil thoughts, murder, adultery, fornication ..." (Mt 15:18-19). Chastity of the body must be the reflection of the interior purity of the desires, affections, and thoughts. "If your eye is sound, your whole body will be full of light" (Mt 6:22); and likewise, if your heart is pure, your body will also be pure.

*Since the flesh has desires that are contrary to the spirit,
and the spirit has desires contrary to the flesh, the struggle is
a mortal one, my God; I do not do what I would like, for I
would like not to have concupiscence, but that is impossible.
Wish it or not, I have it; wish it or not, it flatters, entices,
stimulates and importunes me, and is always ready to raise
its head: it can be restrained, but not stifled ...*

*O God, through your Spirit you have given me the means
to restrain my members ... Stop my feet that they may not
roam toward unlawful things; ... hold back my hands from
every offense; curb my eyes that they may not rest upon evil
objects; close my ears, that they may not willingly listen to
wanton words; restrain my whole body on every side, from
head to toe. (Ser. 128:11-12).*

*O Lord, all my hope is based on your great mercy. Give
me what you command, and command what you will. You
command that we be continent. Someone has said that no one
can be continent unless God grants it, but it is true wisdom to
know from whom this gift comes. Continence brings us
recollection and the restoration of that unity which we have
lost in giving ourselves to too many things. He loves you less
who loves, together with you, anything which he does not
love for you. O love, ever burning and never extinguished, O
charity, O my God, inflame me! You command me to be continent; give me what you command and command what you
will. Almighty God, is your hand perhaps powerless to heal
all the weaknesses of my soul, to extinguish my wanton
movements with a more powerful surge? ... Lord, multiply
your gifts more and more in me, so that my soul, disentangled
from the snare of concupiscence, may follow me to you; that it
may not rebel against itself ... I hope, good Lord, that you
will perfect your mercies in me, even to perfect peace which
my outward and inward being will have with you, when death
shall be swallowed up in victory.*

St. Augustine, *Confessions* X 29,40; 30,42

104 — THE VOW OF CHASTITY

*O that I may comprehend, O Lord, the privilege of perfect
chastity through which man offers himself to you with undivided heart (1 Cor 7:32-34)*

1. There stands out among the evangelical counsels "that
precious gift of divine grace, which the Father gives to some, so
that by virginity or celibacy, they can more easily devote their entire selves to God alone with undivided heart" (LG 42). The vow of
chastity is the creature's answer to God's free gift, who by choosing that soul for himself makes it understand how precious is

perfect virginity "for the sake of the kingdom of heaven" (Mt 19:12). The value of the vow does not lie so much in the renunciation which logically follows it, as in the totality of love, of belonging, and of dedication to the Lord. Only God's infinite love explains his offering us this gift, and only the response of total love on the part of his creature explains the decision to take the vow.

"Each one"—says St. Paul—"has his special gift from God" (1 Cor 7:7); marriage is good, but virginity is better: he who marries "does well" and he who does not, "will do better" (ib. 38). "The unmarried man is anxious about the affairs of the Lord, how to please the Lord; but the married man is anxious about worldly affairs . . . and his interests are divided! So also . . . the virgin is anxious about the affairs of the Lord, how to be holy in body and spirit" (ib. 32-34). The vow of chastity is the outcome of one single love: infinite love, and aims at securing "undivided devotion to the Lord" (ib. 35), that is, at communion with God and a dedication to him which is not distraced by earthly cares. "Chastity which is practiced 'on behalf of the heavenly kingdom' "—says the Council—"deserves to be esteemed as a surpassing gift of grace. For it liberates the human heart in a unique way and causes it to burn with greater love for God and all mankind" (PC 12). The only purpose of the negative aspect of the vow, that is, of the renunciation that accompanies it, is to free the heart to make it capable of all-embracing love; this is the essential value of perfect chastity.

2. Virginity is not a value in itself, but only the virginity that is consecrated to God, because only this latter is the fruit of charity and is animated by love. St. Augustine says that consecrated persons "are not deprived of marriage, because they share, together with the entire Church, in the marriage in which the bridegroom is Christ" (In Io 9:2). Catholic tradition represents the vow of chastity, not as an inhibition, but especially as a consecration, as a nuptial relationship with Christ, and as a joyous, spontaneous decision of the will to belong totally to him. It brings to mind "that wondrous marriage between the Church and Christ, her only Spouse, a union which has been established by God" (PC 12). The vow of chastity thus constitutes a principle which transforms all the affective powers of life, a principle that enlarges the heart and for that reason becomes an inexhaustible source of dedication to God and his concerns. Vatican Council II expressed itself in this sense: "Total continence embraced on behalf of the kingdom of heaven has always been held in particular honor by the Church as being a sign of charity and a stimulus toward it, as well as a unique source of spiritual fertility in the world" (LG 42). The more intense the love that inspires and sustains the vow of chastity, the more it attains its positive value of spiritual fruitfulness, and the more capable the consecrated person becomes of fully offering his life to God and for souls. "To be your spouse, O

Jesus"—wrote St. Therese of the Child Jesus—is ... "by my union with you to be the mother of souls" (Auto. B, p. 192).

When the vow of chastity is completely understood and fulfilled, it neither mutilates nor distorts our capacity for affection, it does not sterilize the fecundity of life nor shut us up in ourselves or create problems or lack of balance, but by making use of our native resources, opens us to a boundless love and dedication. The only indispensable condition is that it be lived in a climate of authentic theological charity. Thus does the Church understand the vow of chastity and thus does she propose it and defend it against the accusations of the world, for she considers it not only "a most suitable way for religious to spend themselves wholeheartedly in God's service and in works of the apostolate", but also "a part of the richness of their whole personality" (PC 12).

O Father of grace, I raise my prayer to you and give endless thanks to your love, because in virgins we see living again here on earth that angelic life that we lost with Eden. What more could you have done to kindle the desire for virginity, to strengthen its power and exalt its glory, than to be born of a virgin? (Educazione delle Vergini 17:104)

And now, O Lord, I beg you to watch every day over these ... [virgins] in each of whom a living temple is consecrated to you ... May every sacrifice which will be offered to you in this temple with ardent faith and sincere piety rise up to you in an odor of sweetness. And when you look upon the sacred Host through which the sins of the world are taken away, so also look upon these victims of chastity. Protect them with your continual help so that they may become hosts, acceptable and pleasing to you. Deign to preserve their spirit whole, their mind and body pure, until the coming of our Lord Jesus Christ your Son. (Esortazione alla Verginita 14:94)

St. Ambrose

Behold I come to you whom I have loved, in whom I have believed, to whom I have given my whole affection. I will follow you wherever you go, my Jesus.

O my God, consuming fire! behold I come to you! Make me the prey of the mighty fire of your love, for I am only a little grain of dust; devour and consume me utterly in yourself. O my dearest light, I come to you. Enlighten me with the shining of your face that my darkness may become as noontide in your presence. O my beatitude, behold, I come to you! Unite me unto yourself by the bond of living love.

What have I to do henceforth with the world, my dear Jesus? Not even in heaven have I desired anything save you. You alone do I love and desire; for you alone do I hunger and thirst; in you do I grow all faint, my beloved! . . . To you my heart turns and says: you are my precious treasure, you are my joy, serene and true, you are the only love and desire of my soul!

St. Gertrude, Exercises 4

105 — CHASTITY AND VIGILANCE

I place my trust in you, O Lord; may your grace sustain me so that I may live like your angels in heaven (Mt 22:30)

1. The vow of chastity leads us to live here on earth "like angels in heaven" (Mt 22:30). But man is not a pure spirit and even when consecrated to God, carries the treasure of chastity "in an earthen vessel" (2 Cor. 4:7), that is, in a body of flesh which feels the impulse toward the pleasures of the senses. The vow of chastity does not change this situation. "Religious, [and thus all consecrated souls . . .], do well to lodge their faith in the words of the Lord; trusting in God's help rather than presuming on their own resources, let them practice mortification and custody of the senses" (PC 12). Perfect chastity is a divine gift; and as a consecrated soul has received it through a particular grace of God, it cannot be preserved without his grace. "Watch and pray" (Mt 26:41), said the Lord, indicating the means for overcoming any difficulty or temptation. Prayer is the great strength of any one who is conscious of his own weakness and, instead of shifting about with excessive fear, throws itself upon God with complete confidence: "In you, O Lord, I seek refuge"—sings the psalmist—"let me never be put to shame . . . Incline your ear to me; rescue me speedily! Be a rock of refuge to me, a strong fortress to save me!" (Ps 31:2-3)

In addition to prayer, the custody and mortification of the senses are necessary means for all Christians, and still more so for those who are pledged not only to the virtue, but also to the vow of chastity. The rule suggested by St. John of the Cross is very useful in this connection: renounce every pleasure of sense which is not "purely for the honor and glory of God" (Asc. I 13:4), and when we cannot avoid the experience of this pleasure, not to employ "all the faculties and senses . . . but only those which are required; as for the others, leave them unoccupied for God" (Maxims on love 38). Enamored with the ideal of perfect chastity, sustained by prayer and the spirit of mortification, those who dedicate themselves "almost by spiritual instinct, will be able to repulse anything that would endanger their chastity" (PC 12).

2. Mortification of the senses is the first bulwark in the defense of the vow of chastity. Then there is another, deeper and more interior: custody and mortification of the heart. The heart of one consecrated must be "a garden locked, a fountain sealed"

(Song 4:12), that is, must be impenetrable to all purely natural love, in order to be faithful to its choice of one only love. After breaking sacred family ties to follow Christ, and giving up the right to have a family, it would be the height of folly to allow the heart to be chained by creatures who have no claim, or by affections which are not holy. To all this, the response of St. Agnes is ever fitting: "God has put a sign on my face that I may admit no other lover. It is to him alone that I plight my troth" (RB). It can take very little to make us yield to the natural desire to feel loved by another, and to become bound, almost inadvertently, by sympathies and affections which become very hard to break. St. John of the Cross speaks of persons who are dedicated to the spiritual life but who "never advance, because they lack the courage to make a complete break with some little satisfaction, attachment or affection. Therefore, even though laden . . . with good works . . . they never reach the port of perfection" (Asc. I 11:4).

This does not mean that consecrated persons must make themselves incapable of loving, and insensitive, as it were, to human love. On the contrary—having put aside all seeking for personal satisfaction—they must be the more open to the love and service of their neighbor, mindful that the vow of chastity is directed precisely to this. Freedom of the heart, the fruit of perfect chastity, should help in the development and exercise of charity. "You were called to freedom"—says St. Paul—"through love, be servants of one another" (Gal 5:13). The freer the heart is from particular affections, the more consecrated persons are ready and open for the love of God and of neighbor; "they more easily hold fast to him and through him to the service . . . of men, they more readily minister to his kingdom with greater effectiveness, and can become all things to all men" (PO 16: cf OT 10).

O my good Jesus, I know well that every perfect gift, and chastity more than any other, depends upon the powerful influence of your providence, and that man, without you, can do nothing. Therefore I beg you to protect with your grace the chastity and purity of my soul and my body. And if I should receive any impression whatever from the senses which could sully chastity and purity, do you who are the supreme Lord of all my powers, cancel it out, so that with a clean heart, I may advance in your love and in your service, offering myself as a chaste sacrifice upon the altar of your divinity every day of my life.

St. Thomas Aquinas, *Preghiere*

Protect me, O Father of love and glory, that I may guard the sanctuary of my purity as in an enclosed garden and in a sealed fountain. Let me find you there, my Beloved, hold fast

*to you and never let you go. Let me be always alert, watching
day and night with all the strength of my spirit, so that you
may never find me asleep. And since you want to be sought
for without ceasing in order to be sure of the sincerity of my
love, let me run after and follow you. Let my faith and my soul
go out to meet your word. Let my heart keep watch, but my
flesh sleep, so that I may not begin again, to my own harm, to
be awake to sin.*

*O Lord, give me the other ornaments of virginity also!
Give me an eager piety; make me know how to keep myself
pure and how to humble myself; help me to preserve love and
to guard the wall of truth and the barrier of modesty. Make
me simple of heart, circumspect in speech, modest with all,
loving toward relations and merciful toward the poor . . .*

*Put your word as a seal upon my heart, and as a seal upon
my arm, so that you alone may shine out in all my feelings
and all my actions, that I may look upon you and speak of
you.*

cf St. Ambrose, *Educazione delle vergini* 17, III-3

106 — PRESENTATION OF OUR LORD

February 2

*Glory to you, O Christ, a light for revelation to the gentiles
(Lk 2:32)*

1. The Liturgy of this feast has a solemn and joyous tone, for
it celebrates Christ's first entrance into the temple; at the same
time, it has a sacrificial note because he comes to be offered.

The prophecy of Malachi sets the tone (3:1-4): "The Lord
whom you seek . . . will come to his temple" (ib. 1). It is easy to apply this text to the act that we commemorate today: the arrival of
Christ at the temple where, forty days after his birth, he is to be
presented by Mary and Joseph, according to the prescriptions of
the Mosaic law. In becoming man the Son of God desired to "be
made like his brethren" (Heb 2:17; 2nd reading); while not ceasing
to be God, he wished to be a true man among men, to be inserted
into our history, and to share our life in every thing, not excluding
the observance of the law prescribed for sinful men. Thus the
fulfillment of the law is the occasion by which Jesus meets in the
temple those of his people who were awaiting him in faith. He is in
fact received by Simeon, "a righteous and just man, looking for
the consolation of Israel" (Lk 2:25), and by the prophetess Anna,
who lived in prayer and penitence. Enlightened by the Holy Spirit,
both recognized the promised Savior in the little one presented by
a young mother with the humble offering of the poor, and they
burst into songs of praise. Simeon took him in his arms and ex-

claimed: "Lord, now let your servant depart in peace . . . for my eyes have seen your salvation" (ib. 29-30); and Anna, filled with joyous enthusiasm, spoke of him to all who were "looking for the redemption of Jerusalem" (ib. 38).

By recalling this event, todays's Liturgy invites us to go to meet Christ in the house of God, where we shall find him in the celebration of the Eucharist, to greet him as our Savior, to offer him the homage of ardent faith and love like Simeon and Anna, and finally to receive him, not in our arms but in our hearts. This is the significance of the "Candlemas" procession: to go to meet Christ, "the light of the world", with the burning flame of a Christian life which ought to be a luminous reflection of his exceeding brightness.

2. According to Malachi's prophecy, the Lord comes to his temple to purify the people from their sins, that they may be able to present to God "just offerings" which are pleasing to him (Mal 3:3-4). The first of these offerings, the one which established perfect worship and made every other offering valid, was precisely the one which Christ made of himself to the Father. For him ransom was not necessary, as it was for all the first-born of the Jews; he was the willing victim who would be sacrificed for the salvation of the world. But in conformity with his condition as a new-born son, Jesus wished to be offered by the hands of his Mother, who appeared here in the role of co-redemptrix. She was not ignorant of the fact that Jesus was the Savior of the world; under the veil of prophecy, she intuitively perceived that he was to fulfill his mission in a mystery of sorrow, in which she, as his mother, would have to share. This was clearly confirmed by Simeon's words: "A sword will pierce through your soul" (Lk 2:35). Mary understood and, in the secrecy of her heart, repeated her "fiat" as at Nazareth. In offering her Son she offered herself, and so began her passion as mother, which would associate her more every day with that of her Son.

Another point of similarity between Mother and Son was the deep humility with which Mary, though conscious of her virgnity, put herself on a level with all the other women, and, standing among them, appeared before the priest for the rite of purification. Jesus had no need of being ransomed, Mary no need of being purified, yet they both submitted to these rites in order to teach us respect and fidelity toward the Lord's precepts and the value of humility and of obedience.

Mary's purification, linked with the presentation of Jesus, is a symbol of that purification that we need so badly, which can only be had through the merits of Christ offered to the Father "to make expiation for the sins of the people" (Heb 2:17). Just as Mary offered her Son, may she also offer each of us to God, and through her motherly mediation prepare us for the purification which must be worked in us. May the holy and immaculate offering of Christ sanctify us and make us capable of offering the Father prayers and sacrifices that will be acceptable to his divine majesty!

We all run to you, O Christ, we who sincerely and profoundly adore your mystery; we set out towards you, full of joy ... carrying lighted candles, as a symbol of your divine splendor.

Thanks to you, all creation is radiant; in truth it is inundated by an eternal light which dissipates the shadows of evil. But let these lighted candles be especially the symbol of the internal splendor with which we wish to prepare ourselves for our meeting with you, O Christ. Indeed, just as your Mother, the most pure Virgin, carried in her arms you who are the true light, and showed you to all who find themselves in darkness, so may we also, who hold in our hands this light that is visible to all, and who are illuminated by its shining, hasten to go to meet you, who are the true light ...

The light that enlightens every man who comes into the world, has come ... All together we come to you, O Christ, to let ourselves be clothed with your splendor and, together with the old man Simeon, to welcome you, O eternal living light. With him we exult with joy and sing a hymn of thanksgiving to God, Father of light, who sent us the true light to lead us out of darkness and to make us luminous.

St. Sophronius of Jerusalem, De Hypapante 3:6-7

O holy Virgin, you offer your Son, the blessed fruit of your womb to the Lord. For the reconciliation of us all you offer the holy victim that is pleasing to God, and God the Father will at once accept this new offering, this most precious victim, of whom he himself says: "This is my beloved Son, in whom I am well pleased ..."

I too, O Lord, will willingly offer you my sacrifice, since you freely offered yourself, not through any need on your part, but for my salvation ... I have only two poor possesions, O Lord: my body and my soul; would I could worthily offer you these two poor pittances in a sacrifice of praise! It would be better, much better, for me to offer myself to you than be left to myself. In fact, if I remain alone, my soul is troubled, but in you my spirit is exultant as soon as it offers itself to you in complete dedication ... Lord, you do not wish my death; shall I not then freely offer you my life? In very truth, that is an offering which appeases your wrath, an offering which pleases you, a living offering.

St. Bernard, *On the Purification of the B. V. Mary*
3:2-3

INDEXES

INDEXES OF ABBREVIATIONS

SACRED SCRIPTURE

The abbreviations used for the various books of the Bible are those given at the beginning of the RSV version of the Scriptures. Unless otherwise noted, all scriptural quotations are taken from the RSV Common Bible.

THE DOCUMENTS OF VATICAN COUNCIL II

The text used is that of The Documents of Vatican II edited by Walter M. Abbott, S.J.

AA	Laity	LG	Dogmatic Constitution of the Church
AG	Missions	NAe	Non-Christians
CD	Bishops	OE	Eastern Churches
DH	Religious Freedom	OT	Priestly Formation
DV	Revelation	PC	Religious Life
GE	Christian Education	PO	Priests
GS	Church in the Modern World	SC	Liturgy
IM	Social Communication	UR	Ecumenism

AUTHORS AND WORKS FREQUENTLY CITED

T.J.	St. Teresa of Jesus	J.C.	St. John of the Cross
F	Foundations	Asc	Ascent of Mt. Carmel
IC	Interior Castle	Cs	Counsels to a religious
Life	Life	Ct	Cautions
Way	Way of Perfection	Dk N	Dark Night
Med	Meditations on the Song of Songs	Fl	Living Flame
Sol	Soliloquies (Exclamations)	Let	Letters
SpTest	Spiritual Testimonies	Say	Sayings of Light and Love
	(Relations)		

Note: The Spiritual Canticle and the Living Flame are generally cited from redaction B; in the rare cases in which A is used, the letter A is added as Sp C A, Fl A.

T.C.J.		E.T.	Sr. Elizabeth of the
	St. Theresa of the Child Jesus		Trinity
Auto	Autobiography, Auto-biographical Mss.	1 R	First Retreat
NV	Last Conversations (Novis-	2 R	Second Retreat
		Let	Letters

MISCELLANEOUS

RB	Roman Breviary	cf	compare
RM	Roman Missal	Let	Letter
RRo	Roman Ritual (old)	p	page
Lect	Lectionary	v	volume

— — — — — —

For the works of St. Teresa of Jesus, St. John of the Cross and St. Theresa of the Child Jesus, the ICS texts have been used throughout. An English version of the works of Sr. Elizabeth of the Trinity is under preparation.

ENGLISH REFERENCES

Augustine, St.

The Soliloquies of, New York Cosmopolitan Science & Art Service Co., 1943

The Confessions of, New York, Sheed & Ward, 1943

Bernard, St.

The Steps of Humility, Cambridge, Ma. Harvard University Press, 1942

Sermons on the Canticle of Canticles, Vol. I Dublin, Browne & Nolan, 1920

Sermons on Advent and Christmas, New York Benziger Bros., 1909

On the Love of God, New York Spiritual Book Associates, 1937

Blosius, Ludovicus

Paradise of the Faithful Soul Benziger Bros., 1926

Bonaventure, St.

The Souls Journey into God, The Tree of Life, The Life of St. Francis, New York, Paulist Press, 1978

Catherine of Genoa, St.	The Dialogue, New York, Sheed & Ward, 1946
Catherine of Siena, St.	The Dialogue of, New York, Benziger Bros., 1925
Chautard, Dom J.B.	The Soul of the Apostolate, Abbey of Gethsemani, Trappist, Ky., 1941
Early Christian Prayers	A. Hamman, Chicago, Regnery, 1961
Eudes, St. John	The Kingdom of Jesus, New York, Kenedy, 1946
de Foucauld, Charles	Meditations of a Hermit, Burns & Oates, London Orbis Books, New York, 1981
Francis de Sales, St.	A Treatise on the Love of God, trans. by John K. Ryan, Image Books, New York, Doubleday
Gay, Mgr. Charles	The Christian Life and Virtues, Vols. I,II,III London, Burns & Oates, 1879
Gertrude, St.	The Exercises of, Westminster, Md., Newman Press, 1956
John XXIII, Pope	Prayers and Devotions, Garden City, New York Doubleday, Image Books, 1969
	Journal of a Soul, New York, McGraw-Hill, 1965
Marmion, O.S.B., Abbot	Christ the Life of the Soul, St. Louis Herder, 1925
	Christ the Ideal of the Monk, St. Louis Herder, 1926
	Christ in His Mysteries, St. Louis Herder, 1924
	The Trinity in Our Spiritual Life, Westminster, Md. Newman Press, 1953
de Montfort, St. Louis Mary	True Devotion to the Blessed Virgin Mary, Bay Shore, New York, Montfort Fathers, 1949

Newman, J.H.	Meditations and Devotions, New York Longman,s Green and Co., 1907
de'Pazzi, St. Mary Magdalen	The Complete Works of, Vols. II,III,IV Carmelite Fathers, Aylesford, Westmont, Illinois 1974
Philipon, O.P., M.M.	The Spiritual Doctrine of Sr. Elizabeth of the Trinity Westminster, Md., Newman Press, 1961
	Spiritual Writings, New York, Kenedy, 1962

Refer to a collection of patristic writings for the works of the Fathers and early ecclesiatical writers.

The quotations from the works of St. Teresa of Avila, St. John of the Cross and St. Therese of the Child Jesus have been taken from the ICS Publications, Washington, D.C.

FOREIGN REFERENCES

St. Ambrose	Commento al Vangelo di S. Luca 2 voll., Citta Nuova, Roma 1966
	Educazione delle Vergini Exortazione all verginita) Scritti sulla verginita, Ed. Paoline, Alba, 2° ed. 1941
Ambrosian Preface	Maria Regina della Chiesa
Bl. Angela da Foligno	Il libro della B. Angela da Foligno, A. Signorelli, Roma 1950
St. Augustine	Commento al Vangelo e alla prima Epistola di S. Giovanni, Citta Nuova, Roma 1968
	Esposizione sui Salmi v. 1° (1967); v. 2° (1971), Citta Nuova, Roma
St. Bernard	De Advento 7:2 In purificatione B.V. Mariae) Sermoni per le feste della Madonna, Ed. Paoline, Roma 1970

St. Bonaventure	Opuscoli mistici, Vita e Pensiero, Milano 1956
J.B. Bossuet	Elevazioni a Dio sui misteri, SEI, Torino 1933
	Meditazioni sul Vangelo v. 1° (1930) v. 2° (1931), V. Gatti, Brescia
G. Canovai, da Mondrone	Suscipe Domino, La Civilta cattolica, Roma 1949
G. Cassiano	Conferenze spirituali v. 1°, Ed. Paoline, Roma 1966
St. Catherine of Siena	Epistolario 6 voll., a cura di P. Misciattelli, Giuntini-Bentivoglio, Siena
P. Charles	La priere de toutes les heures, Desclee de Brouwer, Parigi, 1941
A. Chevrier	Il vero discepolo di Cristo, Vita e Pensiero, Milano 1950
L. Da Ponte	Meditazioni, 2 voll., Marietti, Torino 1852
P. de Berulle	Le grandezze di Gesu, Vita e Pensiero, Milano, 2° ed., 1938
C. de Foucauld	Opere spirituali (Antologia), Ed. Paoline, Milano, 2° ed., 1964
Sr. Elizabeth of the Trinity	Oeuvres Completes, Cerf 1979, 1980
St. Francis of Assisi	Detti di S. Francesco d'Assisi, S. Bartolomeo in Isola, Roma 1933
R. Giordano	Contemplazione sull-amore divino, L.E. Fiorentina, Firenze 1954
St. John Chrysostom	Commento al Vangelo di S. Matteo 3 voll., Citta Nuova, Roma 1966-7
St. John Eudes	Miseria dell-uomo e grandezza del cristiano, L.E. Fiorentina, Firenze 1937
Liturgia Orientali	I giorni del Signore, Ed. Paoline, Milano 1961

Mozarabic Missal	PL 85,187
Pope Paul VI	Insegnamenti
Preghiere di rito bizantino alla Madre di Dio	Ed. Corsia dei Servi, Milano 1966
Aurelio Prudenzio	Inni della giornata, Ed. Paoline, Alba 1954
St. Thomas Aquinas	Preghiere, Firenze 1963